KU-265-175

RAILWAY TICKETS
TIMETABLES & HANDBILLS

This book is gratefully dedicated to my mother, Dorothy Mildred Dagmar Bray, who, by her early endeavours, taught me to read and write, and to love books. She thus enabled me to open the door on the world, which thereby lay revealed to my inquisitive attentions. Because of her devoted teachings I have been able to fulfil my lifetime's dream.

Maurice I. Bray

Also by the author:
Railway Relics and Regalia (co-author) (Country Life, 1975)
Postcard Mail (BRD Publishing, 1978-80)
Bells of Memory (BRD Publishing, 1981)

RAILWAY TICKETS
Timetables & Handbills

Maurice I. Bray

Bray, Maurice I.
Railway tickets, timetables & handbills.
1. Railroads — Equipment and supplies — Collectibles
2. Printed ephemera — Collectors and collecting
1. Title
385'.22 HE1035

ISBN 0 86190 163 0

Published by
Moorland Publishing Co Ltd,
8 Station Street,
Ashbourne, Derbyshire,
DE6 1DF England.
Tel: (0335) 44486

Printed in the UK by
Butler and Tanner Ltd,
Frome, Somerset.

CONTENTS

ACKNOWLEDGEMENTS

It is not until one commences research, collects, edits, and transcribes the mountain of notes for such a book as this, that the full extent of the work necessary comes to be realised. For every statement issued as fact, a hundred have to be dismissed as unverified legend, and railways have as many legends as sleepers. But more important than this realisation, comes the knowledge that considerable help and advice is needed from so many people and organisations.

My good fortune was that their help was unstintingly given, often at personal inconvenience, but of such volume that I was overwhelmed. The publication of this book is their real reward since it sets the seal on their endeavours. For their kindness and consideration I wish to place on record their names. To them all, I can only say, 'Thank you, very much':

The late Reverend E. ('Teddy') Boston, MA, Rector of Cadeby, and 'guiding light' of the Cadeby Light Railway. A friend of many years who cheerfully and generously agreed to write the foreword. For his encouragement and much practical help, I am indebted.

Mr George Dow, FRSA, FCIT, retired British Railways Divisional Manager and leading railway historian, who on the strength of an acquaintance at a railway exhibition, made available to me much valuable material from his personal collection. His advice on avenues of research and final production was heeded with gratitude. The interested and friendly encouragement by himself and his wife made the hard work a lot easier.

The late Mr Richard Bosomworth, ALA, former Borough Librarian, Loughborough, Leicestershire. A friend from schooldays, very much a friend in need, who freely offered help, and the use of much valuable material in the Central Library Archives. To his staff also, I tender my thanks.

Thomas Cook & Son Ltd, 45 Berkeley Street, London W1. A former Archivist, Mr M.F.T. Clasby, and Mr C. Walters, Assistant Press Officer, went to great lengths to help me. The present Archivist, Mr Edmund Swinglehurst, was most enthusiastic and freely placed at my disposal historic Company records. For these gentlemen with their cheerful and friendly generosity, and their practical help, mere words are inadequate to express my gratitude.

Gallaher Limited, and in particular, Miss Jane Calver, Public Relations Manager, for friendly and generous permission to reproduce photographs from 'Senior Service' cigarette cards originally published by Joseph A. Pattreiouex, Ltd.

Michael J. Chapman, a ticket collecting friend whose ideas were the inspiration for this work.

Other friends showed their interest and encouragement in a practical way, without which this book would be lacking illustrations. My thanks for the loan of tickets and other ephemera to: Henry D.Davy, former Managing Director, and Mr W. Morris, Director, Hindson Print Group, Newcastle-upon-Tyne; Gordon Fairchild; Ron Grosvenor; Lesley Jackson; Stuart Underwood; Patrick B. Whitehouse; Peter Wootton.

Mr Rex Beecham, Railway Booking Agent, Loughborough, The generous loan of his first Booking Register provided much interesting material.

Mrs F.A. Walker, County Requests Librarian, Leicester Central Lending Library; also the Archives staff at the Municipal Library, Leicester. Their helpful response to my requests made the research so much easier.

Mr M.J. Moore, Assistant Director, Museum Services, Leicestershire Museums, for permission to use illustrative material.

Mr M.A. Blakemore, Museum Assistant (Library), National Railway Museum, York, for the provision of photographs and offers of help.

Lastly, but by no means the least, my sister Margaret, who wishes to remain anonymous! Without her monumental efforts in deciphering my original draft, and in preparing the final typescript, the efforts of all these kind people would have come to naught.

M.I. Bray

FOREWORD

The extraordinary interest in all matters concerning steam railways is a well known fact. All aspects of the history and operation of Railways seems to have been written about, especially the study of that magnificent machine, the steam locomotive. Its demise, thought by some to be due to shortsighted and unfortunate planning, has brought an extraordinary interest in the preservation movement, and the private ownership of a few of these monuments to mechanical engineering. Following this interest in steam locomotives has come a flood of books on the subject, some technical, some unashamedly popular and pictorial. The steam railway enthusiast, deprived of the real thing, has turned to this literature and the nostalgia of the preservation lines. The hunger is so great that almost anything written on the subject of steam is assured of an avid readership.

The addiction of railway enthusiasts to the steam locomotive, although the most laudable of studies, can at times obscure the fact that there are many other fascinating sides to railway operation. It is only very recently that such subjects as passenger coaches, goods stock, station architecture, permanent way construction, and signalling operations have been covered to any extent. As yet, the mysteries of train control and timetable compilation has remained the preserve of the specialist.

Because of this, it is a great honour to be asked to write a foreword to Mr Maurice Bray's book on the history of railway tickets and timetables. Here is a subject which at first glance would seem to be far removed from the general run of popular interest, but which on examination proves to have all the fascination of a new discovery.

Since there are very few (possibly only three) lines in the world which carry passengers free of charge, it follows that from the earliest days there has been a need for a system of collection of fares and the issue of a receipt for payments given. Mr Bray traces this history in all its many forms from the primitive writing-out of a paper receipt, one copy of which was handed to the passenger, and through to the rather more advanced system of books of printed forms. These latter were torn out as required, with the destination and fare details written by hand; this gave rise to the term 'booking office' which is still in use.

Further developments discussed by the author are the metallic or ivory tokens which were issued and collected on each journey, to the coming of the Edmondson card ticket, and the modern theory and practice of fare collection. Some of the intricacies of the Railway Clearing House are also unravelled. The history includes an explanation of where and how tickets were printed and what happened to them after they had been surrendered to the ticket collector, matters which most people never even consider.

Different types of ticket systems from all over the world are examined, from the trans-continental issues of long folded strips like the popular seaside folding postcards, to tickets issued on tiny and almost unknown preserved railways. There is also revealed the subject of advertising on tickets which is almost a study in itself. Patriotic slogans too, found their place on these small strips of pasteboard, and during World War I travellers on the Kinver Light Railway were exhorted to use a well-known brand of knitting wool to knit for the 'gallant Forces at the Front'. The railway companies also produced tickets with little compartments containing advertisements; some are illustrated herein.

In Great Britain, railway tickets were usually plain in design, consisting of two colours, but in some cases abroad full colour printing and pictorial representation found its place; rarely did tickets printed in this latter fashion rise to the artistic heights of the postage stamp. It is fascinating to think for a moment what might have happened if this idea had taken root in Britain. Obviously, the Great Western Railway would have used prints of cathedrals and castles, stately homes and halls, while the London and North Western Railway might have taken classical mythology, famous men and inventions. What would have been the theme of say, The Garstang and Knot End, or the Southwold Railways?

Tickets of the normal design were issued for all sorts of unusual groups of people and every conceivable occasion. There was a shipwrecked mariner's ticket specially printed for the journey from Grimsby to Sheffield; while the Blakesley Hall Railway (15in gauge) issued a ticket, price 6d, from Blakesley Station on the Stratford-upon-Avon and Midland Joint Railway to the hall, which included admission to the garden fete. A special ticket from Cheltenham to Cadeby, issued privately in connection with a visit by the Gloucestershire Railway Society and illustrated in the book must surely be unique. In the journey of about seventy miles only the last hundred yards from Sutton Lane to Cadeby were over a steam operated narrow gauge railway, the rest having been accomplished by a chartered omnibus!

I recall a party of twelve undergraduate members of the Cambridge University Railway Club, myself among them, making an evening excursion to the Mildenhall Branch of the Great Eastern Railway. We boarded a double-decker Eastern Counties bus to take us to the cemetery, the nearest stop to Fen Ditton Station. The conductor was somewhat exasperated by the time he had supplied twelve separate tickets as we sat in line along the coach. On arrival at Fen Ditton Station (really a halt without a platform) sentries were posted up the line waving bicycle lamps to stop the train. Heeding our signals, the train stopped and the guard let down the steps. We climbed aboard and asked for twelve first-class singles to Barnwell Junction. As we had previously surmised, none were available and so we were given a free ride in style, to steam majestically into Barnwell Junction a full 200yd up the line, whence we caught the same number bus back into Cambridge, arriving in time for hall!

Another section of this interesting book deals with the travelling public and their felonious evasion of fares. There is, in an early copy of the *Railway Magazine*, a complete article on this fascinating subject and its satisfactory prevention. Not all cases, however, are as simple as the rather pompous season ticket holder who was somewhat annoyed by the collector's request for his ticket at the barrier. He answered, 'My face is my ticket'. The reaction of the railway official was simple. He rolled up his sleeves and quietly said, 'Certainly, sir. But I fear that I have instructions to punch all tickets'. History does not relate the end of the story.

Although the subject of railway tickets may seem somewhat prosaic on the surface, this book will show what an interesting subject the author is investigating. It is the first book on the subject since 1939, and our praise and thanks must go out to Mr Bray for producing such a readable and fascinating study of a much neglected branch of railway history.

Rev. E. Boston, MA
The Rectory,
Cadeby, Leicestershire

1
ORIGINS & DEVELOPMENT

The railway passenger ticket is generally rather commonplace in its appearance. Its purchase can involve the would-be traveller in a journey which may range from places as far apart as the next village or the other side of the world.

Although the age of steam is no longer with us, except on a few preserved lines, the start of a journey is much the same. A tremulous 'pheep' from the whistle of the departure officer, an answering 'honk' from the engine by the driver, and the journey begins. The vibrations of the revving diesel-engine shudder through the coupled coaches, perhaps a slight jerk, and the train is on the move. Passengers begin to settle back in their seats, with items of their personal luggage stowed about them on floor, knees, seat, and rack. To each his own; the pleasures of the journey are a private occupation, ranging from stony-faced stares to animated conversation, a quiet read, or a leisurely contemplation of the passing countryside.

But sooner or later the peace of this gently swaying mobile mini-world is shattered. Along the corridors echoes the insistent call, 'All Tickets, Please'.

There can surely be few rail travellers who have not engaged in the frantic search through bags, purse, and pockets in an endeavour to produce the tiny card for inspection and clipping. The inspection of the ticket provides, as it always has done, a spot check on passengers to ensure that all have paid their fares and are correctly seated. It also provides a service for the passenger by checking that he is on the right train for his particular destination.

But how did it all begin, and where? The issue of the first railway ticket is a matter of debate, and there are a number of different opinions on the subject. It must be remembered that railways first came into operation, not for the conveyance of passengers, but for the transport of goods, chiefly coal. The original passengers on the Stockton and Darlington Railway, opened on 27 September 1825, were company guests, formally invited by the board of directors. Their fare-paying successors were most probably the holders of the first railway tickets; to be precise, they held a printed receipt for their fare. Other travellers on those early railways carried metal tallies which had to be surrendered at the end of the journey. Not until 1838, with the first issue of Thomas Edmondson's invention, did the railway ticket, as we now know it, come into being.

But the birth and development of the railway ticket can be found in the days of the stagecoach. The coach was the principal means of travel,

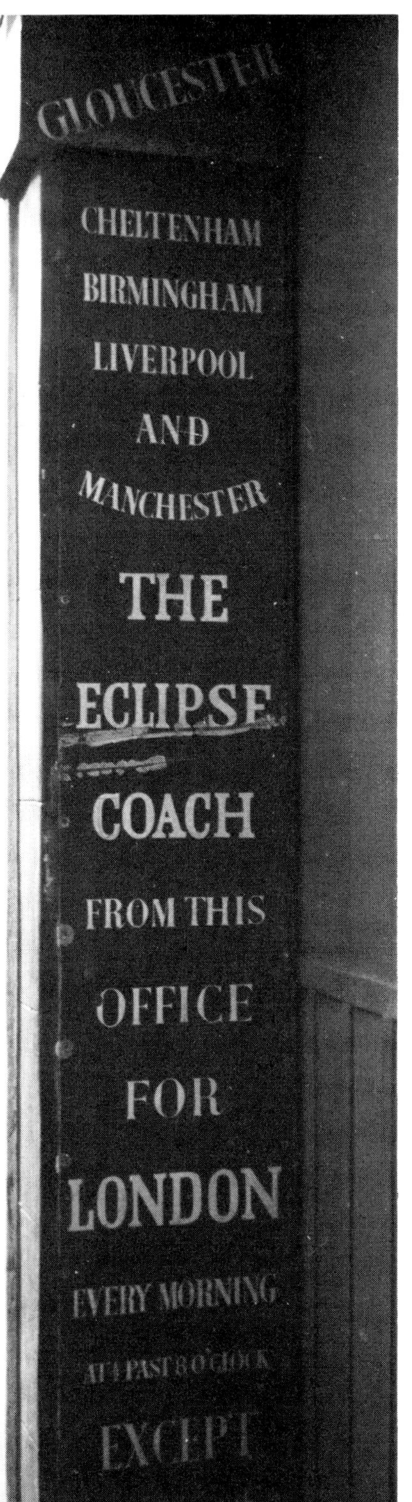
GLOUCESTER
CHELTENHAM
BIRMINGHAM
LIVERPOOL
AND
MANCHESTER
THE
ECLIPSE
COACH
FROM THIS
OFFICE
FOR
LONDON
EVERY MORNING
EXCEPT

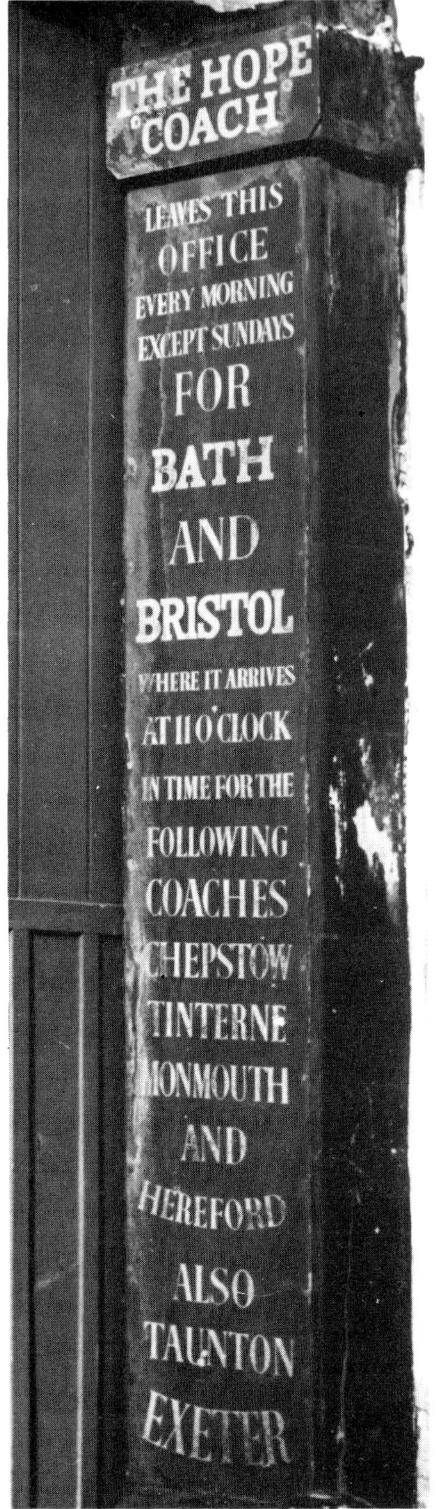
THE HOPE
COACH
LEAVES THIS
OFFICE
EVERY MORNING
EXCEPT SUNDAYS
FOR
BATH
AND
BRISTOL
WHERE IT ARRIVES
AT 11 O'CLOCK
IN TIME FOR THE
FOLLOWING
COACHES
CHEPSTOW
TINTERNE
MONMOUTH
AND
HEREFORD
ALSO
TAUNTON
EXETER

Coaching timetable notices. The entrance pillars to the stableyard of the King's Arms, Calne, Wiltshire, each carry advertisments giving notice of the times and itineraries of coaching runs. Many famous Royal Mail coaches travelled these routes, and in August 1784, John Palmer inaugurated the first mail-coach service, which ran between London and Bristol. Since these photographs were taken, the boards and other reminders of the coaching era have been restored. (Photo: Lesley Jackson)

departure times were uncertain and seating accommodation was very strictly limited. It was essential for the would-be traveller to secure his place in the stagecoach at least twenty-four hours prior to the commencement of his journey. There were no 'stations' on the old coach routes. Instead, inns of good repute were selected to serve this duty. Usually such selected 'stations' were inns where stabling and other accommodation was available. Booking one's seat in advance was done in an office specially set apart for the purpose at the coaching inn. Not until the days of the railways and their use of a similar practice did the term 'booking-office' come into regular use as part of the language. One of the more famous metropolitan coaching inns was The George in Borough High Street, London. In the mid-1930s it was in use by the London and North Eastern Railway as a parcels office.

Staffing these booking-offices was usually undertaken by an employee of the inn specially engaged by the stagecoach proprietors. He was generally required to act as their representative and booking clerk. But the traveller could not merely hand over his money with a request for a ticket to a particular place. The purchase of a ticket was quite a lengthy and complicated process.

The booking clerk was provided with a ledger containing tear-out pages, each third page being permanently bound into the book. Details of the passenger's name, his intended destination, the coach in which accommodation was desired, and even his preference for inside or outside travel, were recorded laboriously in triplicate. Of the two tear-out copies, one was given to the passenger, and the other to the guard of the coach. The third copy was retained in the book as a company record. It was not usual for any money to change hands as part of the booking transaction. The traveller paid his fare to the guard at the end of his journey.

The pioneer railways carried on this practice of booking a journey. Early railway tickets were of paper, very thin, each being filled in and then torn out of a book as required. On to the printed form of the ticket the booking clerk wrote the date, ticket number, and the time of the train for which it was valid. Many of the smaller railways used paper ticket systems until the 1920s. The Welsh Highland Railway conceded to modernity by printing their 'Conditions of Issue' in a panel across the top of the ticket, including a cut-off corner for when the ticket was issued to a child 'not exceeding 12 years of age', and using a simple overprint for special purposes. As can be seen, the system was very similar to the one in operation by the coaching companies.

In the early days of American railroads the practice of booking a journey was similarly continued by using methods employed by the stagecoach companies. But what had sufficed for the Wells Fargo Express was impractical for the Baltimore and Ohio Railroad or the Pennsylvania

Railroad, two of the earliest railway companies. The old booking register for the Phoenixville branch-line of the Pennsylvania Railroad shows entries which indicate that the booking clerk was hurried. It would also seem that he was a local man, and not much worried by supervisors. Instead of writing the passenger's names, as was required, he wrote 'Boy', 'Lady', or even 'Friend'.

The early railway traveller was issued with his ticket as a printed receipt for his fare paid to the booking clerk. He was then allowed on to the station platform where he showed the ticket to a company official. It was the duty of this official to escort the passenger to the seat on the train corresponding with the number written on the ticket. Before the invention of the corridor-coach, it was not an uncommon practice for the doors to be locked as each coach became filled. This system provided an extra tally for the production of passenger statistics and a further check on cash receipts.

But rail travel was a habit that quickly gained popularity. With the growth of this new form of transport it became imperative that the system of passenger bookings was speeded up. The old stagecoach methods could

West Bridge Station, Leicester. This main station of the old Leicester & Swannington Railway was closed 13 March 1893, when the West Bridge terminus was built. The poster in the window refers to the closure, nearly 50 years after the line had been bought by the Midland Railway. The board on the side of the station building bears the legend RAILWAY OFFICE.

The four brass tallies were issued to third class passengers who boarded the train according to the priority shown by the number. These tallies, introduced by the L & S, provided the first break from the cumbersome methods of paper tickets carried over from the stage-coaching era.

not cope, since the number of passengers was too great. The stagecoach passenger could be booked in advance with relative ease since, at the most, only twelve persons could travel on each coach. But a train carried more than 100 passengers. They could arrive at any time of the day at a station requesting transport. It became a lengthy process, both tiring and tiresome, to issue tickets by the old method.

Just before a train was due to depart, the booking office was closed. The opening-day timetable issued by the Grand Junction Railway in 1837 stated: 'The doors of the Booking Office will be closed at the times appointed for starting; after which no Passenger can be admitted.' This was necessary because the booking clerk had to complete a waybill, giving details of the numbers of passengers in each class, together with their destination. The completed form was handed to the guard who proceeded to check the train, coach by coach, against the list.

Clearly, a radical change of method was needed in the booking office. It was on the historic Leicester and Swannington Railway that this change was first recorded.

The old L & S was one of the earliest Midland lines, some sixteen miles in length, with severe gradients, although these were later modified and improved. It was not originally intended that passengers should be carried on the line, but it did so with great success for nearly one hundred years. Out of this line, which was operated from West Bridge Station, Leicester, via Desford, to Swannington, near Ashby-de-la-Zouch, the powerful and important Midland Railway was born. But in those early days the future of

A view of the Glenfield Station on the historic Leicester & Swannington Railway, about 1905. At the far end of the platform can be seen the entrance to the Glenfield Tunnel, at one time the longest in Britain, where a sand-glass was used to regulate the passage of trains through its 1 mile 36yd length.

OPENING

OF

The Leicester and Swannington

RAILWAY,

Tuesday, 17th July, 1832.

The Bearer of this Ticket is entitled to Seat, No. 111 in Carriage No. 4 Entered John Ellis

COCKSHAW, PRINTER.

To judge by this opening day ticket of the historic Leicester & Swannington Railway, the carriages must have been crowded indeed. It is signed by John Ellis, who later became chairman of the Midland Railway. He is commemorated in the name of the mining village, Ellistown, on the edge of the Charnwood Forest. The original ticket is now in Leicester Museum.

railways and their tremendous potential was unsuspected. As a source of revenue, passengers were given little consideration. But success soon became apparent, and the board of directors noted with delight that passenger fares repaid one per cent on the capital outlay.

Brass octagonal checks or tallies were introduced by the Leicester and Swannington Railway in place of the paper slips still being used by other companies. These new metal tickets were issued at the opening of the line on 17 July 1832, and were in use until 1846. They were embossed with the name of the company, the destination station, and a serial number. Their issue was originally restricted to third-class passengers, or 'open carriage passengers', the name being derived from the fact that they travelled standing, in open vehicles. These vehicles were nothing more nor less than high-sided goods wagons generally known as 'tubs'. The tubs had no seats, and their buffers were unsprung. As if the absence of such creature comforts was not enough, the passengers' discomfort was further aggravated by the lack of a roof, a feature most noticeable in bad weather, or when the train was travelling the notorious 1 mile 36yd Glenfield Tunnel.

In exchange for his fare the L & S passenger was issued with one of the brass checks. The fare was $1\frac{1}{4}$d per mile for third-class passengers, and $2\frac{1}{2}$d per mile for those who travelled first-class. The transaction was recorded in a book. Issue of the metal ticket permitted admission to the train, and the passenger's priority was indicated by the embossed serial number. At the end of each journey the guard collected the checks in a special leather pouch for delivery back to the issuing point. The leather pouch was divided into eight separate compartments, one for each station. Receipt of the brass checks was recorded by the booking clerk, and they then became available for re-issue.

The *Leicester Chronicle* of 28 July 1832, contains a reference to the Leicester and Swannington Railway, which in such a short time had become exceedingly popular. It says: 'Since the public opening on Tuesday, an additional carriage for passengers has been added to the train, and numbers of respectable parties have availed themselves of the opportunity to visit Bagworth and its neighbourhood. On Wednesday upwards of 200 passengers went by the conveyance, who speak in high terms of the treat which they experienced.' The paper goes on to list the seemingly moderate fares: to Glenfield 4d, to Ratby 6d, Desford Lane 8d, Mary Lees 10d, Thornton and Bagworth 1 shilling, and 'understands that these fares permit of return also.'

A first class carriage was built within a year of the opening of the Leicester and Swannington Railway. It had a roof, seats, even suspension springs, but still no buffer springs. To ride in this luxurious coach the first-class passenger was issued with a paper ticket, and was allowed the privilege of 'booking' his seat several days in advance. The practice was officially advertised and thus gave formal acceptance of the terms 'booking office' and 'booking clerk' carried over from the days of the stagecoach. They have been in use ever since.

Several other railways copied the example of the L & S by issuing

Metal tallies, tokens, and passes have a complex history, and owe their origins to the Leicester & Swannington Railway tallies. Some of elaborate design on precious metal were minted like coins and reserved for use as directors' passes. From these were evolved the brass tokens illustrated here, which were used as duty and pay checks to establish identity when collecting a pay packet. As such, they are in use on many railways and in various industries today. (Stuart Underwood and Maurice I. Bray collections)

indestructible tickets. The London and Greenwich Railway Company in its early days used circular copper checks. The director's free ticket was of silver-bronze, and carried an artistic representation of the trans-London Viaduct which carried the railway. These coin-type passes were about the same size as the old half-crown piece.

Free tickets made of ivory, numbered, and not transferable, were issued by the Sheffield, Ashton-under-Lyne, and Manchester Railway. This early line was later incorporated into the Great Central Railway.

In 1843, the Newcastle, North Shields and Tynemouth Railway issued an elliptical metal ticket. On one side was embossed the motif of each of the three towns' coat of arms set into an elliptical plaque, and with the name of the company set round the outer edge of the ticket. The reverse side denoted the class of travel for which the ticket was issued.

But commendable though the idea was, the metal ticket represented a cumbersome and costly alternative to the paper coupon and card. As a passenger ticket it enjoyed a relatively short reign. The metal tally was used in the locomotive sheds, even until comparatively recent times, as a token to be exchanged at the end of the week for wages. In later years the big companies preserved the memory of the metal passenger ticket. Honoured directors and managers were issued with gold, silver or ivory medallions in the styles of these early metal tallies.

In general, the paper or card tickets were of greater popularity. The

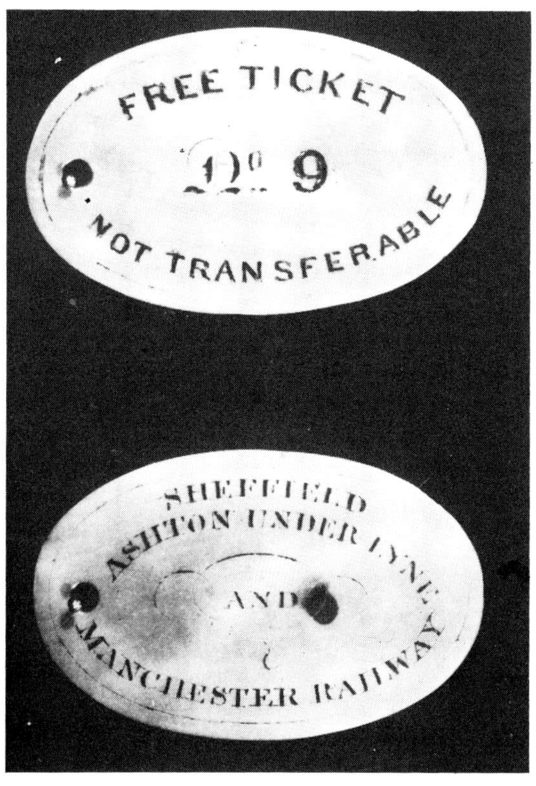

Ivory free ticket of about 1844. The reverse is inscribed with a belt and buckle design, now mostly worn away with constant handling. (George Dow)

different styles available ranged from the most elaborate and highly artistic to the starkly simple. Paper coupon tickets issued in 1832 for travel from Liverpool to Warrington looked very similar to the printed receipts obtainable nowadays from jobbing printers and stationers. These coupon tickets, filled in and issued by the booking clerk, carried a ticket number, the date and time of issue, the fare paid, and the names of both the passenger and the issuing agent. An instruction was printed to inform the passenger that 'This Ticket must be shown at the Station, but must be kept to present to the Guard of the Warrington Coaches at Warrington Junction.' Printed in the bottom right-hand corner of the ticket was the request 'Turn over', whereupon the passenger was given the gentle warning that no gratuity was allowed to be taken by any guard or porter, and other company servants and that smoking in the first-class carriages was also strictly forbidden. A paper ticket issued by the Bolton and Leigh Railway carried a similar warning. On the face of these blue coloured tickets issued prior to 1845 was printed the name of the station of issue with a blank space left for the destination. The attention of the passenger was drawn to a small printed notice which stated that the ticket was issued subject to the provision that there was room on the carriages.

Among the first season tickets ever issued in London were those of the London and Greenwich Railway Company. Printed on cardboard approximately 3½in by 2½in in measurement, these tickets were artistically produced. Beneath the name of the company printed in gothic type-face was depicted the winged messenger Mercury, carrying the shields of the company's coat of arms and motto. The ticket authorised admittance of the passenger (whose name was entered on the card) between specified dates. One such ticket, still preserved, was valid for the period from 19 January 1837 to 19 April 1837. These early season tickets were given a number by the issuing clerk and indicated the class for which they were valid. Each ticket was countersigned by the Company Secretary. The London and South Western Railway Company issued circular season tickets which fitted into card cases with a celluloid window. The case was serially numbered, and was embossed with the legend 'This case is the property of the Company.'

Not unnaturally, the railway companies allowed their staffs to travel between specified stations at reduced rates or on free passes. These tickets were of the simple tear-out type and were issued for monthly and three-monthly periods, and were not transferable. They were made out in the same manner as the ticket issued to ordinary passengers except that they stated the name of the company's department in which the bearer worked, and were printed with consecutive numbers in a special machine. General passes were issued by the Manchester, Sheffield and Lincolnshire Railway in paper form. The booking clerk added the number and date of issue, together with details of the passenger's name, journey, and the period for which the pass was valid. Before issue to the passenger, the general manager countersigned the pass.

Similar free passes were issued by the Lancashire and Yorkshire Railway, and were in the form of the company's standard paper ticket. Together with all the usual details, and the general manager's countersignature, it also showed the reason for its issue.

The press have always enjoyed concessionary fares with the railway, and one of the earliest examples preserved is a free pass issued by the London and South Western Railway in August 1859. This forerunner of the Southern Railway allowed a journalist and his friend the enviable privilege of travelling first-class between London and any station for a period of three months. Renewing of this precious card was made quite simply by

Train indicator boards. For elegance, clarity, and simplicity combined with functional purpose, these examples at Leicester Central Station can have had few rivals. They were the special responsibility of the ticket examiner, seen here at his task on an October afternoon in 1919, resplendent in his frock-coated uniform. (Leicestershire Museums, Art Galleries, and Record Services, from the S.W.A. Newton collection.)

A Great Central Railway ticket examiner at Leicester proudly stands by the upholstered door of a first class carriage. The leather straps, used to raise and lower the windows, were constantly removed by passengers who used the fine quality leather as barber strops for their cut-throat razors. (Leicestershire Museums, Art Galleries, and Record Services, from the S.W.A. Newton collection.)

alteration of the dates for which it was valid, and with a further countersignature by the Company Secretary. Such tickets issued by the London and South Western were elaborate in their design, and carried an embossed motif of the company's crest and motto surmounted by a side-view of one of the locomotives operated by the company.

As may be readily imagined, forgery of these early paper or card tickets was a relatively easy matter, and provided a simple means of evasion of the proper fare. During the late 1920s and early 1930s, forgery was a serious problem for all of the railway companies; so much so that the Great Western Railway adopted bank-note style printing for the issue of their three-monthly first-class season tickets. These were in use right up to nationalisation. They measured approximately 3in by 2¼ and were a fine example of the engraver's art. Provision was made for the over-printing of the ticket number, the duration of validity, the rate or fare, and the destination. At its subsequent issue to passengers, the booking clerk handwrote the issuing date in ink, and rubber-stamped the expiry date in a centrally located panel. The ticket had to be signed by the passenger and was required to 'be produced for examination when it is called for by Officers of the Company, and delivered up on the date of expiry.'

Season tickets were a very early development on English railways, used by all the major companies. They were originally known as 'Periodical Tickets'. As the railway companies began to realise the vast potential of the passenger traffic (the growth in popularity of rail travel was phenomenal) they introduced enterprising techniques of salesmanship. During the 1850s many of the companies, on their lines north-bound out of London, offered a free first-class season ticket to anyone erecting new buildings in residential land adjoining the railways. These gratuitous tickets were eagerly sought since they were, in many cases, available for periods from fifteen to twenty years. As a further inducement to travel, in 1852 the London and South Western Railway issued residential tickets. The occupiers of the houses where building had been encouraged by the railway company could obtain tickets at a 20 per cent discount for a period of seven years.

In the history of the steam locomotive the name of George Stephenson stands supreme; you cannot talk of one without the other. So it is with the railway ticket, where the outstanding figure is Thomas Edmondson. The modern railway ticket system is based on the invention of this Lancashire Quaker. To him belongs the further distinction that his invention was to become the standard adopted by railways the world over.

Born in 1792, Thomas Edmondson served his apprenticeship as a cabinet maker, and then abruptly changed the course of his career to become a grocer. A further change of course occurred in 1836 when he was appointed as station-master at Milton (later Brampton Junction), on the Newcastle and Carlisle Railway, which became part of the North Eastern Railway in 1862. It was not long before he saw the tremendous disadvantages in the existing ticket-issuing system. Being of an inventive nature, he gave considerable thought to the problem. The long periods of spare time between train arrivals and departures gave him the opportunity to perfect a new system. At first, this was a system whereby passengers were identified by number instead of by name.

For this purpose he used a wooden block into which he set printing type.

This simple matrix contained the station name and class of the most frequently issued tickets. A small mallet completed Edmondson's printing press. With the mallet and block he printed rows and rows of tickets upon suitably textured and coloured card. The next stage was the laborious one of giving each ticket a serial number. Having done this, the tickets were cut out of the cardboard strip and carefully placed in a special box ready for issue. There was a marked improvement in the speed with which tickets were issued, but Edmondson was not yet satisfied. He next developed a

A close-up view of Edmondson's ticket dating press. This very solidly constructed piece of apparatus was chiefly criticised because its movable iron jaws were liable to bite at unwary fingers. Later models were made to Edmondson's Patent by John Blaylock, clockmaker, of Carlisle; some can still be seen in use throughout Britain. (Photo: The Museum of British Transport)

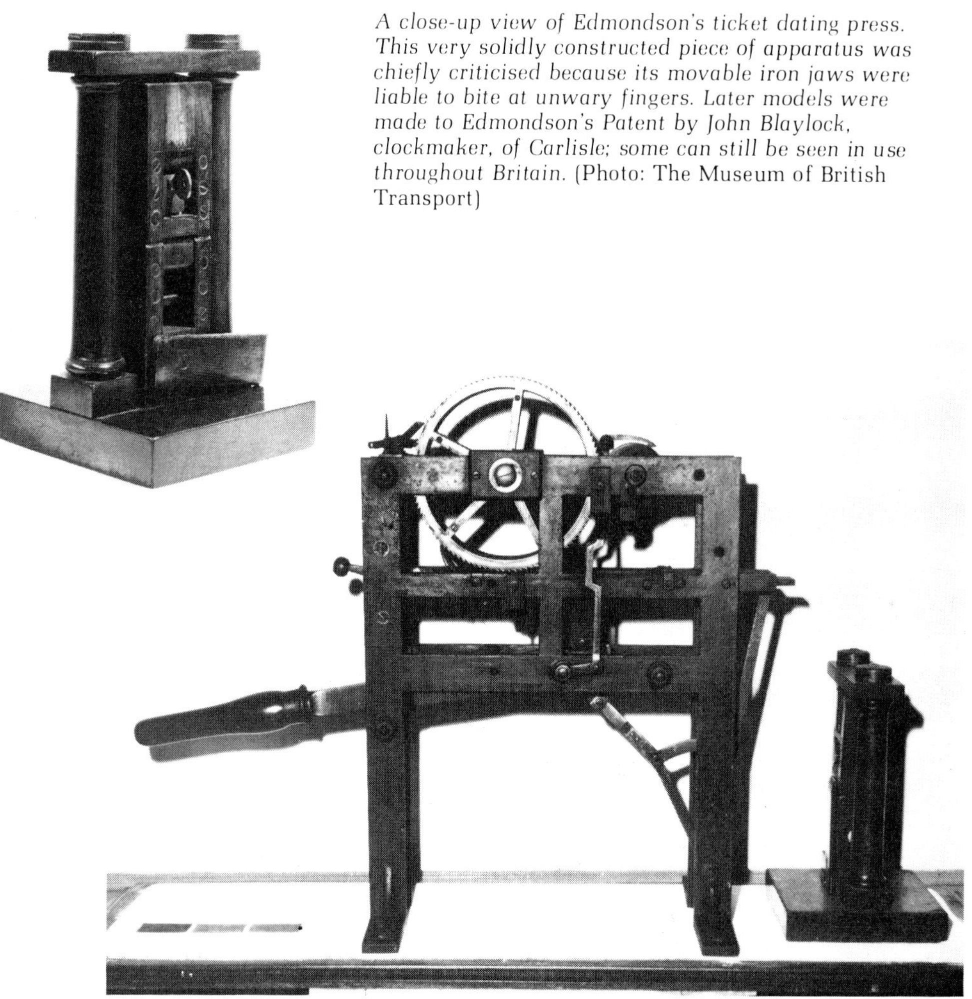

Thomas Edmondson's early ticket-printing machine and date press, about 1848. The press, on the right, contains a movable dating forme at the top and back. By inserting a ticket, a rotating ratchet wheel carried an inked ribbon, simultaneously pressed on the ticket by the date forme. The large contraption separately printed the serial numbers which were carried on the spoked wheel, and rubbed them against a small inkpad wheel. Pressure on the handle slid the ticket into contact with the numbers wheel.

This rarely noticed commemorative plaque was set above a corner betting shop in Stonewell, Lancaster. (Photo: Studio Wayne, Lancaster)

ticket tube in which the pre-printed tickets were stored in numerical order, at the top of the stack being the ticket with the lowest number. At the bottom of the tube was a counter-balanced plate controlled by an arrangement of weighted strings and pulleys. On removal of the uppermost ticket, the remainder ascended in the tube leaving the next ticket ready for issue. Tickets still needed (as they do even today) dating immediately before issue, and to this end Edmondson turned his inventive talents. He contrived a ticket-dating machine constructed of wood. It was in the form of a press, and the ticket was gripped between two movable jaws. One of these jaws held the dating type against a moving ribbon; the chief objection to this machine was that the jaws were unprotected. Later models were improved in 1862 by Edmondson's son.

Prior to his death on 22 June 1851, Edmondson transferred his services from the Newcastle and Carlisle Railway to the Manchester and Leeds Railway, where he introduced his special ticket arrangements. The Midland Railway was also very interested in Edmondson's ideas. For a small consideration he consented that they should be used by the company in extensive trials. Railway tickets as we have now come to know them were first formally adopted on the Birmingham and Gloucester line. Their advantages became publicly known, and eventually Edmondson's ticket machines were to be found in every booking-office.

Of the fact that Edmondson's machine fulfilled a tremendous need, there can be no doubt. At this time rail travel was fast becoming popular, not only with those who could afford first- and second-class fare, but also with third-class passengers. The number of third-class passengers showed a marked increase in comparison with the other two classes. About the year 1857, approximately one third of the entire traffic consisted of third-class passengers; by 1867, this proportion had risen to one half. Six years later they accounted for more than three-quarters of the total number carried, which was nearly four hundred million.

Section 6 of the Regulation of Railways Act, 1889, stated that 'every passenger ticket issued by any railway company in the United Kingdom shall bear upon its face, printed or written in legible characters, the fare chargeable for the journey for which such ticket is issued. . . .' Any railway company which contravened these regulations was liable to a penalty not exceeding 40 shillings for every ticket so issued.

In 1884, anticipating the Act by five years, the Midland Railway began to print the rail fares on the face of the tickets, and by February 1885, when the chairman presented his half-yearly report, more than 7 million such tickets had been issued to the stations. At this time there were about 460 stations on the Midland Railway, of which some 450 had received their quota of the new style tickets. Twelve months later, some of the facts and figures in the chairman's report were a little less heartening. It was his painful duty to inform the board of directors that more than 105,000 fewer first-class passengers had been carried than during the corresponding period of the previous year. The glum faces of the directors were given an uplift when the chairman announced that passenger traffic miles in the past year had increased by 212,233 to a record total of 7,021,997 miles, although the earnings per train miles were down by ⅞th of a penny, to a figure of 3s 7⅛d.

When writing a work of this nature it is sometimes difficult to present a comparison of relevant statistics without descending into a vale of tedium. This is usually because much of the necessary information has to be unearthed from among a pile of dreary, formal company records. However they may solve the problem, few railway historians have the flair and imagination possessed by Fred Williams. This celebrated author/historian, who was responsible for the authoritative history of the Midland Railway compiled in 1876, was very fond of playing with figures. The disciplines and logic of mathematics intrigued him. When visiting a friend he made some rather interesting comparisons which concerned the total issue of tickets on all the country's railways. Williams announced to his somewhat sceptical friend that the number of tickets used on the railways every year would cover an area of one hundred acres. He explained to his friend thus.

'In order to make the calculation easy for you, let us use round numbers. Let us suppose that 100 tickets occupy one square foot. As there are nine square feet in one square yard, that means that we should need 900 tickets for a square yard; or in round figures again, say 1,000.'

'Well, then. There are 4,840 square yards in an acre; but for simplicity's sake let us put it at 5,000 square yards. That would mean 5,000,000 tickets for an acre; since about 500 millions of passengers travel by railway in one year, we may conclude that they require 100 acres of tickets to satisfy their enormous demands. As the gross receipts from passengers amount to about £25,000,000 a year, we may consider that these bits of paper come to be worth about one shilling each on the average.'

The railway historian's friend commented that Williams had an odd way of suiting the laws of arithmetic to his private convenience. 'But,' he said, 'you may be right.'

With the growth in railway travel it became a not uncommon event for friends and family to gather on the station platform to wish the traveller *Bon Voyage*. Such a practice was fraught with disadvantages to the railway companies, not the least being that these well-wishers crowding the platform represented an untapped source of revenue. Technically, they were trespassers, and were of further danger to the railway companies in that some might attempt to ride in a carriage without payment of the proper

MIDLAND RAILWAY.

LEICESTER RACES.

On THURSDAY, September 10th, a Special Train will leave NOTTINGHAM, DERBY, and the under-mentioned Stations for LEICESTER.

Fares there and back and Times of Starting:—

STATIONS.	A.M.	1st Class. s.	d.	Cov. Car. s.	d.
Nottingham	9 30	4	0	2	6
Beeston	9 40				
Trent	9 50				
Derby	9 25				
Kegworth	9 55	3	0	1	9
Loughborough	10 10	2	6	1	0

Leicester, arrive about 10·45 a.m.

Children under Three years of age, Free; above Three and under Twelve, Half-fares.

The Tickets are not Transferable.

The Special Train will leave Leicester in returning at 7-0 p.m. the same day, and the Tickets will be available for returning by this Train only. No Luggage allowed.

Derby, August, 1863. JAMES ALLPORT, General Manager.

A typical advertisement from the Excursionist and Advertiser, 1 September 1863. This was a monthly travel magazine, the forerunner of the travel brochures and newspaper supplements of today, produced and published by Thomas Cook, and printed in Leicester. Note the special fares for passengers who travelled by covered carriage; these carriages had unglazed windows! The reference to the arrival time is significant in that, from the Stockton & Darlington onwards, no railway has been required to guarantee an arrival time, merely that trains would not depart before the time indicated.

fare. Strangely enough, the idea for platform tickets originated on the Continent. The English railways issued platform tickets for which, at the outset, they made no charge. It was not long before they began to imitate the Continental railways, and a charge of one penny or thereabouts became general. Exceptions were made at specified stations or on special occasions. With the advent, in the late 1940s, of 'train-spotters' (young boys who collected train numbers and names), and older railway enthusiasts who travelled on 'Excursion Specials', platform tickets began to be issued for retention as souvenirs. The original charge of one penny stayed for a very long time, and for many years the revenue recovered was considerably less than the cost of printing and issuing; not until 1970 did the nationalised British Rail increase the charge for some platform tickets to one shilling. Platform tickets were issued from slot machines of simple mechanical construction. More sophisticated machines were used extensively at many busy ticket-issuing centres. These machines were a very successful development of the early 1930s, but the use of platform tickets on the railways of Britain has virtually disappeared with the current 'open station' policy.

The first picture in a burlesque series of picture postcards depicting amorous adventures on the railways, about 1900. Comic, romantic, and sentimental innuendoes referring to railway tickets have appeared on picture postcards for the past 80 years.

During these years a number of variations on Edmondson's standard were to be found throughout the railway world. Although his original cardboard ticket dimensions were adopted by many countries, others, while retaining his ticket-issuing system, preferred their own style of ticket. Several European lines issued tickets of a narrow strip of card which measured a mere 1½in by ⅝in; tickets measuring one inch square were quite common in Malta. It must have been an irksome process to retrieve such minute cards from the cluttered depths of handbag or pocket. To the Lithuanian or Persian railway traveller life presented no such problems. The former received in exchange for his fare a ticket which was nearly 5in long; the latter received one of the largest railway tickets in the world, measuring 8in by 4in. Ironically the Persian State Railway at that time was just six miles long. Circular tickets, for obvious practical reasons, were a rarity, but during 1935 they were in use in what was then British North Borneo, now Sarawak. The only hexagonal tickets ever known to have been used were issued as platform tickets on the Paris to Orleans Railway. The logical Eastern mind pondered that a return journey meant doubling the amount of travelling, so why not issue a return ticket made double the size of a single; the Japanese did just this. A similar practice was also quite common to most of the North American railroad companies; at this time some of the American companies also issued rather remarkable paper tickets. These were in strip form, folded zigzag fashion along perforations, and for certain journeys have been known to be an long as 7ft. Appropriate sections were collected en route.

In the years prior to the turn of the century, various measures were adopted for the production of railway tickets, and it is interesting to note the different stages. The cardboard manufacturers supplied to the railway companies boxes of prepared card. In accordance with the individual company's specification, these boxes contained something in the region of fifty thousand cards, each of appropriate size, shape and colour. The cost was approximately one shilling per thousand.

Subsequent to receipt and checking, the boxes of prepared card were sent to the railway company's own printing works, together with full instructions for their ultimate production. At the printing stage, three main processes were necessary in the manufacture of the finished ticket. A rather ingenious machine was used, sophisticated for its day, but somewhat 'Heath-Robinson-ish' by today's standards. Firstly the card was printed on the back with a notice which was intended to draw the passenger's attention to the conditions of sale as laid down in company regulations. After this stage had been completed, the tickets were fed into a hopper which controlled their descent to the printing bed of another machine. From the lower end of this hopper the tickets were mechanically withdrawn, one by one, and printed with the necessary details of destination and class. The ticket then continued its journey to its final stage of production. This was the more difficult one of giving each ticket a number in consecutive order. The numbering machine was automatic in its operation, and was fitted with a mechanical warning device. If any fault occurred during the numbering process, this instrument released a spring which in turn rang a bell. The printer then stopped the machine and investigated the trouble. Extreme care was needed at this stage, since for obvious reasons, no tickets with duplicate numbers could be permitted to be issued.

It was usual for stations to be issued with a six-month's supply of tickets; the actual number which this represented varied considerably, and was governed by several factors. Stocks for a particular ticket could mean only a mere fifty while for another this number could be in excess of ten thousand. Stationmasters sent their demand for more tickets to the company's audit office. A complete specification was listed on a specially designed form (for small orders an ordering ticket was used), which gave details of the issuing station, the route for which the ticket was required, the appropriate colour, class, and description. This latter item referred to the type of ticket, single or return, and the variations thereon. A further item was required on the special form since it was of paramount importance for audit records; this was the last progressive number issued for that particular ticket, together with the last progressive number held in existing stocks. After approval of the requisition it was forwarded to the ticket printing department. This procedure was followed for all standard tickets, but special tickets (for excursions, etc) had to be ordered from the superintendent's office. In its basic essentials, this system remained practically unaltered until fairly recent times.

As may well be imagined, the number of tickets produced for any of the major railway companies was enormous. With the printing machines of the

(continued on page 48)

L. N. E. R.
DAY EXC'N
Newmarket
(M) TO
LIVERPOOL St
Valid as per Bills.
THIRD
For conditions see back
L. N. E. R.
DAY EXC'N
LIVERPOOL ST
(M) TO
NEWMARKET
And thence to Racecourse & Back
By Eastern National Omnibus Co.
Valid as per Bills.
THIRD & MOTOR
For conditions see back

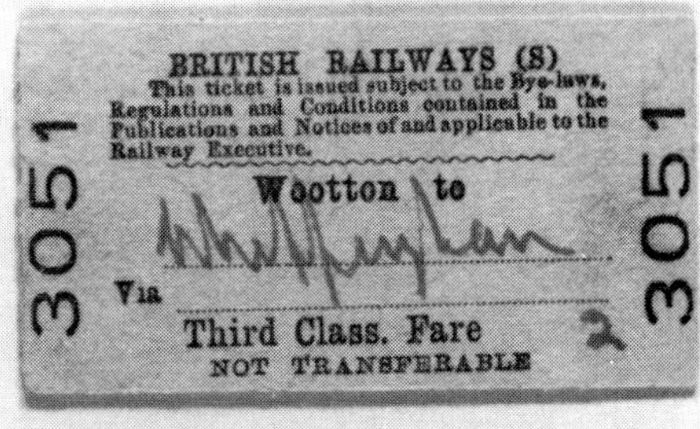

BRITISH RAILWAYS (S)
This ticket is issued subject to the Bye-laws, Regulations and Conditions contained in the Publications and Notices of and applicable to the Railway Executive.
3051
Wootton to
Via
Third Class. Fare
NOT TRANSFERABLE
3051

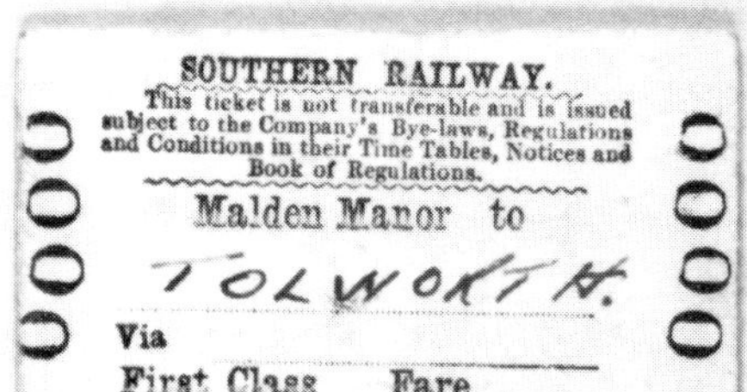

SOUTHERN RAILWAY.
This ticket is not transferable and is issued subject to the Company's Bye-laws, Regulations and Conditions in their Time Tables, Notices and Book of Regulations.
0000
Malden Manor to
TOLWORTH.
Via
First Class Fare
0000

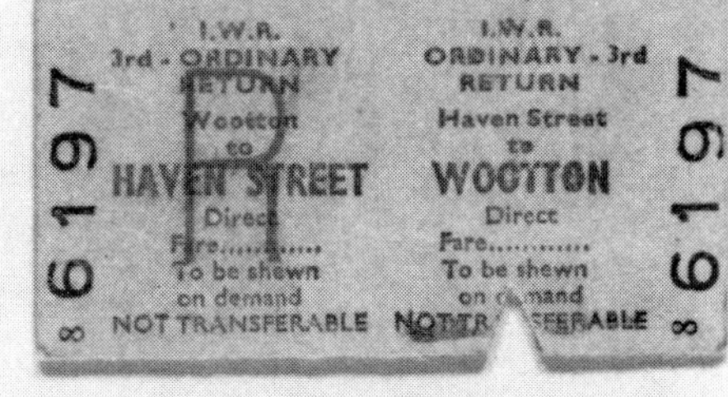

6197
I.W.R.
3rd - ORDINARY RETURN
Wootton to
HAVEN STREET
Direct
To be shewn on demand
NOT TRANSFERABLE
I.W.R.
ORDINARY - 3rd RETURN
Haven Street to
WOOTTON
Direct
To be shewn on demand
6197

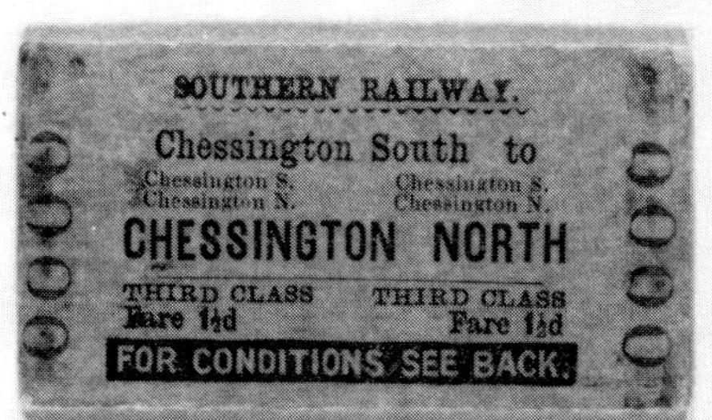

SOUTHERN RAILWAY.
Chessington South to
Chessington S.
Chessington N.
CHESSINGTON NORTH
THIRD CLASS
Fare 1½d
THIRD CLASS
Fare 1½d
FOR CONDITIONS SEE BACK.

0008
SOUTHERN RAILWAY.
WHIPPINGHAM
Third Class.
NOT TRANSFERABLE
SOUTHERN RAILWAY.
CHEAP DAY
CARISBROOKE CASTLE
Third Class.
0008

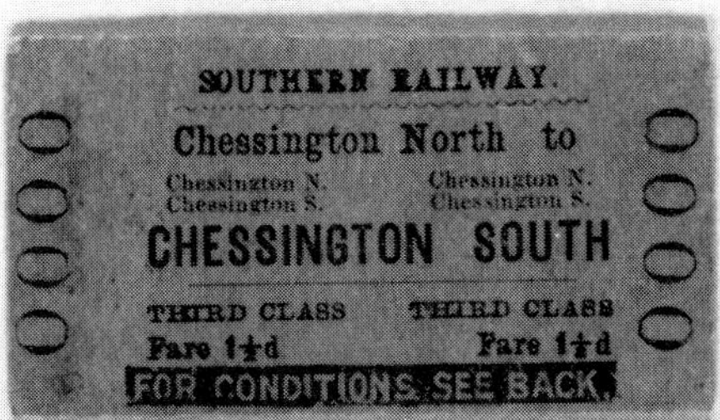

SOUTHERN RAILWAY.
0000
Chessington North to
Chessington N.
Chessington S.
CHESSINGTON SOUTH
THIRD CLASS
Fare 1½d
THIRD CLASS
Fare 1½d
FOR CONDITIONS SEE BACK.
0000

0088
SOUTHERN RAILWAY.
WOOTTON
Third Class
NOT TRANSFERABLE
SOUTHERN RAILWAY.
MONTHLY RETURN
Wootton to
WHIPPINGHAM
Third Class
0088

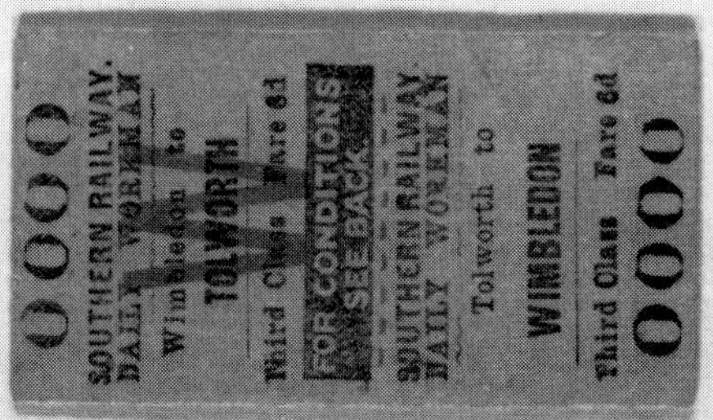

0000
SOUTHERN RAILWAY.
DAILY WORKMAN
TOLWORTH
FOR CONDITIONS SEE BACK
SOUTHERN RAILWAY.
DAILY WORKMAN
Tolworth to
WIMBLEDON
Third Class Fare 6d
0000

SOUTHERN RAILWAY.
3401
Newport to
CEMENT MILLS HALT
Third Class. Fare 1½d.
3401

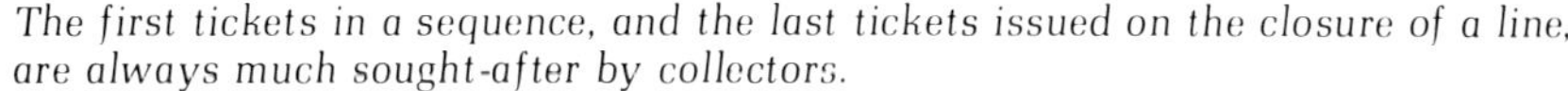

The first tickets in a sequence, and the last tickets issued on the closure of a line, are always much sought-after by collectors.
0000 LNER day excursion. This ticket was used as a specimen by the the booking-office clerk when ordering a further supply of similar tickets.
0000 Four Southern Railway tickets. The Malden Manor and Tolworth branch line was the last to be constructed by the SR, opening on 29 May 1938, and on to Chessington North and South on 28 May 1939; these are the first tickets issued. Also, the first workman's ticket from Tolworth, issued 30 May 1938. The holder, who travelled 9½ miles for his 6d fare, is thought to have been purchasing one of the new houses erected at Tolworth. Such concessionary fares were not unusual when new estates were built.
3051 Wootton Station on the Isle of Wight was closed on the evening of 20 September 1953; this ticket was one of the last to be sold.
6197 Wootton can again be reached by rail, and is the terminus of the Isle of Wight Steam Railway; this ticket was issued in 1980.
0008 SR Child, 'B' for bus overprint, issued 20 September 1953, the last day when the combined rail/bus journey could be made.
0088 SR monthly return, one of the last to be issued from Whippingham to Wootton, on 13 August 1953.
3401 Cement Mills Halt did not appear in public timetables. It served the staff of a cement works between Newport and Cowes and was closed along with the line, early in 1966. This child ticket was one of the last such to be issued on 12 November 1959.

Many early tickets, apart from the historical curiosity of their age, have interesting tales behind the mere destination details.
571 MR bicycle ticket, issued 17 September 1890. This was issued to signify that the passenger had an insured bicycle in the luggage van; a separate ticket was tied to the cycle.
8548 Possibly a cricket enthusiast used this ticket issued on 30 August 1888, by the Manchester South Junction & Altrincham Railway. This particular journey lay on the 1½ miles of the South Junction Line.
1289 Dublin & Drogheda Railway, first class single, issued in 1864, for a journey beyond their own lines, the D & DR acting as agents for other companies. The railway operated on 5ft 3in gauge, opened in 1844, and became part of Great Northern (Ireland) Railway in 1875.
6400 London & South Western Railway and London, Chatham & Dover Railway third class single, issued 22 January 1896.
873 London, Chatham & Dover and London & North Western third class single, issued 9 April 1895. Horizontal green overprint on white card.
3413 Bishop's Castle Railway second class single, issued 13 July 1899. The BCR was a privately-owned line which opened in 1865, and after a chequered history, was closed in 1935, the last trip to Craven Arms made on 21 February, 1937.
2083 Queensland Government Railway first class single. The line was run on a 3ft 6in gauge and was the largest railway in the Commonwealth. This ticket, issued 14 July 1899, had the date impressed into the card.
2442 Metropolitan & Midland Railways third class single, issued 30 July 1894. The Metropolitan was brought underground into London to relieve railway traffic problems in 1863 at the suggestion of Charles Pearson, solicitor. The change from steam to electricity was engineered by Tyson Yerkes, an American, in 1905.
1801 Macclesfield Committee third class single issued 13 April 1897. The original Macclesfield, Bollington & Marple Railway was dissolved in 1871 and reformed under a committee of the Manchester, Sheffield & Lincolnshire and the North Staffordshire Railways. Its name changed again in 1907, and the committee was absorbed jointly by the LMS and LNER in 1921.
498 London & South Western Railway first class single, issued 26 November 1886.

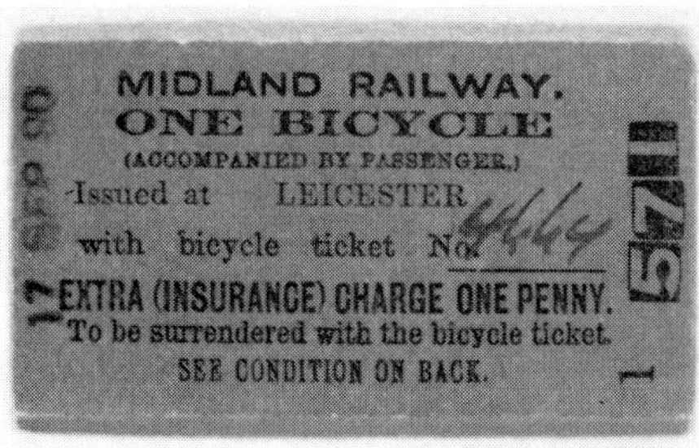
MIDLAND RAILWAY.
ONE BICYCLE
(ACCOMPANIED BY PASSENGER.)
Issued at LEICESTER
with bicycle ticket No
EXTRA (INSURANCE) CHARGE ONE PENNY.
To be surrendered with the bicycle ticket.
SEE CONDITION ON BACK.
1571

Issued by the M.S.J.&A.R.Co., subject to the Company's regulations, and to the conditions in their Time Tables.
AVAILABLE ON DAY OF ISSUE ONLY
Cricket Ground To
Oxford Road
FARE 2d
M
Third Class
Oxford Road
8548

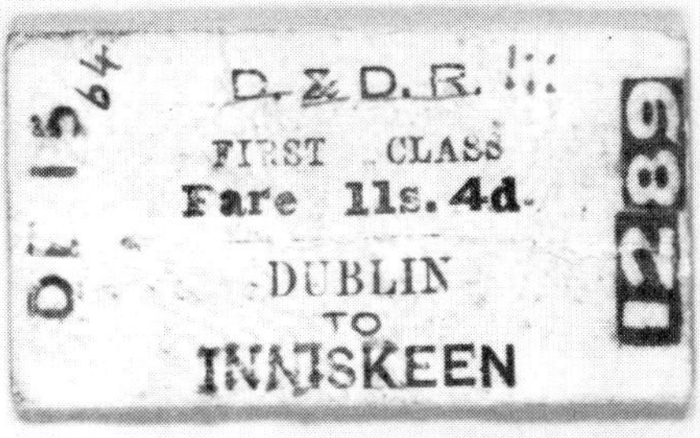
D.&D.R.
FIRST CLASS
Fare 11s.4d
DUBLIN
TO
INNISKEEN
1289

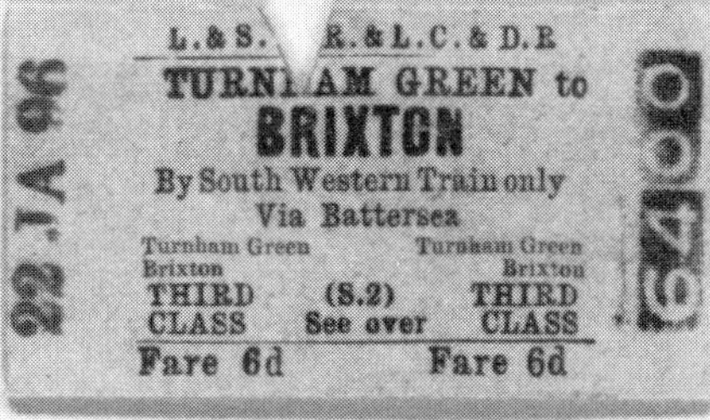
TURNHAM GREEN to
BRIXTON
By South Western Train only
Via Battersea
Turnham Green
Brixton
THIRD CLASS
(S.2)
See over
Fare 6d
22 JA 96

HERNE HILL
HERNE HILL TO HERNE HILL
WILLESDEN JUNC.
Via Victoria & District or L. B. & S. C. Rly's,
to Kensington, thence by L. & N. W. R'ly,
or direct by L. & N. W. train.
THIRD CLASS
7d.
7d.
Available on the day of issue only.
873
873

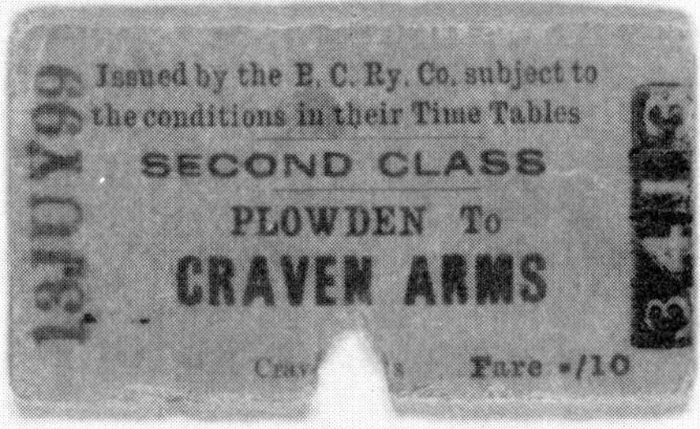
Issued by the B. C. Ry. Co. subject to the conditions in their Time Tables
SECOND CLASS
PLOWDEN To
CRAVEN ARMS
Fare -/10

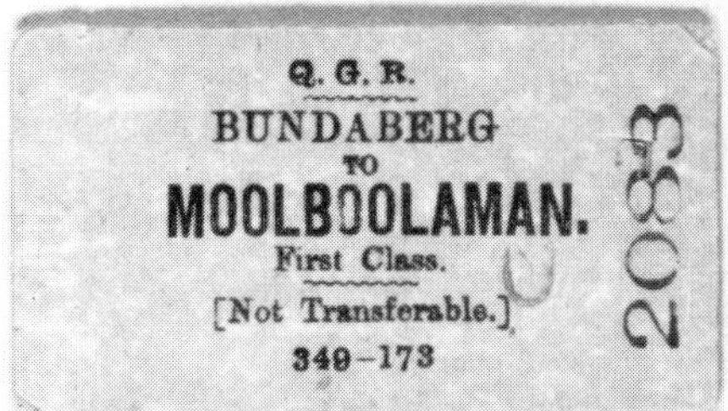
Q. G. R.
BUNDABERG
TO
MOOLBOOLAMAN.
First Class.
[Not Transferable.]
349-173
2083

Met. & Midland Rys.
Available by Midland trains only.
FARRINGDON STREET
Series 6.A
TO
D
KING'S CROSS
FARE 1d THIRD CLASS 1d
2442
2442

MACCLESFIELD COMMITTEE.
Issued subject to the printed conditions and regulations of the Company.
Available on date of issue only
MACCLESFIELD
TO
POYNTON
THIRD CLASS
FARE 6½d

L.& S.W.R.
SOUTHAMPTON
(S.1)
TO
KENSINGTON
FIRST CLASS
(See Back)
(Kensington)
(Kensington)
498

BOW
TO
VICTORIA PARK
Available between the above Stations only,
SECOND CLASS
Issued subject to the Company's
Published Regulations,
856

BELFAST
TO
CASTLEDAWSON
SECOND CLASS

Great Western Railway
ROCK FERRY
TO LIVERPOOL
Via Monks Ferry
FIRST CLASS
464
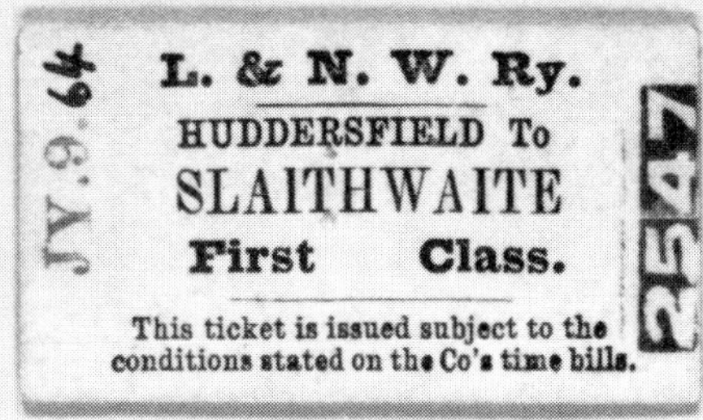
L. & N. W. Ry.
HUDDERSFIELD To
SLAITHWAITE
First Class.
This ticket is issued subject to the
conditions stated on the Co's time bills.
2547
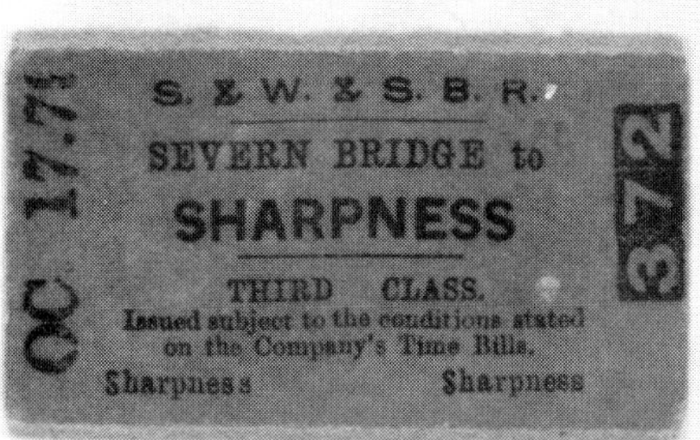
S. & W. & S. B. R.
SEVERN BRIDGE to
SHARPNESS
THIRD CLASS.
Issued subject to the conditions stated
on the Company's Time Bills.
Sharpness Sharpness
3772
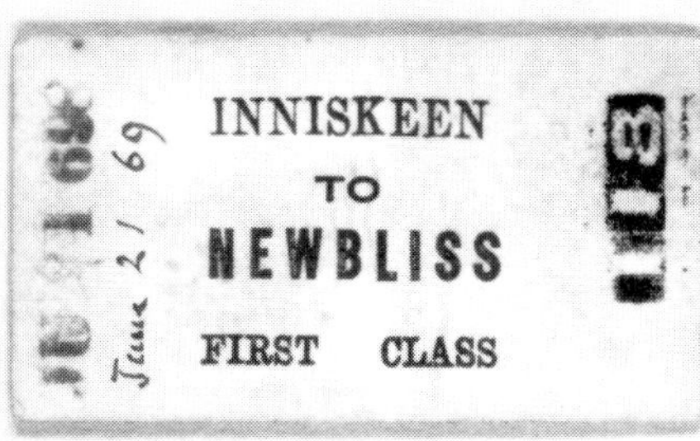
INNISKEEN
TO
NEWBLISS
FIRST CLASS
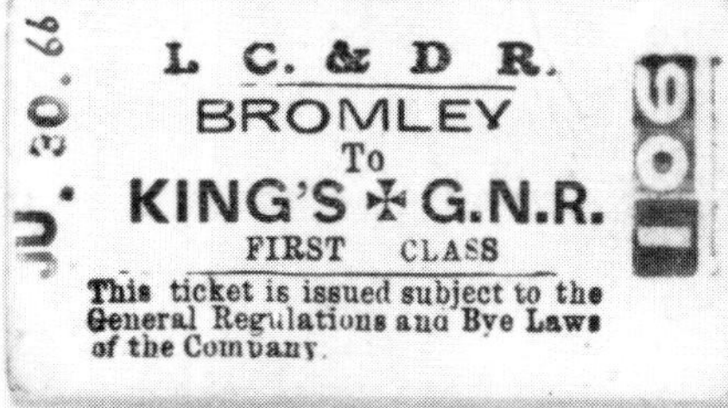
L. C. & D. R.
BROMLEY
To
KING'S ✠ G.N.R.
FIRST CLASS
This ticket is issued subject to the
General Regulations and Bye Laws
of the Company.
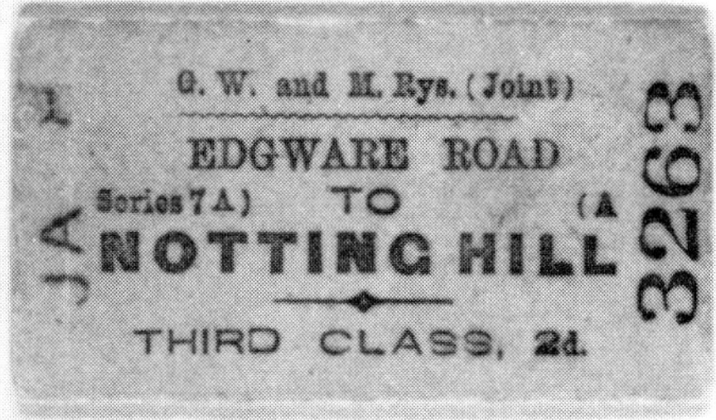
G. W. and M. Rys. (Joint)
EDGWARE ROAD
Series 7 A) TO (A
NOTTING HILL
THIRD CLASS, 2d.
3263
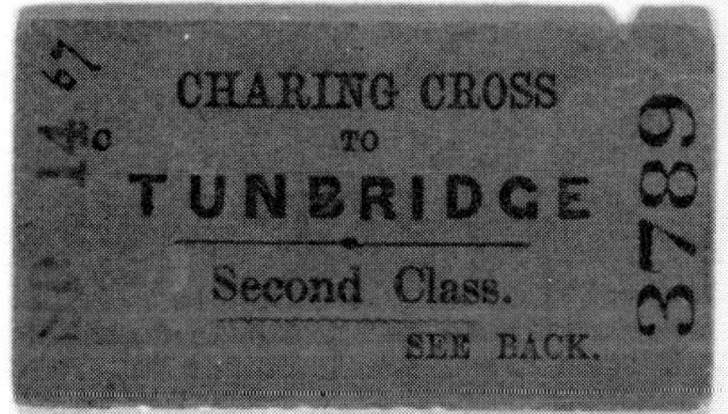
CHARING CROSS
TO
TUNBRIDGE
Second Class.
SEE BACK.
3789

Jersey Railway.
FIRST TOWER
TO
MILLBROOK
FIRST CLASS.
1884

More than 120 years ago the booking clerks who issued these early tickets probably did not suspect that they would later be of historical interest.
856 North London Railway, second class single, issued 9 April 1867. The North London operated on only twelve miles of track, and was opened in sections between 1851 and 1860.
1593 Belfast & Ballymena Railway second class single, issued August 1861. The line was opened in 1848, and the title changed in 1860 to Belfast & Northern Counties Railway.
464 Great Western Railway first class single, issued 12 March 1864. The GWR was publicly opened in 1838, and extended over the Birkenhead Railway in 1860.
2547 London & North Western Railway first class single issued 9 January 1864. In 1864 the Grand Junction and the London & Birmingham railways were amalgamated into the LNWR. Eleven other enactments were required before it was able to absorb other companies into its rail network.
372 Severn & Wye & Severn Bridge Railway third class single issued 17 October 1879. The S & W was originally incorporated in 1809 as the Lydney and Lydbrook Railway. In 1879, on its opening, the Severn Bridge Railway was amalgamated with the S & W into the S & W & SBR.
118 Irish North Western Railway first class single, issued 21 June 1869. The company was originally known as the Dundalk and Enniskillen Railway, and became part of the Great Northern Railway of Ireland in 1876.
106 London, Chatham & Dover Railway first class single issued 30 June 1866. Originally the East Kent Railway, in 1859 its title was changed to LC & DR.
3263 Great Western and Metropolitan Railways (Joint) third class single, issued January 1868. The line was opened in 1863 with mixed gauge tracks, the last broad-gauge rails being lifted in 1869.
3789 South Eastern Railway second class single, issued 14 September 1867. The SER was opened as far as To(u)nbridge in 1842.
1884 Jersey Railway first class, with lilac on white overprint, about 1872. The JR Company was formed in 1862, re-registered in 1896 as Jersey Railways and Tramways, operating on mixed gauge until its closure in 1936.

Free passes were originally issued to railway company directors, their families and friends, and directors of other railways, including those overseas. They first appeared as ivory tokens, later in gold and silver. Probably first appearing in 1880, gold passes of the Great Northern Railway entitled holders to free use of GN and LNWR sleeping saloons in 1891.
265 Southern Railway first class, giving the holder unrestricted travel, but requiring him to pay harbour taxes.
Victorian Railways visitor's free pass, beautifully gold-blocked on mustard yellow leather. No 093, it was issued on 22 September, 1891, to a member of the crew of HMS Orcando, and was available for one month.
41114 San Francisco Municipal Railway Fast Pass allowing unlimited travel for one month. Printed red and black on plastic-covered thin card.

SOUTHERN RAILWAY
FREE PASS 1946 FIRST CLASS
No. F/T 265
Pass MR. G. A. DALTON {SOUTH AFRICAN RAILWAYS}
BETWEEN
ALL STATIONS & STEAMERS.
Each passenger
must pay
Harbour Taxes.
Expires 31 ST MAY 1946
(UNLESS PREVIOUSLY WITHDRAWN OR CANCELLED.)
E. J. MISSENDEN,
General Manager.
Issued by
FOR CONDITIONS SEE BACK.

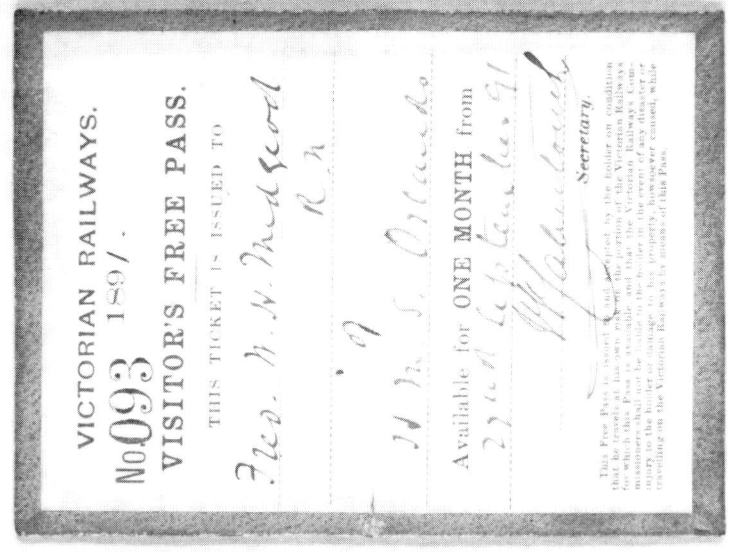
VICTORIAN RAILWAYS.
No 093 1891.
VISITOR'S FREE PASS.
THIS TICKET IS ISSUED TO
Available for ONE MONTH from
Secretary.
This Free Pass is issued to and accepted by the holder on condition that he travels at his own risk on the portion of the Victorian Railways for which this Pass is available and that the Victorian Railways Commissioners shall not be liable to the holder in the event of any disaster or injury to the holder or damage to his property, howsoever caused, while travelling on the Victorian Railways by means of this Pass.

19 MUNI 77
FAST-PASS
GOOD FOR UNLIMITED RIDING
— ALL ROUTES, AT ALL TIMES —
DURING MONTH INDICATED.
May
NAME
41114
GEN. MGR OF MUNICIPAL RWY
$11

FOR CONDITIONS OF ISSUE SEE BACK
L.N.E.R.
Bulwell COMMON TO NOTTINGHAM (VIC
Nottingham (Vic TO BULWELL COMMON
THIRD CLASS
L.M.&.S.R. FOR CONDITIONS SEE BACK
PRIVILEGE TICKET
Valid for Seven Days
THIRD CLASS SINGLE
STOCKINGFORD TO
CHILD
L.N.E.R. PRIVILEGE
SUTTON-ON-SEA TO NOTTINGHAM VIC.
NOTTINGHAM (VIC.) TO SUTTON-ON-SEA
L.M.&S.R. FOR CONDITIONS SEE BACK
PRIVILEGE TICKET
Valid for 7 days Not transferable
PETERBORO EAST TO
IRTHLINGBORO'
L. N. E. R. PRIVILEGE
(For conditions see back)
WHITTLESEA to
PETERBOROUGH EAST
Available within one week of date of issue.
FIRST CLASS
CHILD
L. M. & R. S.
FOR CONDITIONS SEE BACK
PRIVILEGE TICKET
CROFT TO
MARBORO'
L.N.E.R. PRIVILEGE
FOR CONDITIONS SEE BACK.
MARYLEBONE to
LEICESTER CENTRAL
Available within one week of date of issue.
THIRD CLASS
Leicester Cent.
PRIVILEGE RETURN
Bagworth & Ellistown to COALVILLE (Town)
Coalville (Town) to BAGWORTH & ELLISTOWN
L.N.E.R. PRIVILEGE
AYLESBURY TO CALVERT
CALVERT TO AYLESBURY
THIRD
For conditions see back
LM&SR. FOR CONDITIONS SEE BACK
Valid for Seven Days
PRIVILEGE TICKET
BROUGHTON ASTLEY TO

Privilege tickets were, and are, usually issued for a period of one week, but as 0095 British Transport Commission privilege return shows, this period could be extended to one month. The tickets illustrated here were issued subject to the usual conditions which were printed on the orders and vouchers exchanged for them. Although only intended for a relatively limited market, such tickets were not immune to the plague of excess printing. So many thousands were printed that some were destined never to be issued, while others were eventually issued by British Rail for use as ordinary tickets.

5406 On the reverse of this LNER special privilege ticket is printed a warning that it was for issue only to company's servants, their wives or children. Any other person using the ticket was liable to prosecution. This SPT is drab in colour; the official name, although intended for the colour also applied to the card. Even when newly-purchased, a ticket in this brown-grey colour looked soiled.

018 Note that the company is misprinted as LM & RS.

Privilege and pass tickets.

232 A rather impressive looking pass, issued by the Midland Railway of Canada, sometime in 1878, to George Griggs, general superintendent of the Connecticut Valley Rail Road. This line extended through Vermont to Montreal. The holder of the pass was required to assume all risks of accidents and damages.

2082 Issued by the Railway Executive in 1955, this free ticket was available for one day only. The Executive disclaimed any liability for injury or damage to the holder or his property. It was also only available for travel by Pullman cars.

0443 Welsh Highland Railway privilege ticket. Part of the original line was opened in 1877, closed in 1916, re-opened in 1922, and in the following year the title was changed to WHR. It finally closed in 1936, and was dismantled in 1941. This ticket is one of the last to be issued.

568 British Transport Commission locomotive pass. A railway ticket with a difference; this pass was not valid unless the holder was in possession of a railway ticket or free pass available for the journey made by him while riding on the locomotive.

53732 London & North Eastern Railway 'Certificate of Identity and Privilege Ticket Order (Retired Staff)'. It was available annually from 1941 to 1945.

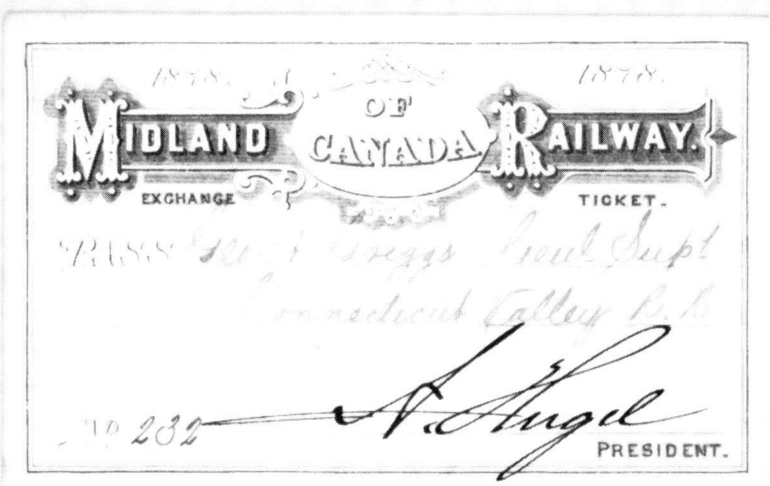
1878. 1878.
MIDLAND OF CANADA RAILWAY.
EXCHANGE TICKET.
PASS
PRESIDENT.

THE RAILWAY EXECUTIVE
FIRST CLASS
FROM GLASGOW
TO MALLAIG & BACK
P. B. WHITEHOUSE
FOR CONDITIONS SEE BACK
2082

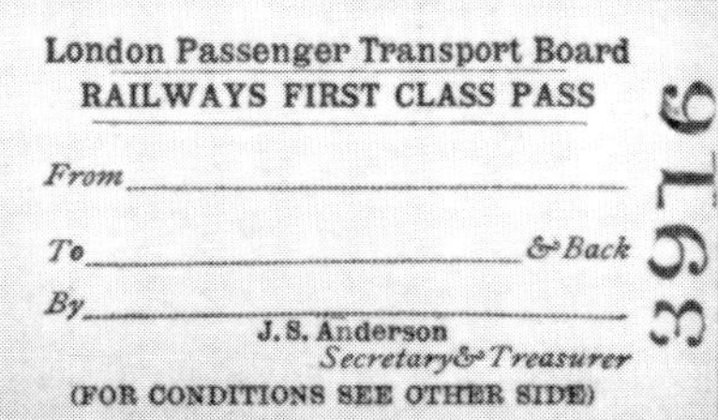
London Passenger Transport Board
RAILWAYS FIRST CLASS PASS
From
To &Back
By
J. S. Anderson
Secretary & Treasurer
(FOR CONDITIONS SEE OTHER SIDE)
3916

G. C. & Mid. Jt. Com.
(FOREIGN)
PRIVILEGE
BELLE VUE (No.2)
Available within one week of date of issue.
THIRD
For conditions see back
087

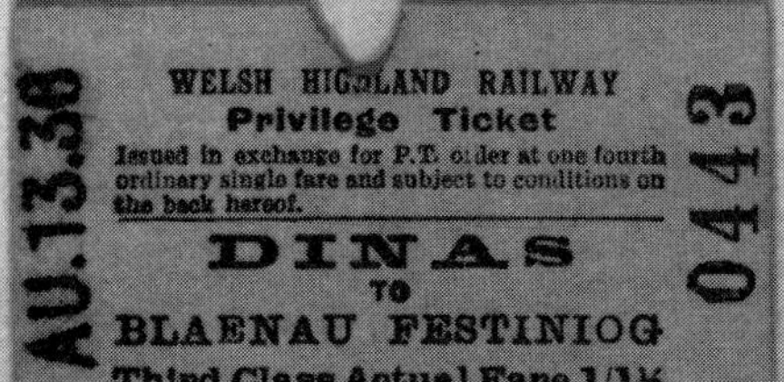
WELSH HIGHLAND RAILWAY
Privilege Ticket
Issued in exchange for P.T. order at one fourth ordinary single fare and subject to conditions on the back hereof.
DINAS
TO
BLAENAU FESTINIOG
Third Class Actual Fare 1/1½
AU.13.38
0443

N. Y. M. R. N. Y. M. R.
GOATHLAND
TO
GROSMONT
SECOND PRIVILEGE
GOATHLAND / SINGLE / GROSMONT
10 AP 77
0166

FOR ISSUE TO OTHER THAN B.T.C. STAFF.

BRITISH TRANSPORT COMMISSION BR 87102

BRITISH RAILWAYS, Scottish REGION.

Motive Power Superintendent's Office,

302 Buchanan Street, Glasgow.

No 568 1st May, 1959.

LOCOMOTIVE PASS.

Allow Mr. P.B. Whitehouse

to ride upon the Locomotive : ~~in the Driving Compartment of Diesel Rail Car.~~

Train Any train.

Between Glasgow

and Mallaig

Date 8th and 9th May, 1959.

Issued for the B.T.C. by FOR C. R. CAMPBELL [signature]

This pass must be exhibited when required, and is issued subject to the conditions printed on the other side.

LNER 1309/2/35 10,000 M 9507

LONDON & NORTH EASTERN RAILWAY.

No. 53732

To the Station Master Airdrie South

Mr. John Sheen

late Clerk : Coatbridge Goods Manager's Dept.

(*Grade*) (*Station*)

is, upon production of this certificate during the **YEAR SHEWN ON BACK HEREOF,** to be supplied with THIRD Class **Local** or **Interchange** Privilege Ticket Orders for himself, wife, and children resident with and wholly dependent upon him if 21 years of age and over, or not earning more than 15/- per week if under 21 (**NOT** applicable to sons or daughters out of employment and temporarily residing at home), or

for ....

(*Insert Name*)

his .... who

(*Insert Relationship*)

is acting as his housekeeper.

All Privilege Ticket Orders are issued **subject to the regulations of this and the other Railway Companies.** (The regulations must be consulted before orders are issued).

R. L. WEDGWOOD,

Chief General Manager.

Signature of Holder John Sheen

This Certificate must be produced whenever Privilege Ticket Orders are applied for at Stations.

It is essential that every care should be taken to preserve it in good condition during the period for which it is available.

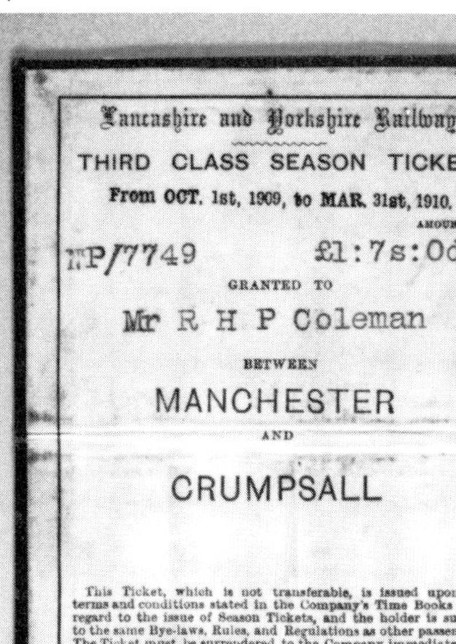
Lancashire and Yorkshire Railway.
THIRD CLASS SEASON TICKET.
From OCT. 1st, 1909, to MAR. 31st, 1910.
AMOUNT
P/7749 £1:7s:0d
GRANTED TO
Mr R H P Coleman
BETWEEN
MANCHESTER
AND
CRUMPSALL
This Ticket, which is not transferable, is issued upon the terms and conditions stated in the Company's Time Books with regard to the issue of Season Tickets, and the holder is subject to the same Bye-laws, Rules, and Regulations as other passengers. The Ticket must be surrendered to the Company immediately on expiration.
R. C. IRWIN, SECRETARY.
Issued by

NOT TRANSFERABLE.
MIDLAND RLY. THIRD CLASS
WEEKLY SEASON TICKET.
Issued subject to the Regulations & Conditions stated in the Cos. Time Tables & Bills, & on BACK HEREOF
Available for use up to SATURDAY NIGHT following date of issue between
HEELEY, ECCLESFIELD, ROTHERHAM (W'gate) ROTHERHAM (Masboro' Stn.) & WOODHOUSE MILL
AND INTERMEDIATE STATIONS.
Issued at TREETON (SEE BACK)
1204

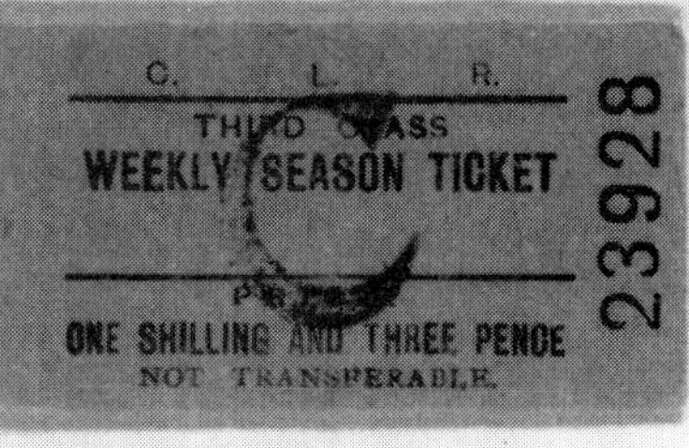
C. L. R.
THIRD CLASS
WEEKLY SEASON TICKET
ONE SHILLING AND THREE PENCE
NOT TRANSFERABLE.
23928

SECOND CLASS SEASON TICKET
No. 47 Date of Issue June 2/36
Holder's Name Mr. D. R. Taylor
Rate, £ 2 : 6 s. 4 d.
This Ticket is not transferable and is issued and accepted subject to the Bye-laws, Regulations and Conditions published in the Companies' Time Tables, Bills and Notices.
Issued at HORNSEY
Initials of Issuing Clerk
This Ticket to be given up immediately on expiry

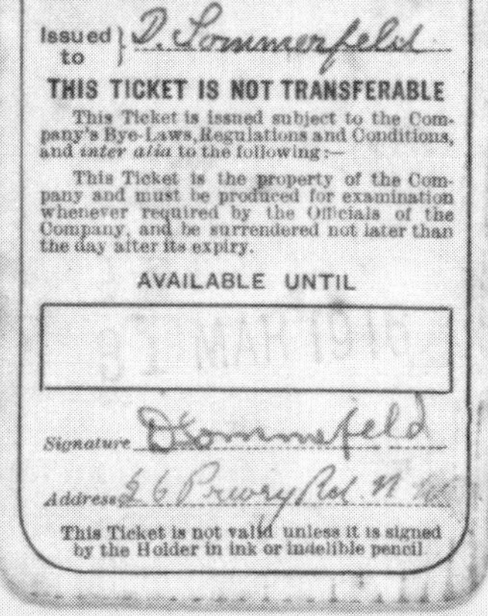
UNDERGROUND
LONDON ELECTRIC RAILWAY.
MONTHLY SEASON
Issued to D. Sommerfeld
THIS TICKET IS NOT TRANSFERABLE
This Ticket is issued subject to the Company's Bye-Laws, Regulations and Conditions, and inter alia to the following:—
This Ticket is the property of the Company and must be produced for examination whenever required by the Officials of the Company, and be surrendered not later than the day after its expiry.
AVAILABLE UNTIL
31 MAR 1916
Signature D. Sommerfeld
Address
This Ticket is not valid unless it is signed by the Holder in ink or indelible pencil

Season tickets are issued for periods from one week to one year, and are a mixture of discount fares and paid privileges. In style they range from very smart and official to very ordinary.
P/7749 Lancashire & Yorkshire third class season, available from 1 October 1909 to 31 March 1910. Mounted in a gold-blocked green buckram case which also has the destination impressed in gold, with an insert showing the expiry date. Known originally as the Manchester and Leeds Railway, three Acts in 1847 gave powers to extend the line and alter the name of the company to L & YR.
1204 Midland Railway weekly season, issued 30 September 1891.
23928 Central London Railway weekly season, unissued, about 1914. The CLR was renowned for the frequency of its services, trains running at ninety-second intervals.
47 London & North Eastern Railway two month second class season. The Metropolitan Great Northern, and City Railway had all been absorbed by the 1923 regrouping.
220 Underground, London Electric Railway monthly season. The LER was incorporated in 1910, and in 1933 was taken over by the London Passenger Transport Board.

Season tickets were like other railway tickets, a target for forgers, and elaborate measures were taken to foil their attempts.
02395 Winnipeg Electric Company monthly transportation ticket, valid for April 1938. A white rabbit and yellow chicken are superimposed upon a background of green and yellow banknote-style design which continues through, printed in red to complete the safety background.
GWR Third class weekly season. A simple banknote-style safety background, printed in brown on biscuit-coloured card. The GWR were one of the first companies to introduce this style of printing, extending the idea to most of their ticket range.
M33 Central London Railway one month season expiring in March 1914. Inside the decorative border pattern the safety background is made up of an endless repetition of the company's name.

Special tickets were issued for particular events and occasions in much the same way as excursion tickets; indeed there was little real difference.
0020 Nailstone Colliery Railway. This was an industrial branch line from the Leicester & Swannington Railway, but it is not known why the Freemasons had a special party train to the colliery.
0017 Navy Week supplementary ticket issued by the Southern Railway. There is no indication on the ticket as to when it was issued nor under what conditions
55 LNER day excursion 28 June 1924. The trip was organised by Dean & Dawson, travel agents, to the British Empire Exhibition. Note the special BEE red overprint.
009 Circular tour on Salter Bros' steamer, issued by the LMSR.
064 Evening river cruise, issued by the Great Central & North Staffordshire Joint Railway acting as agents for the London & North Western Steam Ship Company. In the 1930s the railway-owned steamer, docks, and harbour works was the largest commercial undertaking in Britain.
0103 British Railways Board (Midland Region) control ticket issued in conjunction with the World Cup Final in 1966 when England beat Germany.
031 Great Western Railway to Snowdon summit by the mountain railway. The SMR was opened on Easter Monday, 1896, operating on the Abt rack system and a 2ft 7½in gauge.
207 Londonderry & Lough Swilly Railway second class return to Buncrana fête & gala. A gaily-coloured ticket over-printed blue and yellow on white card to match the occasion.

WINNIPEG ELECTRIC COMPANY
MONTHLY TRANSPORTATION TICKET
APRIL 1938
$6.00
02395
TRANSFERABLE
NOT REFUNDABLE
THIS TICKET MUST REMAIN IN POSSESSION OF PASSENGER DURING ENTIRE RIDE, OR FULL FARE WILL BE COLLECTED
IF THIS TICKET IS LOST, DUPLICATE WILL NOT BE ISSUED
SUBJECT TO INSPECTION BY COMPANY UPON REQUEST
PRESIDENT & GEN'L. MGR.
INSPECTED X X X X X
(See Over)

G.W.R.
WEEKLY SEASON
37
G.W.R.
THIRD CLASS
No 6585
(S.1)
EXPIRES
Rate 3/5
SAT.
BETWEEN
OLTON
AND
BIRMINGHAM
TO BE GIVEN UP IMMEDIATELY ON EXPIRY.

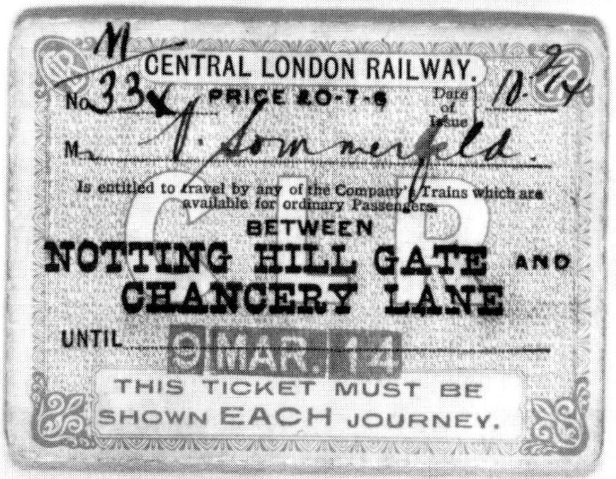
CENTRAL LONDON RAILWAY.
PRICE £0-7-6
Date of Issue
Is entitled to travel by any of the Company's Trains which are available for ordinary Passengers.
BETWEEN
NOTTING HILL GATE AND
CHANCERY LANE
UNTIL 9 MAR. 14
THIS TICKET MUST BE SHOWN EACH JOURNEY.

FESTINIOG RAILWAY.
SPECIAL SERIES
TOUR No 16.
PORTMADOC
TO
CAERNARVON
(Via Crosville Motor Services)
BLAENAU FESTINIOG F.R. Issue
1901
NAILSTONE COLLIERY Railway
June 10th, 1909
FREEMASONS' PARTY
Special Train
Nailstone Colliery to BAGWORTH
First Class
NAILSTONE COLLIERY Railway
June 10th, 1909
FREEMASONS' PARTY
Special Train
BAGWORTH to Nailstone Colliery
First Class
0020
FESTINIOG RAILWAY.
station to which passenger is entitled to travel. Single journey on date of issue only.
NAVY WEEK.
Admit ONE PERSON to
H. M. Dockyard at
CHATHAM, PORTSMOUTH
or PLYMOUTH.
CHARGE 6d
CAMERAS PROHIBITED
Issued by SOUTHERN RLY. Chiswick
0017
L. N. E. R.
NOT TRANSFERABLE
JUNE 28, 192
LEICESTER (Central) (A 70)
to WEMBLEY HILL & MARYLEBONE
AND BACK
THIRD CLASS
ADULT
55
Messrs Salter Bros' Steamer
FOR CONDITIONS SEE BACK
L. M. & S. ISSUE
Available only while the Boat is running
(1) CIRCULAR TOUR NO.115d. (3750)
This Ticket is issued by the L. M. & S. R. Co. as Agents for & on behalf of the Steamboat Owners subject to the conditions printed on the back.
KINGSTON(SUN HOTEL) TO
OXFORD
STEAMER
009
L. & N. W. S. S. CO.
EVENING RIVER CRUISE
From LIVERPOOL (LANDING STAGE
By L. & N. W. S. S. Co. Steamer
Available on date of issue only.
THIRD CLASS
Issued at
2233
L. N. W. S.
Ev. Cruise
H. Poynton
064
British Railways Board (M)
Control Ticket
WORLD CUP 1966
Kensington (Olympia) to
WEMBLEY STADIUM & BACK
For conditions see over
0103
Gt. Western Ry.
July 31. 1930
LLANBERIS to
SNOWDON SUMMIT
By Mountain Railway
THIRD CLASS
A.I. See back
Iss'd in connection with
Half Day Excursion
ABERDOVEY
031
L.&L.S.Ry
RETURN
TICKET
Second Class
Admit
TO
FETE
& GALA.
Buncrana
14th Sept. 1916.
Fare 1s.3d
Buncrana to L'DERRY
L'derry to BUNCRANA
Not Transferable
207

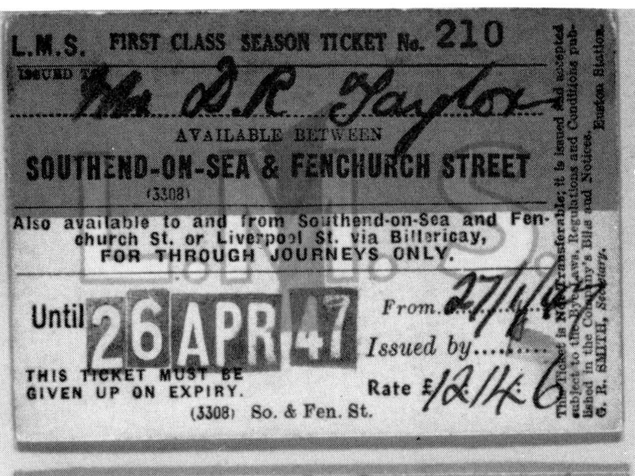

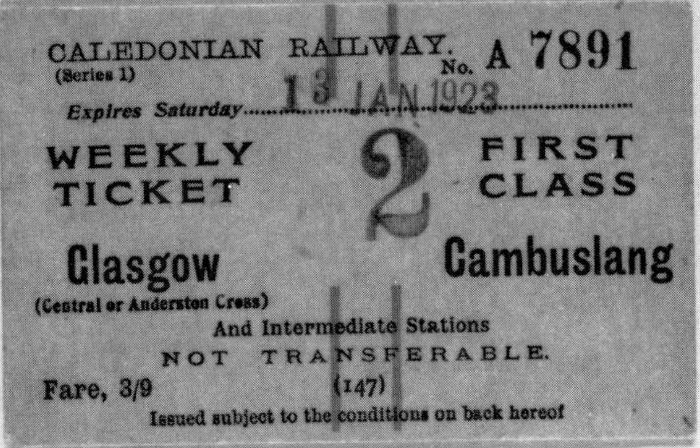

Season and weekly tickets.

210 London, Midland & Scottish first class season. The safety background is formed of the company's initials in outline surrounded by random dots printed in yellow on white card, and with a light green overprint on the top half of the ticket.

A7891 Caledonian Railway weekly ticket, unusual in naming the day as well as the date. Printed black on biscuit-coloured card, with vertical red overprints top and bottom. The first section of the CR from Carlisle to Beattock was ceremonially opened in 1847.

412 North British Railway Company weekly ticket, first class. Printed black on off-white card with a light green diagonal overprint. The NBR was incorporated in 1844, and with the Midland formed the celebrated 'Waverley Route'.

Gt. Western Ry.
SPECIAL TRIP
Sept 4, 1886
SHIFNAL
TO (WL)
BIRMINGHAM S.H
Via Wolverhampton
First Class
SEE BACK
Gt. Western Ry.
SPECIAL TRIP
Sept 4, 1886
RETURN SAME DAY
Birmingham S.H.
TO (WL)
SHIFNAL
Via Wolverhampton
First Class
SEE BACK
022
022
GREAT N RN RAILWAYS
DUBLIN (Amiens St.) To
MYSTERY
DESTINATION ST'N
Third Class & RETURN
Available Only On
9th. JUNE 1937
For Conditions of Issue See back
0501

L. M. & S. R.
No. 004
LONDON, MIDLAND & SCOTTISH RAILWAY COMPANY
GLENEAGLES
HOTEL
COMBINED RAIL AND HOTEL, &c., TICKET
WEEK-END
(Friday night to Monday night)
FIRST CLASS
LONDON (Euston)
Inclusive Charge
£12-0-0
McCorquodale & Co., Ltd., London.

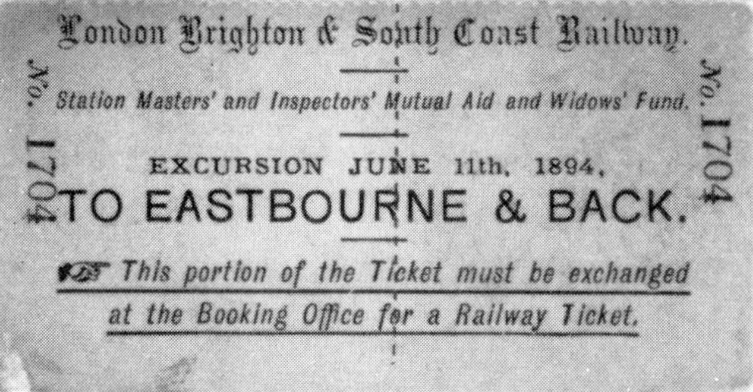
London Brighton & South Coast Railway.
No. 1704
Station Masters' and Inspectors' Mutual Aid and Widows' Fund.
EXCURSION JUNE 11th, 1894,
TO EASTBOURNE & BACK.
This portion of the Ticket must be exchanged
at the Booking Office for a Railway Ticket.
No. 1704

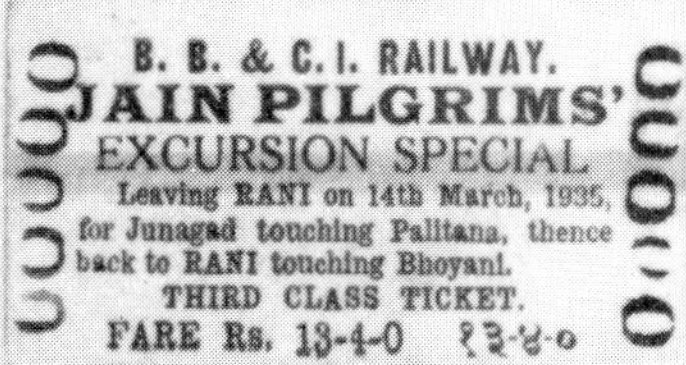
B. B. & C. I. RAILWAY.
JAIN PILGRIMS'
EXCURSION SPECIAL
Leaving RANI on 14th March, 1935,
for Junagad touching Palitana, thence
back to RANI touching Bhoyani.
THIRD CLASS TICKET.
FARE Rs. 13-4-0

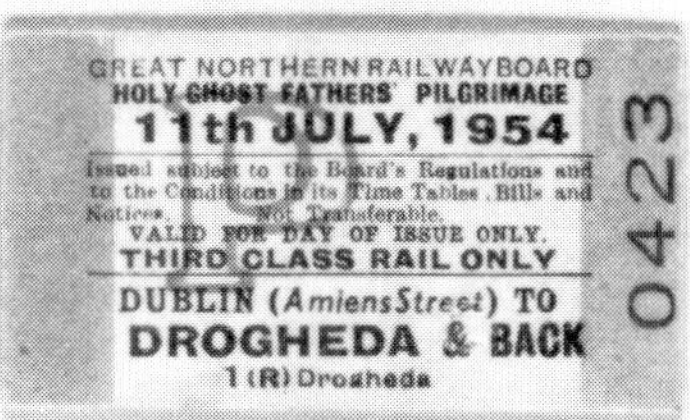
GREAT NORTHERN RAILWAY BOARD
HOLY GHOST FATHERS' PILGRIMAGE
11th JULY, 1954
Issued subject to the Board's Regulations and to the Conditions in its Time Tables, Bills and Notices. Not Transferable.
VALID FOR DAY OF ISSUE ONLY.
THIRD CLASS RAIL ONLY
DUBLIN (Amiens Street) TO
DROGHEDA & BACK
1 (R) Drogheda
0423

THE DART VALLEY RAILWAY
The Shell
Vintage Special
Buckfastleigh to Ashburton and Return
DAY OF ISSUE ONLY
TUESDAY, 24th MARCH, 1970
Issued subject to Company conditions
YOU CAN BE SURE OF SHELL

B. H. R.
JUBILEE TICKET
The Queen's Silver Jubilee
1952 - 1977
First Class
0059
0059

Special occasions.
022 Great Western Railway special trip return, overprinted red on white card.
0501 Great Southern Railways third class return to a mystery destination. Mystery trips by railway, coach and charabanc were popular, especially in the 1930s.
004 LM & SR weekend ticket (coupon book) blank. For the inclusive fare of £12 (sometime in the mid-1930s) the holder was conveyed from Euston to Gleneagles in a first class sleeping carriage, with a hotel bus from the station, hotel meals throughout the weekend, use of the golf courses, and all appropriate facilities on the return journey.
1704 London, Brighton & South Coast Railway excursion exchange voucher. It is hoped that the occasion was less sombre than its title.
00000 Bombay, Baroda & Central India Railway Excursion Special. A train-load of Jain pilgrims must have been a colourful spectacle indeed.
0423 Great Northern (Ireland) Railway Board pilgrimage return.

Punch types. Not all railway tickets were of pasteboard, and although similar to the Edmondson standard in size, many were of paper. They were of the Bell Punch type and issued bus and tram style by a conductor with a hand-held rack of tickets. As with ordinary railway tickets, many colours were used, and in most cases the reverse of the ticket was used for local advertising. The Midland Railway, Burton & Ashby Light Railway carries the following instruction:
'SAFETY FIRST. Conductors could devote more time to safeguarding passengers from accidents if they were not asked for change so often. Please provide yourself with EXACT FARE before boarding the Car'.
C2 2384 The Ashover Light Railway was opened in 1926 and closed to passenger traffic in 1937.

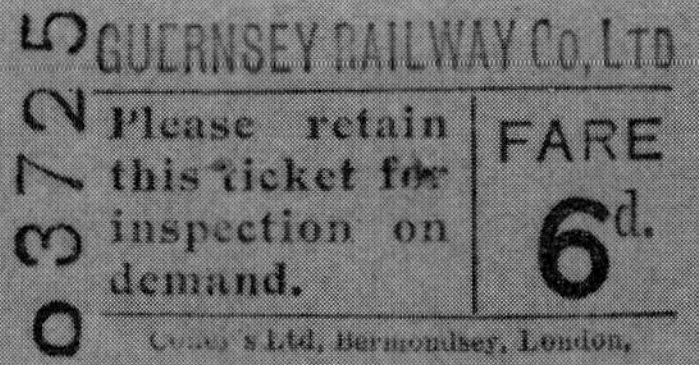
03725
GUERNSEY RAILWAY Co, LTD
Please retain this ticket for inspection on demand.
FARE
6d.

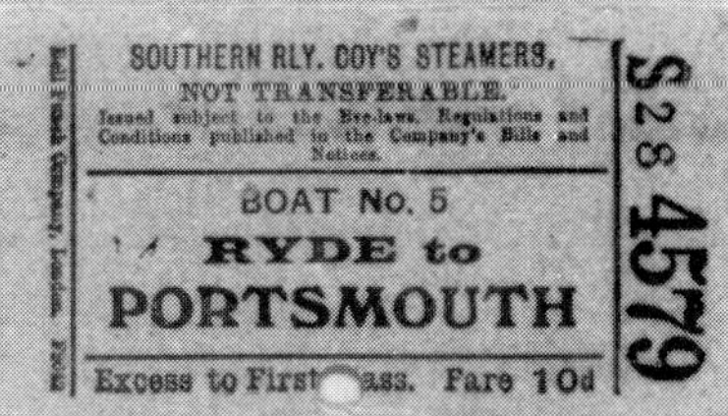
SOUTHERN RLY. COY'S STEAMERS,
NOT TRANSFERABLE.
Issued subject to the Bye-laws, Regulations and Conditions published in the Company's Bills and Notices.
BOAT No. 5
RYDE to
PORTSMOUTH
Excess to First Class. Fare 10d
S28 4579

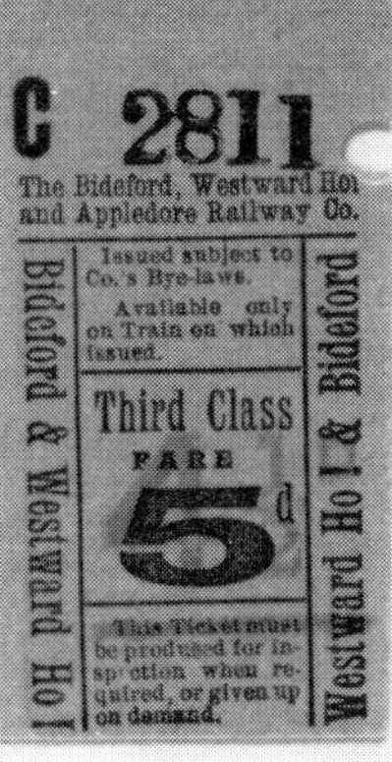
C 2811
The Bideford, Westward Ho! and Appledore Railway Co.
Issued subject to Co.'s Bye-laws.
Available only on Train on which issued.
Third Class
FARE
5d
This Ticket must be produced for inspection when required, or given up on demand.
Bideford & Westward Ho!
Westward Ho! & Bideford

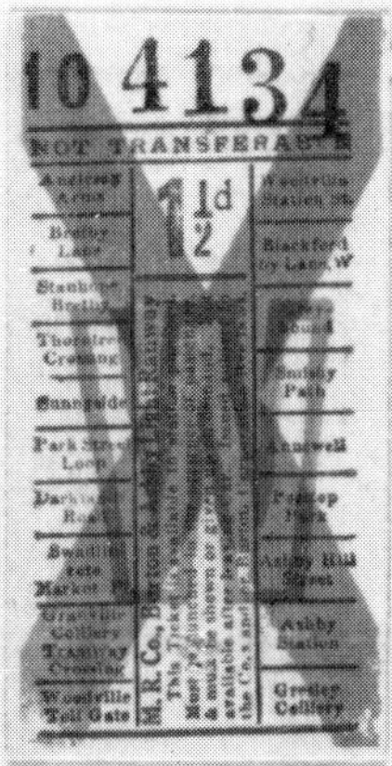
10 4134
NOT TRANSFERABLE

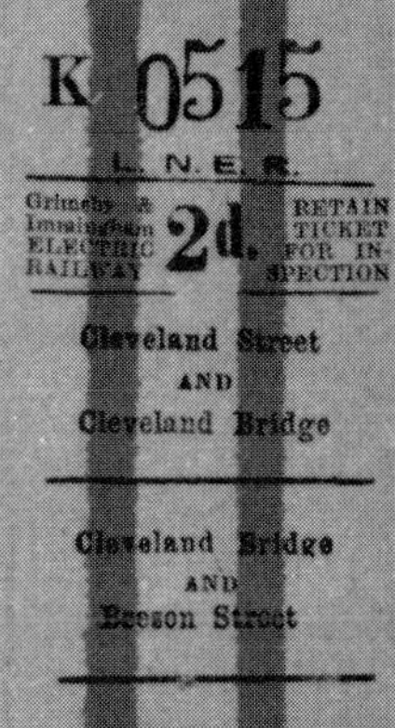
K 0515
L. N. E. R.
Grimsby & Immingham ELECTRIC RAILWAY
2d.
RETAIN TICKET FOR INSPECTION
Cleveland Street
AND
Cleveland Bridge
Cleveland Bridge
AND
Beeson Street

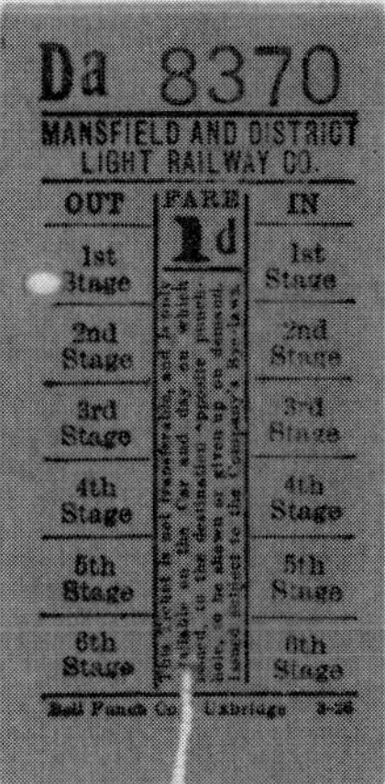
Da 8370
MANSFIELD AND DISTRICT LIGHT RAILWAY CO.
OUT
FARE
1d
IN
1st Stage
2nd Stage
3rd Stage
4th Stage
5th Stage
6th Stage
Bell Punch Co. Uxbridge

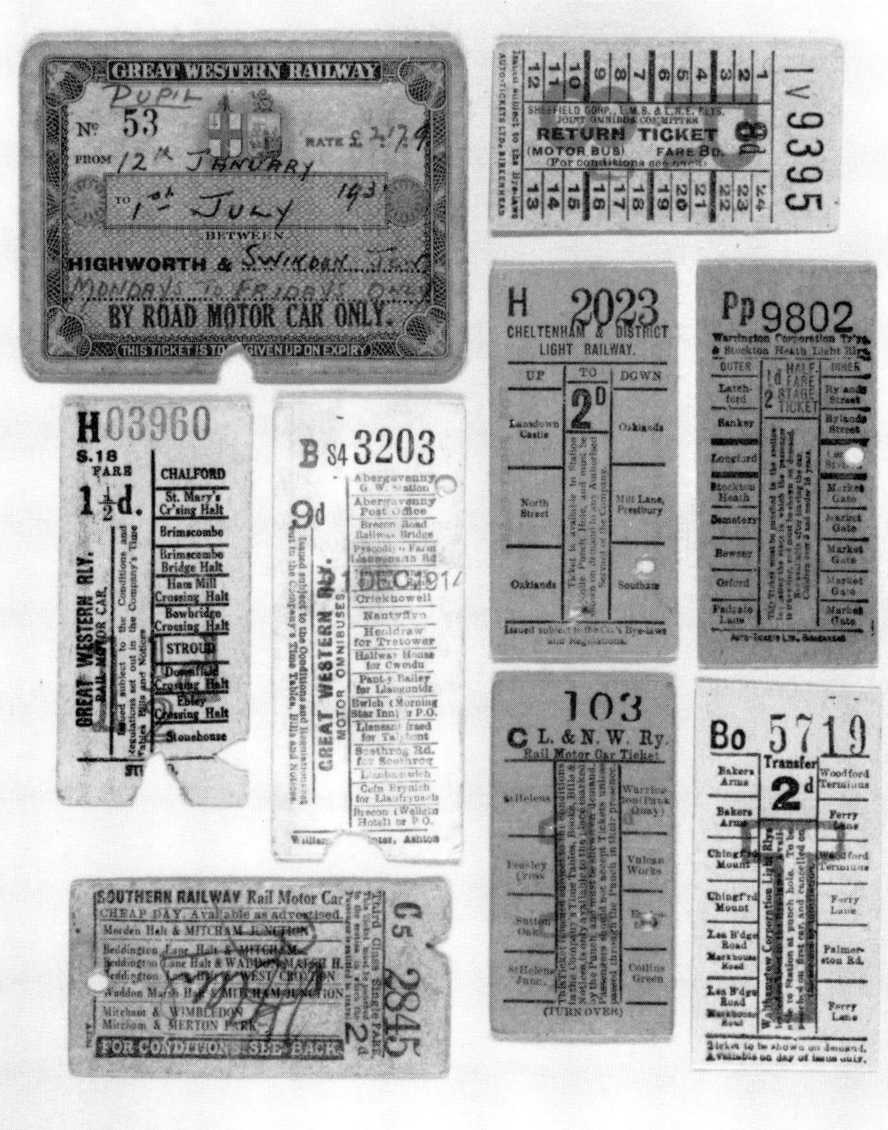

Road/rail motor & punch. Although the Great Western Railway pioneered the use of the rail motor, the first recorded RM coach was built for the Eastern Counties Railway in 1847. The year following, the GWR built a combined coach and engine, the latter with a 4ft 6in diameter driving wheel. Very little is known of the performance of either of these rail motors.

53 GWR Road Motor Car season ticket with restricted use. Printed dark green on light green card with bank-note safety design.

Several railway companies experimented with the idea of an omnibus on rails, the flanged wheels being between the pneumatic-tyred wheels. Other companies operated their own conventional bus service, particularly in village areas, or had a commercial arrangement with local bus companies. Most of the tickets issued were of the vertical Bell Punch type.

103 L & NWR rail motor car ticket. This issue is unusual, being an Edmondson standard pasteboard printed and punched like a bus ticket.

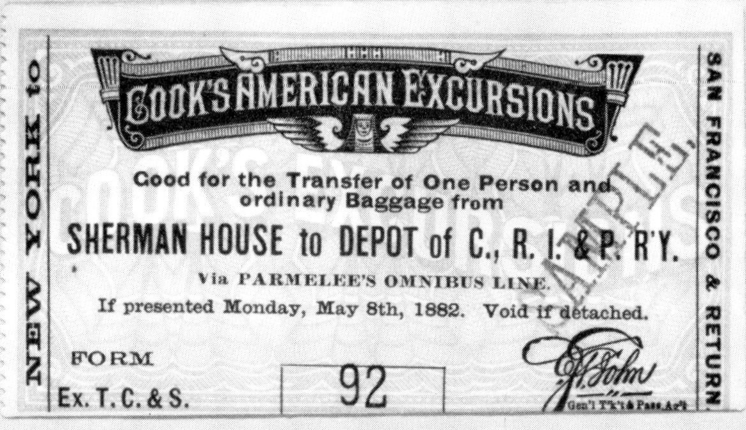

NEW YORK to

COOK'S AMERICAN EXCURSIONS

Good for the Transfer of One Person and ordinary Baggage from

SHERMAN HOUSE to DEPOT of C., R. I. & P. R'Y.

Via PARMELEE'S OMNIBUS LINE.

If presented Monday, May 8th, 1882. Void if detached.

FORM Ex. T. C. & S.

92

Gen'l Tk't & Pass. Ag't

SAN FRANCISCO & RETURN.

SAMPLE.

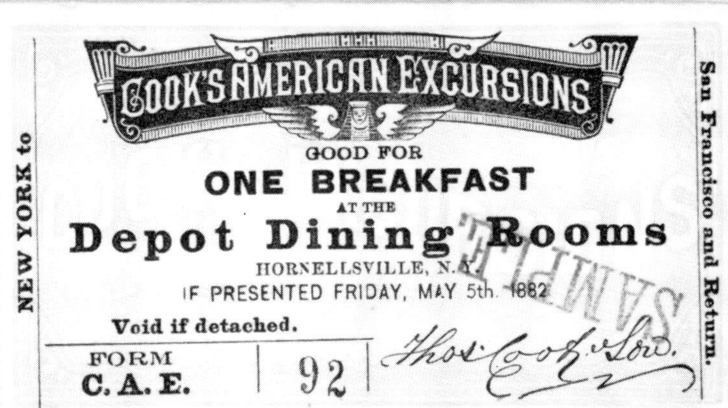

NEW YORK to

COOK'S AMERICAN EXCURSIONS

GOOD FOR

ONE BREAKFAST

AT THE

Depot Dining Rooms

HORNELLSVILLE, N.Y.

IF PRESENTED FRIDAY, MAY 5th. 1882

Void if detached.

FORM C. A. E.

92

Thos Cook & Son.

San Francisco and Return.

SAMPLE.

NEW YORK to

COOK'S AMERICAN EXCURSIONS

GOOD FOR ONE DOUBLE BERTH IN PULLMAN SLEEPING CAR

From NEW YORK to CHICAGO.

On Through Train leaving New York at 7.00 P. M.,

THURSDAY, MAY 4th, 1882.

Via ERIE and CHICAGO LINE.

Double UPPER LOWER Berth No. .... Car ....

Void if detached.

FORM C. A. E.

92

Thos Cook & Son.

San Francisco and Return.

SAMPLE.

Coupon tickets. The 'Cook's American Excursions' tickets illustrated here are from a set of supplementary tickets issued in book form. They covered the various stages and facilities of a journey from New York to San Francisco; the railway tickets were also issued in coupon form. The first stage of the journey was by the Erie & Chicago Line, and continued from Chicago by the Chicago, Rock Island & Pacific Railway; there was no through route in 1882, the date of these tickets. In an attempt to foil forgers and ticket sharks, the coupons were printed in pink to a bank-note style design on high quality paper with heavily gilded edges.

day, an output of 6,000 an hour per machine was possible. This was achieved despite the fact that frequent changes were necessary during the printing process; sometimes, only a small number of tickets were printed before the type had to be changed, while on other occasions the machine could be left undisturbed during the production of several thousand tickets. A total of more than 20 million tickets could be required by any one company during a year.

On completion of the printing, the new tickets were forwarded to the station, where they were formally received and checked. They then became the responsibility of the booking clerk. In his custody, the tickets were stored, and later arranged in order and class so that they were immediately accessible for issue to the passengers.

Because of the heavy demands made upon the booking-office staff by the increasing volume of passenger traffic, many ingenious devices were in use to assist in the speedy issue of tickets. One such device was the ticket box or tube. Conveniently mounted, these boxes or tubes were affixed to the walls of the booking-office. Made of wood and with metal rims, these tubes were so contrived that when tickets were fed into them, the column sloped downwards in front. At the front at the bottom was a small opening through which one ticket could slide. Since the weight of the column always pressed upon the sloping ticket at the bottom, it sprang forward at a touch to give an immediate issue. A similar principle was used in the chocolate vending machines which later were installed on station platforms throughout the country.

2
COLOUR, CLASS & COLLECTION

The nineteenth-century author, Robert Louis Stevenson, brought to life a character called Father Apollinaris, in *Travels with a Donkey*. This quaint and itinerant character stated that '. . . if landscapes were sold, like the sheets of characters of my boyhood, one penny plain and twopence coloured, I should go the length of twopence every day of my life.' He was referring to a widespread pleasure of the Victorian era, when old and young, rich and poor, delighted in playing at theatricals. Toy theatres were assembled, and for these, sets of scenery were available together with the cast of popular plays. These were printed on to sheets of card, to be cut out later, and according to the price paid for them were uncoloured outline drawings, or elaborately coloured pictures. Father Apollinaris might almost have been talking about railway tickets.

Colour coding systems now extensively used in modern business management had their roots in the humble railway ticket. Various colours were used, according to the class of carriage for which they were available, and the ordinary service or special trip for which they were required. The use of colours was determined by the fact that relatively few of the railways' employees could read fluently; compulsory education was still nearly forty years hence. The Midland Railway, for example, used seven plain colours as standard, for tickets of a uniform colour. Because of the many and varied services which the company offered to its passengers, there were several permutations of these seven colours used on different types of ticket.

Some were half-white and half-yellow, red and blue, or buff and green, while other tickets were available with a strip of one colour crossing one or more other colours. It was not uncommon for some tickets to have as many as seven alternating bands of colour. The 'down line' trains were accorded certain colours, with different colours being used for the 'up line' trains.

The more outstanding colours tended to be used for excursion trains, with yet more variations of colour for the different classes of excursionists. As has been previously mentioned, even banknote style printing was adopted by the Great Western Railway. It was quite a common practice on all the railways to organise excursions to particular places or for special events on successive days. By issuing a different coloured ticket for each day, the collector or the examiner was able to tell at a glance that the ticket handed to him was the correct one for that day. Special tickets were a nightmare to the booking-clerk and the examiners because of the ever-present threat of forgery and fare evasion. Confusion was even more

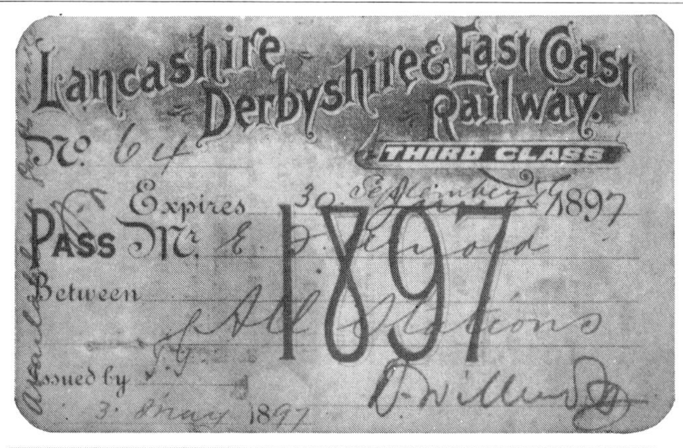
Lancashire Derbyshire & East Coast Railway.
No. 64
THIRD CLASS
Expires 30 September 1897
1897
PASS Mr.
Between All Stations
Issued by

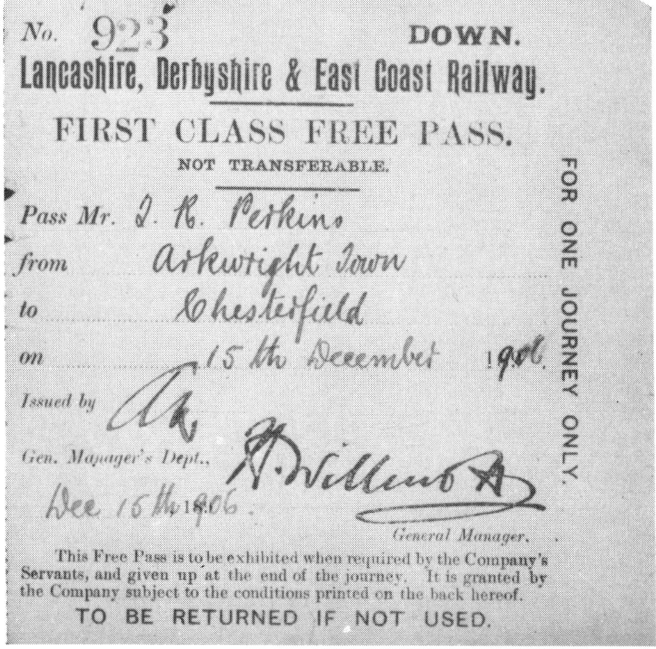
No. 923 DOWN.
Lancashire, Derbyshire & East Coast Railway.
FIRST CLASS FREE PASS.
NOT TRANSFERABLE.
FOR ONE JOURNEY ONLY.
Pass Mr. J. R. Perkins
from Arkwright Town
to Chesterfield
on 15th December 1906.
Issued by
Gen. Manager's Dept.,
Dec 15th 1906.
General Manager.
This Free Pass is to be exhibited when required by the Company's Servants, and given up at the end of the journey. It is granted by the Company subject to the conditions printed on the back hereof.
TO BE RETURNED IF NOT USED.

Dukeries Route.
L. D. & E.C.RY.
DAY
Excursion Return
Lincoln (G.N.)
TO
CHESTERFIELD
Third Class
See back
3901

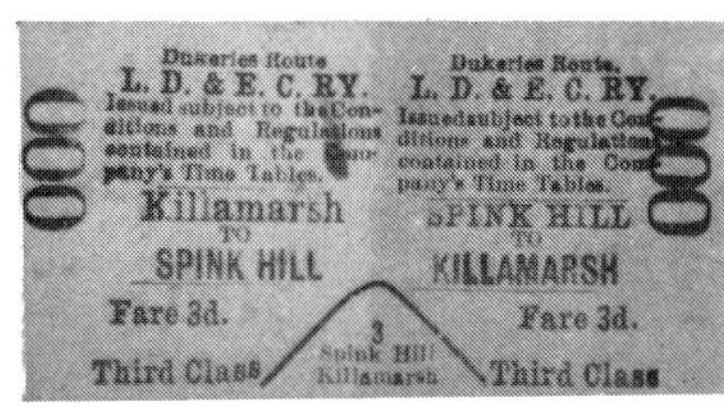
Dukeries Route
L. D. & E. C. RY.
Issued subject to the Conditions and Regulations contained in the Company's Time Tables.
Killamarsh
TO
SPINK HILL
Fare 3d.
Third Class
000

Dukeries Route.
L. D. & E. C. RY.
Issued subject to the Conditions and Regulations contained in the Company's Time Tables.
SPINK HILL
TO
KILLAMARSH
Fare 3d.
Third Class
000

Lancashire, Derbyshire & East Coast Railway tickets are rare because stocks at stations were withdrawn and replaced by those of the Great Central the day that company took over.
Third class pass No 64 printed in pale blue, the year 1897 in red.
First class free pass No 923, printed black on cream paper.
Third class day excursion return (half) 3901 with crossed red lines and skeleton R red overprint on buff card.
Third class return 000, buff left half, pale green right half. (George Dow)

compounded with the issue by some stations of market tickets, or picnic tickets, which were ordinary day tickets with the appropriate endorsement.

Before continuing with descriptions of some of these coloured cards, and the special reasons for their issue, let us diverge once again. All rules and regulations are made to be broken, and those of the various railway companies were no exception. Almost every ticket examiner there has ever been could draw on a fund of stories about fare-dodging passengers. In his history of the Midland Railway, Frederick Williams relates a splendid example of rural repartee. A ticket collector on his rounds enquired of a country woman, 'Is this your boy?' The lady nodded assent. Looking from the boy to the ticket offered for him, and then back to the mother, the collector exclaimed, 'He's too big for a half ticket.' Protective maternal instincts rose as the woman bristled with indignation. 'Oh, is he? Well, perhaps he is now, but he wasn't when he started. The train is ever so much behind time, and he's a growing lad.'

From the earliest days, forgery was one of the many ways used to evade the payment of the proper fare. But forgery can only be a paying game if there is an assured black market, and ample time in which to produce the merchandise. During the two World Wars, servicemen and women travelled extensively on the railways while on weekend leaves. Limited service pay and hastily arranged leave are hardly the best foundation for effective forgery. But the need and the circumstance provided the necessary spur to the inventive minds of men more interested in their destination and its pleasures, rather than the tiresome journey there.

Wartime weekends could generally be reckoned to be hectic at railway stations. Numerous guises were used to get two people past the ticket barrier after the purchase of a ticket for one. After safely but furtively boarding a train, it then became the job of one of the twosome to evade the ticket examiner. The usual methods were to hide behind the toilet door, or to lie on the luggage rack under a pile of coats. Eventually, the ticket examiner would make his visit and clip the legally purchased ticket produced by the other conspirator. All that was then required, after the railway officer had gone his way, was the skilful use of a razor-blade or a thin penknife. The ticket was carefully sliced through its thickness, thus producing (or rather, apparently so) two correctly clipped tickets. In the rush at the out-going ticket barrier, there was hardly time for the collector to inspect each piece of card thrust with hasty abandon into his hand, let alone for him to identify the donor. Two for the price of one, and the war was safely left behind, while pleasures temptingly beckoned.

It would have been interesting to see how 'Nan o' the Train' would have dealt with some of these fare dodgers. She was a conductress on the Campbeltown and Machrihanish Light Railway in Argyllshire. It was the practice for many years for the Campbeltown and Machrihanish Light Railway to employ pretty girls as conductresses, the most celebrated of whom was Miss Nancy Galbraith. When she left the service of the Company, 'Nan o' the Train' was succeeded by Miss Margaret Leyden. This young Scottish beauty, who is regarded to have added considerable pleasure to the journey, also held as large a place in the respect of the passengers as did her predecessor. Cardboard tickets were issued by the conductresses who collected the fares directly from the passengers. Issue was made from wooden racks fixed to a leather shoulder strap, and each ticket was cancelled by a plier type punch. In those far-off days around the turn of the century, corridor coaches were not used on light railways, and so, after collecting the fares from one coach, the conductress climbed to the next while the train was still in motion. She swung from the footboard of one carriage to the next, collected her fares, and so on, until the entire train-load had been accounted for.

Prior to 1844, poorer people received little consideration from the railway companies, but the Railway Act of that year required their recognition. Up to this time, third class passenger traffic was generally reckoned by the humanists to be a social disgrace for which all of the railway companies were of equal guilt. The differences in the degradation

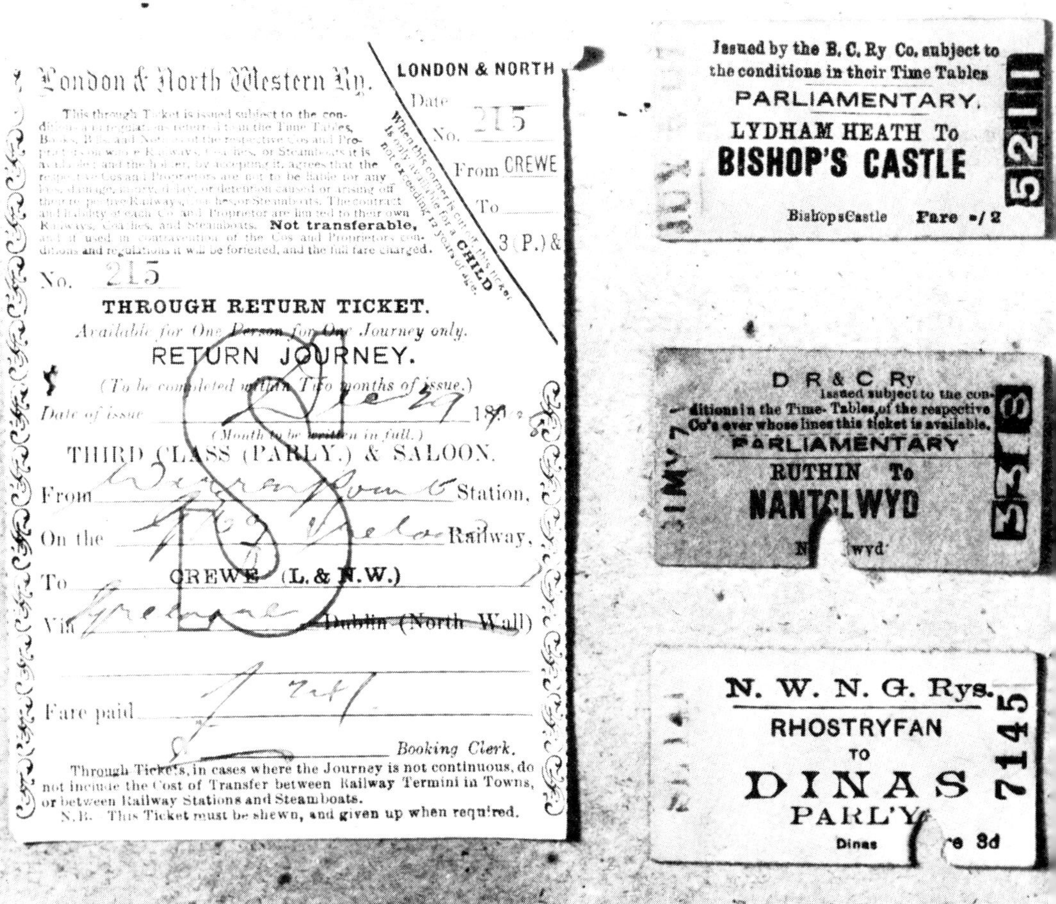

Parliamentary tickets. These tickets, issued repectively by the London & North Western; Bishop's Castle; Denbigh, Ruthin & Corwen; and the North Wales Narrow Gauge Railways were in accordance with Parliamentary requirements. The 'Parly' trains were run at minimum speed and inconvenient (to passengers) times, merely to comply with regulations. (P.B. Whitehouse collection)

of the passengers was an academic distinction when most were herded like cattle; some were even forced to travel standing for as long as sixteen or seventeen hours, regardless of the weather.

Quite a different story was told in the *Railway Traveller's Handy Book* for 1862 when referring to American railways. These were declared to 'present the very acme of comfort and convenience. You can buy your railway ticket in the carriage;...' With the Railway Act, the 'Parliamentary' train then became a standard feature of English railways, but while fulfilling the Statute by running once daily, the various companies arranged for it to be run as slowly and as inconveniently as possible. At this time, the ticket (printed on green card by the Great Western Railway, for instance) was labelled simply as 'Parliamentary', with no reference to class. Members of Queen Victoria's staff, some fifty years later, travelling from Windsor to Sandringham, were issued with a ticket which specified the class, but also identified it as a 'Parly' ticket, this being a colloquialism of the day. The tickets were, of course, valid for third class travel only, for Royalty staff or not, the bearers were merely servants. In the very early days of railway travel passengers were carried at speeds which varied according to the class or the fare charged. Many travelled in their own coaches which were placed on special trucks provided by the company; these passengers and those who travelled by the company's first or second class were conveyed more rapidly than the 'Parliamentary' passenger.

This short-sighted and rather degrading state of affairs continued until the early 1870s. By this time, the Great Western Railway, with some reluctance, was carrying third-class passengers as a class in their own right. For the privilege they paid a fare in excess of the 'Parly' rate of one penny per mile.

The Parliamentary Act of 1844, sometimes known as 'Gladstone's Act', is worthy of brief mention here, since it was generally regarded as the third-class passengers' charter. In this important Act, which became law in 1845, Clause VI sought to 'secure to the poorer class of travellers the means of travelling by railway at moderate fares, and in carriages in which they may be protected from the weather....' Provision was made for children under three years of age accompanying passengers, on these trains to be carried without charge. Children aged three and under twelve years of age could be carried at half adult fare. It soon became the universal custom for railway companies to carry children by all trains and by all classes on these terms.

The railway companies were required to provide such improvements on at least one train per day on all lines. Such provision was to include junction and branch lines as well as main sections; the specified 'one train' had to operate on both 'outward' and 'return' directions. In seeking to give the third-class passenger a more dignified status, Parliament was also mindful that he should not be exploited; to this end they specified the fare that he should be charged: 'The fare or charge for each third-class passenger by such train shall not exceed one penny for each mile travelled.' Unfortunately, the Act made no precise provision for charges where the journey involved fractions of a mile. Not until the Public General Act of 1858, the Act 'to amend the Law relating to Cheap Trains' which was applicable to all railways in Great Britain, was this undesirable state of affairs removed. In Clause I of the 1858 Act, a proper basis was laid down by which charges could be made for fractions of a mile travelled on the Parliamentary trains. It must be remembered that the halfpennies and farthings about which Parliament concerned itself represented not insignificant sums of money to the Victorians.

For a period of about twenty years until 1882, the Great Western carried first-class passengers in express trains, and special fares were charged for this mode of travel. The ticket was white top and bottom, with a central band of a light yellow-brown, running from end to end. In an early attempt to prevent ticket forgery, the destination station name was printed in a mixture of gothic and sans serif capital letters.

In 1872, the general manager of the Midland Railway made a rather startling announcement; he declared that all trains would carry accommodation for the conveyance of third-class passengers. At this time the company were using Pullman coaches on first-class trains for which a supplementary fare was charged. The abolition of second-class carriages, and the reduction of first-class fares almost to second-class level, occurred in 1875. As with most of the major railway companies, fares had originally been fixed on the basis of 3d, 2d, and 1d per mile, for each of the three classes respectively. One by one, each railway company abandoned second-class carriages, or else retained them for use on restricted services, and reduced their first-class fares. Thus, 1d per mile for third-class passengers and 2d per mile for those who travelled first-class became general throughout the country. All fares were increased in 1917 as a direct consequence of World War I. With the exception of workmen's, season, and London Underground fares, this increase was a staggering 50 per cent. The financial crisis of 1920 produced a further increase to 75 per cent above the pre-war level. When the Railways Act (Re-grouping), 1921, came into force in 1923, the later addition was removed, and fares were stabilised at 50 per cent over the pre-war figure.

Railway travel continued to increase in popularity throughout the nineteenth century, and well into the twentieth; but all the companies seemed to share a lamentable lack of statistics on ticket production. With the adoption of Edmondson's standard by all the major companies, most of the tickets produced were of a very similar style and colour. To the layman, knowing little of railways or English place-names, they could easily be mistaken for the production of one company. They were produced in thousands, far in excess of actual requirements, and tickets are now preserved that were printed in the 1850s, but which were not issued until the early 1920s.

The fare structures of most of the railway companies allowed for the conveyance of special categories of passengers. Each company differed in its preferences, but one category was common to all. This was the passenger who travelled at 'Government Agreed Rate'; a typical passenger who was allowed this concession was a volunteer soldier on manoeuvres. The Great Western Railway used at least two styles and colours for these Government Rate tickets; one was a uniform light green with a large overprint in black outline of the letters GR, and the other was bright green top and bottom, with the destination printed on a central band of light brown. Many of these came to be issued, in overprinted form, during World War II. The Southern Railway issued its Government Rate ticket on a pale

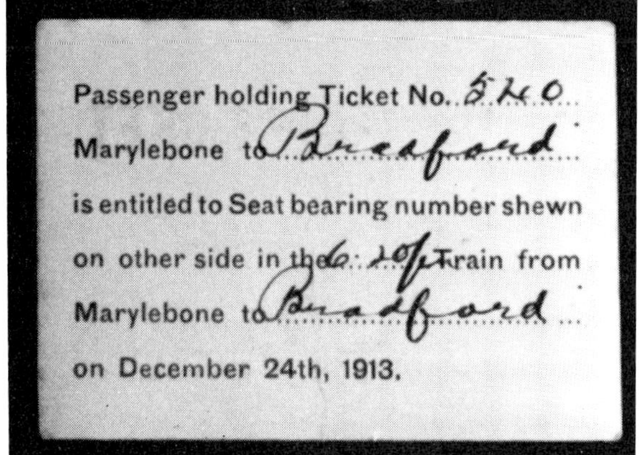
Passenger holding Ticket No. 540
Marylebone to Bradford
is entitled to Seat bearing number shewn
on other side in the 6.10 pm Train from
Marylebone to Bradford
on December 24th, 1913.

The passenger who held ticket No 450 occupied seat no B4 for the journey, as specified on this Great Central Railway reservation ticket. This type of special ticket was issued in advance of the journey at the same time as the ordinary service ticket.

green card; likewise, so many were printed that they were used for issue to other categories of passengers, with a suitable overprint.

Boats and trains have always had a close association. It is perhaps ironic that in the later development of the railways there should have been such close liaison between the steamship companies and the railways, since in the beginning there was fierce competition between the slow narrowboats of the canal and newly invented steam locomotive. Eventually, most of the railways ran their own steamship lines, with coastal and inland ferries, and collier fleets. In the early 1930s, the London and North Eastern Railway was advertising Humber Ferry River Cruises by the company's own paddle steamer. They were merely carrying on the commercial practice of the Great Central Railway who, to quote one example, operated a paddle steamer ferry service between Kingston-upon-Hull and New Holland at the turn of the century. About 1910, the Campbeltown and Machrihanish Light Railway were issuing steamer express tickets. These were paid for and issued on the boat, whereas on other trains of the company, the issue of tickets was by the guard or conductress.

A rather tragic and dramatic slice of history is preserved in a Great Western Railway ticket, printed in 1912, but never issued. The ticket series was titled 'Ocean Passenger', with the colour of the card varying according to the class for which it was valid. Issuing station and destination were Plymouth (Divisional Office) and London (Paddington) respectively. The route was via Dawlish, for which a third-class passenger was intended to pay fifteen shillings. At the bottom of the ticket is the legend: 'Issued on Board White Star Line SS "Titanic" '; on the night of 14 April 1912, she struck an iceberg, and sank on her maiden voyage. These GWR tickets were bulk-issued from the booking offices on the docks at Plymouth, and would have been sold on board ship.

By the beginning of the 1930s, production of colour coded, over-printed, special issue tickets had reached astronomical proportions. The system had got out of hand, not only in Great Britain, but in most other countries of the world which operated a major railway network. Tremendous efforts were made, through the use of organisation and method studies, to reduce

A splendidly-engraved picture advertises the services of the Lake Shore & Michigan Southern Railway; it is on a ticket agent's card and dates from 1876. The card was a centennial business card blank designed by Clay, Cosack & Co of Buffalo, and registered in 1875 in the Library of Congress at Washington. It bears portraits of Presidents George Washington and Rutherford Hayes.

the colossal number of special types of passenger ticket. Even so, there was issued in Great Britain a vast number of special tickets, which catered for the needs of cyclists, shoppers, battlefield pilgrims, and commercial travellers; in fact, for practically every class of person imaginable, there was a special ticket available. They were issued with distinguishing overprints of letters or words, solid or in outline, large or small, on various coloured cards. Some of these tickets included admission to carnivals, exhibitions, and the like; on the old Maryport and Carlisle Railway provision was made for special travellers to be admitted to the Carlisle Hospital on visiting days. The London and North Eastern had similar schemes — on presentation of a special voucher at the booking-office, tickets were issued to patients visiting the Cheshire Joint Sanatorium. On the Nizam State Railway in India, there was an issue of a special ticket which covered breakfast for soldiers. In the Federated Malay States, coolies could obtain tickets which entitled them to a special rice ration. Such similar tickets were echoes of the dining car and luncheon voucher tickets issued on European railways.

The practice of using outside booking agents was adopted by most railways, and for these special imprints were made. Tickets frequently carried the name or initials of the sellers, and sometimes a special colour was used which indicated the agent from whom the tickets had been bought. Inns of good repute had been used as stations and booking offices during the stagecoach era in England; light railway companies in Holland during the early 1930s copied this practice, with the inn-keepers acting as the official agents for the sale of tickets. These agents bought tickets in bulk at discount prices, and made their profit by reselling the tickets at standard passenger rates. On some of the English country branch lines, it was not an economical proposition to have a full-time booking office in operation at the station. Indeed, with perhaps only one train (outward and return) per day, the 'station' was merely a halt, being little more than a platform, sometimes not even that! In such cases, intending passengers had to purchase their tickets elsewhere; for example, at Collingbourne Kingston near Marlborough, on the old Midland and South Western Junction Railway, tickets for the halt were obtainable from a house nearby.

The famous 'Torbay Limited' express was hauled, in its time, by such equally famous locomotives as *Western Star* and *King Charles II*, en route to Kingswear for Dartmouth. In 1930, the station consisted of one double-sided platform with a covered way leading to the pier. From this pier, the Great Western Railway ferry steamer plied across the River Dart to the town of Dartmouth on the opposite bank. The Dartmouth pier-head was equipped with a booking office, and tickets were issued as though it were a railway station proper. It was described in 1901 as a 'Curious Railway Station'; people living in Dartmouth had to obtain their tickets on one side of the river and board the train on the other side.

While we may commiserate with the British old-time booking-clerk, bent under a deluge of special tickets and bedazzled by their kaleidoscopic colours, we should also remember that the tickets he issued were printed only in English. It was quite a common practice in many countries for railway tickets to be printed in bi-lingual and poly-lingual form. In what was known, prior to World War II, as Palestine, and now known as Israel and Jordan, tickets were printed in English, Turkish, and Hebrew. For issue on the Indian railways, the production of passenger tickets presented quite a problem, since they had to be printed in a variety of languages and dialects. In Belgium, it is still customary for tickets to be printed in both French and Flemish; certain types of Swiss railway tickets are worded in Italian, French, and German.

The Great Western rail car ticket was issued for travel on the AEC rail coach and similar vehicles. These businessmens' trains operating in the Cheltenham area offered fast services. LMS excess fare ticket.

At speed on the Great Western Railway. The AEC rail coach was introduced by the GWR in 1934; as pioneers of the streamlined railcars, they soon became the biggest users of these light and speedy units. Each car carried up to sixty-nine passengers on the cross-country routes between Birmingham, Oxford and Cardiff, and travelled at speeds in excess of 60mph.

Even when looking at a well set-out ticket collection with types and groups presented in orderly array, the complexity of the ticket system, further confused by the distinctive issues of the different companies, is staggering. To the booking clerk of the day it must surely have been a nightmare. Special tickets in special colours seem to have been produced and issued merely for the sake of so doing. Workman's daily, weekly, and return were commonplace, as were also children's and privilege tickets. In 1865 the South Eastern and Chatham Railway inaugurated what were called 'Workmen's Penny Trains'. These ran between Ludgate Hill and

Victoria, but because of their popularity, the company had to institute tight security measures to ensure that all passengers holding the special ticket were entitled to travel at the specially reduced rate. Intending passengers were required to apply one week in advance for a weekly season ticket, giving at the same time, the name and address of their employer. The passenger specified two stations en route, between which he wished to travel, and a ticket was issued which was valid as per specification only. The ticket, which cost one shilling, allowed the passenger one journey per day in each direction; tools to a weight limit of 28lb were allowed to be carried, but luggage was prohibited. In the mid-1930s, the Great Western Railway ran a businessmen's diesel railcar service for which supplementary tickets were issued to third-class passengers only. The fare for this service was 2s 6d irrespective of class.

Race-goers were handsomely catered for, but were regarded with some suspicion by the companies. In an attempt to prevent misuse and forgery, differently coloured tickets were issued for each day of the meeting, and each ticket was over-printed with the date set in bold type face. Sometimes these special tickets were for examination only on the train, since the outward half was required to be surrendered to the conductor on special buses which were arranged to convey passengers to and from the racecourse.

Another type of ticket which had a brief reign in the mid-1930s was the advertisement card. It was not too popular, either with the public, or the booking clerks. Apart from its slightly increased bulk, with the obvious restrictions on stacking space, it also had the full complement of colours and overprinting. Essentially, the ticket was made of two thin cards cut to Edmondson's standard, and glued together at the edges of both ends and at the bottom. This made a simple pocket, with the usual ticket information printed on the front and the reverse. A small finger notch was cut into the top edges and a tiny advertisement card, measuring approximately 1½in by ⅞in, was slotted into the pocket. Corresponding with the finger notch in the ticket, a tiny segment was printed on the advertisement card inviting the bearer to 'PULL'.

Quite naturally, the railway companies were in business to make money, and they objected to others using railway property for the same purpose. Taxicabs were tolerated as long as they brought potential passengers to the station, but plying for hire among the newly-disentrained travellers was not encouraged. A toll was levied on each cab which entered the station forecourt, and a ticket was issued (special and coloured, of course) which, dated and numbered, would 'Admit One CAB on ONE OCCASION to . . . STATION'. Quite understandably, the taxicab owners retaliated by boycotting the stations, and in about 1917 the toll was abolished.

During the 1930s, the publicity-cum-snob value of the famous named trains of the different companies was exploited to the full. Tickets for a journey by one of these glamorous trains were of a special issue, with the name of the train a prominent feature; they were, of course, valid only for the appropriate class and on the specified train. At one time Britain's fastest train, the 'Cheltenham Flyer', hauled by the famous *Castle* class locomotives, was operated by the Great Western Railway on its Paddington to Swindon run. It was the first train in the world to be scheduled for a

Special trains and special labels. Passengers would purchase separate tickets for accompanied luggage and each item would carry a delightfully pictorial label. Some splendid labels were issued for such trains as 'The Cheltenham Flyer', the 'Golden Arrow', and the 'Cornish Riviera Express'. British Railways adopted and adapted the idea of pictorial labels. The GWR label is for a charter flight by Imperial Airways for the railway company. In 1934, Railway Air Services was formed by the 'Big Four'. (Stuart Underwood collection)

regular service at the then quite remarkably high average speed of more than 70 miles per hour. For the privilege of travelling on the 'Flyer', first-class passengers were charged a bargain fare of 7s 6d return.

Passengers on the 'Capitol Limited' of the Baltimore and Ohio Railroad received every kind of luxurious attention when they purchased a ticket for the 991-mile trip between New York and Chicago. At different stages during the journey passengers could avail themselves of Pullman cars, diners, observation sun-coaches, sleepers, or individual seat coaches; among the many attendants in this completely air-conditioned paradise were secretaries, hairdressers, valets, and maid-manicurists.

In the late 1920s, the celebrated *Flying Scotsman* was the only train in Great Britain with hair-dressing salon facilities, a ladies' room, and a cocktail lounge. Passengers could connect with steamers to the Western Islands, or travel round the coast to Oban, and through the Caledonian Canal to Inverness. It was possible to make special tours, such as the then world-famous 'Trossachs' trip, or to visit part of the West Highlands, by using the Loch Lomond steamers from Balloch to Ardlui. This famous locomotive, on Friday 30 November 1934, attained an officially recorded speed of 100 miles per hour, the first locomotive so to do. The London and North Eastern Railway made the official announcement, revealing that

Santa Fe, the Chief Way. The Atchison, Topeka & Santa Fe Railroad introduced two 'Super Chief', stainless steel streamlined transcontinental flyers in 1937. Later with two 'El Capitans', they became four of the world's fastest trains, making the Chicago to Los Angeles 2,227-mile trip, twice weekly, in 39 hours 45 minutes.

Tickets for these all-Pullman trains were contained in a pictorial envelope, printed blue and red on silver. The tickets, of coupon form, were for coach reservation, the journey, and every service offered on the train. The envelope listed the passenger's name, carriage bedroom, all services and meals, together with the itinerary and an itemised record of the fares paid.

A popular Eastern Counties excursion express hauled by a 4-6-0 B12 class locomotive introduced in 1911. The 'Eastern Belle' ran on a different route every day to one of the East Coast resorts; cheap day and weekly season tickets were issued. The engines were very efficient, and after the re-grouping of 1923 were used extensively throughout the Scottish areas of the LNER'.

during the high speed experimental train run from London to Leeds and back, examination of the dynamometer car records showed that the 'magic' 100 miles per hour had been achieved. The speed was maintained for a distance of 600yd, in the neighbourhood of Little Bytham Station, between Grantham and Peterborough.

The 'Eastern Belle', also of the LNER, operated on a different route every day among the East Coast resorts of England. Cheap day tickets were issued, with weekly and season tickets also being available.

In the flood of tickets printed for issue to commercial travellers, boys on training ships, and shipwrecked mariners (the Great Western Railway issued such tickets, and even tickets for paupers!), there was still room for more. The passenger might wish to park his motor cycle, three-wheeled vehicle, or motor car before embarking on his journey. If he was not affluent enough to own one of these machines, then for payment of a suitably low sum his bicycle could be propped up in an open shed in the station yard. But maybe this bicycling passenger had a further journey beyond his destination station; in which case he purchased a special ticket which enabled him to take his bicycle with him. The ticket was so designed that one third was torn off, this section carrying duplicate information to that on the remaining two-thirds, ie type, number, date, issuing station, and destination. A hole was punched in a corner of the tear-off section to enable it to be tied to the bicycle. The ticket, issued within zonal or regional limits as specified, was available to any station above fifty and not exceeding seventy-five miles distant, and back. It was overprinted 'BR' for bicycle return.

In a law suit of 1871 (Macrow v Great Western Railway) the judgement suggested that an item could be classed as personal luggage if it was for the immediate personal use of the passenger at the end of the journey. However, in 1899 (Britten v Great Northern Railway Co), it was decided that a bicycle was not ordinary luggage, and a passenger could not require a railway company to carry it without extra charge. The judge also commented upon the difficulty of defining what is luggage, and how much easier it would be to say what is not luggage.

Railway companies issued tickets to commercial travellers on favourable terms, and allowed them to take their trade samples free of charge, as if they were personal luggage. This privilege was granted on the understanding that the companies were relieved of liability for loss and damage, etc. In the case of neglect or default by the company, then the conditions of section 7 of the Railway and Canal Traffic Act, 1854, applied.

At the request of the insurance companies, the North Staffordshire Railway (affectionately known as the 'Knotty') introduced in 1920 a scheme for cycle insurance. The special tickets cost one penny and covered loss or damage due to railway accidents and/or the company's proven negligence. As with similar schemes operated by most of the other companies, it was not very popular, and was destined to die a natural death. For a pram or 'Mail Cart (Accompanying Passenger)', a similar style of ticket was issued; the rate was cheaper, and the length of the journey for which it was valid was fifteen miles.

The railway companies were aware of the fondness of many people for their dogs, so they printed special tickets to enable dogs to be taken on train journeys. Like bicycle and pram tickets, there was a distance restriction, usually about ten miles. Dogs were allowed to travel on the understanding that they did so either at their owners' risk, or for a limited liability to the company of about two pounds. Immediately after re-grouping, the Great Northern and London and North Western Companies Joint Railway carried dogs which accompanied passengers, and the ticket bore the following legend on the reverse side:

> The London and North Eastern Rly. Coy. [they apparently could not make up their minds whether or not they had been re-grouped] are not, and will not be, Common Carriers of Dogs, nor will they receive Dogs for conveyance except on the terms that they or any other Company or Companies over whose Lines the Dog may pass shall not be responsible for loss, injury, or delay thereto, except upon proof of negligence, on the part of their Servants; nor in any case for any greater amount of damages beyond the sum of £2, unless at the time of Booking the Dog be declared of a higher value and a percentage of 1¼ p.c. be paid upon the higher value so declared.

On the London, Midland and Scottish Railway the Dog Ticket carried a warning of similar intent:

> The Dog to which this ticket relates is accepted for carriage (1) subject to the Regulations and Conditions contained in the Railway Companies Book of Regulations relating to traffic by Passenger train or other

RAILWAY EMPLOYEES' PRIVILEGE TICKET ASSOCIATION

£400 **INSURANCE** **3d.**

The Ocean Accident and Guarantee Corporation Limited

Incorporated in England and Empowered by Special Act of Parliament — Head Office 36-44 MOORGATE LONDON E.C.2

WILL PAY

£400 to the legal personal representative of the *bona fide* holder of this Coupon-Insurance-Ticket if such holder shall be fatally injured by an accident, within Great Britain, Ireland, the Channel Islands or the Isle of Man or on the Continent of Europe, directly occasioned by or to any railway passenger train (including a railway staff train) in which such holder is at the time of such injury travelling as a passenger* and not as one of the crew of the train, or directly occasioned by or to any goods train in which such holder is at the time of such injury travelling to or from any point of duty in connection with railway service but not as one of the crew of the train, or directly occasioned by or to any tramcar, omnibus, cab or motor car, which is licensed to ply and at the time of being entered or hired is plying for public hire and is being driven by a driver licensed to ply for public hire in or on which such holder is at the time of such injury travelling as a passenger,* or directly occasioned by or to any motor charabanc in or on which such holder is at the time of such injury travelling as a passenger*; or by an accident directly occasioned by or to any passenger-steamship, within Great Britain, Ireland, the Channel Islands or the Isle of Man or plying between Great Britain, Ireland, the Channel Islands or the Isle of Man and the Continent of Europe, in which such holder is at the time of such injury travelling as a passenger* and not as one of the crew of such passenger-steamship;

OR will pay to such holder should any such accident cause non-fatal injury to such holder:—

£400 for (*a*) the loss of Two or more Limbs by actual separation at or above the wrist or ankle or the total and irrecoverable Loss of all sight of Both Eyes or (*b*) the Loss as herein defined of One or more Limbs and all sight of One or Both Eyes: OR

£200 for the Loss as above defined of One Limb or of all sight of One Eye: OR

£1 15s. 0d. **PER WEEK** during temporary or permanent total disablement from earning a livelihood; **OR will pay** to the legal personal representative of such holder:—

†**£100** if such holder shall within Great Britain, Ireland, the Channel Islands or the Isle of Man be fatally injured by an accident to any passenger, goods, ballast or empty carriage train, or light engine, or train or engine undergoing a trial run, in which such holder is at the time of such injury travelling in performance of his duties as one of the crew of such train or engine, or by an accident to a Railway Company's road-vehicle in which such holder is at the time of such injury travelling in performance of his duties, or if such holder shall be fatally injured by an accident to any British Railway Company's passenger-steamship, dredger, mud hopper, tug, floating crane or lighter in which such holder is at the time of such injury travelling in performance of his duties as a member of the crew of such passenger-steamship, dredger, mud hopper, tug, floating crane or lighter; OR

£25 if such holder shall die from injuries which shall be accidentally received by such holder whilst such holder is on any railway passenger platform within Great Britain, Ireland, the Channel Islands or the Isle of Man; OR

£10 if such holder shall be fatally injured within Great Britain, Ireland, the Channel Islands or the Isle of Man, or, if he (she) be there as a member of the crew of a British Railway Company's steamship therein, within any Port of the Continent of Europe: (*a*) by an accident arising out of his (her) occupation as an employee of a Railway Company during the period of his (her) hours on duty, whether or not there may be contributory negligence: (*b*) by being accidentally knocked down or run over whilst a pedestrian on a public highway by a horse, cycle or vehicle: or (*c*) by accident whilst pedal-cycling by direct route from home to work or vice versa.

Provided that the above undertaking is subject to the following special conditions, which are of the essence of the contract, namely, that:—

(*a*) Such death, loss or disablement shall occur within ninety days after and as the direct result of the injury independent of any other cause; (*b*) the Corporation shall be under no liability in respect of any accident caused by or occurring while such holder is getting on or getting off or falling from any such conveyance; (*c*) notice in case of injury shall be given to the Corporation at its Head Office in London within seven days or in case of death within fourteen days after the accident; (*d*) medical certificates and other information shall be furnished by the person claiming upon request for the same by the Corporation; (*e*) the Corporation shall not be liable for more than one of the respective sums or allowances stated herein in respect of injury sustained by such holder in any one accident; (*f*) such holder shall, prior to the accident, have written his usual signature in ink, in the space provided underneath, in the presence of a witness, and this Coupon-Insurance-Ticket, so signed, shall be forwarded to the Corporation with the notice of injury or death; and (*g*) this Insurance applies only to persons over twelve and under seventy years of age, is limited to six Coupon-Insurance-Tickets for any one holder, and holds good only for twelve months from the date of issue, inserted beneath, expiring in any event, however, on the 31st December, 1952.

This Insurance entitles the holder to the benefit of, and is subject to, the conditions of the "**Ocean Accident and Guarantee Company, Limited, Act, 1890**", except so far as the same are altered by the terms and special conditions above stated.

The possession of this Coupon-Insurance-Ticket is admitted to be the payment of a premium under Sec. 33 of the Act. A Print of the Act can be seen at the Head Office of the Corporation.

This Insurance does not include any consequence of War.

Eire Insurance Act 1936. If this Coupon-Insurance-Ticket is issued to a person who is ordinarily resident in Eire all moneys which become or may become due and payable by the Company hereunder shall in accordance with Section 93 of the Eire Insurance Act 1936 be payable and be paid in Eire.

Coupon-Insurance-Ticket No. 601,461/ 728182

DATE OF ISSUE Feb 7/49

(to be inserted by issuer before this Coupon-Insurance-Ticket is issued.)

Signature of Holder ....

Signature and Address of Witness J H Kenney, 26 oak street, Leicester

The term "train" includes the brake van.

*** The term "passenger" includes the holder of a free or duty pass, holiday or residential pass, privilege ticket, privilege contract ticket, excursion, ordinary or workmen's ticket or a railway servant travelling as a passenger without ticket or pass.**

The term "a Railway Company's road-vehicle" includes road-vehicles owned by the London Passenger Transport Board or by any Company in which a British or Irish Railway Company has a financial interest.

†N.B.—Unless the Holder of this Coupon-Insurance-Ticket is in or on the train, engine, vehicle, ship, etc. at the the accident thereto this benefit is not payable.

An interesting coupon insurance ticket issued in 1949, but although witnessed, it does not carry the signature of the holder. An endorsement on the reverse increased the price of the coupon to 4d from the first day of November 1948, and the benefit of £1 15s 0d per week is limited to a payment not exceeding £400 in any one accident.

More than 100 years of British railway history is covered by this colourful array of tickets. The variety of colour and design demonstrate how necessary it became to distinguish between categories and contingencies as railway travel became more popular. The date of issue of the Dursley to Bristol ticket, 1348, is unknown, but it was probably stock-printed about 1860. Dursley was on the Western Union and Bristol & Gloucestershire Joint Lines, the latter becoming part of the Dursley & Midland Junction Railway in 1856, passing into the Midland Railway in 1861. The Manchester South Junction and Altrincham Railway (Dog Ticket 2119) was incorporated in 1845, and taken over in succession by the LNWR, the MSLR, the Great Central, and the LNER, but the ticket was not issued until November 1940!

0042
L.N.E.R.
CIRCULAR TRIP
Wroxham
(A 918) TO
LIVERPOOL ST
BY RAIL
including
Pullman
Supplement.
THIRD
G. Smith & Sons
BOAT TRIP
(A 918) on
NORFOLK
BROADS
By
Messrs Smiths
Motor Boat.
L.N.E.R.
CIRCULAR TRIP
LIVERPOOL ST
(A 918) TO
WROXHAM
BY RAIL
including
Pullman
Supplement.
THIRD
0042
Available on day of issue.
For conditions see back

2119
M. S. J. & A. R.
ONE DOG
Accompanying Passenger
OLD TRAFFORD to
ANY M. S. J. & A. STATION
Rate 3d.
Validity same as Passenger Ticket
FOR CONDITIONS SEE BACK
2119

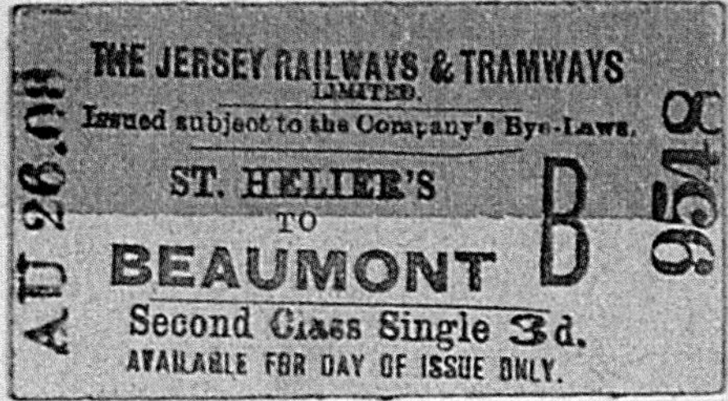
AU 26.08
THE JERSEY RAILWAYS & TRAMWAYS
LIMITED.
Issued subject to the Company's Bye-Laws.
ST. HELIER'S
TO
BEAUMONT
B
Second Class Single 3d.
AVAILABLE FOR DAY OF ISSUE ONLY.
9548

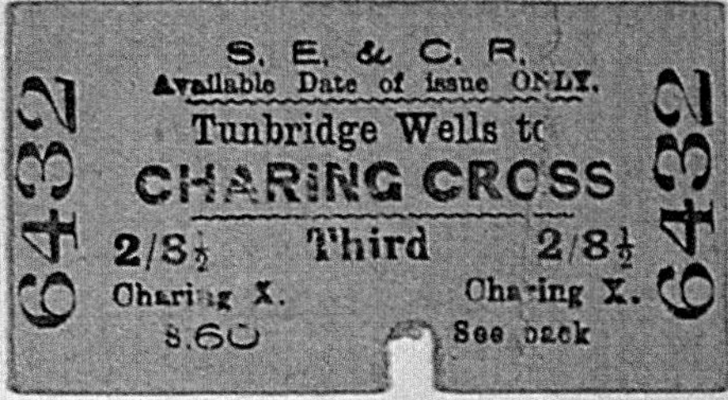
6432
S. E. & C. R.
Available Date of issue ONLY.
Tunbridge Wells to
CHARING CROSS
2/8½ Third 2/8½
Charing X. Charing X.
8.60 See back
6432

037
Great Western Railway
Issued in connection with Matinee
Excursion Birmingham to London
AVAILABLE FOR ONE
LUNCHEON
IN RESTAURANT CAR.
This ticket to be surrendered to
Restaurant Car Conductor.
CHARGE 2/9
Iss'd at B'ham 28.
037

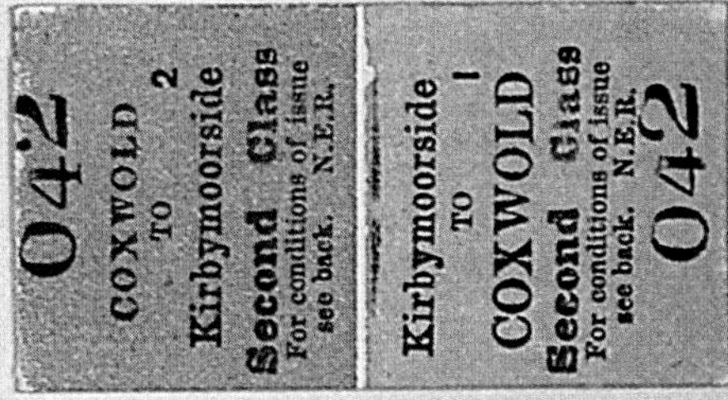
042
COXWOLD
TO
Kirbymoorside 2
Second Class
For conditions of issue
see back. N.E.R.
Kirbymoorside 1
TO
COXWOLD
Second Class
For conditions of issue
see back. N.E.R.
042

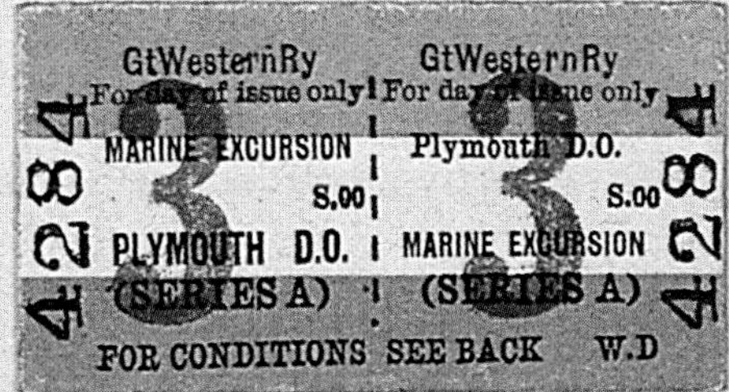
4284
GtWesternRy
For day of issue only
MARINE EXCURSION
S.00
PLYMOUTH D.O.
(SERIES A)
GtWesternRy
For day of issue only
Plymouth D.O.
S.00
MARINE EXCURSION
(SERIES A)
3 3
FOR CONDITIONS SEE BACK W.D
4284

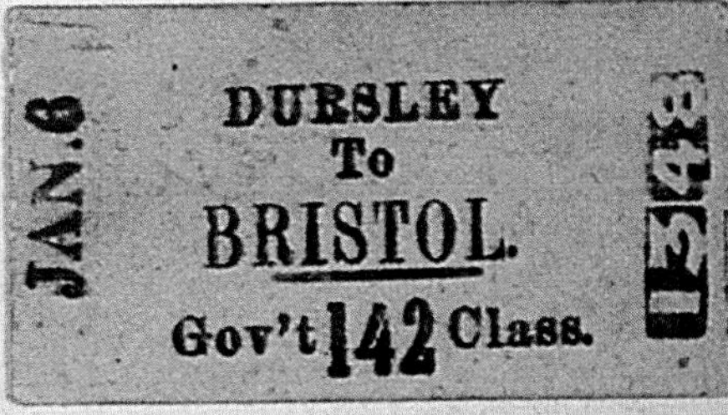
JAN.6
DURSLEY
To
BRISTOL.
Gov't 142 Class.

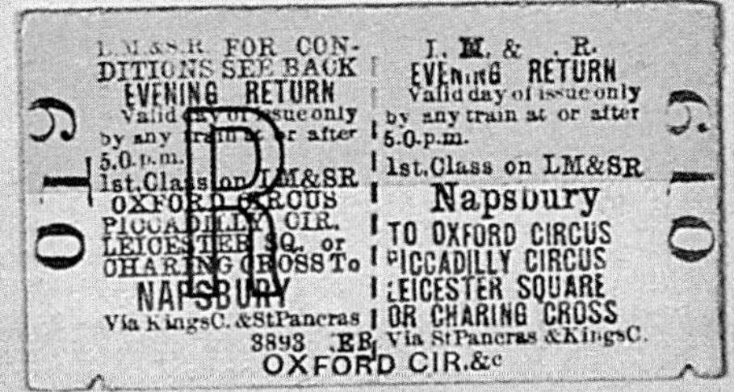
019
L.M.&S.R. FOR CONDITIONS SEE BACK
EVENING RETURN
Valid day of issue only
by any train at or after
5.0-p.m.
1st.Class on LM&SR
OXFORD CIRCUS
PICCADILLY CIR.
LEICESTER SQ. or
CHARING CROSS To
NAPSBURY
Via KingsC. &StPancras
3893
R
L.M.&S.R.
EVENING RETURN
Valid day of issue only
by any train at or after
5.0-p.m.
1st.Class on LM&SR
Napsbury
TO OXFORD CIRCUS
PICCADILLY CIRCUS
LEICESTER SQUARE
OR CHARING CROSS
Via StPancras &KingsC.
OXFORD CIR.&c
019

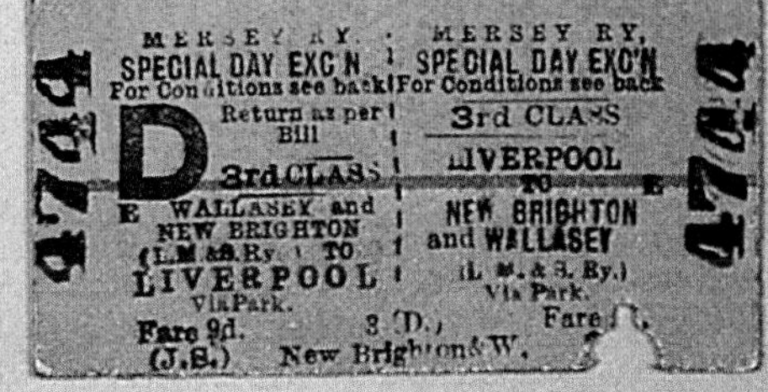
4744
MERSEY RY.
SPECIAL DAY EXC'N
For Conditions see back
Return as per
Bill
D
3rd CLASS
E WALLASEY and
NEW BRIGHTON
(L.M.&S.Ry.) TO
LIVERPOOL
Via Park.
Fare 9d.
(J.S.)
MERSEY RY.
SPECIAL DAY EXC'N
For Conditions see back
3rd CLASS
LIVERPOOL
TO E
NEW BRIGHTON
and WALLASEY
(L.M.&S.Ry.)
Via Park.
3 (D.)
New Brighton&W.
4744

OAKHAM
To
MANTON.
THIRD 225 CLASS.

G.C.Ry (Excursion) G.C.Ry
CHEAP CHEAP
NOV. 13. 09
Handsworth
(A.70) TO
LEICESTER(C)
THIRD CLASS
2/3
Leicester(C)
TO (A.70)
HANDSWORTH
THIRD CLASS
2/3

MIDLAND RAILWAY.
FIRST CLASS.
MIDLAND RLY.
No. 4) Birmingham to
FIRST CLASS.

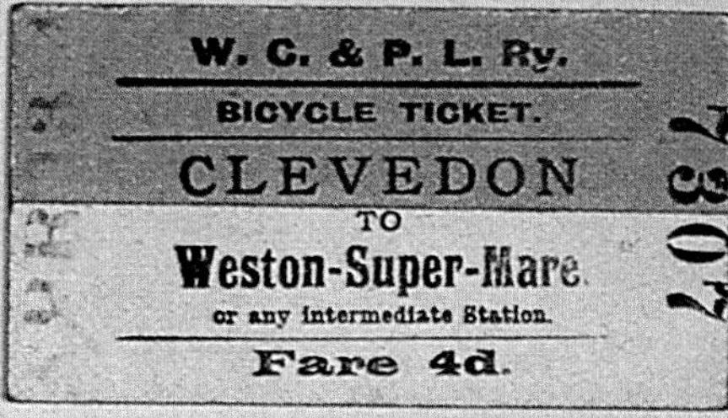
W. C. & P. L. Ry.
BICYCLE TICKET.
CLEVEDON
TO
Weston-Super-Mare
or any intermediate Station.
Fare 4d.
4097

L.N.E.R.
DAY EXCN.
LEICESTER (Cen.)
to
PILSLEY
Valid as per Bills.
FIRST
FOR CONDITIONS SEE BACK.
L.N.E.R.
DAY EXCN.
PILSLEY
to
LEICESTER CEN
& thence to
Racecourse & back
by MIDLAND RED
MOTOR OMNIBUS
Valid as per Bills.
FIRST & MOTOR
FOR CONDITIONS SEE BACK
0004

MS&LR Return Half
Rotterdam to
SOUTHPORT
Saloon & First Class
MS&LR Outward Half
EXCURSION
Southport
ROTTERDAM
First Class & Saloon
Fare 35s.
26

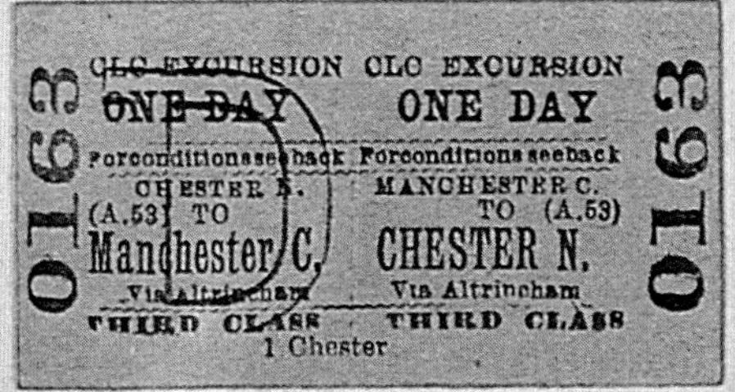
CLC EXCURSION CLC EXCURSION
ONE DAY ONE DAY
For conditions see back For conditions see back
CHESTER N. MANCHESTER C.
(A.53) TO TO (A.53)
Manchester C. CHESTER N.
Via Altrincham Via Altrincham
THIRD CLASS THIRD CLASS
0163

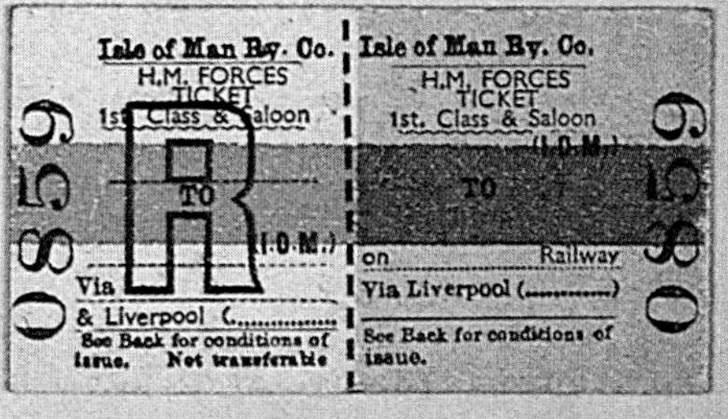
Isle of Man Ry. Co.
H.M. FORCES
TICKET
1st. Class & Saloon
Isle of Man Ry. Co.
H.M. FORCES
TICKET
1st. Class & Saloon
Via Liverpool
See Back for conditions of issue. Not transferable
0859

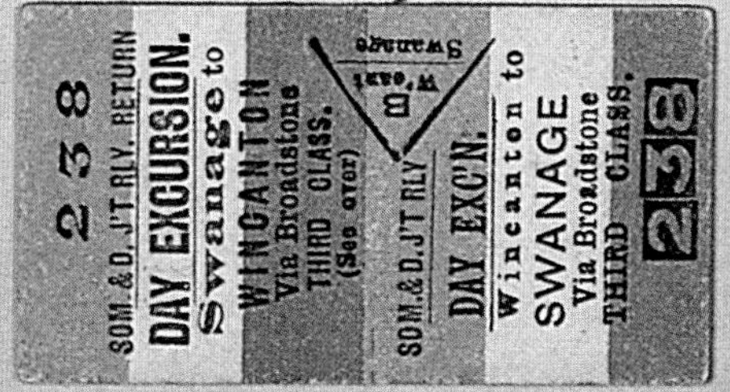
238
SOM.&D.J'T RLY. RETURN
DAY EXCURSION.
Swanage to
WINCANTON
Via Broadstone
THIRD CLASS.
SOM.&D.J'T RLY
DAY EXCN.
Wincanton to
SWANAGE
Via Broadstone
THIRD CLASS.

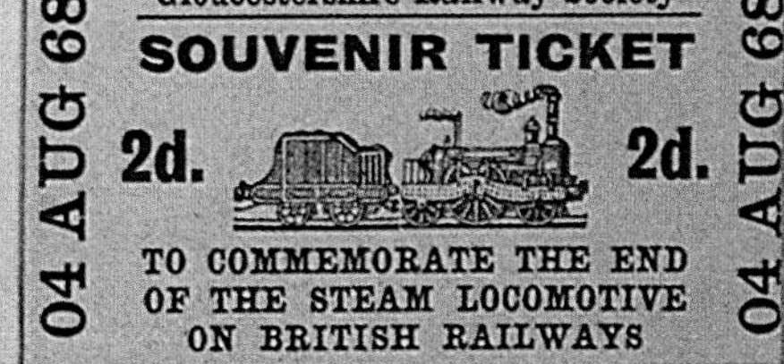
Gloucestershire Railway Society
SOUVENIR TICKET
2d. 2d.
TO COMMEMORATE THE END
OF THE STEAM LOCOMOTIVE
ON BRITISH RAILWAYS
04 AUG 68

similar service, and (2) at a reduced rate at Owner's Risk and subject to the limitations of liability contained in the Standard Terms and Conditions of Carriage of Live Stock by Passenger Train.
NOT TRANSFERABLE.

As well as the generally unsuccessful cycle insurance, all of the major companies issued special tickets which covered insurance against personal risks, and luggage insurance tickets. Although in most other aspects of insurance, the railway companies worked in close co-operation with the insurance companies, with regard to the issue of the special insurance tickets they worked alone. The railway companies assumed the risks involved. This raised an important question which never needed to be posed in a court of law. When issuing tickets which allowed reduced fare concessions, most of the companies printed a proviso in which all liability for accident was declined, whatever the cause; sometimes limited liability was admitted. The Midland Railway set a limit of £100 for a journey covered by the issue of a workman's ticket. Clearly, the issue of the insurance ticket was a contradiction of the companies' limitation.

The special insurance tickets, which were cut to Edmondson's standard, had, like the advertisement tickets, a finger-notch in the top edge. They could be purchased for as little as twopence, and were in effect an insurance policy. For such a small sum, the Great Western Railway guaranteed as much as £500 in the case of death, or £3 per week where permanent injury occurred. Double these benefits could be obtained with the purchase of a 6d insurance ticket for a return journey.

Railway companies throughout the world were beset by the problem of liability in the case of accident, since in the ordinary run of business they were not insurers, but transporters. If the company was negligent in its duties, during which a passenger received injury, then claim for damages could be made. The company was required to exercise reasonable care when transporting a passenger and his luggage, but could not be held responsible for a so-called 'Act of God'. The rules and regulations excerpts printed on ordinary tickets (referred to later on) laid down the limited risks for which the company held itself to be liable. The law of the land, in whatever country the ticket was issued, determined the interpretation of that liability. Various companies accepted responsibility as soon as the ticket was purchased, while others withheld such acceptance until the

---

Modern colour-coded business systems have their origins in the railway ticket, which used many variations in colour and design. Covering more than a century, they are a decorative reminder of companies scarcely known, long-forgotten, or well-loved.
The Oakham to Manton ticket was stock-printed about 1860; the stations were on the Syston & Peterborough Line of the Midland, and opened for passenger traffic on 1 May 1848.
Dated and multi-coloured on the face, the unusual Great Central cheap excursion ticket was coloured lilac on the reverse in an attempt to deter ticket forgers.
Originally named the Weston-super-Mare, Clevedon and Portishead (Steam) Tramway Company, the WC & P was the subject of much ribaldry. It was re-named as a light railway in 1899, and closed in 1940; this ticket, 7307, was one of the last to be issued.
As one of the most colourful tickets issued for the use of HM Forces, that of the Isle of Man Railway Company, 0859, can have had few challengers.
The Gloucestershire Railway Society Souvenir Ticket tells its own sorry tale.

journey had commenced.

Special tickets were issued which induced the passenger to waive his rights to compensation. A typical example was the Workmen's Ticket which carried a notice on the following lines:

> NOT TRANSFERABLE. Workmen's Tickets are subject to the Company's Bye-laws, Regulations, Conditions, and Notices. They are available only on the day of issue, and by advertised trains. Tickets issued under Section [here was quoted various reference numbers], subject to those provisions and in other cases to the condition that neither the holder nor any other person shall have any right of action against the Company or any other Railway Company for injury (fatal or otherwise), or loss, damage, or delay of or to person or property, however caused, but the carriers may without prejudice to this condition make a voluntary payment of not exceeding £100.

Despite the issue of these special tickets, the companies realised that they could not evade their obligations, moral or legal. It was the traveller's right to purchase any ticket he chose: in other words, he had the choice of making the same journey for which he could purchase an ordinary ticket at an increased tariff. In such a case, the company assumed full liability.

The issue of cheap day excursion tickets was similar in effect to that of the workmen's tickets in that the company was able to partially, or completely, disavow responsibility. During the early 1930s, platform tickets issued by the London and North Eastern Railway carried the following notice: 'This ticket is issued on the condition that the Company will not be liable to the holder for any injury or loss, personal or otherwise, however caused.'

The fortnightly notice of 'Instructions to Stationmasters, Booking Clerks, and all others concerned', is a rather interesting source of information. These sheets of instructions, later bound into six-monthly volumes, contained details of train arrangements, and many other miscellaneous items. The pages of one such typical volume, the London and North Eastern Railway, Great Northern Section, Special Train Arrangements, January to June 1936, reveal many interesting facets of rail travel and its organisation. The volume starts with a message from the Chairman

> Now that the Christmas holidays are over, the Chairman wishes to convey to the staff of all Departments his appreciation of their successful efforts to cope with the heavy passenger traffic which passed during the holiday period under extremely unfavourable weather conditions. In passing along this message from the Chairman, the Chief General Manager also desires to thank the staff for the cheerfulness and efficiency which they displayed under very difficult circumstances. This opportunity is taken to wish everybody throughout the System a very Happy New Year.

The railway companies also undertook the carriage of horses, and the fortnightly notice refers to the Percheron Horse Society's Stallion Parade at Histon, Cambridge, on 11 March 1936. It states: 'It has been agreed that Horses entered for the above, if unsold, may be carried back to the station whence the animals were sent, at ½ the rate charged on the outward journey, at Owner's Risk. Free conveyance of the Attendant is not included.'

In 1936, by arrangement with the London and North Eastern, a London firm was organising trips to Bournemouth and other seaside resorts, for the demonstration of 'Television and Radio-Grams'. Special tickets were issued on the surrender of a voucher, the style of which was set out in the instruction sheet.

Bound into book form, the instruction sheets carried a year's record of notices of the issue of passes, the persons to whom they were issued, and the period for which they were valid. Details of missing or unissued tickets, and tickets or warrants which were lost or presumed stolen, were also listed. Tickets were requisitioned according to instructions laid down in the fortnightly sheets, and eventually were despatched to the station originating the requisition; but they sometimes became lost in transit, perhaps with a load of voucher stocks intended for various stations along the delivery route. The notices listed details of number sequences, and all receiving offices and agencies were requested to look for them. To assist in the prompt despatch of tickets, the attention of agents and station clerks was called to the necessity of requisitions being legibly written (especially figures), carbon copied and separate requisitions sent for specified categories of tickets.

Stationmasters and booking clerks were also reminded that dilapidated season tickets were to be regarded as invalid, and were required to be returned, together with a renewal fee of one shilling, for the issue of a new ticket.

On Saturday 5 September 1936, the Railway Employees' Carnival was held at the Belle Vue Gardens, Manchester. The London and North Eastern issued specially printed blue privilege tickets, at reduced rates, which admitted the bearer to the carnival. The outward halves were examined, but not collected, on the train, and were surrendered at the entrance to the gardens. With the railway's passion for colour, and bearing in mind the destination and its famous reputation, it is a wonder that the tickets were not printed like the flamboyant labels on boxes of fireworks.

The random turn of a page in the January to June, 1936, volume of LNER Train Arrangements revealed the somewhat grim humour, albeit unintentional, in a telegraph instruction, which referred to the LNER Telegraph Code Book, dated January 1929:

Code : FUNCO
Subject : Corpse
Interpretation : Vehicle with funeral party and corpse.

In life, as in death, all of the companies paid attention to the welfare of their passengers; business sense dictated that they should, and the various Railway Acts ensured that they did. Evidence of their concern is reflected in the 'Rules and Regulations for the Guidance of the Officers and Men in the Service of the North Eastern Railway Company, From 1st January, 1920'.

Any ladies who purchased tickets for a journey on the North Eastern could be assured that company servants were bound by company rules if not by gentlemanly honour to attend upon their comfort. Rule 195 is concerned with smoking in the carriages. It finished with this noble sentence: 'Guards must, before starting, see that they have a sufficient number of compartments reserved for smokers, and be careful not to place ladies in the compartments so reserved'.

'Ladies travelling alone' is the heading to Rule 197, which indicates the chivalrous attention expected of their guards:

> When ladies are travelling alone, the Guards must pay every attention to their comfort; and, in placing them in the train they must, if requested, endeavour to select a compartment for them (according to the class of their tickets) in which other ladies are travelling. If ladies wish to change compartments during the journey, the Guards must enable them to do so.

Naturally enough the company had quite firm rules to deal with passengers who might attempt evasion of the proper fare. In Rule 20 (a), it was insisted that 'No person must be allowed to travel on the Railway, unless provided with a proper ticket or free pass.' Section (b) of the same rule also dealt with the contingency of persons travelling by goods train without special authority. A further rule required the guards to assist the station staff in preventing passengers travelling in a superior class, or leaving a train to evade payment of the proper fare. Their duties also included assisting the staff generally in detecting fraudulent travelling. If a passenger was desirous of changing from an inferior to a superior class, the guard had to notify the stationmaster, who made the necessary arrangements. The collection or examination of tickets also had its covering rules. When a train arrived at a ticket-collecting station, the guard requested the passengers to have their tickets ready, and assisted the ticket-collector by opening and closing the carriage doors. Except under special instructions, the guard was not allowed to collect or examine tickets.

The prevention of fraudulent evasion of payment of the proper fare was one of the reasons for the extensive use of colour in any company's production of passenger tickets. In the early days of the North Staffordshire Railway, care rather than colour was the watchword. Apparently some fare dodgers were inclined to be violent when apprehended, and company instructions were issued which advised staff to be careful when detaining them. It was advised that the safest course was to take such fare dodgers before the magistrate as quickly as possible.

As with the early railways in England, the American railroad companies were plagued by forgers; the paper coupon tickets then in widespread use were an easy target. Not until 1855 did the American companies install the Edmondson-type ticket system. The firm of Sanford, Harroun, and Warren, of Buffalo, who printed serially numbered tickets to the Edmondson standard, received a consignment of machinery sent over from England. With the new English equipment came a Mr George Bailey, who acted as a supervisor and consultant.

The paper coupon-type tickets, which were a familiar feature on American railroads, were devised by a Mr Hebbard. They were primarily intended for use by travellers who needed to continue their journey over the metals of other companies. The passengers considered them a nuisance, but initially they were the only practical method of proportionally dividing

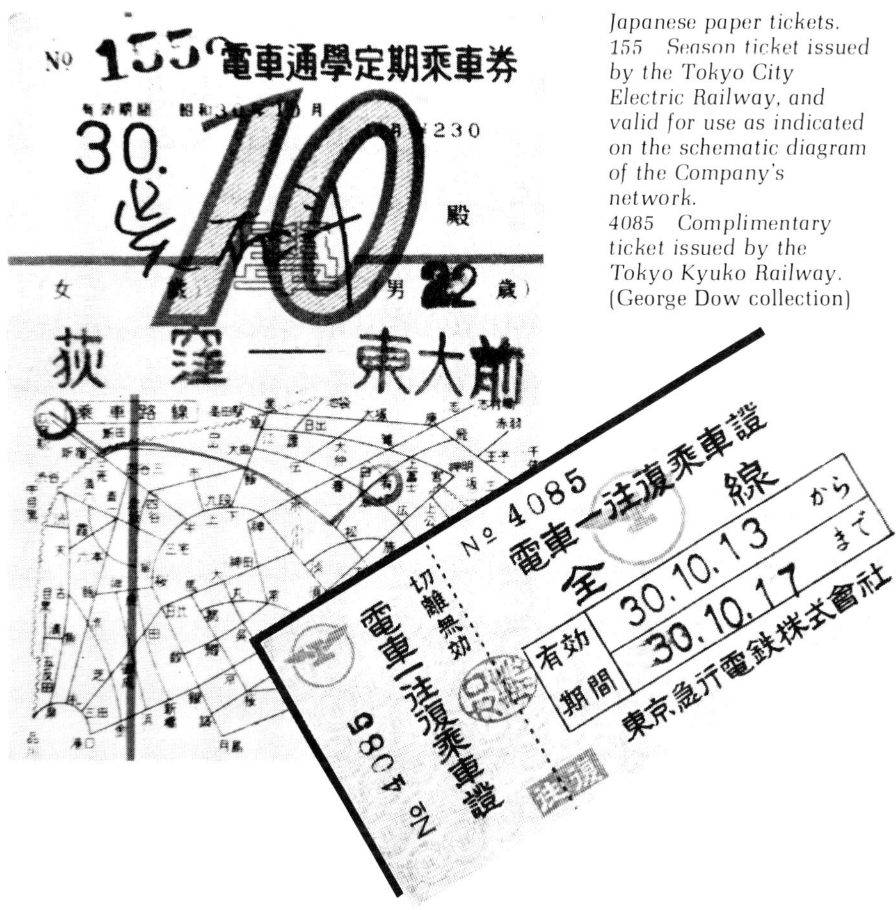

Japanese paper tickets.
155 Season ticket issued by the Tokyo City Electric Railway, and valid for use as indicated on the schematic diagram of the Company's network.
4085 Complimentary ticket issued by the Tokyo Kyuko Railway.
(George Dow collection)

the income of the issuing company between the other companies involved.

In America, to avoid fraud with the Edmondson-type of ticket, the printing of tickets was done in several colours, using a safety background; the colours varied from week to week. Each week was accorded a number, not necessarily corresponding with its calendar order, which was printed on to the ticket along with the date and a special checking symbol. This symbol was also subject to weekly change, and could refer to route, week, or class. From time to time, the style of printing was altered, and secret markings were also included. The safety backgrounds used in ticket production were in themselves highly complicated. They ranged from elaborate and interlaced geometric designs, machine-lithographed intaglio or guilloche patterns, to repetitions of the company's name or initials. Throughout this galaxy of colour printing, all railway companies held one principle supreme: — that the aspect of the ticket should remain constant. This was achieved by the regular use of standard paper and identical colours, and the printing of the necessary ticket information in the same style.

In the stagecoach era, booking clerks had written a number on to each ticket they issued; Edmondson had continued the practice with his pre-printed tickets. The serial numbering of a ticket allows several checks to be made. Deliveries from the printer to the various stations can quickly be assessed, and rapid checks can be made of ticket stocks, numbers sold, and the money received for them. With the introduction of return tickets the serial number had to be printed twice on the ticket, and it was usual for this to be done at either end. For a few years during the 1850s, return tickets with separable halves had the serial number printed in the middle of the card on either side of the 'tearing' line. Sometimes, each half would also be printed '1' and '2' in small type to distinguish 'outward' and 'return' sections.

On British railways the serial number had progressed from the three-figure numbers introduced by Edmondson, to numbers containing four and five figures. Right from the start of the system, the number had commenced with a '0', for example, the twenty-first ticket issued in a particular series would carry the number '0020'; on the Continent, the serial number started at '1'. The British system was both logical and practical, since it allowed the full number of a series to be issued, without requiring the addition of an extra digit for the final ticket.

Railway tickets were soon recognised as being the perfect display board for advertising material. As stated earlier, the insert ticket did not last for very long, despite the companies offering prizes to persons collecting them. The railway companies sometimes advertised, on the backs of their tickets, special train services or fares. This direct form of advertising cost very little, and was of course to the company's own advantage. The indirect form of advertising was much more satisfying financially, and was naturally more effective, since it related to the particular journey for which the ticket was issued. Special tickets were issued for organised visits to exhibitions, engineering works, and the like. As related earlier, they were also issued to popularise famous named trains; such trains operated on journeys to coastal resorts which the company wished to promote. Commemorative tickets were issued, printed on some of the earliest Edmondson presses, for the Railway Centenary in 1925. This was valuable propaganda, and the tickets, printed and numbered in familiar style, carried a simple legend across the card. The number occurred at either end, with the legend reading, 'CENTENARY OF RAILWAYS. 1825-1925. SAFETY FIRST, TRAVEL BY RAIL', set in bold type.

The introduction of the use of colour on railway tickets was a distinct advantage, but its choice was important; ready distinction by both daylight and gaslight was essential. Confusion of the colours had to be avoided, and on multi-coloured tickets contrasting shades were used. As the printing of the necessary information relating to destination was most important, it is obvious that the colour chosen must not detract from the clarity of the message. As a further safeguard, only non-fading or standard colours were used. The need to distinguish between classes and categories led to the frequent use of colour. Such tickets were readily identified, but the system got out of hand, causing great confusion. The riot of multi-coloured tickets issued by the London, Brighton and South Coast Railway, while possibly pleasant to the traveller in their aspect, were a nightmare to the collector or examiner.

Many of the major companies attempted to standardise this riot of colour. For example, in 1905, the Lancashire and Yorkshire Railway standardised the colour of its tickets issued for regular services. The Single tickets were: First Class — white; Second Class — red; Third Class — green; the Return tickets were: First Class — white and yellow; Second Class — red and blue; Third Class — green and brown.

On the amalgamation in January 1899 of the South Eastern Railway with the London, Chatham and Dover Railway, into the popularly known title of South Eastern and Chatham Railway, the LC&D ticket standards were adopted. To unify ticket practice, the colours white, pink and green for First, Second and Third classes were used. A few early SER section tickets in the obsolete colours of yellow, blue and buff are known to have been issued, but these are rare.

A convention of the International Railway Congress Association, together with a mutual agreement between the major British companies, led to the standardisation of colours. In the mid-1930s, the following colours were used for normal tickets:

First class : yellow, white
Second : green, blue
Third : brown, buff or green
Dogs : vermilion
Various : orange

While these colours were generally agreed, the British railway companies still continued to use different sets of colours for local and special trains.

On bi-coloured tickets, transverse, longitudinal, or diagonal bands were often used. In an attempt to lower printing costs, frequent use was made of white card on which a coloured band was printed. It was reasoned that the ticket was neater in its aspect, and the type stood out bolder. The scheme was false economy since the time involved in 'setting-up' usually outweighed the savings in printing ink. As the colour coding system became exploited to the very limits of its potential, tickets were issued which not only indicated the superiority of class, but also the direction of travel, together with an indication of any special rate; and all on one ticket! While bi-coloured tickets were common to most railway systems throughout the world, the multi-coloured ticket (printed to Edmondson's standards) was seldom used outside Great Britain. The card for such tickets was equally divided into three or four colours; on return tickets, the pattern was repeated in the same or reverse order for each half.

Most types of ticket, in Britain and on the Continent, could also be issued with special markings in addition to their already coloured background. Extensive use was made of circles and squares (in Britain these were used to designate certain categories of return tickets), oval rings, lozenges, St Andrew's crosses, etc. Narrow stripes set diagonally, vertically, or longitudinally, were also used, sometimes in repeat patterns; strictly speaking, such devices constitute an overprint, and therefore cannot be classed as part of a 'coloured' ticket. On a coloured ticket, the standard details, company, destination, class, etc. can be seen to have been printed over the colour.

In the production of some ticket series, typography of one or more colours was used, but this was relatively rare in Great Britain. The use of open or 'outline' type was widespread for overprinting, since it did not obscure the main legend of the ticket. Its most frequent use was for indicating the class of ticket, or on the return half where the ticket had been issued for a round trip. The use of overprinting on Edmondson tickets was a simple method of using excess stocks, or for making amendments to the existing legend. Thus, any ticket could receive an overprint, which thereby cancelled or augmented the particulars previously printed. A number of different items were used for overprint purposes, eg the fare, the class, the period of validity, zone numbers (for the carriage of dogs, bicycles, etc), destination station numbers, to list but a few. If, for some reason, supplies of one type of ticket were unavailable, then another series of a similar type could be overprinted for issue as a substitute.

Quite naturally, the most frequent use of overprinting was for alterations to the fare. Company regulations could alter tariffs, and thereby lead to changes in the fare; the revisions so effected did not alter the other details on the ticket. However, if the main categories (class or route) were altered by overprinting, then it was necessary also to change the stated fare.

The backs of the tickets were used to accommodate various items of information, chiefly company regulations and bye-laws extracts, and advertisements. Tickets issued by road transport companies were more likely to carry advertisements than those issued by the railways. The near-hysteria of some of these adverts seems quaintly comical, even pathetic, when viewed from a distance of nearly sixty years. One such ticket issued by the Dudley and Stourbridge Electric Traction Co Ltd, carries the following message:

BE PATRIOTIC!	
Wear	Popular Prices Of All Drapers
TWILFIT	Made in Portsmouth by the wives and
CORSETS	sweethearts of our gallant Jack Tars

Most railway tickets were issued, and indeed still are, with a reference to the company's regulations and bye-laws printed on the back. The issue of a ticket was subject to these regulations, and its acceptance by the passenger implied that he was bound by the conditions as laid down. In the early years, very few tickets carried any reference to company rules, but by about 1862 such references came into regular use.

Whether or not the passenger scrutinised the conditions before purchasing a ticket, they were held to be contractually binding by a law suit of 1869; another suit in 1876 upheld this decision.

At one time, the conditions of an ordinary ticket were generally displayed in the station booking hall and elsewhere; detailed reference was also contained in the company's published timetables. In the case of excursion tickets, and other special tickets, there were usually special conditions. These were printed on the appropriate handbills, and even on the ticket itself. These special conditions were also held to be legally binding, and in an 1895 lawsuit the judge said, 'When a passenger takes a special ticket to a named place and back at a cheap fare, the carriage of the passenger to that place and back is the only service which the railway company contracts to perform; it cannot if the passenger goes on to another

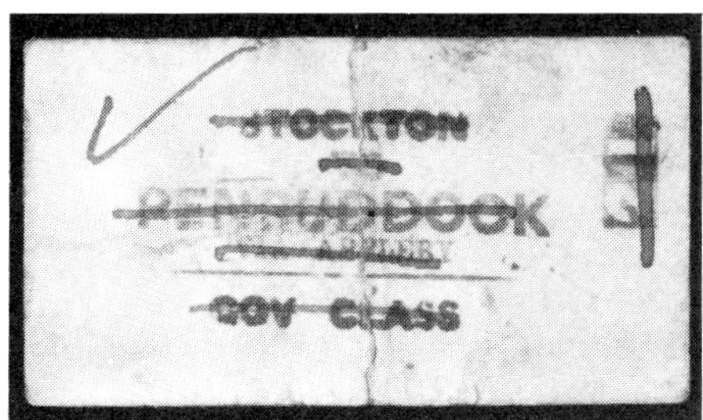

A ticket issued on the famous Stockton & Darlington Railway and bearing the signature of George Stephenson. It appears to have been issued for use as a free pass ticket, since the destination details, the ticket number, and the category 'Government Class' on the face have been cancelled. The original ticket is in Chesterfield Museum.

station, be treated as part of the service rendered by the company in taking him to a place to which they did not contract to carry him.'

Initially, extracts from the more important clauses were printed on the tickets, since, for obvious reasons, the entire rule-book and constitution of the company could not be contained within the small dimensions of the ticket. The printing of such conditions of issue, or reference thereto, gave greater strength to the companies' legal standing. By 1875, with the addition of special clauses for certain types of tickets, the entire back of the ticket was used. The front of the card carried a small notice, such as, 'See conditions on back'. This was designed to draw the passenger's attention to the fact that conditions were imposed, and he could not thereafter claim that he knew nothing of them.

It is interesting to examine in brief some parts of a typical set of such regulations. In the *Official Illustrated Guide to the South Eastern Railway*, published in 1858, is printed a list of general regulations for the benefit of passengers. The list, together with the rest of the information, was applicable to the company's branch lines which included the North Kent and Greenwich Lines.

Passengers were requested to check their tickets and change before leaving the booking office counter, since mistakes could not thereafter be rectified. The practice of re-booking at intermediate stations was not allowed. Return tickets which were issued for travel within a distance of sixty miles were valid for the day of issue only. Certain exceptions were allowed; if, for instance, tickets were purchased on Saturday or Sunday, they could be used on the following Monday.

At this time, different fares were levied for travel on ordinary trains and express trains over the same route. A ticket valid for the ordinary train service could not be used on the return journey for express trains, except upon payment of the difference in fare.

Under the clauses of section 15 of the Regulation of Railways Act, 1868, it was provided that 'every company shall cause to be exhibited in a conspicuous place in the booking office of each station on their line, a list or lists painted, printed, or written in legible characters, containing the fares of passengers by the trains included in the timetables of the company from that station to every place for which passenger tickets are there issued.'

Provision was made for those passengers who wished to travel in private carriages, and naturally there was a price for the privilege. Any such passengers, not being servants, were required to take first-class tickets; the servants were charged at second-class rates.

Two British lawsuits — Thompson v London, Midland & Scottish Railway, 1930, and Penton v Southern Railway, 1931 — gave precedents which confirmed the implied acceptance of a company's regulations. The court's decision in both cases was that, provided the printing clearly drew the attention of the passenger to any condition in force, this was sufficient to make their intent legally binding upon the passenger. It was upheld that even though the full list of regulations was kept at company headquarters, the passenger, if he so desired, could inspect them before purchase of a ticket. From about the time of these court cases, tickets began to be printed with a phrase which implied a contract between the passenger and the company; the manner of the wording removed the necessity for the printing of clauses and extracts. Typical wording, taken from a London, Midland and Scottish Railway ticket, states: 'Issued subject to the conditions & regulations in the Co's Time Tables Books Bills & Notices & in the Railway Co's Book of regulations relating to traffic by Passenger Train or other similar service.'

One of the most important statutory enactments relating to offences by passengers was Section 5 of the Regulation of Railways Act, 1889. This provided that every passenger should, on request by a railway company's servant, produce a ticket, or pay his fare from whence he started, or supply his name and address. If he failed to do any of these things he was liable, 'on summary conviction, to a fine not exceeding 40s.' Thus, if he could not, or would not, produce a ticket, he could pay the appropriate fare without any offence being committed; if he was willing to give his name and address after refusing to produce a ticket or pay in this case also no offence was committed against the provision of the Act. All companies exacted penalties for evasion of payment; a typical regulation referred to on tickets is this, by the South Eastern Railway; which reads as follows:

> PAYMENT OF FARE — PENALTIES.
>
> Under the Provisions of the Acts relating to this Railway, any Person who shall travel, or attempt to travel, in any Carriage used on the Railway, without having previously paid his Fare, and with intent to avoid payment thereof, or who, having paid his fare for a certain distance, shall knowingly and wilfully proceed in any such Carriage beyond such distance, without previously paying the additional Fare for the additional distance, and with intent to avoid payment thereof, or who shall knowingly and wilfully refuse or neglect on arriving at the point to which he has paid his Fare, to quit such Carriage, is for every such offence liable to a penalty of Forty Shillings.

Some tickets carried a note stating that it was 'Not Transferable', while

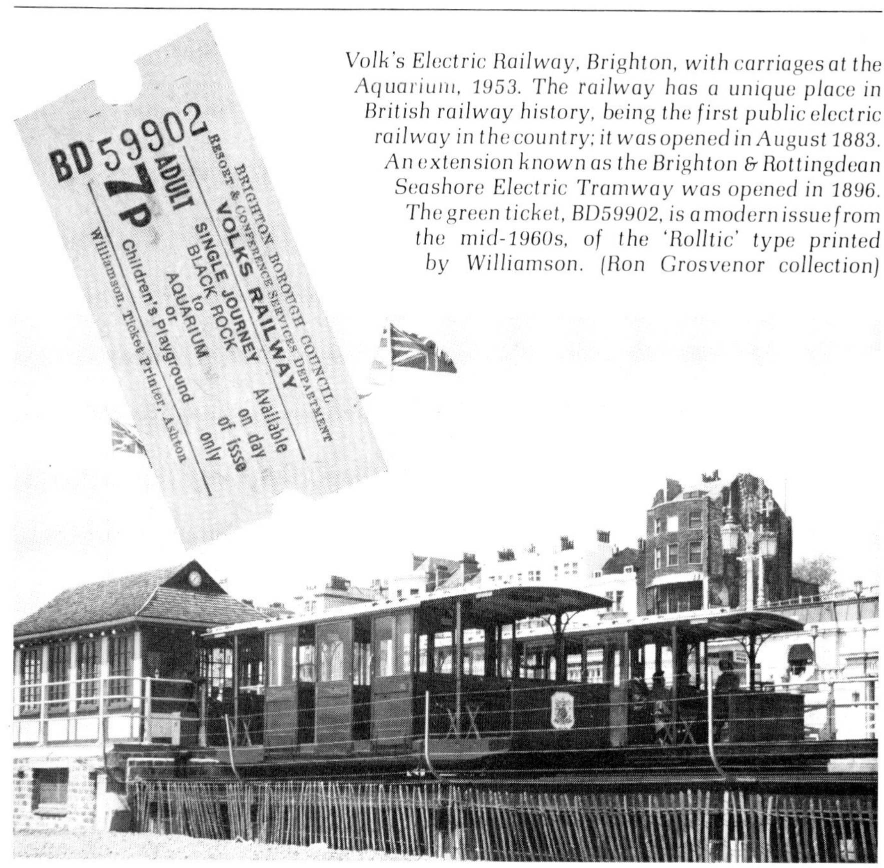

Volk's Electric Railway, Brighton, with carriages at the Aquarium, 1953. The railway has a unique place in British railway history, being the first public electric railway in the country; it was opened in August 1883. An extension known as the Brighton & Rottingdean Seashore Electric Tramway was opened in 1896. The green ticket, BD59902, is a modern issue from the mid-1960s, of the 'Rolltic' type printed by Williamson. (Ron Grosvenor collection)

others added a phrase to the effect that the acceptance of the ticket was evidence that the holder understood the rules and regulations of the company. How he was supposed to understand was never stated. The essential and overriding fact was that the passenger was given the chance of inspecting the company's regulations if he so wished; it was then up to him whether or not he purchased a ticket.

Railway guides and handbooks were always urging the passenger that his ticket should be guarded with care, 'as it is demanded at the end of the journey, and those who cannot produce it are compelled to pay again.' Also 'A ticket may be demanded during any part of the journey. The object, therefore, is to have it always safe and always handy.'

By the early 1930s, the world's railway companies were printing tickets is such exceedingly large numbers that serious attention was given to the very real problems of storage and subsequent issue. The tremendous advantages of self-printed tickets (ie those printed at the time of issue) were not lost upon those concerned with research into the vast problem. Such tickets relieved the necessity for carrying large stocks of pre-printed tickets, and also made it possible to issue them far more quickly. The ever-present threat of fraud was at once removed, and accountancy and audit checks were greatly simplified. Considerable economies at various levels could be effected in the production costs of tickets. Wastage on ticket stocks could be practically eliminated, while the labour of handling, checking, sorting and stocking could be drastically reduced.

Against such very considerable savings was the high cost of the printing machines, and their installation in booking offices. It was found, after detailed cost analysis, that it was only viable to install these special machines in the major stations, since large sales of tickets were necessary to offset their purchase.

One such machine, used extensively for British and European railway ticket production, was the AEG Multi-Printer manufactured by the Allgemeine Elektrizitäts Gesellschaft of Germany. The underframe, of cast iron, carried a printing plate magazine, the size of which depended upon the number of different tickets the machine was required to produce. Several machines were manufactured around a basic specification, which enabled magazines carrying 100 to 2,500 printing plates to be used. Printing could be effected by either push-button or manual control, and the printing carriage also contained a numbering mechanism and a date stamp. Two control strips were fixed to the printing carriage, which registered every item printed on the machine. One of the control strips was forwarded to the chief accountant's office, while the other strip provided the booking clerk with a visible check of ticket issues. A later development was the Totalisator Unit which kept a mechanical record of all the tickets printed. Six counting units operating on the cyclometer principle were housed in a small box, which came into contact with the printing plate during the printing and issuing process. Spot checks could be undertaken whenever required by the simple means of inserting a piece of paper into a special slot, and operating a small lever at the top of the unit, thereby obtaining a carbon duplicate record.

The London and North Eastern Railway Company used several of these AEG machines, adapted to its own requirements. Although the machines produced tickets to Edmondson's standards, since the machines were automatic in their operation, only card roll of a single colour could be used. This meant that tickets so produced had to be entirely different from any others in the company's galaxy of cards. After deliberation, the LNER finally chose pale mauve.

The use of such tickets meant that the type-face had to indicate all the details of the ticket category, and in order to help the collectors, the ticket had to present these details in an easily read aspect. The card was printed with the text parallel to the short edges, and the class was indicated by a large, solid numeral on the extreme right-hand side. The use of this German machine meant that the tickets could only be printed on the front, and therefore, the reference to company regulations also had to appear among the destination and fare details. Where the LNER operated the zone system, as many as four destination stations were listed; together with identification marks (plate and machine number), this made for a rather crowded ticket face. Altogether, there were fifteen separate items listed on a Single ticket issued from the AEG machine. A Return ticket was similar in layout, although somewhat compressed, with the outward portion being the smaller of the two sections. The general aspect of the Return ticket was much clearer than the single card.

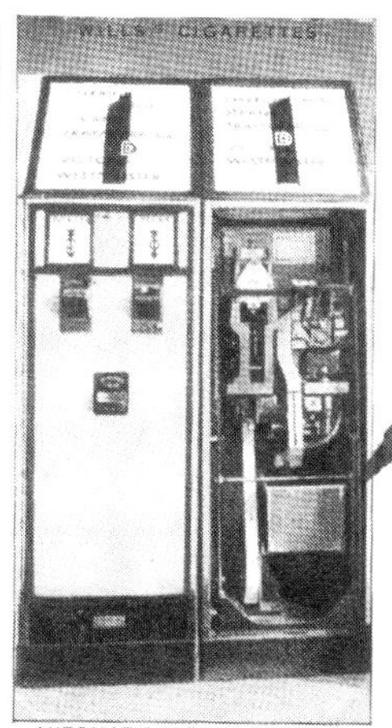

This type of automatic ticket-printing machine, installed at stations on the Underground Line of the London Passenger Transport Board, could also give the appropriate change. Tickets were issued at one penny fares, with change available for coins up to 2s 6d. The machine was loaded with a roll of pasteboard long enough for 2,000 tickets.

To avoid congestion at the booking office windows, Passimeter equipment was used by the LPTB. A turnstile was operated from inside the office as each ticket was issued (at the rate of four a second), the tickets being dated and cancelled mechanically.

A development of the AEG Multi-Printer was the Rapid Printer, which could issue four tickets every second. The entire operation, which was electrical and controlled from a keyboard of typewriter style, although complex, was trouble free. With text and fare as constants, the machine printed the date, serially numbered the ticket, guillotined it to size, recorded its issue, and transported the blank ticket roll into place ready for the next printing. It could print any type of ticket to cover any journey from the station of issue, and in less than one minute the date could be changed, and a new ticket roll inserted. Its installation effected considerable savings in time, labour, and money, and was generally reckoned to have revolutionised booking office practice and ticket printing methods.

It is impossible to discuss ticket machines without some reference to the Central Line of the London Underground, originally called the Central London Railway. During the period 1920-30 there was no railway system in the world which made such extensive use of mechanical aids in the booking office. The 'Twopenny Tube', so called because after its opening in 1900, the fare for a journey in any direction was 2d, had suffered the same fate as most other railways — booking office congestion caused by keeping large stocks of a wide variety of tickets under inadequate storage conditions. Business was so good that tickets were being manually issued at the rate of more than one every three seconds. Most of the passengers requesting tickets were also in need of change, and so it became imperative to devise some means of speeding-up and simplifying ticket issue, and giving change where necessary.

The Scheme Ticket was introduced on the Bakerloo Line in 1911, and extended to all the Underground lines by 1927. This innovation was quite simple and allowed the passenger the choice of about a dozen separate terminal stations to which the fare was applicable. The immediate effect of the new ticket system was to bring about a 60 per cent reduction in the number of tickets needed in stock.

The London Underground was no stranger to mechanised issue of tickets. In 1904 a coin-slot machine, with a pull bar operated by the passenger, issuing ready-printed tickets, was installed on the Central London Line. Four years later, an electrically operated coin-slot machine was in use. Another early device in use on the Underground was the Passimeter, a form of turnstile-cum-ticket machine. The passenger inserted the appropriate coin, whereupon the machine issued, dated, and cancelled the ticket, and then freed the flapper-arm of the turnstile. After the passenger had negotiated the turnstile, the flapper-arm was automatically reset. The first Passimeter was installed at Kilburn Park Station in 1921. Although it could not dispense change, it was such a success that it became standard equipment for all new stations.

Early in June 1922 an entirely new type of ticket issuing machine, the Rolltic, was installed at Oxford Circus Station; at a later date these machines were installed at other principal stations on the Bakerloo Line. Three continuous rolls of ticket card were loaded into the machine and were fed past the appropriate printing stereo by the simple method of turning a miniature handle. The automatically dated tickets were guillotined and fell through a glass tube of rectangular section into a convenient pick-up tray for the passenger. The machines were very fast in operation and represented a tremendous saving of time in comparison with other methods. One such old-fashioned method required the booking clerk to wet his finger on a suitable sponge pad, withdraw the ticket from a tube dispenser, and then to date it in a separate machine before issuing it to the passenger.

One of the most familiar machines in use on the Underground was the Brecknell, Munro and Rogers ticket and change dispenser. The machine was operated by a fractional horse-power motor, and was mounted in a sheet-metal case of pleasant design. An inclined and illuminated sheet of opaque glass listed in black letters against a white background the names of destination stations. These were available for a particular fare, which was indicated in the style of an overprint, and in red, also on the glass sheet. There were three types of machine in use according to the price of tickets issued. The coin mechanism was quite remarkable. For fivepenny fares, the machine would accept coins up to a total of one shilling; if a sixpence or a shilling was inserted the change was dispensed at the same time as the ticket. Where fares were in excess of sixpence, the machine would accept coins to a total value of two shillings, dispensing the necessary change without affecting the overall operating speed. Coins of all values up to two shillings could be inserted, either in orderly fashion or completely haphazard, without detriment to the normal operation of the machine. It was even possible for other passengers to insert their money before the first had been issued with his ticket. As many as thirty tickets could be issued in one minute in this manner, and each with change if required. After coins were inserted into the machine, they were counted, the printing mechanism switched on, and the ticket roll transported, the change delivery mechanism set in motion if necessary, and the coins stored in the change hoppers. Finally, the ticket was printed and issued. Such machines, although basically expensive, soon saved their cost by the very speed of their operation. Unnecessary queues at the booking office window were prevented, and the public benefited from the improved service.

3
TIMETABLES & PUNCTUALITY

Also necessary for the efficient running of a railway is the complicated maze of timetables and excursion notices. To most people, railway timetables are dull affairs, completely impossible to understand. With their cross-referenced columns of times, they have been the butt of many a vaudeville comic's barbs. Nowadays, railway enthusiasts are becoming more and more interested in the operational side of their hobby. Since they provide a hardcore of workers on most preserved lines, this is not really surprising, and the old timetables are a valuable source of information. Reprints of some of the rarer versions have, in recent years, sold well, while early originals have become collectors' items, with some rare specimens fetching very high prices at auction.

In the early years of the railways, timetables were not published by the companies. Indeed, so unreliable were the running times of the trains that in most cases, any attempt at publication would have been a waste of time and money. In the first ten years or so of passenger railways' operation, local solar time was in general use throughout Great Britain, and this created further complications. A Great Western Railway timetable of 1841 gave specific information concerning the differences in times between its major stations and London. One of the earliest known examples of a timetable was published by the London and Birmingham Railway. This was for the Euston to Tring section of the line, and gave details of the 'Hours of Departure, Commencing 29th October, 1837'. For the most part, however, the railway companies had not yet appreciated the vast potential and increasing popularity of rail travel. Passenger train services were announced on station posters and in the local newspaper on the initiative of the stationmaster.

The timetable announcing the opening of the Nottingham-Derby-Leicester section of the Midland Counties Railway was typical of many other such notices. The heading shows a one-coach train being hauled by a steam engine for which there is no apparent means of propulsion, while two persons are shown standing in the coal tender since the locomotive has no footplate. It is in fact a crudely executed wood-cut which quite clearly shows that the artist had not yet come to terms with this new-fangled form of transport. The notice states, 'The Public are informed, that this Railway, from Nottingham and Derby to Loughborough, Leicester, and the intermediate Stations, will be Opened for the Conveyance of Passengers, Parcels, Gentlemen's Carriages, Horses, and Van Goods, on TUESDAY, the 5th of May.' The hours of departure are listed below, and show four trains per weekday running between Nottingham and Leicester, with half that number operating on Sundays.

A Midland Counties Railway timetable first appeared in the *Leicester Journal and Midland Counties General Advertiser*, published for 31 December 1841. The simple timetable was printed one column width (about 3in) together with the account of weekly receipts. There was shown an operating schedule for six trains per weekday, and three on Sundays; these trains operated between London, Birmingham, Leicester, Nottingham, Derby and Manchester. Two weekday trains and one Sunday train also operated as Mail Trains.

In May 1839, the Great Western Railway published a timetable for its London to Maidenhead services, to announce the opening of the new Southall Station, for 'Passengers and Parcels'. This informative document provides a rather interesting slice of social history. The prospective passenger was told that 'An Extra Train to Slough will leave Paddington on Sunday Mornings, at Half-past 9 o'clock', and was further informed of the various stations en route at which the train would call. The timetable was evidently aimed at the wealthier passenger who would wish to ride in his own carriage, as was the custom of the day. It was possible in these early days of railways for a passenger to travel in his own carriage, which was loaded on to an open wagon, in preference to riding in a company coach. Carriage owners were advised, on this early GWR timetable, that their 'Horses and Carriages, being at the Paddington and Minehead Station ten minutes before the departure of a Train, will be conveyed upon this Railway.'

For the conveyance of a four-wheeled carriage the charge was 12s; for one horse the charge was 10s, while a pair of horses was charged at 16s. The Great Western Railway Company realised that a carriage owner might not wish to tire his horses with what must have been a dreadfully uncomfortable journey, and so they intimated on the timetable that company horses were available. These post horses were kept in readiness at both Paddington and Minehead, and provided sufficient notice was given (the exact period of such notice was not stipulated), they were sent to bring 'Carriages from any part of London to the station, at a moderate charge.'

Business was evidently fairly brisk, since train services from Paddington were in operation from eight o'clock in the morning until eight o'clock in the evening. From Minehead to Paddington the service commenced at six o'clock in the morning. This, the first up train of the day, called at Southall on Wednesday mornings, for the convenience of persons attending the market. Trains departed every hour, on the hour, but neither the up nor the down line carried a train at eleven o'clock in the morning, nor at one o'clock and three o'clock in the afternoon. Short trains ran from Paddington to West Drayton at half past the hour of nine, one, four and eight, while trains in the opposite direction left at one quarter before nine, eleven, three, and seven. A pointing hand gave special notice that there were no second class carriages in the short trains. A further note stated: 'Passengers and Parcels for Slough and Maidenhead will be conveyed from all the stations by means of the short Trains, waiting to be taken on the succeeding long Train, as above [referring to the time-table].'

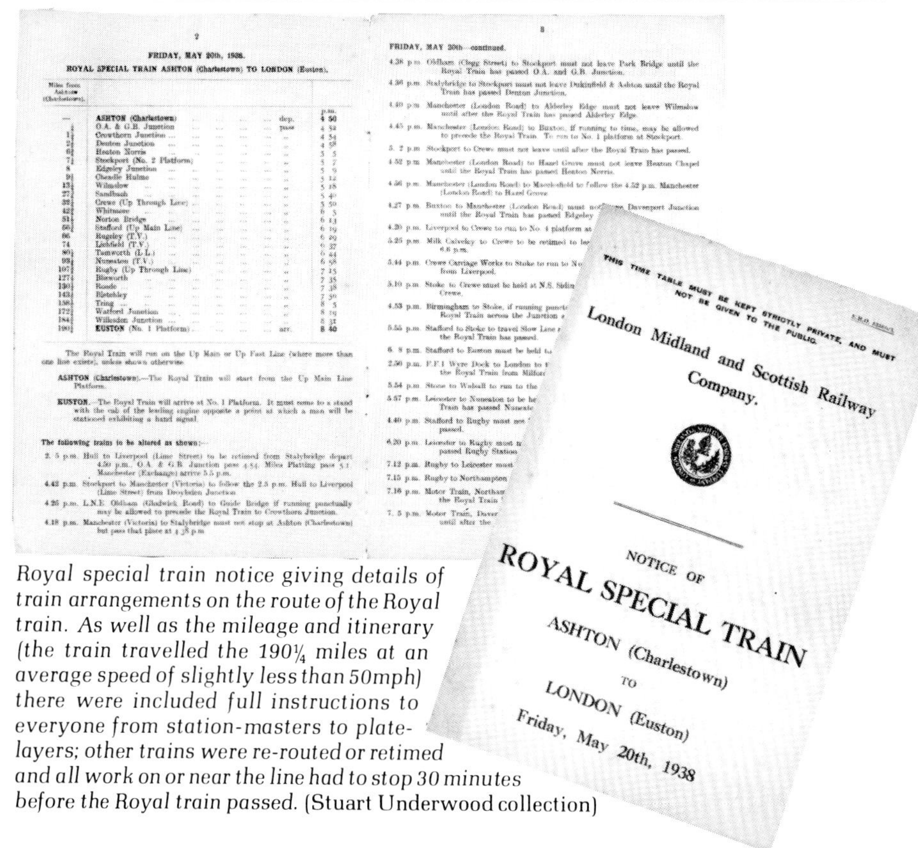

FRIDAY, MAY 20th, 1938.

ROYAL SPECIAL TRAIN ASHTON (Charlestown) TO LONDON (Euston).

FRIDAY, MAY 20th—continued.

THIS TIME TABLE MUST BE KEPT STRICTLY PRIVATE, AND MUST NOT BE GIVEN TO THE PUBLIC.

London Midland and Scottish Railway Company.

NOTICE OF

ROYAL SPECIAL TRAIN

ASHTON (Charlestown)

TO

LONDON (Euston)

Friday, May 20th, 1938

Royal special train notice giving details of train arrangements on the route of the Royal train. As well as the mileage and itinerary (the train travelled the 190¼ miles at an average speed of slightly less than 50mph) there were included full instructions to everyone from station-masters to plate-layers; other trains were re-routed or retimed and all work on or near the line had to stop 30 minutes before the Royal train passed. (Stuart Underwood collection)

One hour before the departure of each train, omnibuses and coaches left Princes Street, calling at the Angel Inn, Islington, the Bull Inn, Holborn, and various other places en route for Paddington Station. The fare, without luggage, was 6d.

The timetable gave a list of fares, the first-class, of course, being for travel by coach, while the second-class passengers had a choice of 'Open' or 'Close' travel. For 5s 6d a passenger rode in a first-class coach from Paddington to Minehead. His less fortunate fellow-traveller did the same journey in a second-class 'Open' for 2s less.

Almost sixty-two years later, on Saturday, 2 February 1901, on the occasion of the funeral of Queen Victoria, the train services in and out of Paddington and Southall were curtailed. A special timetable was produced, bordered in black, which stated that Sunday service conditions would operate throughout the Great Western Company's system. The early morning newspaper trains to Plymouth and Swansea ran as usual, and details of connections were given. The route of the Royal Funeral Train was from Paddington to Windsor, and so the Windsor station was closed for public traffic on the Sunday. The steamer service from Waterford to New Milford on the Friday was suspended, as was also the return trip on Sunday morning, 3 February 1901. This special timetable finished with the comment that the issue of weekend excursion tickets to Windsor, and the half-day excursion tickets to London 'will be suspended'. Passengers were advised to see special announcements issued locally for particulars of any additional local arrangements.

Fortunately, not all timetables were so sombre. Indeed, many of the old timetables, before the companies were re-grouped into the 'Big Four', were fine works of art. The Great Western Railway was justly renowned for its artistic publicity, and the summer 1889 edition of the company's timetable is a splendid example. The company was very proud of its royal associations, and featured as a centre-piece to the cover a fine engraving of Windsor, overlooked by the castle with the Sovereign's flag flying. Brown and black on a white background was the colour scheme of the cover which was entitled *GREAT WESTERN RAILWAY & other Railways in Connection.* Above the picture of Windsor is a view of Plymouth harbour, flanked by the cathedrals of Gloucester and Worcester. To the left and right of the centrepiece are views of Cardiff and Salisbury respectively. Underneath are views of Tintern Abbey, the Mumbles Lighthouse, and Llangollen Bridge, with the company's coat of arms providing a support for the superb pictorial layout. The price of this attractive book was one penny.

For a similar sum one could purchase the timetable of the North Eastern Railway, which in November 1891 published an edition with a most attractive cover in black and white. A map of the system was shown with all the principal stations marked, and the map was surrounded with illustrations of notable places on the various routes. Such places included Fountains Abbey, York Minster, Scarborough, and Edinburgh. A rather interesting inclusion was a picture of the Forth Bridge in an aspect which must surely have set the fashion for all future views. At the time, the bridge was barely eighteen months old, and was in the territory of the North British Railway, in whose east coast route the North Eastern Railway was a joint operator.

A very colourful cover embraced the April 1900 timetable issued by the London & North Western Railway. Blue-green, red, and black were attractively used to show the company's rail network, and panels on either side of the map proudly asserted that the company operated the 'Shortest and Quickest Route between London, Liverpool, Manchester and Glasgow' and the 'Royal Mail Route to and from Scotland, Wales and Ireland'. A small scroll on the right of the map listed some of the fastest schedules in operation at that time. The time taken between London and Manchester was 4 hours and 10 minutes, while a journey to Birmingham took only 2¼ hours. In contrast, the journey to Inverness took 13½ hours, so perhaps it was not without significance that the scroll concluded with the information: 'Sleeping Saloons on the Night Trains'.

The multi-coloured timetable issued in October 1911, by the South Eastern and Chatham Railway, is another artistic gem. In the top right-hand corner of the cover is the heraldic device of the company surmounting its name, while in the left-hand corner is a picture of one of the company's cross-channel steamers. Across the centre-spread is a map of the company's rail network, together with its connections to France; filling the bottom section of the cover is a picture of an express train hauled by a James Stirling 4-4-0 type locomotive. The pictures of the steamer and the train are particularly attractive.

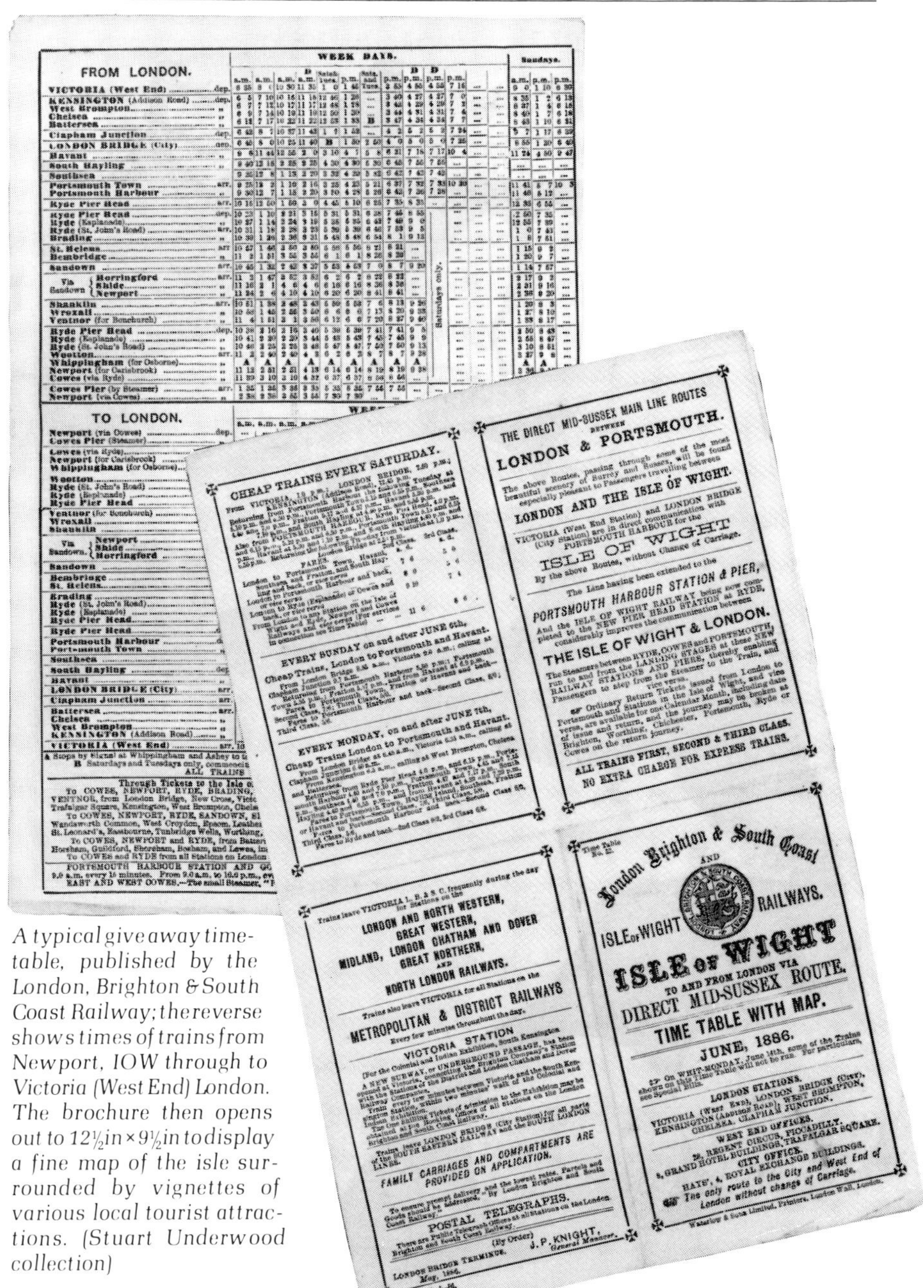

FROM LONDON.

WEEK DAYS.

Sundays.

TO LONDON.

CHEAP TRAINS EVERY SATURDAY.

EVERY SUNDAY on and after JUNE 6th,

EVERY MONDAY, on and after JUNE 7th,

THE DIRECT MID-SUSSEX MAIN LINE ROUTES BETWEEN LONDON & PORTSMOUTH.

LONDON AND THE ISLE OF WIGHT.

ISLE OF WIGHT

PORTSMOUTH HARBOUR STATION & PIER,

THE ISLE OF WIGHT & LONDON.

ALL TRAINS FIRST, SECOND & THIRD CLASS. NO EXTRA CHARGE FOR EXPRESS TRAINS.

LONDON AND NORTH WESTERN, GREAT WESTERN, MIDLAND, LONDON CHATHAM AND DOVER GREAT NORTHERN, AND NORTH LONDON RAILWAYS.

METROPOLITAN & DISTRICT RAILWAYS

VICTORIA STATION

FAMILY CARRIAGES AND COMPARTMENTS ARE PROVIDED ON APPLICATION.

POSTAL TELEGRAPHS.

(By Order) J. P. KNIGHT, General Manager.

Time Table No. 21.

London Brighton & South Coast AND ISLE OF WIGHT RAILWAYS.

ISLE OF WIGHT TO AND FROM LONDON VIA DIRECT MID-SUSSEX ROUTE.

TIME TABLE WITH MAP.

JUNE, 1886.

LONDON STATIONS.

WEST END OFFICES.

CITY OFFICE.

The only route to the City and West End of London without change of Carriage.

A typical giveaway timetable, published by the London, Brighton & South Coast Railway; the reverse shows times of trains from Newport, IOW through to Victoria (West End) London. The brochure then opens out to 12½in × 9½in to display a fine map of the isle surrounded by vignettes of various local tourist attractions. (Stuart Underwood collection)

Not all the companies produced such works of art, thinking perhaps that function and art did not go well together. Some companies did ornament their timetables with a simple representation of their coat of arms, but others so filled the cover with masses of wordy titles that no space was left for artwork. During the early years of World War I, printing costs and paper restrictions resulted in the issue of very plain covered editions, and

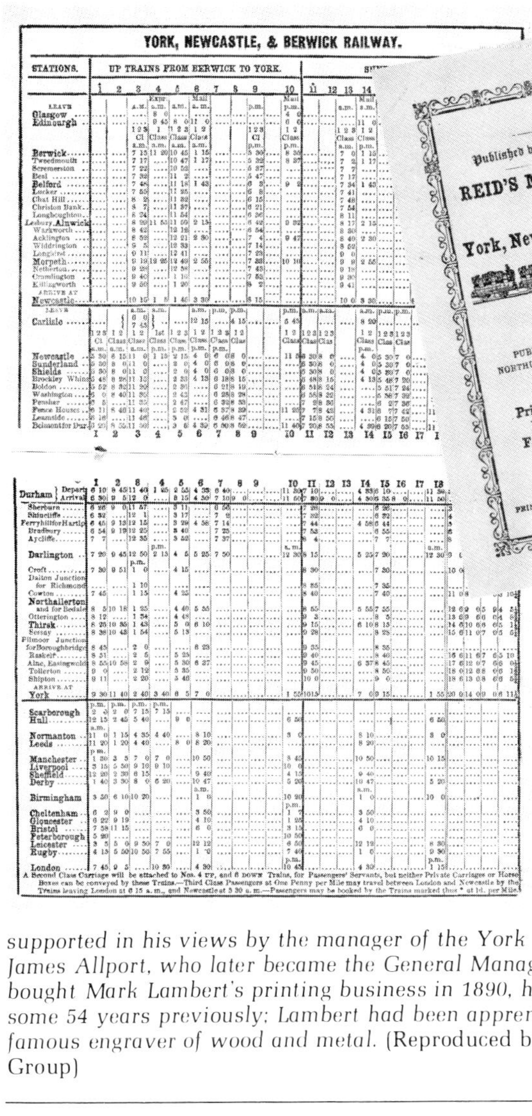

YORK, NEWCASTLE, & BERWICK RAILWAY.

UP TRAINS FROM BERWICK TO YORK.

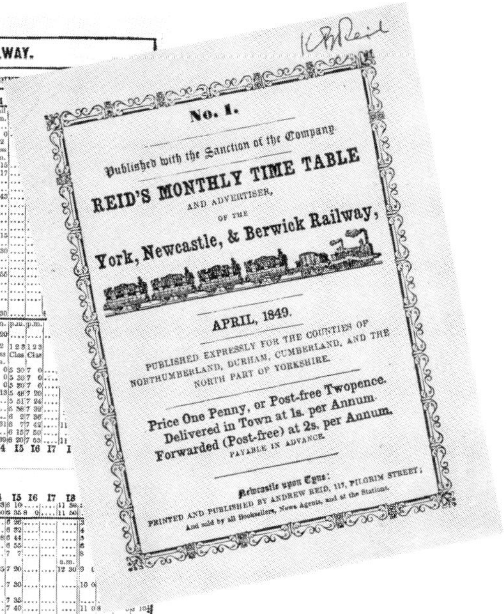

No. 1.

Published with the Sanction of the Company.

REID'S MONTHLY TIME TABLE

AND ADVERTISER,

OF THE

York, Newcastle, & Berwick Railway,

APRIL, 1849.

PUBLISHED EXPRESSLY FOR THE COUNTIES OF NORTHUMBERLAND, DURHAM, CUMBERLAND, AND THE NORTH PART OF YORKSHIRE.

Price One Penny, or Post-free Twopence.
Delivered in Town at 1s. per Annum.
Forwarded (Post-free) at 2s. per Annum.
PAYABLE IN ADVANCE.

Newcastle upon Tyne:
PRINTED AND PUBLISHED BY ANDREW REID, 117, PILGRIM STREET;
And sold by all Booksellers, News Agents, and at the Stations.

Cover and inside page of the No 1 issue of Reid's Monthly Time Table. Andrew Reid, the founder of the well-known Newcastle printing company (later to become part of the Hindon Print Group) was convinced that a railway timetable in this form was much in demand; he was supported in his views by the manager of the York Newcastle & Berwick Railway, James Allport, who later became the General Manager of the Midland Railway. Reid bought Mark Lambert's printing business in 1890, having been apprenticed to him some 54 years previously; Lambert had been apprenticed to Thomas Bewick, the famous engraver of wood and metal. (Reproduced by permission of Hindson Print Group)

eventually the companies gave up issuing public timetables. After the war, the re-issue of public timetables, with a heritage of restrictions, produced covers of severe simplicity. This severity continued after the re-grouping in 1923, and each of the four big railways chose a colour for its timetable covers which closely resembled the colour of its passenger stock. The Southern Railway cover was green, that of the London, Midland and Scottish was dark red, and the Great Western used its famous 'chocolate and cream'. To avoid confusion with the Southern, the LNER, whose livery was also green, used an orange tint to suggest the varnished teak of its carriages, for which the company was famous.

With the growing popularity of the railways in the 1830s, a passenger who wished to travel extensively had to encumber himself with half-a-dozen or so timetables issued by the different companies. An attempt to solve the problem was made by George Bradshaw with a book which was a collection of all the timetables in Britain.

The renowned statesman and Parliamentary orator, John Bright, was once asked, 'What books do you consult most?'The Bible and *Bradshaw*', was the reply of the great Quaker. Bradshaw's *General Railway and Steam Navigation Guide* became a British institution like *The Times* and *Punch*. Like all great institutions, it became the target for libel and detraction, and its very accuracy was questioned. The novelist, Charles Dickens, once said, 'It has driven countless British lieges to lunacy. Our retreats for the insane are said to be invariably provided with a "Bradshaw ward" filled with the unhappy victims of the famous guide. But, seriously, "Bradshaw" — like the Bench of Bishops — can afford to be indulgent in the knowledge that it is indispensable. What should we do without "Bradshaw"?' Dickens went on to say that Londoners had their *ABC* (of which more later), but London was only a tenth of the kingdom, and *Bradshaw* had all of Europe for its province. He thought that the origin and early progress of *Bradshaw* was interesting enough to be better known to the world.

A Railway Traveller's Handy Book, published in 1862, stated that *Bradshaw* was a work containing 'a mass of information compressed into the very smallest compass, but on that account, and by reason of various signs and symbols having to be made use of, it is not so easy of interpretation as it might be.'

George Bradshaw was a Quaker, and a map-maker by profession. Long before the days of the railways he had employed himself on the production of maps showing the canal networks of Lancashire and Yorkshire. But by 1839 the country was becoming intersected by a different kind of network, that of the steel rail. Stephenson's iron horse was clanking its way between London, Manchester, and Liverpool. Passengers — who had received small account in Stephenson's original calculations when he inaugurated his first railway in 1825 — began to popularise this new form of transport in increasing numbers. Their demands became more clamorous, and it was obvious that a knowledge of train arrivals and departures was essential.

In 1837, the year in which Queen Victoria succeeded to the throne, there were few railway 'guides' really worthy of the name. Indeed, one of the most comprehensive guides was that available to patrons of the Birmingham and Liverpool Line, better known as the Grand Junction Railway. This unique guide was in the form of a large pewter medal, and it was intended that the passenger could carry it in his pocket for handy reference. The obverse of the medal carried the inscription:

Grand Junction Railway Opened July 4, 1837

The trains leave:

BIRMINGHAM		LIVERPOOL & MANCHESTER	
Hour	Min.	Hour	Min.
VII	0	VI	30
VIII	30	VIII	30
XI	30	XI	30
II	30	II	30
IV	30	IV	30
VII	0	VI	30

The reverse was inscribed:

Time and distance from Birmingham

To	Miles	H	M
Wolverhampton	14½	0	40
Stafford	29¼	1	15
Whitmore	43¾	1	55
Crewe	54	2	24
Hartford	65¾	2	59
Manchester			
Liverpool	97¼	4	30

There were just seven railways operating in 1837, and Bradshaw reasoned that the monthly leaflets published by each on their own account would be better collected and re-printed in handy form like a little book. The idea was not an original one, and so Bradshaw lost little time between the thought and the action. A Manchester printer by the name of Gadsby had a similar idea, but missed priority of publication by a few weeks. On 19 October 1839, the first *Bradshaw* came off the printing presses in Manchester. The last *Bradshaw* was printed in June 1961; British Railways issued their first and only *Bradshaw*-type guide in June 1962.

As Bradshaw produced a number of separate publications and several changes in title, it is as well to summarise the sequence of publication, which can otherwise become somewhat confusing. The very first volume was a modest and unobtrusive affair bound in green, ribbed cloth, with the title *Bradshaw's Railway Time Tables,* surrounded by a foliate wreath stamped in gilt. No 1, dated 19 October 1839, included only the northern railways; No 2, dated 25 October 1839, dealt with only the southern railways; but No 3, also dated 25 October 1839, was the first national guide and was a combination of Nos 1 and 2. It was obtainable from railway companies and most booksellers for the sum of 6d. The title page read:

Bradshaw's
Railway Time Tables
and Assistant to
Railway Travelling
with
Illustrative Maps & Plans.

Also included on the title page were details of *Bradshaw's Map and Section of the Railways of Great Britain,* together with prices.

The introduction to the first volume acknowledged the assistance of the several railway companies, 'on which account the information it contains may be depended upon as being correct and authentic. The necessity of such a work is so obvious as to need no apology; and the merits of it can best be ascertained by a reference to the execution both as regards the style and correctness of the maps and plans with which it is illustrated.' The last comment causes little surprise when one remembers that Bradshaw was first and foremost a map engraver; he obviously lost no opportunity publicly to advertise his professional skills. Also included were different fares for 'Inside and Outside passengers.

The railway companies were not very enthusiastic in their reception of

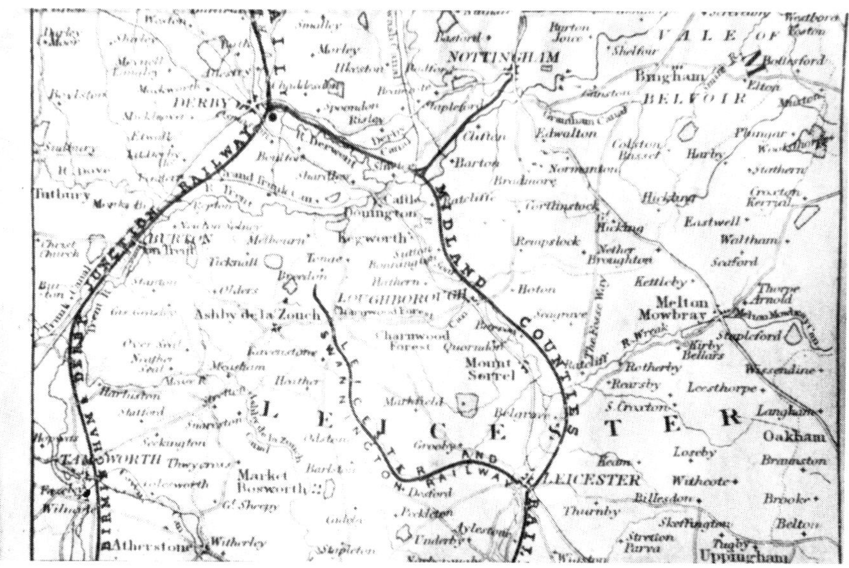

The routes of the Birmingham & Derby Junction Railway, Midland Counties Railway, and the Leicester & Swannington Railway, are shown on this map contained in Bradshaw's Railway Guide, *published in 1844. The railways later became constituent companies of the Midland Railway.*

the first general railway guide. When they learned of the use to which Bradshaw was putting their timetables, they refused him further supplies. They claimed that continued publication of the timetables would make punctuality a kind of obligation, with penalties for failure. It is strange to think that a commercial operator could be so lax; even stranger still to offer the following excuse for unbusinesslike methods:

> Whereas at present, if the ten minutes past three steams gently out at twenty minutes to four, or even four o'clock, we do not fall much in the esteem of the public, accustomed to the free and easy methods of the stage-coach'.

But Bradshaw was not easily deterred. He needed the timetables, and so he pestered the railway boards, even going to the extent of purchasing stock in the hostile companies, so that he could continue his enterprise.

Bradshaw's Railway Timetables was not a regular publication, and the London agent, Adams, recommended that it should be so. The first such regular volume appeared in December 1841, with the new title of *Bradshaw's Railway Guide*, which was retitled *Bradshaw's Monthly Railway Guide* in February 1842. It differed from its predecessors in being bound in paper, and having only thirty-two pages. By this time, Bradshaw had evidently convinced the hostile railway companies of the advantages of his *Guide*, since he was able to announce its monthly publication 'under the direction and with the assistance of the railway companies'. He was further able to claim that every reliance could be placed on the accuracy of its details.

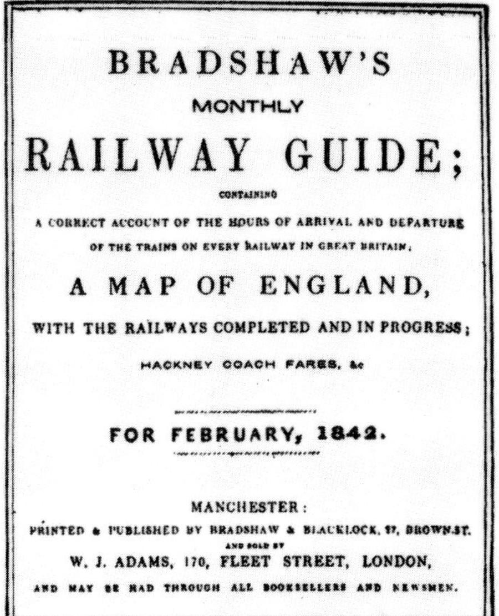
BRADSHAW'S

MONTHLY

RAILWAY GUIDE;

CONTAINING

A CORRECT ACCOUNT OF THE HOURS OF ARRIVAL AND DEPARTURE OF THE TRAINS ON EVERY RAILWAY IN GREAT BRITAIN;

A MAP OF ENGLAND,

WITH THE RAILWAYS COMPLETED AND IN PROGRESS;

HACKNEY COACH FARES, &c

FOR FEBRUARY, 1842.

MANCHESTER:

PRINTED & PUBLISHED BY BRADSHAW & BLACKLOCK, 27, BROWN ST.

AND SOLD BY

W. J. ADAMS, 170, FLEET STREET, LONDON,

AND MAY BE HAD THROUGH ALL BOOKSELLERS AND NEWSMEN.

The title page of the first 'Bradshaw' to be issued with the designation, Monthly Railway Guide.

Bradshaw may have been able to enlist the assistance of the railway companies, but they evidently continued in their unpunctual ways long after the issue of his new monthly *Guide*. For instance, *Pleasant Days in Pleasant Places*, published in 1878, has the following discourteous, but damning, comment: 'although the said line is no longer called the "Eastern Counties", but the "Great Eastern", it has not changed its nature with its name; it is still by far the worst managed line in the kingdom, the most unpunctual in its arrangements, the slowest in speed, the most churlish in its courtesies, the most indifferent in its servants.'

The new monthly edition was presented in a much simpler form. The pages were arranged in broadsheet style, 'exhibiting at one view the hours of departure and arrival of the trains on every railway in the kingdom, and are particularly adapted for counting-houses and places of business'. The broadsheets could be purchased separately at only 3d, but if they were mounted on stiff board, the price was 2s 9d.

By 1843, the popularity of railways, or, as one fashionable London magazine described it, 'the mania which has enriched and beggared thousands', had increased. There were in that year forty-eight railway companies operating throughout Britain, with a keenly interested public. The title of *Bradshaw* was again altered, this time to the *Monthly General Railway and Steam Navigation Guide*. It contained much more in the way of reading matter, including a list of shares, together with their dividends and market values.

For some reason there is a break in numbering in the early life of the monthly *Guide*. With the publication in March 1845 of No 40, there is a sudden jump to No 141 with the April 1845 issue. The error was never corrected, and it was probably deliberate, to make the *Guide* appear to be more established than it actually was.

London and Luton.] 585 [Midland.

LONDON, HENDON, St. ALBANS, and LUTON.—Midland.

Down.	Week Days—Continued. aft	aft	aft (Except Saturdays)	aft	aft (Except Saturdays)	aft	aft	aft	aft	aft (Except Saturdays)	aft	aft (Except Saturdays)	aft	aft	aft	aft	aft	aft	aft (Saturdays only)	aft (Except Saturdays)	aft	aft
ST. PANCRAS ....dep.	5 8	5 25	5 45	5 50	6 5	6e10	6 17	6 33		6 55		7 10	7 20	7 45	7 50	8 5	8 40	8 50	9 40	9 45	1040	1140
Moorgate Street dep.		5h11	5g34			5h50	6g3	6h15	6 26		6 47		7g3		7g19	7g47		8g21	9g25	9g25		11g7
Aldersgate Street		5h13	5g36			5h52	6g4	6h17	6 28		6 49		7g5		7g21	7g49		8g23	9g27	9g27		11g9
Farringdon Street		5h15	5g38			5h54	6g6	6h19	6 30		6 51		7g7		7g23	7g51		8g25	9g29	9g29		g1111
King's Cross (Met.)		5h19	5g42			5h58	6g10	6h23	6 34		6 55		7g11		7g27	7g55		8g29	9g33	9g33		g1115
Camden Road ......dep.		5h24	5g47			6h3	6g15	6h28	6 39		7 0		7g16		7g32	8g1		8g34	9g38	9g38		g1120
Kentish Town	5 15	5 31	5 51	5 56		6e16	6 23	6 39	6 42		7 3	7 16	7 26		7 56	8 11		8 56	9 46	9 51	1045	1146
Haverstock Hill							6 26		6 45		7 6	7 19			7 59			9 0	9 49	9 54	1050	1149
Finchley Road							6 30		6 49		7 10	7 23			8 3			9 4	9 53	9 58	1054	1153
West Hampstead				6 3			6 32		6 51		7 12	7 25			8 5			9 6	9 55	10 0	1056	1155
Cricklewood		5 38		6 6		6e23	6 36		6 54		7 15	7 28			8 8	8 18		9 10	9 58	10 3	1059	1158
Hendon		5 43		6 11		6e27	6 41		6 58		7 19		7 38		8 12	8 24		9 15	10 3	10 8	11 4	12 3
Mill Hill		5 48		6 17	6 24		6 46			7 11			7 43			8 29		9 20	10 8	1013	11 9	12 8
Elstree		5 54		6 23	6 31		6 53			7 18			7 49			8 36		9 27	1014	1019	1116	1214
Radlett		6 0		6 29	6 37		6 59			7 24			7 55			8 42		9 33	1020	1025	1122	1220
Napsbury							7 6						8 2									
St. Albans 373, 437	5 42	6 8	6 19	6 37	6 45		7 10	7 5		7 34			8 6	8 12		8 50	9 9	9 41	1030	1035	1132	1228
Harpenden 603	5 51		6 30					7 15		7 43				8 23			9*19		1039	1046	1143	
Chiltern Green †	5 57		6 37					d						8 29								
Luton 347, 538 ....arr.	6 3		6 46					7 26		7 54				8 35			9 30		1048	1055	1152	

Down.	Week Days—Continued. ngt.	ngt.	ngt.			Sundays. mrn	mrn	mrn	aft	aft	aft	aft	aft	aft	aft	aft	aft	aft	aft	aft	aft	ngt.	
ST. PANCRAS ....dep.	12 5	1215	1222			8 0	9 30		1 0		2 15		4 10		5 30			8 40		9 50		1215	
Moorgate Street dep.			g1140					1039		1g13		2 37		5 10		6 40	8 5		8 45		1033		
Aldersgate Street			g1142					1041		1g15		2 39		5 12		6 42	8 7		8 47		1035		
Farringdon Street			g1144					1043		1g17		2 41		5 14		6 44	8 9		8 49		1037		
King's Cross (Met.)			g1148					1047		1g21		2 45		5 18		6 48	8 13		8 53		1041		
Camden Road ......dep.			g1153			8 4	9 35	1052	1 4	1g26		2 50	4 15	5 23	5g29	6 53	8 18		8 58	9 54	1046		
Kentish Town		1221	1228			8 7	9 37	1054	1 6	1 33	2 20	2 52	4 17	5 25	5 35	6 55	8 20		9 0	9 57	1048	1221	
Haverstock Hill						8 10	9 41	1057	1 9	1 38		2 55	4 20	5 28		6 58	8 23		9 3	10 0	1051		
Finchley Road						8 14	9 45	11 1	1 13	1 42		2 59	4 24	5 32		7 2	8 27		9 7	10 4	1055		
West Hampstead						8 16	9 47	11 3	1 15	1 44		3 1	4 26	5 34		7 5	8 29		9 9	10 7	1057		
Cricklewood						8 19	9 51	11 6	1 18	1 47		3 4	4 30	5 37		7 8	8 32		9 12	1011	11 0		
Hendon			1239			8 25	9 57	1112	1 23	1 51	2 31	3 9	4 35	5 41	5 46	7 13	8 37		9 16	1017	11 4		
Mill Hill			1244			8 30	10 3	1117	1 28		2 36	3 14	4 41		5 52	7 19	8 43			1022			
Elstree			1251			8 37	1010	1124	1 35		2 43	3 21	4 48		5 58	7 25	8 49			1028			
Radlett			1257			8 43	1016	1130	1 41		2 49	3 27	4 54		6 4	7 31	8 55			1034			
Napsbury							1023	1137	1 48			3 34	5 1										
St. Albans 373, 437	1234		1 5			8 53	1029	1141	1 54		2 59	3 38	5 5		6 14	7 40	9 3	9 9		1042		1248	
Harpenden 603	1243					9 3	1039		2 3		3 8				6 23			9 19					
Chiltern Green †						9 9	1045								6 29								
Luton 347, 538 ....arr.	1254					9 17	1053		2 12		3 17				6 37			9 30				1 4	

c Arrives at 5 12 aft.
d Stops to set down from London.
e Except Saturdays.
g Change at Kentish Town.
h Except Saturdays, changing at Kentish Town.
s Saturdays only.
† Station for Luton Hoo.

☞ For **OTHER TRAINS** between **St. Pancras, Moorgate Street, and Kentish Town, see pages 588 and 590.**

MANSFIELD and PYE BRIDGE.—Midland.

Miles.	Up.	Week Days. mrn	mrn	mrn	mrn	Thurs. mrn	Thurs. mrn	mrn	mrn	Sats. aft	aft	aft	aft	aft	aft	Thurs. & Sats. aft		Sundays. mrn	aft	
	Mansfield ....dep.	6 0	6 35	6 53	7 56	9 20	9 40	10 6	1140	1 5	1 35	3 43	4 38	6 30	7 40	9 35		6 30	6 25	
2¼	Sutton Junction	6 7	6 41	6 59	8 2	9 25	9 47	1012	1145	1 12	1 41	3 49	4 44	6 36	7 46	9 40		6 36	6 31	
3¾	Kirkby-in-Ashfield......	6 11	6 45	7 3	8 6	9 29	9 51	1016	1149	1 16	1 45	3 53	4 48	6 40	7 50	9 44		6 40	6 35	
7	Pinxton and Selston.....	6 18	6 52	7 10	8 13	9 38	9 58	1023	1157		1 52	4 0	4 55	6 47	7 58	9 52		6 48	6 43	
9¼	Pye Bridge 597 .....arr.	6 23	6 57	7 15	8 18	9 43	10 3	1032	12 2	1 26	1 57	4 5	5 0	6 56	8 4	9 58		6 53	6 48	

Miles.	Down.	Week Days. mrn	Thurs. mrn	mrn	aft	aft	aft	aft	aft	aft	aft	aft	Thurs. & Sats. aft	aft					Sundays. mrn	aft	
	Pye Bridge ....dep.	8 27	1049	1127	12 9	2 25	2 58	4 33	6 26	7 32	8 35	9 30	1025	11 1					1030	7 40	
2¼	Pinxton and Selston	8 33	1054	1132	1215	2 31	3 4	4 39	6 32	7 38	8 41	9 36	1032	11a6					1036	7 46	
5½	Kirkby-in-Ashfield 583..	8 41	11 2	1140	1222	2 39	3 13	4 47	6 40	7 46	8 49	9 44	1042	1120					1044	7 54	
7	Sutton Junction 575	8 45	11 6	1144	1226	2 43	3 17	4 51	6 44	7 50	8 53	9 47	1046	1125					1048	7 58	
9¼	Mansfield 601 ......arr.	8 50	1111	1149	1231	2 48	3 22	4 58	6 49	7 55	8 58	9 53	1052	1130					1053	8 4	

a Wednesdays, Fridays, and Saturdays.

☞ For **OTHER TRAINS** between **Mansfield and Pye Bridge, see page 600; between Mansfield and Kirkby-in-Ashfield, see page 583; between Mansfield and Sutton Junction, see page 575.**

LEICESTER (West Bridge) and DESFORD.—Midland.

Miles.	Down.	Week Days. mrn	Except Sats. aft	Sats. aft	aft			
	West Bridge Sta., Leicester .....dep.	9 2	1 0	1 15	5 30			
2¾	Glenfield	9 9	1 8	1 23	5 38			
4¼	Ratby	9 15	1 14	1 29	5 44			
6¼	Desford 593 ..arr.	9 21	1 20	1 36	5 50			

Miles.	Up.	Week Days. mrn	Except Sats. aft	Sats. aft	aft			
	Desford ......dep.	8 30	2 5	2 15	7 22			
2	Ratby	8 37	2 12	2 22	7 29			
3½	Glenfield 549, 572	8 43	2 18	2 28	7 35			
6¼	Leicester 538, arr.	8 50	2 25	2 35	7 42			

A typical page from the 1909 issue of Bradshaw's Railway Guide, *which showed the departure and arrival times of every train run by every company in Britain. The frequency of trains, every quarter of an hour or so, is quite amazing.*

Another publication, which first appeared on 1 January 1840, was *Bradshaw's Railway Companion.* Although similar to the *Time Tables* it was a separate work, with thirty-eight pages of maps and letterpress. The *Companion* merged with the *Guide* in 1848.

Some entertaining and very interesting facts are to be gleaned from the early issues of *Bradshaw's Railway Guide.* Trains were described as 'first class', 'second class', 'mixed', 'fast', or 'mail', but never as 'express', which was a title which came into fashion many years afterwards. It goes without saying that a 'first class' train would only stop at a first-class station.

Third-class passengers travelled on the roof in a clear space among the luggage on the second-class coaches, or in open wagons. At the other end of the scale of luxury, one reads of 'glass' coaches — ie carriages with glazed windows, and plush upholstery. Passenger tickets were referred to as 'passes' or 'check tickets', and the passenger was reminded that his ticket would be demanded from him at the penultimate station to London or Birmingham; failure to produce it could mean repayment of the fare.

At the time, there was no overall standard by which fares were charged, and it is curious to read that fares were liable to fluctuation according to day or night travel, or the number of passengers who occupied a carriage. A lone traveller from London to Birmingham in a first-class coach was charged 32s 6d, but if six passengers travelled inside by day, the tariff was reduced to 30s. Second-class passengers enjoyed a similar reduction. The season ticket system was familiar to most rail travellers, and was fairly popular; nonetheless, it must have been quite a shock to read that 'An annual subscription ticket from London to Brighton and back is £100.'

With most railway companies it was the practice to allow each passenger to take hand-luggage into the carriage, usually to a weight limit of 28lb; other luggage had to be stored on the roof. An extract from an early *Guide* reads: 'Passengers are especially recommended to have their names and address or destination written on each part of their luggage, when it will be placed on the top of the coach in which they ride. If the passenger be destined for Manchester or Liverpool, and has booked his place through, his luggage will be placed on the Liverpool or Manchester coach, and will not be disturbed until it reaches its destination.'

A revolutionary timetable was introduced in one of the early *Guides*. The two terminal stations and the intermediate stations were listed in a vertical column, with the accumulative mileage written at the side; across the page were printed columns with 'Time' headings. Going across the page level with each station name the 'Time' columns were entered with a dotted (...) or a dashed (---) line. It was explained: 'Where the space is dotted the trains call; where a blank, thus ---, they do not.'

Children in arms, provided they were unable to walk, were allowed to travel free, while others were required to tender the appropriate fare. No doubt, while travelling through the countryside the passenger would wish to admire the view, but he was warned not to lean upon the door of the carriage.

Bradshaw started out in life with thirty-two pages, but by the turn of the century contained more than twelve hundred of increased dimensions; its weight had increased from a mere two ounces to a pound and a half.

The work involved in the monthly production of this collated timetable was tremendous, needing all the resources of a large staff of editors and printers. They had to be continually aware of the almost perpetual, and sometimes minute changes that the various railway companies chose to initiate. It should be remembered that there was no telephone to give an instant answer to any query. Each page was packed almost to bursting with type, approximately 3,000 characters per page. Every change, however small, inaugurated by the traffic superintendent of any of the country's railways, had to be instantly set down. The inclusion of a new train service had to be crowded into an already overcrowded page — for the style of layout could not allow 'over-running' on to the next page. It is small wonder that *Bradshaw* acquired a reputation for being so difficult to understand. So much so that it was referred to as 'a recondite treatise on the subject of railway times', and the wit George Cruikshank, along with others, called it an 'Aid to Bedlam'. It was regularly lampooned in *Punch*, and in the issue of 24 May 1856, was a two-page feature entitled 'Bradshaw — a Mystery', in which two lovers, parted by distance, seek to unite by means of the *Guide*.

But although Bradshaw tried, generally successfully, he did not entirely solve the problem of timetables for some travellers. For such people the *ABC* was devised, first appearing for sale in 1853. It was different in that it made London the hub of the railway network, and all other stations were listed in alphabetical order. Fares were calculated from London, and all train routes in and out of the capital were shown together with departure and arrival times. Small stations were cross-referenced to the larger ones, so that even the lowliest halt could boast a reference. Because of its arrangement, this railway guide was claimed to be 'as easy as A.B.C.' Other guides were produced which combined the alphabetical arrangement with the Bradshaw-type timetable, but these for the most part were purely local in their application.

During the mid-1930s, many of the major stations introduced a mechanical timetable. This consisted of a metal cabinet with an illuminated window, and was known as the 'Mechanical Informator'. The simplification of the timetables was its purpose, and an intending traveller pressed a key, after having selected his destination station from a numbered list. There were fifty such keys, each of which was connected to a time-sheet, showing departure and arrival times, and which was viewed through the window.

With the re-grouping of the railways in 1923 the number of company timetables diminished almost overnight from several dozen to four. Their bulk increased, and instead of being issued every month, the new timetables were issued for the 'Spring', 'Summer', and 'Winter' seasons.

Perhaps not unnaturally, railway services had deteriorated during World War I, and after the cessation of hostilities, each of the companies embarked upon a recovery programme. Train services were improved over pre-war days, and the achievement of a standardised timetable was a common goal. Several years before the war, many express services had operated at reasonably regular intervals, but afterwards the railway companies were more concerned with the problems of national reorganisation than with the day-to-day details of running trains on time. The Great Western Railway attempted to run its expresses to Birmingham, Exeter, and South Wales at ten minutes, thirty minutes, and at fifty-five minutes past the hour; the times must have been too regular, because they did not achieve lasting popularity with the travelling public. The greatest success was achieved by the Southern Railway who standardised their electric train services to Brighton and to Eastbourne. Indeed, so successful were they that the company could announce that 'time-tables are unnecessary'. Suburban trains were arranged to run within a few minutes of one another.

Railway staff had need of something far more detailed than the public timetable, and this was produced in several volumes as a 'Service' or 'Working' timetable. These books, of tremendous length and size, could run to more than 2,500 pages, and were up to 5in thick. When one realises that these working timetables dealt with every type of traffic movement, their size is not difficult to understand. Every sort of train, passenger and goods, was listed, together with its reasons for being in a particular area at a given time. Perishable foodstuffs and empty rolling-stock received mention, and there were even details of trains stopping to take on water. Information was included about trains which were to run on 'fast' or 'slow' lines, and the differentiation between weekday running and the operation of weekend schedules, with every train given a working or reporting number. All companies issued copies of these working timetables to appropriate members of their staff; since it was, in effect, their working Bible, they were required to be fully acquainted with its contents. The notice printed in the 1909 issue of the London and South Western Railway Company's working timetable was typical of most other company's directives. It read as follows: 'Each person supplied with a Copy of this Time-Table will be held responsible that he reads carefully, and obeys all Notices and Instructions contained therein so far as they concern him. No excuse of want of knowledge can be admitted for any Failure or Neglect of Duty.' Even though the railways in Great Britain have been nationalised, the pattern of operation is basically the same, and the various regions still produce working timetables.

The design of a timetable was, as it still is, a highly complicated and specialised task. Essentially, any timetable is a series of diagrams upon which is plotted the paths of all trains. The correct use of the diagrams shows the paths of existing trains, and also gives an indication of where extra trains may be injected into the system, and the limits under which they may operate. The density of stations per route mile must be taken into consideration, as must also track capacity and layout; another factor which makes for complication is that some stations operate both as terminal points and through-traffic centres.

One of the heaviest short-distance passenger routes in the world during the mid-1930s was on the London and North Eastern Railway between Liverpool Street and Romford; it also had to cater for long-distance expresses and goods traffic. A three-in-one timetable had to be produced which indicated the platform number of either arrival or departure. The operating conditions required extensive use of footnotes on practically every relevant page. For example, 'a section for . . . will be attached in front', 'attach empty milk tanks', and various running times and operating dates were listed in great profusion. Although the timetable was for a suburban section, it needed to give details of all trains passing through. A random page reveals information about ordinary passenger, express passenger, goods class 'A', goods, and Continental trains. That was a timetable which dealt with a small section on a system which had a route length of nearly 7,000 miles.

Although the working timetable was important, it was not the final authority, and was supplemented by the weekly and fortnightly notices of special train arrangements mentioned previously. These notices dealt with exceptional traffic movements, such as those for a race meeting, a carnival, or a special excursion. During the normal operating times of the various trains, track maintenance programmes were instituted, and notice had to be given; on a busy section as many as one hundred such announcements would be necessary. Drivers of trains were instructed to reduce speed at certain points, and to keep a sharp look-out for hand signals from the line ganger.

The extensive company traffic, heavier than most people realised, also had to be listed in the fortnightly notices. Coal trains working between the locomotive depots and the collieries needed large numbers of wagons set aside for their exclusive use; since the trains were not used for general merchandise, their operation necessitated using one empty train for every loaded one. For every commodity which could be carried by train, and for every engine which shunted along the permanent way, a notice had to be published.

4
EXCURSIONS, HOLIDAYS & CONCESSIONS

Certain types of train arrangements were printed on separate handbills, and for the most part, their details were eagerly sought by the travelling public. These special arrangements were called excursions, and were organised by the railway companies for race meetings or conventions.

But long before the railways were organising excursions there were passengers riding in special trains. Although it is commonly thought that Thomas Cook first organised railway excursions, strictly speaking this is not correct. Arguments have raged over this subject since 1840, and as yet they have not been resolved satisfactorily.

Thomas Cook (1808-92). A photograph of the pioneer of railway excursions and travel, of about 1870.

The last resting place of Thomas Cook, the man who brought travel to the millions, in Welford Road Cemetery, Leicester. The grave lay neglected for years, covered with ivy and grass, Its masonry falling apart. The directors of his now-nationalised travel firm decided to refurbish it. At the same time they added the open Book of Tribute at the base of the headstone. (Photo: Leicester Mercury)

Unusual tickets. The RAP Transfer 1/- ticket was issued to a person named Strange. With a light brown horizontal overprint, it is believed to have been issued in about 1880, but has so far defied identification.
6737 Servant's ticket, third class, issued along with a first class ticket in 1917, on the Great Indian Peninsular Railway.
0378 Issued by the St Kilda Bus Lines Pty Ltd, acting as agents for the Victorian Railways Commissioners; the return half is 100 years out of date!
1773 This American railroad ticket gives no clue to indicate exactly what constituted 'One Load of Cinders'.
0463 This Sligo, Leitrim, and Northern Counties Railway ticket is quite plainly printed as an 'Extorsion Ticket'! It was issued in 1957 as an exchange ticket.
11021 Southern Railway ticket for 'One Hot Bath'. After a journey through the rice fields around Madras the traveller would welcome such a luxury.
0001 Bengal Nagpur Railway Christmas concession ticket issued on Christmas Eve, 1916. The BNR had a 5ft 6in gauge and used Beyer-Garratt 4-8-0+0-8-4 locomotives.
04 Manchester South Junction & Altrincham Railway voter's through ticket, overprinted light blue on white card, unissued. Perforated for return use, there are no conditions or indications that it was for Parliamentary, local, or railway AGM elections.
17119 Commonwealth Government Railways owned the Central Australian Railway which, in August 1929, brought the first passenger train to Alice Springs. The reverse of this single berth sleeping car ticket bears details of berth and carriage number, rail ticket number, and date of issue.

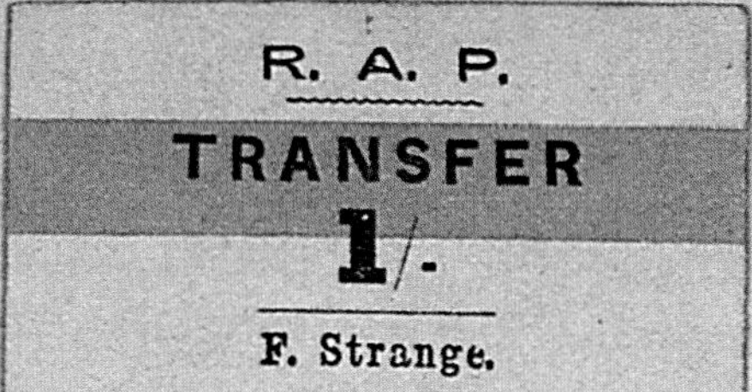
R. A. P.
TRANSFER
1/-
F. Strange.

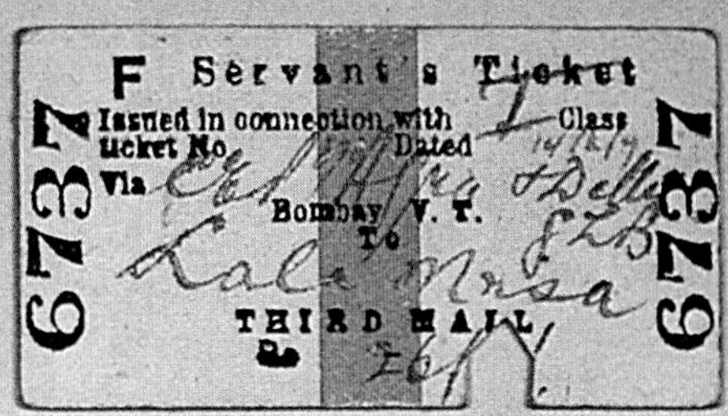
F Servant's Ticket
Issued in connection with Class
ticket No. Dated
Via
Bombay V. T.
To
THIRD MAIL
6737

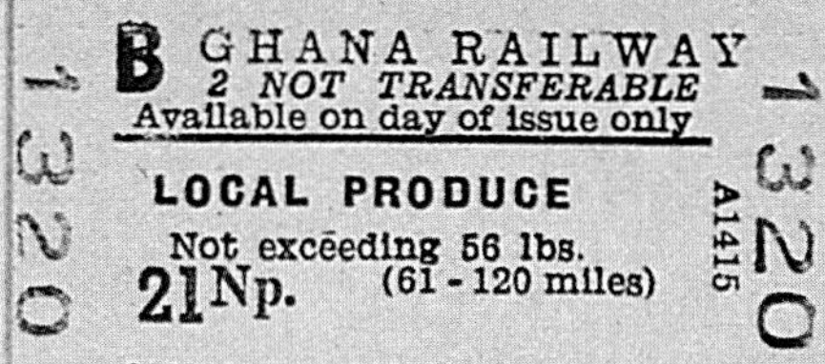
B GHANA RAILWAY
2 NOT TRANSFERABLE
Available on day of issue only
LOCAL PRODUCE
Not exceeding 56 lbs.
21Np. (61 - 120 miles)
A1415
1320

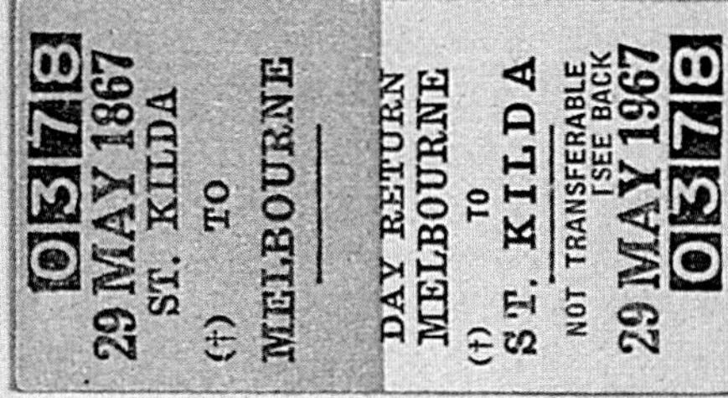
0378
29 MAY 1967
ST. KILDA TO MELBOURNE
DAY RETURN
MELBOURNE TO ST. KILDA
NOT TRANSFERABLE (SEE BACK

ST. FRANCOIS COUNTY
RAILROAD COMPANY.
GOOD FOR
One Load of Cinders.
BED 10 FEET BY 25 INCHES.
Traffic Manager.
1773

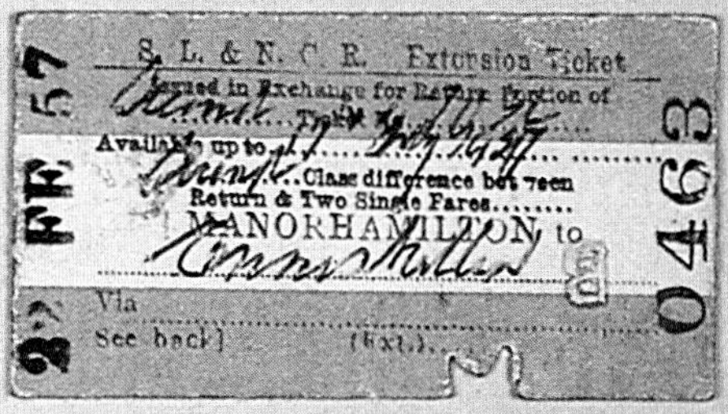
S. L. & N. C. R. Extension Ticket
Available up to
Class difference between
Return & Two Single Fares
MANORHAMILTON to
Via
See back
0463

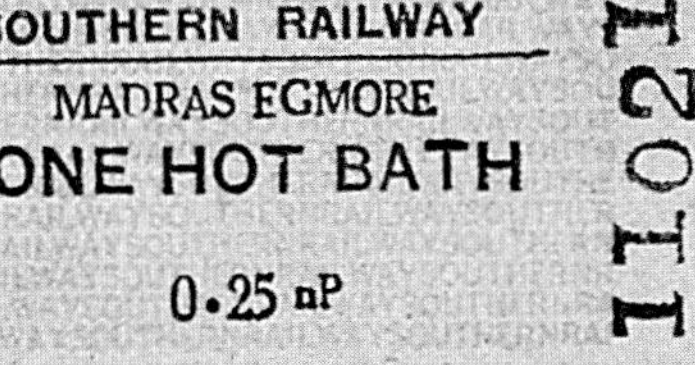
SOUTHERN RAILWAY
MADRAS EGMORE
ONE HOT BATH
0·25 nP
11021

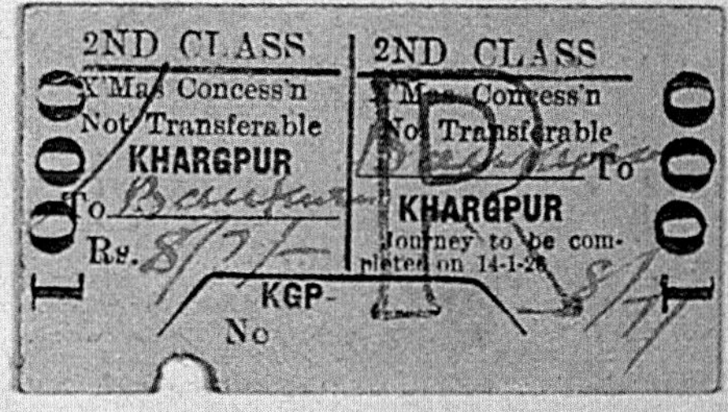
2ND CLASS
X'Mas Concess'n
Not Transferable
KHARGPUR
To
Rs.
2ND CLASS
X'Mas Concess'n
Not Transferable
To
KHARGPUR
Journey to be completed on 14-1-28
KGP-
No
1000

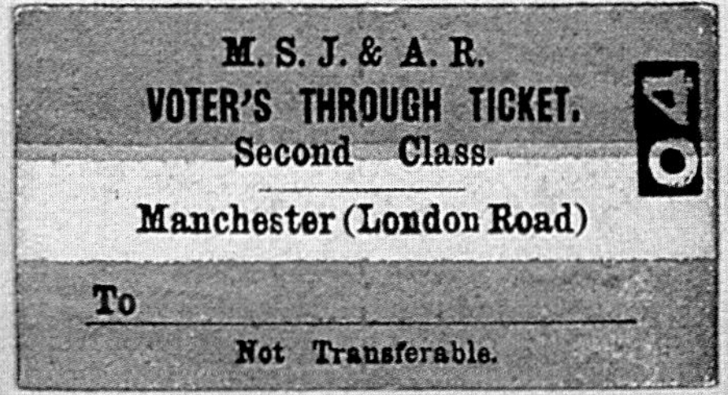
M. S. J. & A. R.
VOTER'S THROUGH TICKET.
Second Class.
Manchester (London Road)
To
Not Transferable.
04

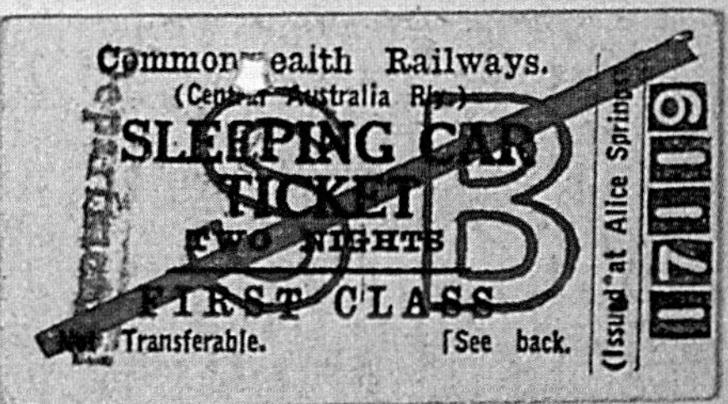
Commonwealth Railways.
SLEEPING CAR
TICKET
TWO NIGHTS
FIRST CLASS
Transferable.
See back.
(Issued at Alice Springs
01709

MONTANA WESTERN RAILWAY CO.
ONE CONTINUOUS PASSAGE
VALIER
—TO—
MANSON
Value of baggage transported on this ticket shall not exceed $100.
Form 7.
Prest.
1071

min de Fer Funiculaire
TERRITET
A
GLION
Fr. 1. 00.

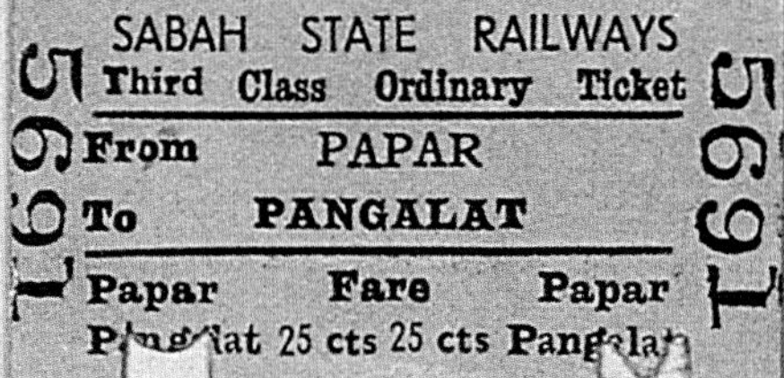
Georgia Railroad
ATLANTA, Ga. to
AUGUSTA, Ga.
Good for One Passage within thirty (30) days in addition to date of sale stamped on back. Subject to tariff regulations.
P.T.M.
GOOD IN COACHES ONLY
N 6082

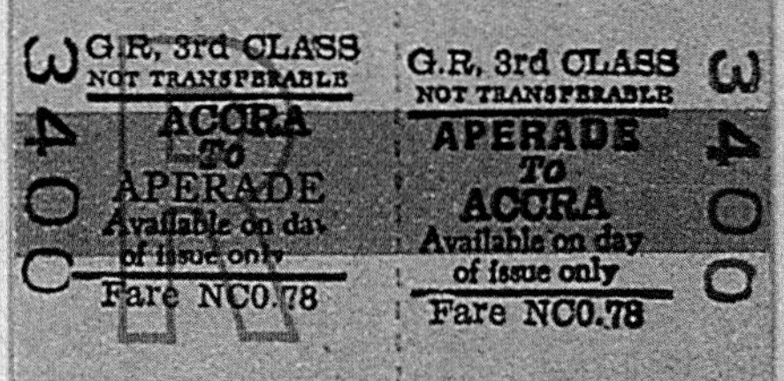
Vevey
Montreux
Valable 1 jour
III. Cl. Fr. — 40.
Vevey-Montreux
6551

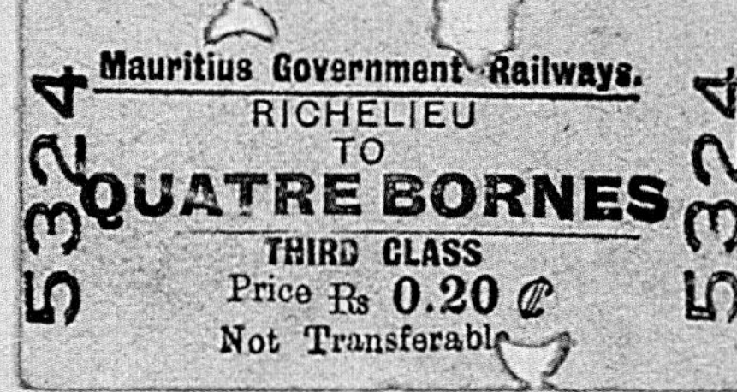
SABAH STATE RAILWAYS
Third Class Ordinary Ticket
From PAPAR
To PANGALAT
Papar Fare Papar
25 cts 25 cts
T695

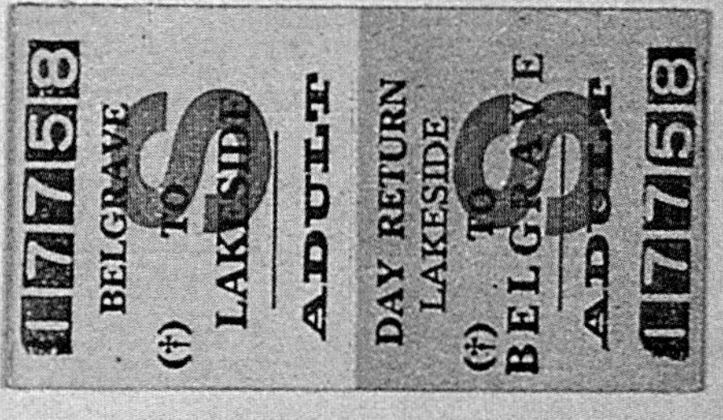
G.R. 3rd CLASS
NOT TRANSFERABLE
ACCRA
To
APERADE
Available on day of issue only
Fare NC0.78
G.R. 3rd CLASS
NOT TRANSFERABLE
APERADE
To
ACCRA
Available on day of issue only
Fare NC0.78
3400

Mauritius Government Railways.
RICHELIEU
TO
QUATRE BORNES
THIRD CLASS
Price Rs 0.20 c
5324
BELGRAVE TO LAKESIDE
ADULT
DAY RETURN
LAKESIDE TO BELGRAVE
17758

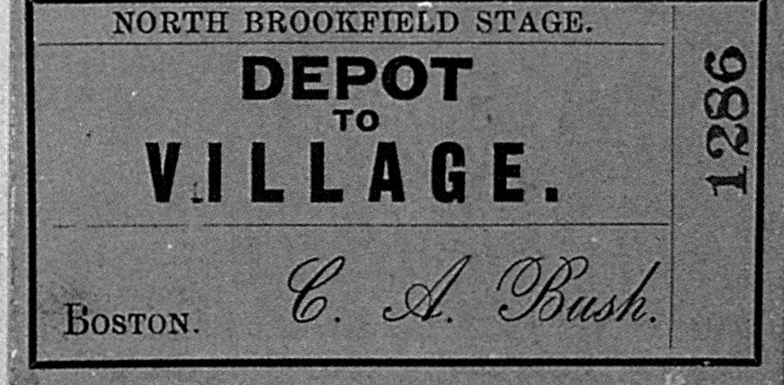
Napierville Junction R'y Co.
One First Class Passage
Un Passage En Premiere Classe
MONTREAL W ST. STN. (3)
— TO — — A —
LACOLLE Que.
NON TRANSFERABLE.
Gen. Pass. Agt.
Form O.W.
NORTH BROOKFIELD STAGE.
DEPOT
TO
VILLAGE.
BOSTON.
C. A. Bush.
1286

The first record of an excursion train was on 20 July 1840, when members of the Nottingham Mechanics' Institute wished to visit a Leicester exhibition. Having received a list of intending passengers, the Midland Counties Railway Company arranged to run a train at half fares; it was so successful that one week later the Leicester Mechanics' Institute was granted reciprocal facilities for a visit to Nottingham. Following upon the immense success of these two trains, in August the railway company ran excursions of its own in both directions between Leicester and Nottingham, stopping at intermediate stations. On one train from Nottingham more than 2,400 passengers were booked for the trip; sixty-five coaches were needed to carry them, and the train was 'hauled by numerous engines' although the exact number is not quoted.

Surprisingly enough, the railway company did not realise the potential of this new style of railway travel. It was left to the vision of a Market Harborough wood-turner, twelve months later.

Thomas Cook was born of humble parentage on 22 November 1808, at Melbourne, in Derbyshire. At the age of ten he had to leave school to help support his widowed mother who kept a small bookshop. His labours in the gardens of a local estate earned him the sum of one penny a day. He had a desire for self-betterment, and thought that working for an uncle in his wood-turning business would help him to achieve quickly the independence he desired. Accordingly, he was apprenticed to his uncle, John Pegg. But Thomas Cook preferred fishing to wood-turning. The woodwork still had to be done, however, and the summer months found Thomas rising at two o'clock in the morning so that he could spend the greater part of the day with rod and line on the banks of the River Trent.

Eventually, his itching feet led him to Loughborough, in Leicestershire, where he was employed by Joseph Winks, a printer and publisher of Baptist books. Here, Thomas's religious views were encouraged to the full, and he was appointed in 1828 as a Bible reader and village missionary for Rutland. He was indefatigable in his new calling, and in his diary for 1829 he records that he travelled 2,692 miles as a missionary, and of these he had

---

As can be seen from this selection of overseas railways' tickets, the influence of Thomas Edmondson's simple idea spread world-wide. But, as in Britain, there were always some companies who preferred to be independent.

3867 Territet-Glion Railway (Funicular), issued 11 August 1884, with the date impressed into the ticket.

6551 Jura-Simplon Railway third class single, issued 5 August 1892, the date impressed. The J-SR ran through the famous Simplon Tunnel, the first section of which was opened in 1906, eleven years after the company was formed.

5324 Mauritius Government Railways third class single, issued 16 August 1955. This small island had more than 100 miles of standard gauge track, and one of the oldest established railway systems in the British Crown Colonies. In 1867 it introduced the famous Sharp, Stewart eight-coupled saddle-tank engines.

17758 Victoria Railways (Australia) return, unissued. The ticket is printed brown and yellow on both sides, the red overprint 'S' also appearing on the reverse. The VR operates on two gauges, 4ft 8½in and 5ft 3in; the first railway in Australia was from Flinders Street, Melbourne to Port Melbourne in 1854.

1286 Boston & Albany Rail Road, stage-coach ticket issued 21 May 1870.

MR. THOS. COOK'S EXCN
LEICESTER
TO
LOUGHBORO'
AND BACK.
JULY 5th. 1841.
THIRD CLASS.
570

A slate-blue exhibition 'mock-up' of the world's first railway excursion ticket, used by Thos Cook & Son Ltd. It is of Edmondson standard size, although there is reason to believe that the original ticket was light orange in colour and approximately of the size shown.

walked 2,106 miles.

In 1832 he married the daughter of a Rutland farmer, settled in Market Harborough, and began a wood-turning business. The following year, the Irish temperance movement came to England, and found in Thomas Cook a devout supporter. He printed and published at his own expense many pamphlets relating to the cause, and founded a magazine called the *Children's Temperance Magazine.*

On 9 June 1841, he walked from Market Harborough to Leicester, about fifteen miles, to attend a temperance meeting in the Leicester Amphitheatre. As he walked he read, and as a result of what he read, the course of railway history was changed. At this time, the papers were full of reports about the recent opening of the Derby-Leicester-Rugby section of the Midland Counties Railway. The Derby to Nottingham section had been opened in 1839, and with the reports of this new and larger section, the Leicestershire people were wildly excited. The thought occurred to Cook that the new railway might be employed to good effect in the service of the temperance cause.

The Temperance Society had arranged to hold a public meeting at Loughborough, so if the Midland Counties Railway could be persuaded to run a special train from Leicester, then, reasoned Thomas Cook, the meeting would have an assured success. He put his thoughts to the Leicester meeting, presided over by Lawrence Haworth, a temperance reformer who became famous as a railway director, and received a majority approval. He stayed in Leicester to negotiate with the company secretary, John Fox Bell, for a train. His comment to Cook was, 'I know nothing of you or your society, but you shall have the train', and he even gave him a contribution towards the preliminary expenses!

The next step was to further arrangements at Loughborough. Those who undertook the journey would need to be refreshed; after all, twelve miles by rail in those days was a long, tiring, and uncomfortable trip. Plans were finalised, and on the morning of 5 July 1841, the world's first publicly-advertised excursion train set out from Leicester to carry its passengers to Loughborough. In his book, *The Business of Travel*, specially commissioned by the firm of Thomas Cook and Son to celebrate their jubilee, Mr W. Fraser Rae perpetuates a legend which persists to this day. He quotes the number of passengers on that original train as 570, probably taking as his authority a mock-up of the original ticket which is kept in the company's archives and is used for exhibition purposes. A contemporary newspaper reporter quotes a lower figure as being exact; it is probable that Thomas Cook purchased an option on 570 tickets at bulk prices, but was unable to sell them all. There is nothing in Thomas Cook's archives, other than the mock-up ticket, to substantiate the number of passengers.

But let history be its own recorder. The following extracts are taken from the *LEICESTER CHRONICLE: or COMMERCIAL and AGRICULTURAL ADVERTISER*, for Saturday 17 July 1841:

> LOUGHBOROUGH TEETOTAL DEMONSTRATION. — The generally quiet town of Loughborough wore quite a bustling look on Monday — during the whole of the day — in consequence of the Teetotallers of that place holding, we believe, their first annual festival, in which they invited their brethren of Leicester, Nottingham, and Derby, to be partakers — . . .
>
> The festival was announced to be held in the park (commonly called South Fields) belonging to W. Paget, Esq., who had in the kindest manner placed it at the entire disposal of the Loughborough Society and their friends for the whole of the day.

The excursion was well advertised in the local press, and the *Temperance Messenger*, of which Thomas Cook was both editor and publisher. That the occasion of the first excursion train was an 'event' can be gauged from the newspaper report which tells of the crowds in both Leicester and Loughborough. Nowadays, we can only smile at such a fuss over a twelve-mile journey; but to many of the crowd who had never set foot outside their town in their lives, it must have seemed like the journey of a lifetime.

The crowds waited in Leicester for the special train which 'the Directors of the Midland Counties Railway had, in a very handsome manner, put on to convey the whole party to and from Loughborough, at the low charge of 1s. per passenger.' This sum represented something less than half-price on the standard third-class fare. The reporter then states: 'The number who availed themselves of this train was, we learn, exactly 485; and as many came at a later hour by the regular train, there could not be fewer than 500 Leicester folk present at the festival.'

Some 2,000 to 3,000 spectators assembled at the Leicester station to witness the departure of these teetotal adventurers setting out on their unique expedition. 'Every bridge along the line was crowded to have a peep at the train in its progress.' On their arrival at Loughborough, several thousands more stood near to the station to welcome them. Travelling with the Leicester Temperance excursionists was the Leicester Independent brass band, who along with the teetotallers, occupied one second-class and nine third-class carriages.

Since the passengers all travelled at a one-class excursion fare of one shilling, it is strange that Thomas Cook's mock-up tickets quotes 'Third Class'. Railway historian George Wade, writing in the April 1905 issue of *The Railway Magazine*, quotes the colour of this ticket as green; it was then in the possession of Mr John Mathieson, Manager of the Midland Railway.

On arrival at Loughborough station, the teetotallers, their friends, and the band, formed into a huge procession, carrying banners and waving flags, and marched through the town to their meeting place. A local paper reports that Nottingham Road, from the canal to near the barracks was 'one crowd of human beings'. The reporter certainly seems to have had a gift for colourful description. He tells of the Dragoons of the barracks who, stripped to their shirts and wide, white trousers, climbed astride the roof to watch the procession — 'their fine proportions appeared swelled to those of Patagonians'.

Further extracts from the *Leicester Chronicle* point to the whole event as being a most joyful occasion. 'The Teetotallers on arrival at South Fields formed a circle in front of the house, and were most cordially welcomed by Mr. Paget.' After a short rest, during which time the National Anthem was played by the Leicester band, the crowd returned to the station to greet the Derby and Nottingham contingents who numbered some 150 to 200 persons. On arrival back at the park, by way of the Market Place where the Teetotal National Anthem was sung, the crowd sat down to tea in several sections, 'for there were too many to partake of the meal all at once'.

After tea, the crowd of about 3,000 people stayed for the temperance meeting, speakers from Wolverhampton, Wellingborough, Nottingham, and Derby addressed the meeting along with Thomas Cook, and two unnamed gentlemen from London and Manchester.

> Prior to the end of the meeting at nine o'clock, votes of thanks were passed with acclamation to the Midland Counties Railway Directors — both at Leicester and Derby — for their kindness in conveying the Teetotallers to Loughborough at half price; and to William Paget, Esq., for so generously granting them the use of his park.

With so many people arriving at and departing from the Loughborough Midland Station, one wonders what arrangements, if any, were made for the inspection and collection of the tickets.

In the same issue (17 July 1841) of the *Leicester Chronicle* there appears the following interesting item:

Midland Counties Railway
(Passenger) Receipts for the week ending, July 10, 1841.

First Class	2,038½	
Second Class	5,151½	11,875½
Third Class	4,685½	

The fares from these passengers amounted to £2,058 19s 10d and the carriage of merchandise, etc, added another £871 5s 6d.

Whatever may be the opinions about the first excursion train, the facts as just related cannot be denied. Nothing that has yet been proven detracts from the fact that Thomas Cook was a pioneer. Others followed his example, and made use of his experience and ideas, but at best they could only be imitators. Thomas Cook declared, 'The whole thing came to me as by intuition, and my spirit recoiled at the idea of imitation.' Certainly, before the excursion train organised by Cook, there had been trains run for the members of various Mechanics' Institutes between Birmingham and Cheltenham, Gloucester and Liverpool, Leicester and Nottingham. These trains were exclusively reserved for members of the institutes, while Cook's excursion train was open to the public at large. It was a special train, as well as an excursion train; the others were special trains only, such as any party could have hired from any railway company. There does

Five Days' Trip to the West of England

T. COOK, Excursion Agent, Leicester, has received authority from the Directors to announce a

CHARMING EXCURSION

TO

CHELTENHAM, GLOUCESTER,

BRISTOL,

EXETER & PLYMOUTH.

TUESDAY, JUNE 18, 1850,

SPECIAL TRAINS

Will run from NOTTINGHAM and LEICESTER and thence to BURTON, where they will be united and attached to a Train from Macclesfield, and proceed, *via* Birmingham, to Bristol.

TIME OF STARTING AND FARES THERE AND BACK.

PLACES and TIME of STARTING.	To Cheltenham or Gloucester. 1st.	2nd.	3rd.	To BRISTOL. 1st.	2nd.	3rd.
Nottingham, 8-40 a.m.; Leicester, 8-30; Ashby, 9-20.	12s. 6d.	9s.	7s.	18s.	12s. 6d.	9s. 6d.
Derby, 9-30; Burton, 10; Tamworth, 10-30	11s. 6d.	8s. 6d.	6s. 6d.	17s.	12s.	9s.

A SPECIAL TRAIN WILL LEAVE BRISTOL FOR EXETER & PLYMOUTH,

On WEDNESDAY MORNING, JUNE 19th, at 7 a.m.

FARES from BRISTOL to EXETER & BACK:—First Class, 12s. Second Class, 8s. Third Class, 7s.
FROM EXETER to PLYMOUTH & BACK:—First Class, 7s. Second Class, 5s. 6d. (No Third.)

Passengers may return from Plymouth to Exeter, or Exeter to Bristol, by the ordinary Trains (Express and Mails excepted) on payment of an extra Shilling to each company, at any time previous to the hour fixed for the return of the Special Train, which will leave Plymouth at 3-30 p.m., and Exeter at 6 on Friday, June 21.

The Train will return from Bristol on Saturday June 22, at 9 a.m.; from Gloucester at 10-30; and from Cheltenham at 10-45. Passengers may return on Friday, June 21, on payment of 1s. extra, by the Trains leaving Bristol at 11 a.m. Gloucester at 12-35, p.m. Cheltenham at 12-55, and Birmingham at 3-30.

TICKETS are issued at the Stations and any additional particulars may be had on application by letter, with stamp for reply, to the **Manager** of the Trip,—T. COOK, 28, Granby-street, Leicester.

T. COOK will be in attendance at GIRAUD'S Victoria Temperance Hotel, Corner of Bath-street, Bristol, on Tuesday Evening, after the arrival of the Special Train, for the purpose of issuing Tickets for Exeter and Plymouth.

N.B.—By the arrangements of this Trip, Tourists will be introduced to districts full of natural, artistical, commercial and historical interest and importance. The bare mention of the names of the deeply interesting Cities of CHELTENHAM, GLOUCESTER, BRISTOL, BATH, EXETER, &c., call up a thousand pleasing associations which cannot be set forth in a handbill. Visitors to Cheltenham will have the privilege of attending the Great HORTICULTURAL EXHIBITION, which takes place on the 20th Instant. From Bristol, River and Sea Trips may be made to CHEPSTOW, TENBY, and other places of note on the Western Coast. Excursions may also be made to various places in SOUTH WALES, such as MONMOUTH, TINTERN ABBEY, &c. &c. The Plymouth tourist will be conveyed over the most astonishing Railway in the world, running along the Coast, over Craggs, Promontories, &c. extending into the sea. The Docks, Arsenal, Fortifications, &c. of PLYMOUTH and DEVONPORT, will be viewed with intense interest; and should the tourist desire to reach the "Land's End" in Cornwall, he may accomplish that object, and return in time to avail himself of an arrangement of the Manager of the Trip, in the month of July, for an Excursion to "John o' Groat's House," at the extreme northern point of Scotland! Such are the glorious facilities afforded by Railways and Steamboats. Let the people appreciate and rejoice in them!

T. COOK, PRINTER, 28, GRANBY-STREET, LEICESTER.

An early excursion handbill by Thomas Cook, its five-day trip billed as a 'Charming Excursion'. The footnote to this attractive notice is also rather quaint. It advertised a July excursion to John o' Groats: 'Such are the glorious facilities afforded by Railways and Steamboats. Let the people appreciate and rejoice in them!'

not appear to be any record of special ticketing arrangements for these other excursion trains. Although Thomas Cook laid claim to being the originator of excursion trains, the idea which occurred to him on his lonely walk from Market Harborough was not original. Three days after he had attended the historic meeting in Leicester, the Birmingham Mechanics Institute placed a notice in the *Birmingham Journal.* It stated that an excursion for their members would take place by rail to Cheltenham on 29 June. Not until many years later did Thomas Cook learn of the appearance of the notice; he had not seen it at the time. Hence his claim to have been the first in the field really remains indisputable.

The success of Cook's excursion train to Loughborough soon spread far and wide, and other societies consulted him when they wished to arrange special journeys. His services were most in request during the summer months, and for the next three years he was fully occupied with other temperance excursions and Sunday school outings. Although local newspaper advertisements and numerous handbills gave details of these trips, the idea of issuing special tickets for them does not seem to have occurred to either Thomas Cook or the railway company. He organised special trains to Birmingham, Derby, Rugby and Nottingham from Leicester, and visits were made to places of interest, such as Matlock and Mountsorrel. In September 1843, Thomas Cook decided to give the Leicester children a treat by taking them on a trip to Derby at the time of the races. The number of children and adults who went on the trip was nearly 4,600; the children paid 6d, and the adults paid 1s. From the success of this pleasure trip he decided that conducting such trips might well form a business of its own.

Other railway companies, about this time, were looking into the excursion business. From being the exclusive haunt of the wealthy, Brighton was being opened up to the general public. The London, Brighton, and South Coast Railway ran the first excursion train to the popular resort on Easter Monday 1844. At about 1.30pm it steamed into Brighton, having completed the 50-mile journey in something like four and a half hours. The number of passengers is not generally quoted since the train itself was more worthy of mention. When it left London Bridge, four locomotives hauled forty-five open carriages, and on its arrival at New Cross, one more locomotive and six more carriages were added. As if all these were not enough, when this enormous train arrived at Croydon, another six carriges and one more locomotive were coupled on, to give a total length of nearly a quarter of a mile. This type of train evidently became popular on the Brighton Line, for on 6 June 1846, the *Illustrated London News* gave details of an excursion train to the resort which was made up of forty-four carriages carrying more than 4,000 passengers. Ticket details do not appear to have been documented.

By now, Thomas Cook was firmly established in the travel business. He had applied to the directors of the Midland Railway to make arrangements to place trains at his disposal; he, in turn, undertook to provide the passengers. He organised a trip from Leicester to Liverpool in 1845, and it was now that his experience in printing and publishing stood him in good stead. Being something more than a return trip to Liverpool, arrangements had been made for special crossings to the Isle of Man, and even to Dublin. The steamer, *Eclipse,* was chartered to convey the railway excursionists along the Welsh Coast. For the benefit of his travellers, Cook compiled, printed, and published a small guide, which listed places of interest en route, and gave details of worthwhile sights to visit. One fact which ensured the popularity of the Liverpool trip was that the journey of 500 miles was made at the low cost of 14s first class, and 10s second class. Cook's *Handbook of the Trip to Liverpool* was a masterpiece of clarity and precision, together with minutely detailed information. The opening sentences make interesting reading:

> The train will leave Leicester at Five o'clock in the morning of Monday, August the 4th, reaching Syston at Ten Minutes past Five; Sileby, Twenty minutes past Five; Loughborough Half-past Five; Kegworth, a Quarter before Six; arriving at Derby at Ten minutes past Six. A train will leave Nottingham at Half-past Five, uniting with the Leicester train at Derby. Parties will have to be 'wide-awake at an early hour, or they will be disappointed. Promptitude on the part of the Railway Company calls for the same from passengers.

It is strange that Cook was asserting the punctuality of the railways, apparently without adverse comment from them, and yet when Bradshaw had published their timetables they had risen in their wrath.

The Leicester to Liverpool train, a novelty in its day, was the forerunner of many thousands which started from stations all over the world throughout the year. It was also unique in another important way. Previous excursions had been confined to one railway, but this tour, for which Cook had provided the tickets and accommodation, was run over the lines of several companies. The receipts from the sale of passenger tickets had to be apportioned through the Railway Clearing House, which had been established three years earlier. There were four companies involved: the Midland Counties Railway, the North Midland Railway, the Lancashire and Yorkshire Railway, and the Manchester and Liverpool Railway.

With the idea of the special excursion train by now well established, it is strange that no special tickets were issued. Although Thomas Cook was also his own printer, it is probable that such extra tickets would have added confusion to the already complex system operating in the Clearing House.

That the excursion was a success can be gauged from the fact that all tickets were sold one week before, and many persons bought tickets from the original purchasers, paying double price for them. As a result of the tremendous demand for the pleasure trip, a second train was run on 20 August 1845. It was organised under the same conditions as the first, and was just as crowded. It is interesting to note that when the 350 passengers who had decided to visit Wales in the steamer *Eclipse* landed at Caernarfon, only one man among the locals could speak enough English to act as guide.

It was while in North Wales that Thomas Cook had another far-reaching idea. He wrote in his diary: 'From the heights of Snowdon my thoughts took flight to Ben Lomond, and I determined to try to get to Scotland.' To arrange such a pleasure trip was to engage upon an undertaking which was startling in its novelty. Scotland was then an unknown country to most English people. It proved to be a difficult country to reach, and taxed Cook's ingenuity to the limit. At that time there was no direct rail link into

(continued on page 122)

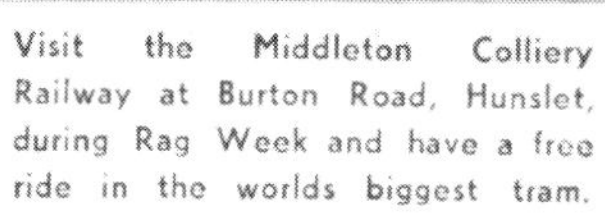

NOEL & PORTER LTD. NEW CARPETS, NEW LINOLEUMS, Now Showing. KING STREET.

NOEL & PORTER LTD. READY TO WEAR BOYS' & YOUTHS CLOTHING. KING STREET.

GREENSILL'S MONA BOUQUET, The most acceptable souvenir our visitors can purchase.

8FE07

METROPOLITAN — RAILWAY. — PARCELS DESPATCHED By EVERY TRAIN From ALL STATIONS To ALL PARTS CHEAP RATES. PROMPT DELIVERY

A. C. ELLIS, General Manager, 32, Westbourne Terrace, W.

VISIT MUNICIPAL— GOLF COURSES TENNIS COURTS — AND — BOWLING GREENS

OUR AIM!!! QUALITY HIGH PRICES LOW Jersey's Most Noted Meat Purveyor HUMPHRIES, 9, 10 & 11, New Market Deliveries Everywhere Everyday Telephone No. 70

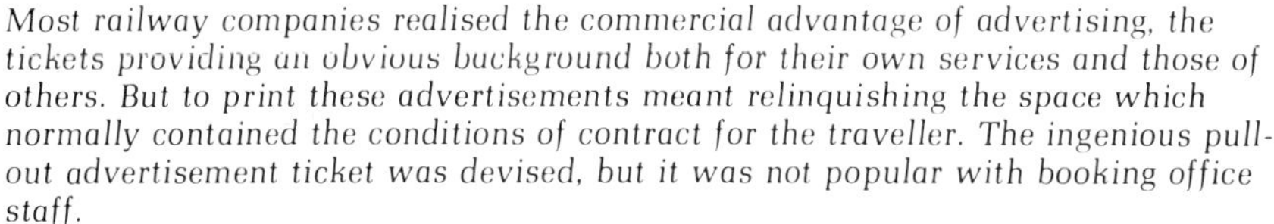

Most railway companies realised the commercial advantage of advertising, the tickets providing an obvious background both for their own services and those of others. But to print these advertisements meant relinquishing the space which normally contained the conditions of contract for the traveller. The ingenious pull-out advertisement ticket was devised, but it was not popular with booking office staff.
From top to bottom from the left, these advertisements are on tickets of the following companies:
LM & SR (three); Middleton Railway Preservation Society; Jersey Eastern Railway Co Ltd; Manx Northern Railway Co; Metropolitan Railway; Great Orme Railway (two); The Jersey Railways & Tramways Ltd.

Special concessions were offered to travellers, either individually or as members of a party, or charter group. The rarest in this selection is ticket No 11, second class family ticket (overprinted 'Child'), blank, printed red on dark green card. It would have been issued by the Eastern Counties Railway in the 1860s; the ticket half valid for the 'up' or outward journey has been removed by the ticket collector.
2429 Western Australia Government Railway family concession, overprinted red on white card. The WAGR started in the 1860s with a 3ft 6in gauge.
0079 Shropshire & Montgomeryshire Railway half-day excursion, issued 28 October 1932. The S & MR came into being in 1911, but was closed to regular passenger traffic in 1933.

No matter how a system is standardised and categorised, there are always situations and circumstances which seem to rise above the scheme of things.
215 London, Tilbury & Southend Railway tender ticket, lilac paper, date of issue unknown. The Tilbury Docks were part of the Port of London Authority. 'Boat Specials' were trains run by several companies which connected with shipping lines such as Cunard and the Peninsular & Oriental.
829 Buxton Improvements Company Limited, yellow, issued 25 May 1880 to Mrs Turner, who appears to have pencilled several train times on the reverse. The company was formed in 1870 for the purpose of securing lands at Buxton for concert halls and pleasure grounds. The Duke of Devonshire, who initiated the scheme to take advantage of the passenger traffic from the Midland Railway which ran through his lands, held the majority shares. The company was allowed to issue tickets for local use on the railway.
Ordering ticket, company unknown, possibly LMS. Most companies used similar tickets to order small stocks of infrequently issued categories.
7529 Llyn Tegid Railway, light blue. A bilingual card from Wales. The reverse, in pink, announces that the ticket is a commemorative issue for the first year of service.
0038 Surrey Border & Camberley Railway, a little known line, part of the London, Brighton & South Coast Railway.
006 Dundalk, Newry & Greenore Railway, light blue overprint on white. Issued in connection with a first class return, this hotel ticket was valid for three days' accomodation and services. Compare with LMS Weekend ticket (coupon book) (page 43).
431 Great Central Railway request stop ticket blank, overstamped LNER.

11
DOWN
SECOND CLASS,
FAMILY TICKET,
Broxbourne to Lowestoft
Date 186
Name
CHILD

British Railways Board (E)
SPECIAL PARTY
REGULATION TICKET
ONE PASSENGER
OUTWARD & RETURN
Date of Travel
2090

SOCIÉTÉ NATIONALE DES CHEMINS DE FER FRANCAIS
The Locomotive Club of Great Britain
LA CÔTE DU NORD RAIL TOUR
DIMANCHE 19 MAI 1968 2e Cl.
ALLER ET RETOUR
CALAIS (MME) - NOYELLES
via Boulogne—Etaples
Voir au verso—See over
0076

L. & N. W. R.
RETURN HALF
PLEASURE PARTY
THIRD CLASS
L. & N. W. R.
OUTWARD HALF
PLEASURE PARTY
(Local Series)
THIRD CLASS
Leicester
TO
Lichfield
TURNOVER
Fare
721

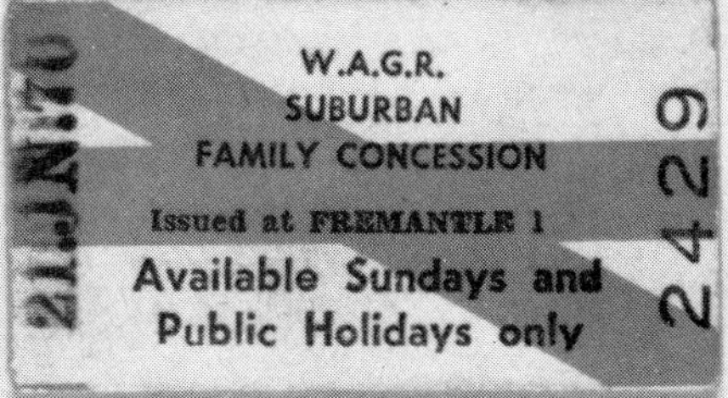

W.A.G.R.
SUBURBAN
FAMILY CONCESSION
Issued at FREMANTLE 1
Available Sundays and
Public Holidays only
2429

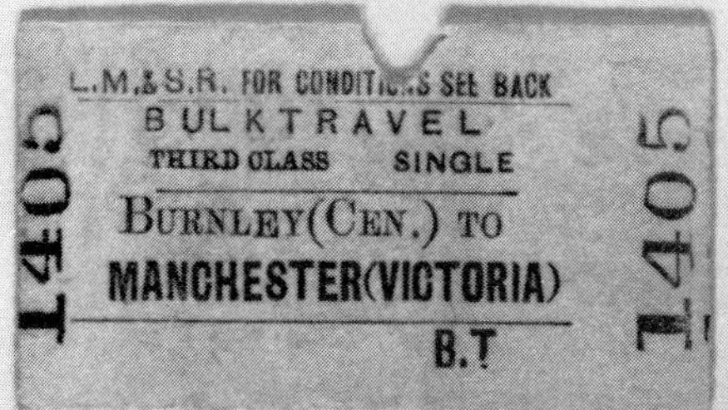

L.M.&S.R. FOR CONDITIONS SEE BACK
BULKTRAVEL
THIRD CLASS SINGLE
BURNLEY(CEN.) TO
MANCHESTER(VICTORIA)
B.T
1405

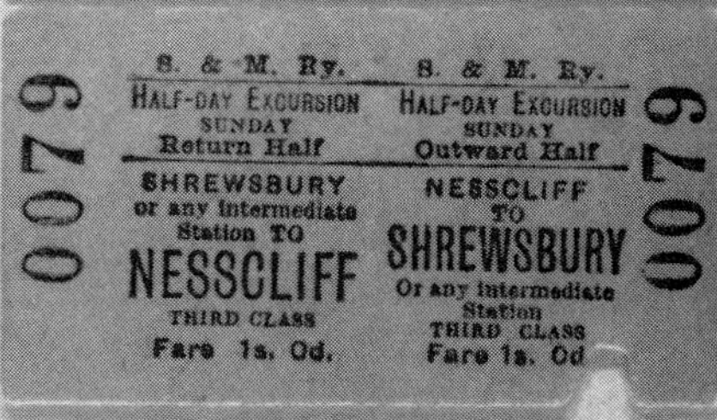

S. & M. Ry.
HALF-DAY EXCURSION
SUNDAY
Return Half
SHREWSBURY
or any intermediate Station TO
NESSCLIFF
THIRD CLASS
Fare 1s. 0d.
S. & M. Ry.
HALF-DAY EXCURSION
SUNDAY
Outward Half
NESSCLIFF
TO
SHREWSBURY
Or any intermediate Station
THIRD CLASS
Fare 1s. 0d
0079

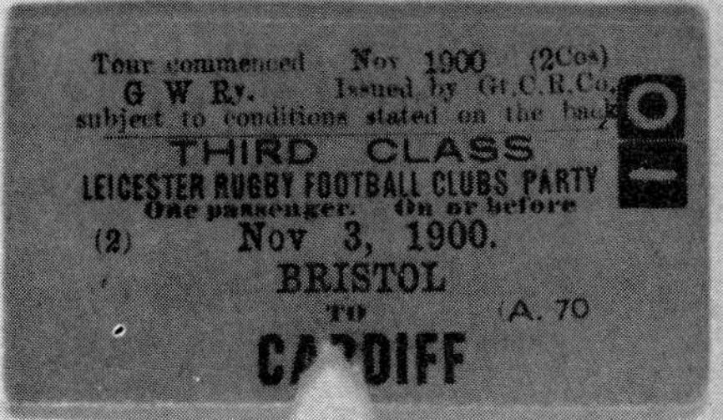

Tour commenced Nov 1900 (2Cos)
G W Ry. Issued by Gt.C.R.Co.
subject to conditions stated on the back
THIRD CLASS
LEICESTER RUGBY FOOTBALL CLUBS PARTY
One passenger. On or before
(2) Nov 3, 1900.
BRISTOL
TO
CARDIFF
(A. 70
10

BRITISH RAILWAYS (E) (S.T. D.207)
THE RAILWAY CORRESPONDENCE AND TRAVEL SOCIETY TOUR
14 APRIL 1951
FENCHURCH STREET to
STRATFORD
Via Millwall, Bromley, Woolwich, Stratford Mkt., Stepney & Woodgrange Pk.
THIRD CLASS
FOR CONDITIONS SEE BACK.
0114

London Tilbury & Southend Railway.

No. 105/215

DOUBLE JOURNEY.

TENDER TICKET

BETWEEN

TILBURY AND A SHIP IN THE RIVER.

FARE 1/6

This Ticket is issued subject to the provisions of the Merchant Shipping Acts, 1854 and 1862, as regards the limitation of the Company's liability.

Waterlow & Sons Limited, Printers, Dunstable and London.

The Buxton Improvements Company (LIMITED)

Single Weekly Ticket.

For Week-Ending. May 31

NOT TRANSFERABLE

This Ticket is issued subject to the printed Regulations of the Company.

829

ORDERING TICKET ONLY
From
To
Via
Class Description
NOT AVAILABLE FOR TRAVEL

7529

* Rheilffordd Llyn Tegid Cyf

Llanuwchllyn I Langower ac yn ôl.

TOCYN I DDATHLU'R FLWYDDYN GYNTAF O WASANAETH

PRIS 30 cn

Rheolau i'w gweld yn Llanuwchllyn.

Williamson, Printer, Ashton

7529

S. B. C. R.

FARNBOROUGH GREEN

TO

CAMBERLEY

Single Fare 1/6

PULLMAN & or EXPRESS

Issued subject to Company's Rules & Regulations. Available day of issue only.

Bell Punch Company, Limited, London.

0038

Dundalk Newry & Greenore Ry.

HOTEL TICKET.

This Ticket entitles the holder to Hotel accommodation for Three days at the Co's Hotel at Greenore, including Afternoon Tea, Dinner & Bedroom on day of arrival, Breakfast, Luncheon, Afternoon Tea, Dinner and Bedroom on the Two following days, & Breakfast on day of departure

Issued in connection with a special First Class Railway Return Ticket from NEWRY (B.ST.) to GREENORE

006

GREAT CENTRAL RAILWAY.

L. N. E. R. L. N. E. R.

to Guard of Train

STOP AT STATION.

Issued at Brackley (C)

0902
W. C. & P. RLY.
W. C. & P. RLY.
RETURN
TICKET
WESTON-SUPER-MARE TO WORLE
WORLE TO Weston-s-Mare
Available on day of issue only
FARE 4d
SECOND CLASS
SECOND CLASS
0902

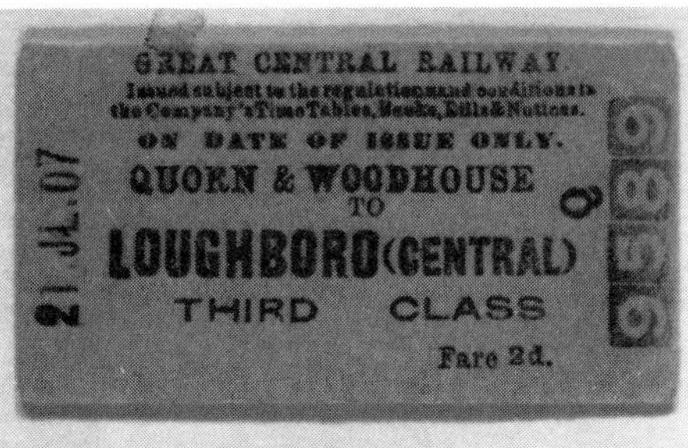
GREAT CENTRAL RAILWAY
ON DATE OF ISSUE ONLY.
21 JL.07
QUORN & WOODHOUSE
TO
LOUGHBORO (CENTRAL)
THIRD CLASS
Fare 2d.

L. C. & D. R.
9886
ST. PAUL'S
ST. PAUL'S
ST. PAUL'S
TO
SHORTLANDS
Via Herne Hill
THIRD CLASS
9½d
9½d
Available on the day of issue only.
See Other Side.
SHORTLANDS
SHORTLANDS
9886

EAST KENT RAILWAY.
250
ASH TOWN
TO
STAPLE
Third Class
Fare-3½d.

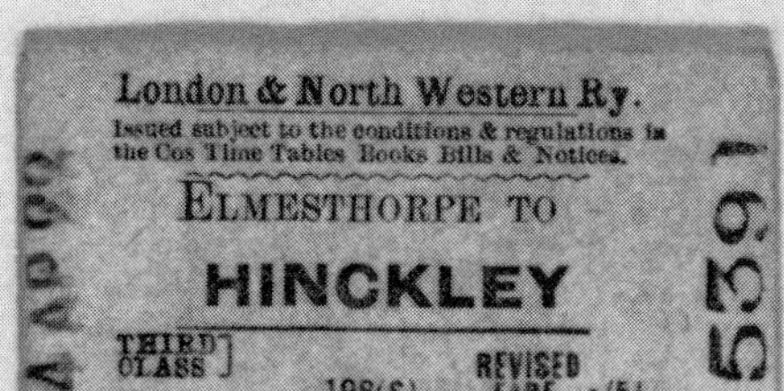
London & North Western Ry.
Issued subject to the conditions & regulations in the Cos Time Tables Books Bills & Notices.
ELMESTHORPE TO
HINCKLEY
THIRD CLASS
REVISED FARE -/5½
HINCKLEY
5391

O. & I. JOINT
SPECIAL SINGLE TICKET
Available on day of issue only.
1331
ILKLEY to
LEEDS (CITY)
Via ARTHINGTON
FOR CONDITIONS SEE BACK
Fare
FIRST
CLASS
LEEDS (CITY
1331

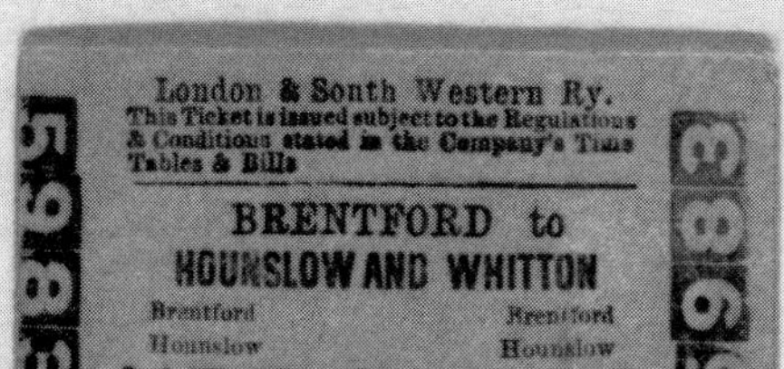
London & South Western Ry.
This Ticket is issued subject to the Regulations & Conditions stated in the Company's Time Tables & Bills
5983
BRENTFORD to
HOUNSLOW AND WHITTON
Brentford
Hounslow
Brentford
Hounslow
3rd CLASS
(S.25)
3rd CLASS
Fare 2½d
Fare 2½d
5983

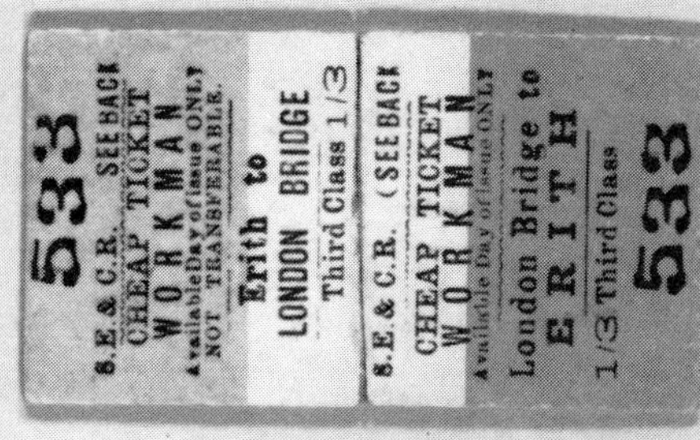
533
S.E.& C.R.
SEE BACK
CHEAP TICKET
WORKMAN
NOT TRANSFERABLE.
Erith to
LONDON BRIDGE
Third Class 1/3
S.E.& C.R.
SEE BACK
CHEAP TICKET
WORKMAN
London Bridge to
ERITH
1/3 Third Class
533

H. & B. Rly. This Ticket is issued subject to the Regulations and Conditions stated in the Company's Time Tables and Bills.
HULL (Cannon Street) to
HULL (Beverley Road)
790
Fare 1d.
Third
HULL (BEVERLEY-RD)
Class

Issued by the B. C. Ry Co. subject to the conditions in their Time Tables
PARLIAMENTARY.
LYDHAM HEATH To
BISHOP'S CASTLE
BishopsCastle
Fare -/2
5211

Prior to the Railways Act of 1921 which brought into being the 'Big Four' (GWR, LNER, LMS, SR) there were several hundred railways operating in Britain, most of which are now all but forgotton.

0902 Weston, Clevedon & Portishead Railway second class return, blue overprint on white card, issued 13 April 1914.

9589 Great Central Railway third class single, green, issued 21 July 1907.

9886 London, Chatham & Dover Railway third class single, green, issued 14 July 1898.

251 East Kent Railway third class single, light brown, issue date unknown. The EKR was incorporated in 1853, the first section of its line being completed in 1860, by which time it had become part of the LC & DR.

5391 London & North Western Railway third class single, green, issued 24 April 1922, just one year before the Grouping came into operation.

1331 Otley & Ilkley Joint first class single, unissued. In 1861 the Midland Railway was granted powers to extend from Arthington to Otley and Ilkley; the line was opened in 1865.

5983 London & South Western Railway third class single, pink, issued 10 December 1900. The L & SWR started in 1834 as the London and Southampton Railway, the title of which was changed in 1839.

533 South Eastern & Chatham Railway cheap ticket (workman), overprinted in red and blue on white, issued 19 December 1915. The company received authority in 1836 as the South Eastern Railway, amalgamated with the LC & DR in 1899, and became the Eastern Section of the Southern Railway in 1921.

790 Hull & Barnsley third class single, blue-green, issued 13 December 1904. The line opened for traffic in 1885, and assumed its title in 1905.

5211 Bishop's Castle Railway parliamentary single, light green, issued 5 July 1907. In 1866 the property of the company was sold by bailiffs to the Midland Wagon Company, who continued to run the line.

1343 Wirral Railway third class single, red overprint on off-white card, issued 9 January 1904. The WR was incorporated in 1891, taking over the 1884 Wirral Company and the 1863 Seacombe, Hoylake, and Deeside Railway.

246 Oxford, Worcester & Wolverhampton Railway second class single, deep blue, unissued. Known as the 'Old Worse and Worse', the line was opened in 1852 with broad gauge track being laid between Oxford and Abbots Wood.

5649 Great Northern Railway third class single, slate-blue, issued 7 April 1913. Incorporated in 1846, the GNR was originally named the London & York Railway, and in the same year amalgamated with the Direct Northern Line to form the GNR.

1149 Vale of Towy Joint Committee third class single, light brown, issued 1 July 1911. Opened in 1858, the VTR became the joint property of the GWR and the LN & WR in 1884.

6627 Macclesfield Committee first class single, white, issued 2 January 1867. Originally incorporated in 1864, the line was absorbed jointly by the LNER and the LM & SR in 1921.

0084 Cheshire Lines Committee third class single, light green, issued 12 September 1907. The CLC came into being with the Cheshire Lines Transfer Act of 1865, and remained in force, operated between the LNER and the LMS until nationalisation.

5924 London, Tilbury & Southend Railway third class single, light green, issued 8 May 1907. The LT & SR was incorporated in 1862, having originally been built by the Eastern Counties Railway and the London & Blackwall Railway, and leased to a private company.

4255 Midland Railway third class single, drab, issued 1 June 1911. The MR was the first big railway company, formed in 1844 by the amalgamation of the North Midland, Midland Counties, and the Birmingham and Derby Junction railways.

011 Cheadle Railway Company third class single, light green. The original name of the company, incorporated in 1882 and 1887, was the Cheadle Railway, Mineral, and Land Company. It was taken over by the North Staffordshire Railway in 1908.

320 Manchester, Sheffield & Lincolnshire Railway, blue-green, issued 22 January 1904. Formed of four railways amalgamated in 1846, and a fifth in 1847, the Consolidation Act of 1849 also brought together the two companies of the Manchester and Lincoln Union Scheme under the new name.

WIRRAL RAILWAY
New Brighton To
LIVERPOOL (JAMES ST.)
THIRD CLASS
Available for one journey on day of issue only
[Series D
Turn over Liverpool J St
1343

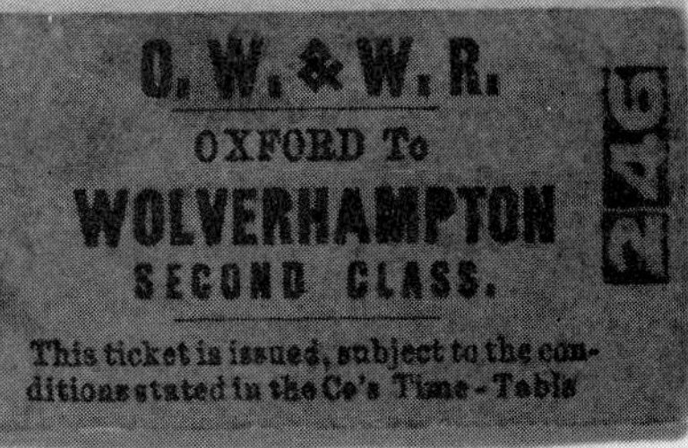
O. W. & W. R.
OXFORD To
WOLVERHAMPTON
SECOND CLASS.
This ticket is issued, subject to the conditions stated in the Co's Time-Table
246

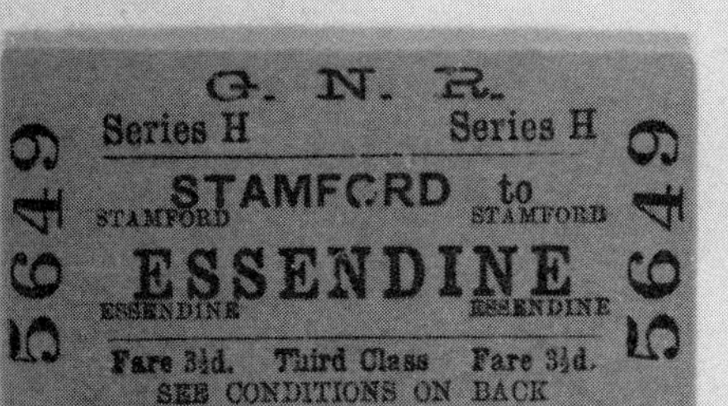
G. N. R.
Series H Series H
STAMFORD to
ESSENDINE
Fare 3½d. Third Class Fare 3½d.
SEE CONDITIONS ON BACK
5649 5649

Vale of Towy Joint Committee.
LLANDILO LLANDILO
LLANDOVERY
11d THIRD CLASS 11d
Llandovery
1149 1149

MACCLESFIELD COMMITTEE
MACCLESFIELD
TO
BOLLINGTON
FIRST CLASS
Macclesfield Macclesfield
Bollington Bollington
FARE 4d
6627

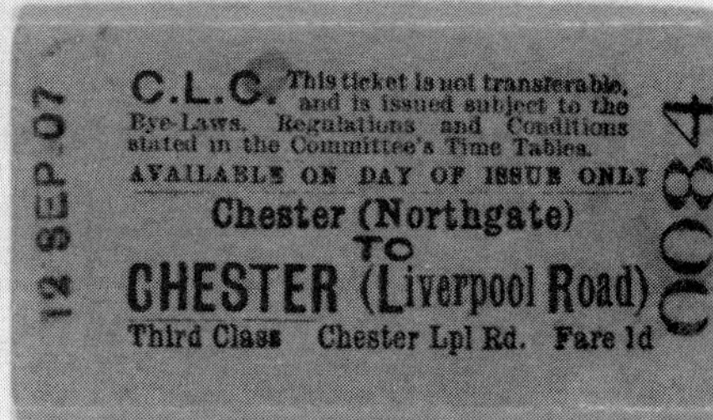
C.L.C.
AVAILABLE ON DAY OF ISSUE ONLY
Chester (Northgate)
TO
CHESTER (Liverpool Road)
Third Class Chester Lpl Rd. Fare 1d
12 SEP 07
0084

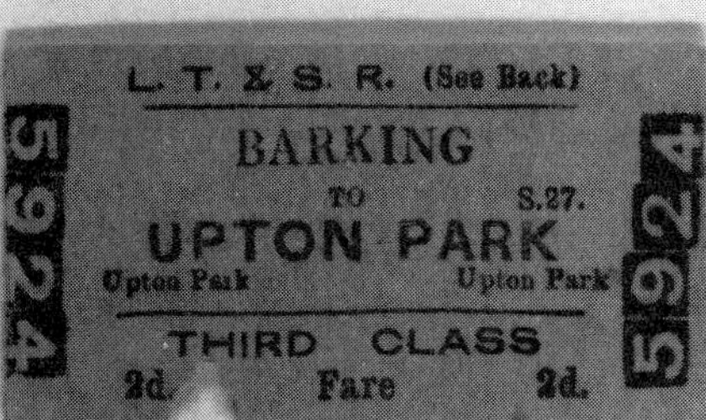
L. T. & S. R. (See Back)
BARKING
TO S.27.
UPTON PARK
Upton Park Upton Park
THIRD CLASS
2d. Fare 2d.
5924 5924

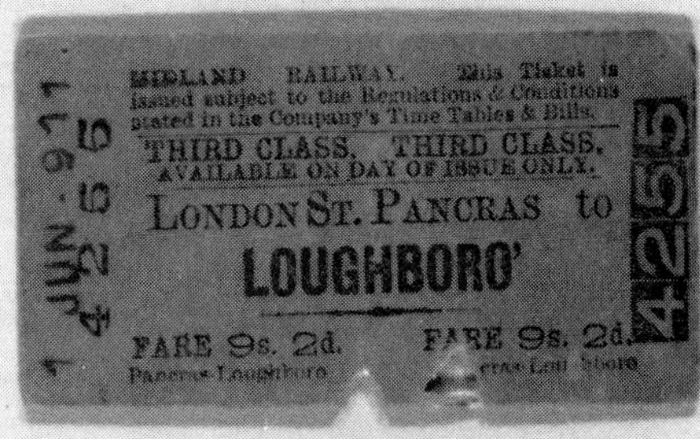
MIDLAND RAILWAY.
THIRD CLASS. THIRD CLASS.
AVAILABLE ON DAY OF ISSUE ONLY.
LONDON ST. PANCRAS to
LOUGHBORO'
FARE 9s. 2d. FARE 9s. 2d.
1 JUN 911
4255

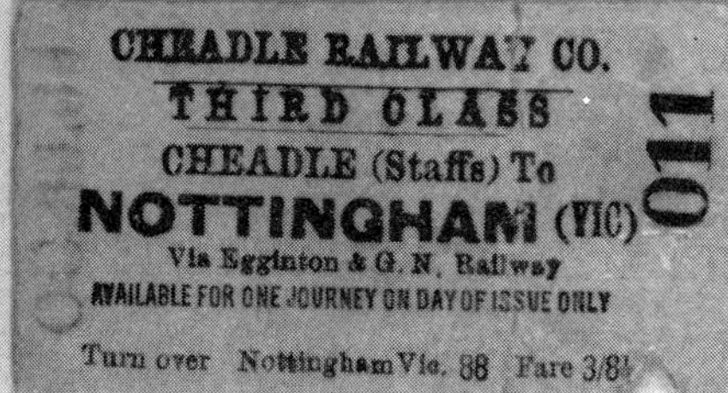
CHEADLE RAILWAY CO.
THIRD CLASS
CHEADLE (Staffs) To
NOTTINGHAM (VIC)
Via Egginton & G. N. Railway
AVAILABLE FOR ONE JOURNEY ON DAY OF ISSUE ONLY
Turn over Nottingham Vic. 88 Fare 3/8½
011

M S & L R
HULL(Paragon St) To
WORKSOP
THIRD CLASS
FARE 4/5½
Hull P St Hull P St
Worksop Worksop
320

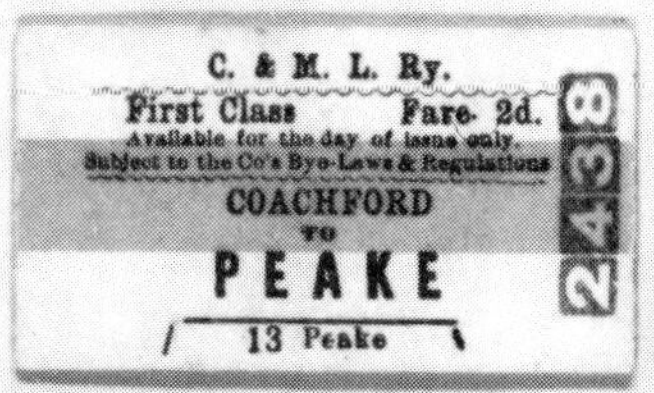

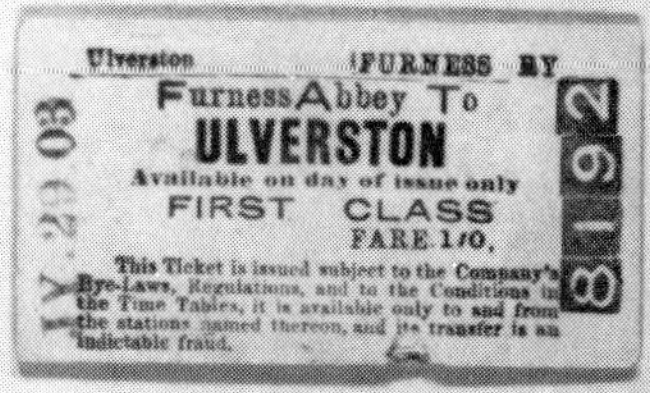

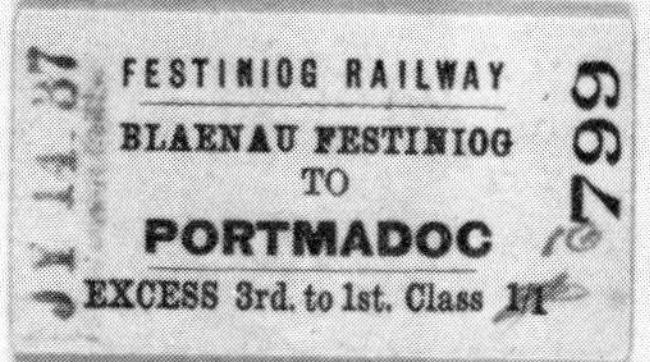

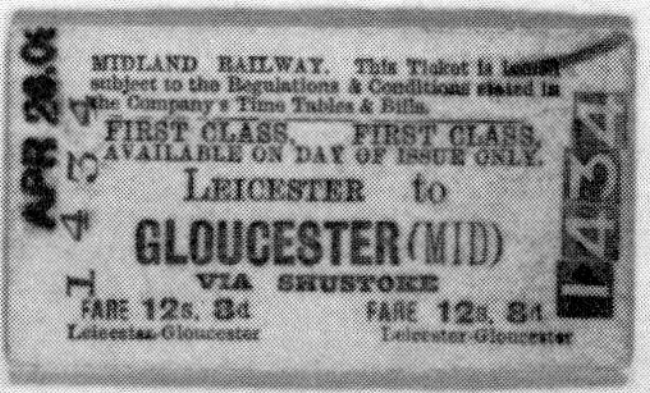

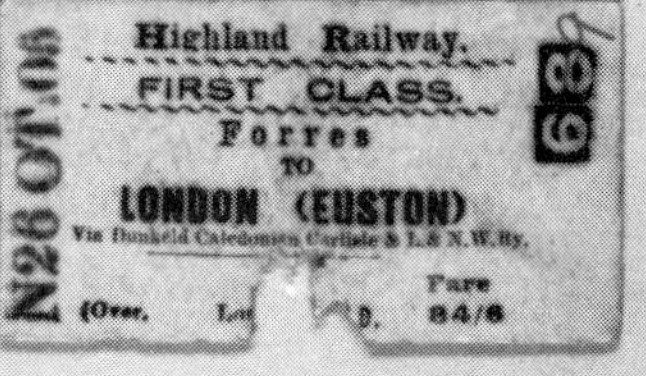

First class singles.

2438 Cork & Muskerry Light Railway, red horizontal overprint on white. The company was incorporated in 1883 by the Tramways Act, the Coachford branch being opened in 1888. It was transferred to the Great Southern Railway in 1925, and ceased operations in 1934.

8192 Furness Railway, issued 29 July 1903. The line opened in 1846, and in 1857 an extension was built from Dalton to a junction with the Ulverston & Lancaster Railway.

799 Festiniog Railway, excess fare, issued 14 July 1937.

3310 District Railway, overprinted red circle and skeleton 'J', issued 7 March 1899. With the Metropolitan, the District formed the original Underground Railway; they were well-known for their 4-4-0 tank locomotives.

0096 LNER Privilege with red overprint 'P'. This ticket was issued 18 years after nationalisation.

1434 Midland Railway. Unusual in being non-standard yellow, this ticket was issued 26 April 1909.

1686 Hull & Barnsley Railway, issued 28 October 1896. In 1910 the company's rolling stock consisted of 150 locomotives and 80 passenger carriages.

68 Highland Railway, issued 26 October 1905. For some reason the ticket number appears to have been altered to 69. The HR was incorporated in 1865 as an amalgamation of the Inverness & Aberdeen Junction and the Inverness & Perth Junction Railways.

W. C. & P. L. RY.
CLEVEDON
TO
COLEHOUSE LANE.
SECOND CLASS, FARE 1d.
COLEHOUSE LANE
COLEHOUSE LANE
02886
Taff Vale Railway
Second Class 3/-
TREFOREST
TO
PORTHCAWL G.W
Via LLANTRISSANT
SEE NOTICE ON BACK
MIDLAND & GT. WESTERN JOINT RLY.
SECOND CLASS. SECOND CLASS.
AVAILABLE ON DAY OF ISSUE ONLY.
SEA MILLS to
CLIFTON DOWN
FARE 3d
FARE 3d.
1646
SEAHOUSES
(North Sunderland Railway)
Seahouses
TO
Seahouses
CHATHILL
Chathill
Chathill
Fare 9d.
Fare 9d.
SECOND CLASS SECOND
4107
MET. & S. E. & C. RYS.
MOORGATE STREET to
SNOW HILL
SNOW HILL
SNOW HILL
3087
GLASGOW
TO
LARBERT
SECOND CLASS.
JOINT RAILWAY STEAMER.
PORTSMOUTH HARBOUR
TO
RYDE [Esplanade
5611
P. & T. R.
PEMBROKE DOCK
To
LLANELLY
via Whitland
Second Class.
FOR CONDITIONS SEE BACK OF TICKET
BRITISH & IRISH STEAM PACKET CO. LTD.
DUBLIN (North Wall) (164)
TO
LONDON (EUSTON)
CLASS STEAMER & RAIL
04380
EAST LONDON RAILWAY.
Available on the Date of issue ONLY.
NEW CROSS
TO
DEPTFORD R'D
0047

Second class singles.
02886 Weston, Clevedon & Portishead Railway, white, issued 8 October 1906. One year later the extension to Portishead was built, making a total length of 14¼ miles. The line closed in 1940.
155 Taff Vale Railway, light blue, date of issue unkown. The TVR was authorised in 1836, provided that its locomotives did not exceed a speed of 12mph. The original section of the line, an inclined plane operated by a stationary steam engine, was opened in 1840.
4107 North Sunderland Railway, pink, issued 7 June 1911. By a Light Railway Order in August 1898, authorisation was given for a 4 mile line between Chathill Station and Seahouses. The line opened for passenger traffic in mid-December 1898, and was closed in 1951.
7860 Edinburgh & Glasgow Railway, dark blue, issued 17 July 1928. Authorised in 1838, the line was opened in 1842, with further extensions between 1846-50. The reverse of the ticket carries a safety symbol in the form of the company's initials derived from a thistle and its leaves.
5611 Joint Railway Steamer, light blue, issued 2 June 1913. The London & South Western and the London, Brighton & South Coast Railways jointly operated five small steamers between Portsmouth and the Isle of Wight. Between them they owned more than forty ships, including three paddle-steamers.
87 Pembroke & Tenby Railway, lilac, unissued. The original line was opened in 1863 to connect with the New Milford Line of the South Wales Railway; it became part of the GWR in 1897.
0047 East London Railway, light blue, issued 13 June 1906. The ELR was authorised in 1865 to link the north and south Thames through Sir Mark Isambard Brunel's Thames Tunnel, the line opening in 1869.

Third class singles.
045 Neath & Brecon Railway, light brown, issued 10 June 1908. The N & BR started as the Dulas Valley Mineral Railway from a junction with the Vale of Neath Railway. With the authorisation in 1863 of an extension to Brecon it became the N & BR, and passed into the ownership of the GWR in 1922.
7457 Isle of Wight Central Railway, green, issued 5 June 1913. The company was formed of the amalgamation in 1887 of the Isle of Wight (Newport Junction), the Cowes & Newport, and the Ryde & Newport Railways.
6127 GWR & Midland, Severn & Wye Joint Railway, light brown, issued 20 August 1910. In 1857 the Severn & Wye operated on broad gauge track, and after amalgamation in 1879 with the Severn Bridge Railway it became a joint company with the GWR and Midland in 1894.
2946 Manx Northern Railway, dark blue, unissued. Authorised in 1878, the line opened in 1879, and was absorbed by the IOMR in 1904.

Third class singles.
4718 The Harton Coal Company Limited, South Shields, Marsden & Whitburn Colliery Railway, pink, date of issue unknown. The ticket is from a perforated roll. The line was opened by the Harton Colliery in 1870, and fifty years later, a Light Railway Order authorised the working to Whitburn in 1926.
9616 Knott End Railway, light blue, issued 21 May 1910. The Company was incorporated in 1898 to take over the old Garstang and Knot End Railway. It had a chequered history before being taken over by the LMS in 1923.
3301 Kent & East Sussex Railway, pink, issued 16 April 1906. Originally the Rother Valley Railway (1896), the company went into liquidation in 1932.
Lancashire & Yorkshire Railway, green, issued 30 March 1904. This ticket is unusual in two ways; in its vertical format, but principally because it has no number. It is also much thinner card than standard Edmondson Tickets. In 1846 the Manchester & Leeds Railway amalgamated with the Manchester & Bolton Railway, changing its name to the L & YR the following year.

Isle of Man Railway Co.
THROUGH SINGLE TICKET
3rd. Class and Fore Cabin
(I.O.M.)
To
Via Liverpool ( ) and
See Back for conditions of issue
Not transferable
3472
NEATH & BRECON RY.
This Ticket is issued subject to the regulations and conditions stated in the Company's Time Tables and Bills.
THIRD CLASS THIRD CLASS
AVAILABLE ON DAY OF ISSUE ONLY
BRECON To
CRADOC
Fare 3d. Fare 3d.
Brecon Cradoc Brecon-Cradoc
045
L. & N. E. R.
Series A Series A
NOTTINGHAM (R.C.St'n) to
BASFORD & BULW'LL (L&N.E)
Via Bagthorpe Junc.
Fare 4½d. Third Class Fare 4½d.
SEE CONDITIONS ON BACK
6479
I. W. Central Railway.
THIRD CLASS THIRD CLASS
Parliamentary Parliamentary
Available day of issue only.
Freshwater Freshwater
TO
NEWPORT
Newport Newport
Fare 1/0 Fare 1/0
7457
JY.5.07 JY.5.07
L. T. & S. R. (See Back)
PLAISTOW
TO
BROMLEY
Bromley Bromley
THIRD CLASS
1d Fare 1d
G.W.R. & Mid. Severn & Wye J'nt Ry.
Lydney Town Lydney Town
TO
LYDNEY JUNC.
1d, THIRD CLASS 1d,
Issued subject to the conditions and regulations set out in the Company's Time Tables, Bills and Notices
Lydney Junc Lydney Junc
6127
Isle of Wight Ry.
SANDOWN
Series 9 TO
RYDE ST. JOHN'S ROAD
THIRD CLASS FARE 5½d
Not Transferable. Issued subject to the Co's Bye Laws & Published Regulations
5165
ST. GERMAINS
TO
SULBY GLEN
Third Class.
2946
District Railway.
Issued subject to the Companies' Bye-laws, Regulations and advertised Conditions.
VICTORIA
TO
WESTMINSTER
SLOANE SQUARE
or intermediately
1d. THIRD CLASS FARE. 1d.
Available day of issue only.
5913
G. N. & L. & N. W. J'nt Ry
FOR CONDITIONS SEE NOTICES
MELTON MOWBRAY TO
TILTON
THIRD CLASS
761(S)
TILTON
7195

The Harton Coal Company Limited.
South Shields, Marsden & Whitburn Colliery Railway.
MARSDEN COTTAGE to
SOUTH SHIELDS
Third Class Single Journey
FARE 2d
4718
Metropolitan Railway.
Available for one journey on day of issue only.
(A.M.4)
King's Cross (1) to
ALDERSGATE STREET,
BAKER STREET
or Intermediate Station (Series 31.
FARE 1d. THIRD CLASS
1344
KNOTT END RAILWAY.
AVAILABLE ON DAY OF ISSUE.
GARSTANG & CATTERALL
TO
GARSTANG
Fare 2d.
Third
Class
Garstang
9616
KENT & EAST SUSSEX RAILWAY.
TENTERDEN TOWN
TO
HIGH HALDEN ROAD
THIRD CLASS. Fare 3d.
[SEE BACK]
High Halden Rd. High Halden Rd.
3301
L. M. & S. R.
FOR CONDITIONS SEE BACK (E.0)
Available for one journey only to be completed within Seven days of issue. HARVESTMAN
CHESTER TO
BALLINA
ViaHolyh'dLM&SRCo'sBoattoKingstown
& Dublin (W.R. & Broadstone)
3rdRAIL&
STEAMER
FARE
Gt. Western & L.& S. Western Rys
RODWELL RODWELL
TO
WESTHAM
HALT
THIRD CLASS
1½d Actual Fare 1½d
REVISED FARE
Westham Westham
5370
1904 MAR 30
L. & Y. R.
SANDHILLS
TO
KIRKDALE
3RD CLASS
Fare 1d.
Issued subject to regulations and conditions in Co.'s Time Tables, &c.
Available on day of issue only.
FOR CONDITIONS SEE NOTICES
Rail Motor Car Ticket.
3rdClassCHEAPSINGLE
4071
GREAT EASTERN RAILWAY
Issued subject to Regulations in the Company's Time Tables.
[E.O.] FOREST GATE to
Forest Gate [E.O] Forest Gate [E.O]
MARYLAND POINT
Maryland Point Maryland Point
1d. Fare 1d.
Third Class
8757
L.N.E.R.
FOR CONDITIONS SEE BACK. Available for three days, including day of issue.
MARYLEBONE to
HARROW-ON-THE-HILL
Fare THIRD S 885 10d.N CLASS
HARROW-ON-THE-HILL
1124

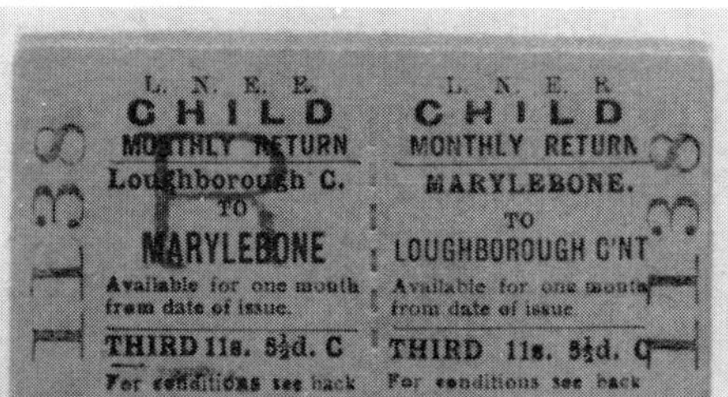
1138
L. N. E. R.
CHILD
MONTHLY RETURN
Loughborough C.
TO
MARYLEBONE
Available for one month from date of issue.
THIRD 11s. 5½d. C
For conditions see back
L. N. E. R.
CHILD
MONTHLY RETURN
MARYLEBONE.
TO
LOUGHBOROUGH C'NT
Available for one month from date of issue
THIRD 11s. 5½d. C
For conditions see back

0216
L. N. E. R.
HALF DAY EXC'N
LEICESTER (CENT.)
TO
QUORN & WOODHOUSE
Valid as per Bills
THIRD
For conditions see back
L. N. E. R.
HALF DAY EXC'N
QUORN & WOODHOUSE
TO
LEICESTER CEN.
Valid as per Bills
THIRD
For conditions see back

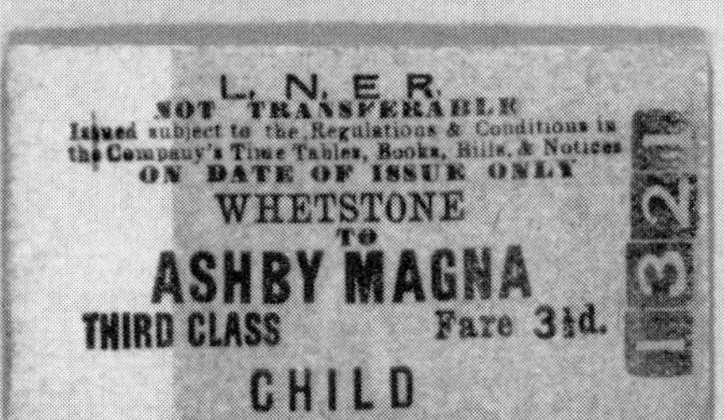
L. N. E. R.
NOT TRANSFERABLE
Issued subject to the Regulations & Conditions in the Company's Time Tables, Books, Bills, & Notices
ON DATE OF ISSUE ONLY
WHETSTONE
TO
ASHBY MAGNA
THIRD CLASS
Fare 3½d.
CHILD

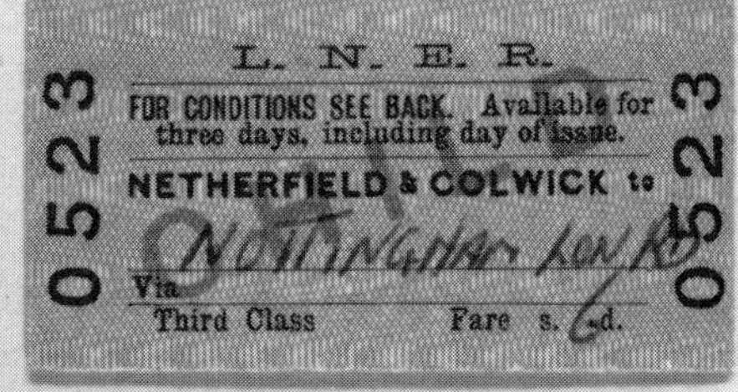
0523
L. N. E. R.
FOR CONDITIONS SEE BACK. Available for three days, including day of issue.
NETHERFIELD & COLWICK to
Via
Third Class
Fare s. d.

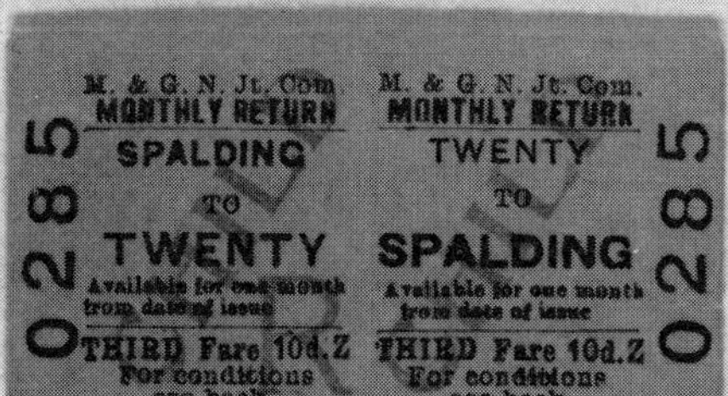
0285
M. & G. N. Jt. Com.
MONTHLY RETURN
SPALDING
TO
TWENTY
Available for one month from date of issue
THIRD Fare 10d.Z
For conditions see back
M. & G. N. Jt. Com.
MONTHLY RETURN
TWENTY
TO
SPALDING
Available for one month from date of issue
THIRD Fare 10d.Z
For conditions see back

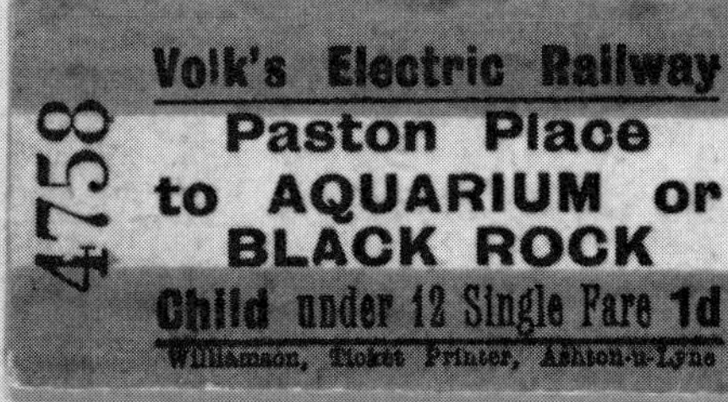
4758
Volk's Electric Railway
Paston Place
to AQUARIUM or
BLACK ROCK
Child under 12 Single Fare 1d
Williamson, Ticket Printer, Ashton-u-Lyne

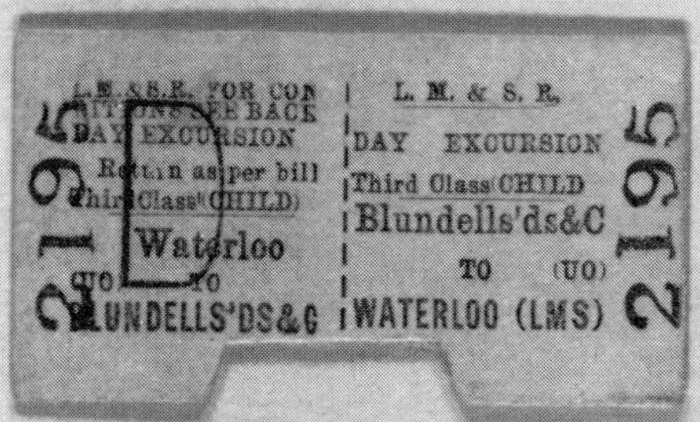
2195
DAY EXCURSION
Waterloo
TO
L. M. & S. R.
DAY EXCURSION
Third Class CHILD
Blundells'ds&C
TO (UO)
WATERLOO (LMS)

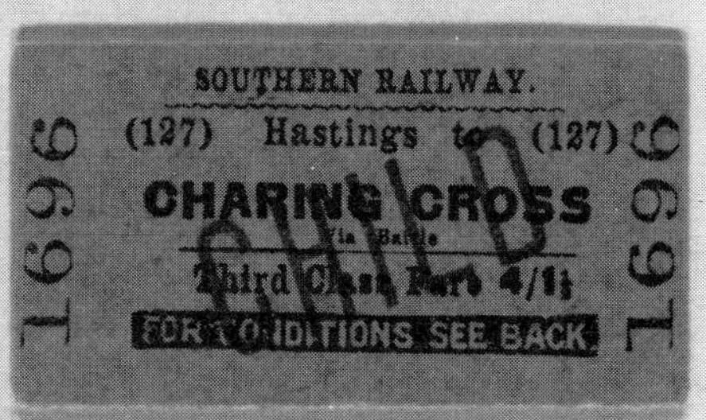
1696
SOUTHERN RAILWAY.
(127) Hastings to (127)
CHARING CROSS
Third Class Fare 4/1½
FOR CONDITIONS SEE BACK
CHILD

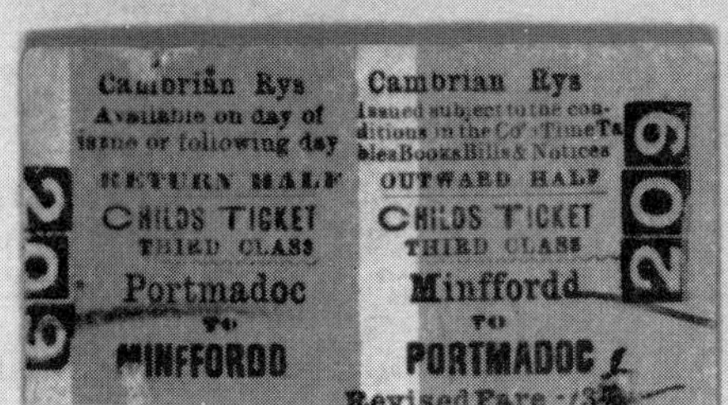
Cambrian Rys
Available on day of issue or following day
RETURN HALF
CHILDS TICKET
THIRD CLASS
Portmadoc
TO
MINFFORDD
Cambrian Rys
Issued subject to the conditions in the Co's Time Tables Books Bills & Notices
OUTWARD HALF
CHILDS TICKET
THIRD CLASS
Minffordd
TO
PORTMADOC
Revised Fare -/3½
209

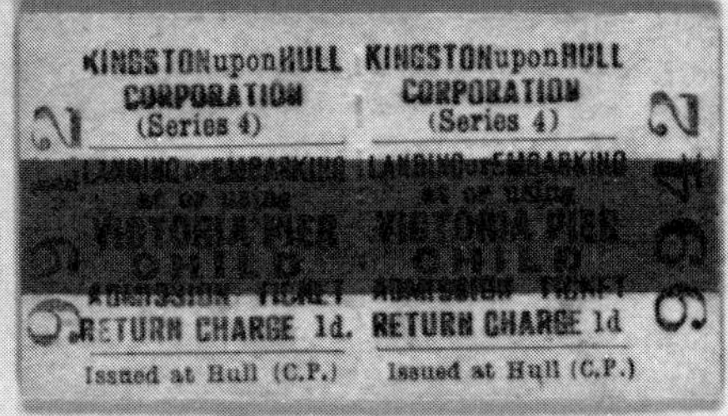
KINGSTON upon HULL
CORPORATION
(Series 4)
VICTORIA PIER
RETURN CHARGE 1d.
Issued at Hull (C.P.)
KINGSTON upon HULL
CORPORATION
(Series 4)
VICTORIA PIER
RETURN CHARGE 1d
Issued at Hull (C.P.)

Child tickets. Differing styles, even within one company's issue, can be seen in this selection. The four LNER tickets are standard issues of different categories.
1138 Monthly return, light green with red overprint.
0216 Half-day excursion, light brown with red overprint.
1321 Third class single, ¾ light blue overprint on white.
0523 Third class single blank, light green safety background on white with red overprint.
0285 Midland & Great Northern Joint Committee, light green with red overprint. This ticket was not issued until 1959.
4758 Volk's Electric Railway, two horizontal light blue bands on white card. This railway, opened in August 1883, was the first public electric railway in Britain; it predates the City & South London Railway, the world's first underground electric railway, by seven years.
2195 LM & SR day excursion, light brown, issued 17 September 1941. Although specially printed as a 'Child' ticket it could be mistaken for an ordinary issue. It was clipped in this distinctive manner to simplify identification. At one time, most companies printed a special segment at the bottom of the ticket containing a codified form of the ticket details. The idea was to obviate the necessity for specially printing or overprinting 'Child' tickets, but it did not seem to have been closely observed when tickets were ordered.
209 Cambrian Railways third class return, printed as 'Childs Ticket', Outward half overprinted light green on white, return half brick red on white, issued 10 July 1929. The CR was formed in 1864 by the amalgamation of five railways, comprising about 230 miles of track, some with very steep gradients.
9942 Kingston-upon-Hull Corporation, dark blue horizontal band on white, issued 24 June 1981. This was the last day of the Humber Ferry Service; Sealink UK Ltd issued a souvenir pictorial ticket to commemorate the last public sailing after 150 years of crossing the Humber Estuary.

The promotion of day excursion tickets has always been an extensive part of the railway business. Special destinations and occasions were not necessary to increase trade; but the issue of the tickets brought a kaleidoscope of colour to the booking office and ticket barrier.
1481 Belfast & County Down Railway, light blue with red overprint to signify validity of ticket. Incorporated in 1846, the line was opened in sections between 1848 and 1861, and became part of the Great Northern of Ireland Railway.
218 Liskeard & Looe, overprinted light orange on slate-blue card. The line was originally incorporated, and was also re-incorporated, in 1858. Under an Act of 1909 it was worked by the Great Western Railway, and amalgamated with it in 1923.
081 Isle of Man Railway, yellow vertical stripe on outward half and light blue vertical stripe on return half.
0230 LNER, lilac with red 'R' overprint. A day at the races, with the trip to the racecourse by Midland 'Red' included in the fare. Date unknown.
1625 Mersey Railway, light orange with red overprint. The original name of the company was the Mersey Pneumatic Railway Company, and the line under the Mersey was opened by the Prince of Wales in 1886.
4382 Northern Ireland Railways, stone coloured with red overprint.
991 Welsh Highland Railway, slate blue overprint on white. Parts of the line were opened between 1877 and 1881, but it closed in 1916. Reopened in 1922 and 1923, its name was established as the WHR, and it closed for passenger traffic in 1936, being dismantled in 1941.
3611 LNER, lilac with red overprint.
298 British Railways, stone coloured with red overprint.
191 Liverpool Overhead Railway, yellow overprint on return half with light blue horizontal band right across.

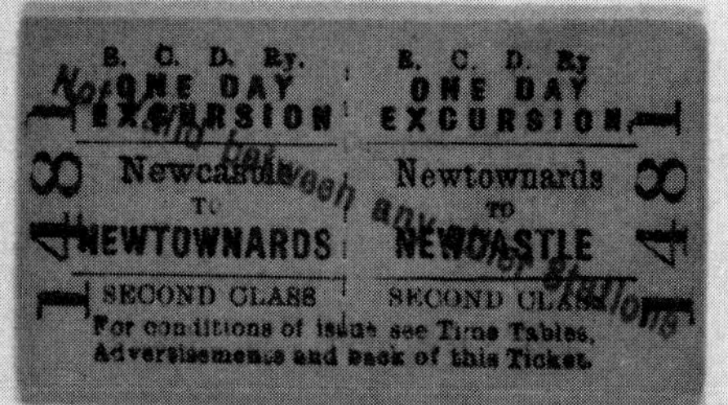
B. C. D. Ry.
ONE DAY EXCURSION
Newcastle TO NEWTOWNARDS
SECOND CLASS
B. C. D. Ry
ONE DAY EXCURSION
Newtownards TO NEWCASTLE
SECOND CLASS
For conditions of issue see Time Tables, Advertisements and back of this Ticket.
1481

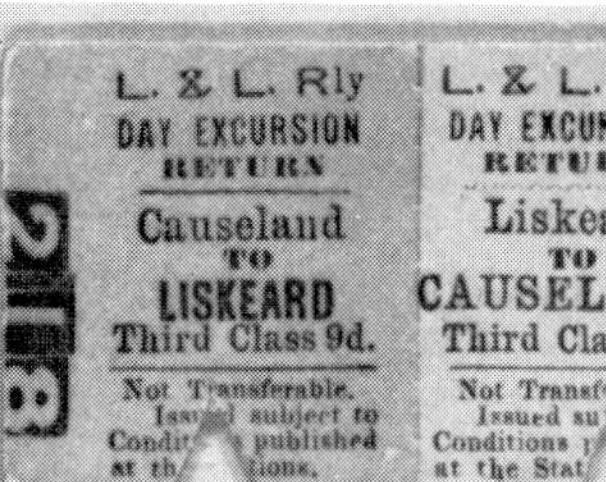
L. & L. Rly
DAY EXCURSION
RETURN
Causeland
TO
LISKEARD
Third Class 9d.
L. & L. Rly.
DAY EXCURSION
RETURN
Liskeard
TO
CAUSELAND
Third Class 9d.

218

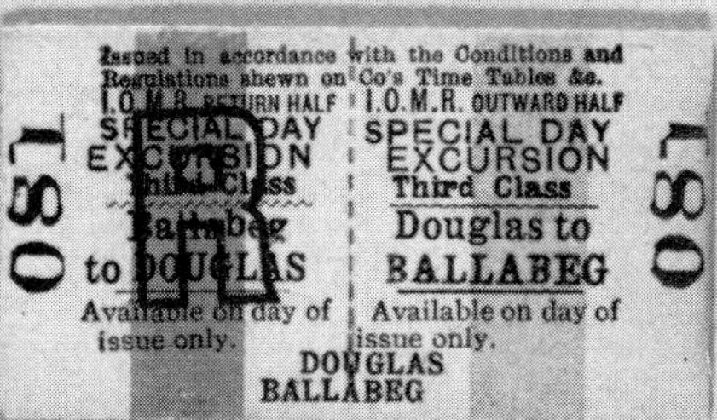
Issued in accordance with the Conditions and Regulations shewn on Co's Time Tables &c.
I.O.M.R. RETURN HALF
SPECIAL DAY EXCURSION
Third Class
Ballabeg to DOUGLAS
Available on day of issue only.
I.O.M.R. OUTWARD HALF
SPECIAL DAY EXCURSION
Third Class
Douglas to BALLABEG
Available on day of issue only.
DOUGLAS
BALLABEG
081

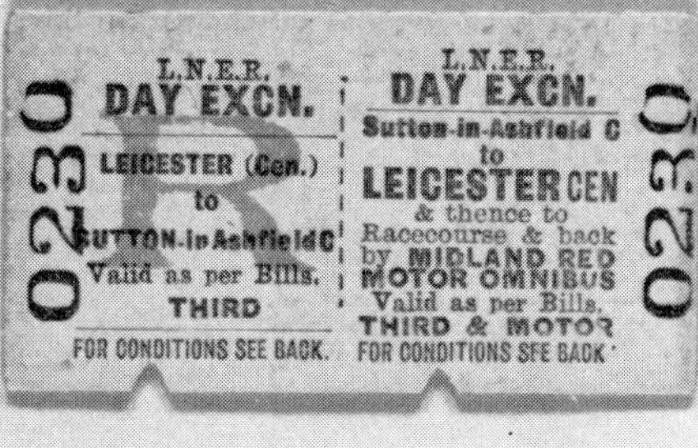
L.N.E.R.
DAY EXCN.
LEICESTER (Cen.)
to
SUTTON-in-Ashfield C
Valid as per Bills.
THIRD
FOR CONDITIONS SEE BACK.
L.N.E.R.
DAY EXCN.
Sutton-in-Ashfield C
to
LEICESTER CEN
& thence to Racecourse & back by MIDLAND RED MOTOR OMNIBUS
Valid as per Bills.
THIRD & MOTOR
FOR CONDITIONS SEE BACK
0230

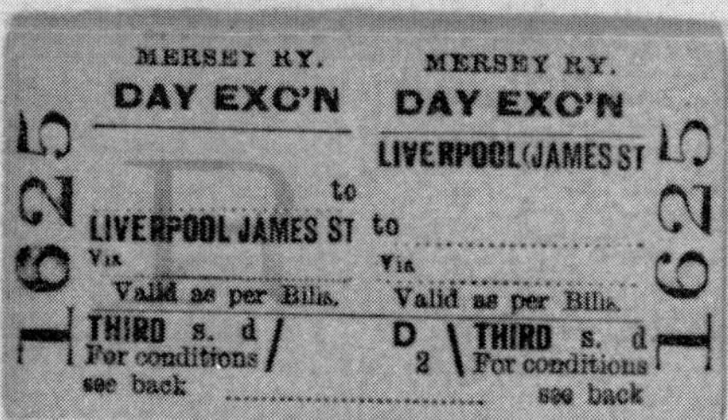
MERSEY RY.
DAY EXC'N
to
LIVERPOOL JAMES ST
Valid as per Bills.
THIRD s. d
For conditions see back
MERSEY RY.
DAY EXC'N
LIVERPOOL (JAMES ST
to
Valid as per Bills.
THIRD s. d
For conditions see back
1625

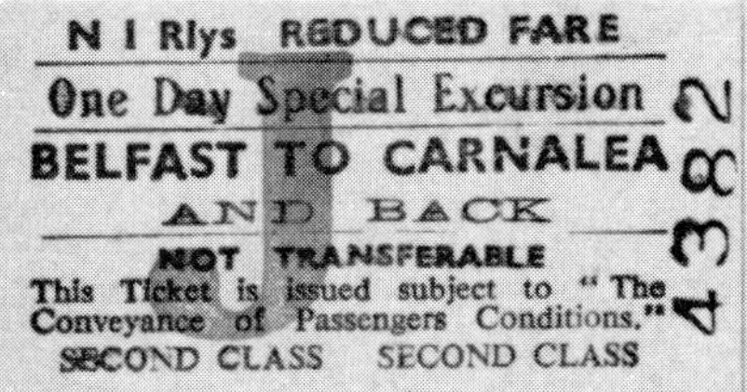
N I Rlys REDUCED FARE
One Day Special Excursion
BELFAST TO CARNALEA
AND BACK
NOT TRANSFERABLE
This Ticket is issued subject to "The Conveyance of Passengers Conditions."
SECOND CLASS SECOND CLASS
4382

WELSH HIGHLAND RY.
DAY EXCURSION
RETURN HALF
BLAENAU FESTINIOG
TO
DINAS
THIRD CLASS
Over
WELSH HIGHLAND RY
DAY EXCURSION
OUTWARD HALF
Dinas
TO
BLAENAU FESTINIOG
THIRD CLASS
Over
991

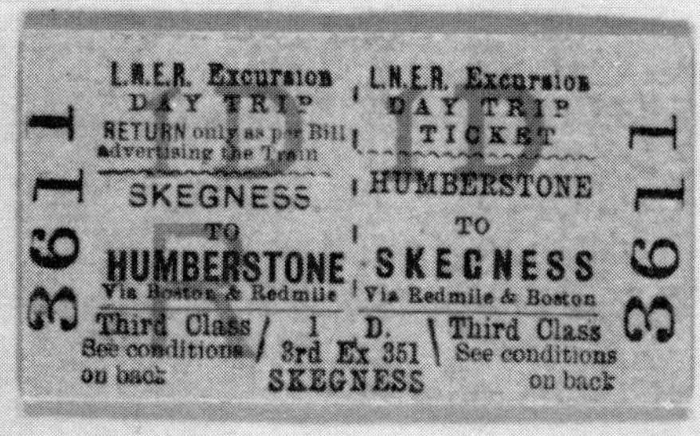
L.N.E.R. Excursion
DAY TRIP
SKEGNESS
TO
HUMBERSTONE
Via Boston & Redmile
Third Class
See conditions on back
L.N.E.R. Excursion
DAY TRIP TICKET
HUMBERSTONE
TO
SKEGNESS
Via Redmile & Boston
Third Class
See conditions on back
1 D.
3rd Ex 351
SKEGNESS
3611

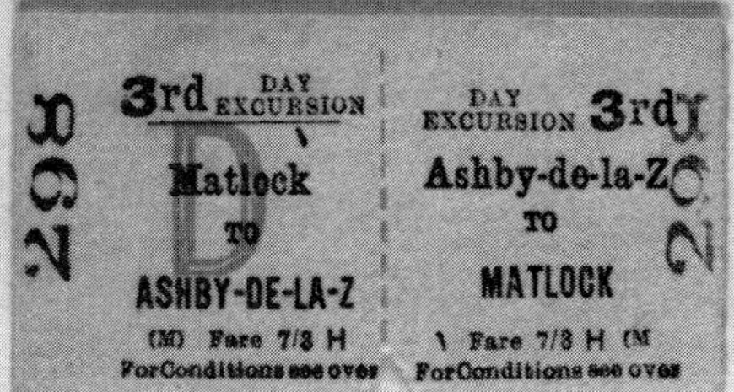
3rd DAY EXCURSION
Matlock
TO
ASHBY-DE-LA-Z
Fare 7/3 H
ForConditions see over
DAY EXCURSION 3rd
Ashby-de-la-Z
TO
MATLOCK
Fare 7/3 H
ForConditions see over
298

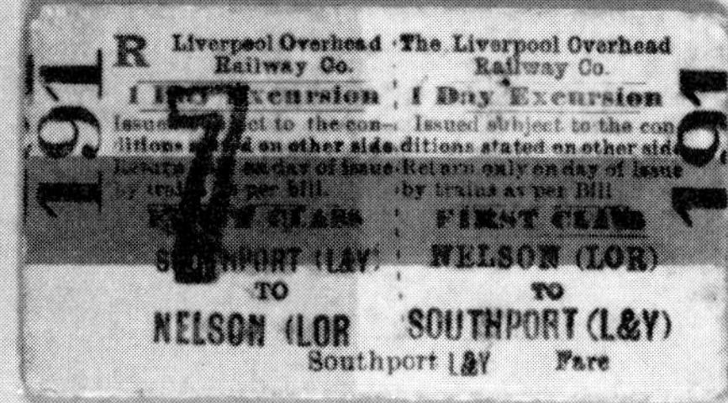
Liverpool Overhead Railway Co.
The Liverpool Overhead Railway Co.
1 Day Excursion
Issued subject to the conditions stated on other side.
Return only on day of issue by trains as per Bill.
FIRST CLASS
NELSON (LOR)
TO
SOUTHPORT (L&Y)
TO
NELSON (LOR
Southport L&Y
Fare
191

M. S. J. & A. R.
CHEAP TICKET.
AVAILABLE ON DAY OF ISSUE ONLY
FOR CONDITIONS SEE BACK.
LONDON ROAD to
WARWICK ROAD
or OLD TRAFFORD
Fare THIRD
CHEAP T. S. 10
3d. CLASS
WARWICK RD. etc.
8081
3rd - SPECIAL CHEAP DAY
SPECIAL CHEAP DAY - 3rd
Helpston TO PETERBOROUGH (East)
Peterborough (East) TO HELPSTON
(E) Fare 1/5
Fare 1/5 (E)
For conditions see over
0139
G.N.& L.&N.W.Jnt. Ry
CHEAP DAY
TILTON to GREAT DALBY
GREAT DALBY to TILTON
Via
Available on day of issue only as per Bills.
Available on day of issue only.
THIRD
For conditions see back
5773
GtWesternRy
CHEAP RETURN
CHEAP
For day of issue by trains as advertised
Aberavon Town to DUFFRYN RHONDDA HALT
Duffryn Rhondda HALT to ABERAVON TOWN
THIRD CLASS
FOR CONDITIONS SEE BACK
1243
M.T.R. OUTWARD HALF
3RD CLASS
CHEAP DAY TICKET
Hamilton Square TO ROCK FERRY
HAMILTON SQUARE
6430
D. W. & W. R.
Third Class
FARE-ONE PENNY.
CHEAP SUNDAY TRAIN
DALKEY TO KINGSTOWN
389
Kent & E.S. Rly
CHEAP
Bodiam
Robertsbridge Jct.
BODIAM
THIRD RETURN
Fare 9½d
Williamson, Ticket Printer, Ashton-u-Lyne
5045
O. & I. JOINT
CHILD
SPECIAL SINGLE TICKET
Available on day of issue only.
ILKLEY to
BURLEY-in-W'DALE
FOR CONDITIONS SEE BACK.
THIRD CLASS
Fare 2½ d.C
3322
L. O. R.
3rd CHEAP DAY
CHEAP DAY 3rd
For c'nditions see back
Southport (L.M.R.) TO JAMES STREET (L.O.R.)
James Street (L.O.R.) TO SOUTHPORT (L.M.R.)
Fare 2/8
3 C.D. 11
SOUTHPORT (L.M.R.)
1582
Gt. Western Ry.
SPECIAL SINGLE
OLTON
ACOCKS GREEN & S. Yardley
THIRD CLASS
7617

As with excursion tickets, the railway companies made great use of special cheap day singles and returns; there is very little real difference betwen the two categories. Prior to World War I they were issued in large numbers, but after the 1923 grouping they were more standardised. Even so, by the late 1920s there were more than twenty forms of cheap day tickets available. In this selection of standard Edmondson tickets there is a colourful array.
8081 green, issued 12 September 1888
0139 British Railways, lilac with red overprint
573 light green with red overprint
1243 green
6430 Mersey Tunnel Railway, outward light blue, return, purple
389 Dublin, Wicklow & Wexford Railway, light brown horizontal overprints on white. This company, formed in 1846, changed its name in 1860 to DW & WR, and yet again in 1906 to Dublin & South Eastern Railway, before becoming part of the Great Southern of Ireland in 1923.
5045 brick red overprint on light brown card
3322 light green
1582 pink with red overprint
7617 deep red, issued 3 May 1938.

Liverpool Overhead Railway.
The LOR began operations in 1893 as a copy of the New York Elevated Railway (known as the 'El'). The El commenced operations with steam engines, but the LOR was electric from the start. The LOR was brought into being by the Mersey Docks and Harbour Board who had statutory powers through three Overhead Railway Acts of 1882, 1887, and 1888. The undertaking remained independent, outside the nationalisation scheme, until its closure in 1957.
1457 light brown
0025 red horizontal overprints on white
0552 lilac with red overprints
2338 cream with red overprints
6617 slate grey with red overprints
2898 light orange with red overprints
1867 lilac with red overprints (the right-hand portion had to be surrendered in exchange for a 6d return ticket issued by the Birkenhead Bus Corporation).
0404 lilac
1732 light green with red overprints
1719 green.

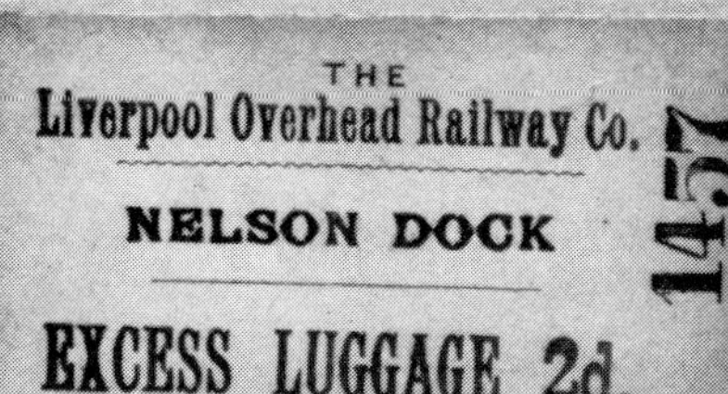
THE
Liverpool Overhead Railway Co.
NELSON DOCK
EXCESS LUGGAGE 2d.
1457

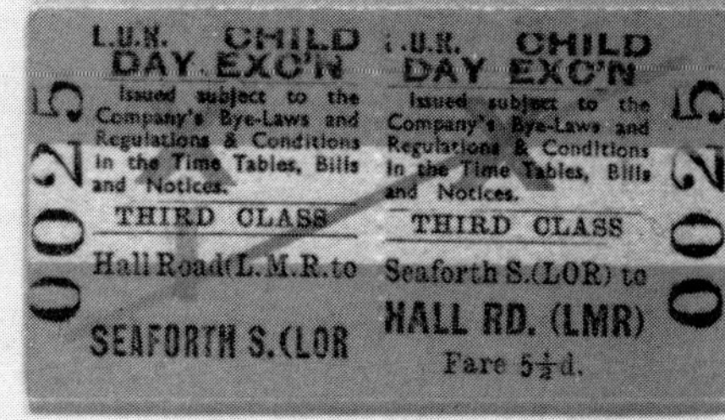
0025
L.O.R. CHILD DAY EXC'N
Issued subject to the Company's Bye-Laws and Regulations & Conditions in the Time Tables, Bills and Notices.
THIRD CLASS
Hall Road(L.M.R.to
SEAFORTH S.(LOR
L.O.R. CHILD DAY EXC'N
Issued subject to the Company's Bye-Laws and Regulations & Conditions in the Time Tables, Bills and Notices.
THIRD CLASS
Seaforth S.(LOR) to
HALL RD. (LMR)
Fare 5½d.
0025

0552
L.O.R.
DAY EX'CN
THIRD CLASS
PIERHEAD
to
SEAFORTH S. L.O.R.
L.O.R.
Available on day of issue only
New Brighton to LIVERPOOL Landing Stage
This Portion to be given up at the Contractor's Gate New Brighton
L.O.R.
DAY EX'CN
THIRD CLASS
SEAFORTH S. L.O.R.
to
NEW BRIGHTON FERRY
Via Wallasey F's
Fare 1/10
FOR CONDITIONS SEE BACK
0552

2338
L. O. R.
DAY EX'CN
FIRST CLASS
PIERHEAD
TO
SEAFORTH S'DS
L. O. R.
Available on day of issue only.
SEACOMBE
TO
LIVERPOOL LANDING STAGE
This Portion to be given up at the Contractor's Gate
SEACOMBE
L. O. R.
DAY EXC'N
FIRST CLASS
SEAFORTH S'DS
TO
SEACOMBE FERRY
Via Wallasey F's
FOR CONDITIONS SEE BACK
2338

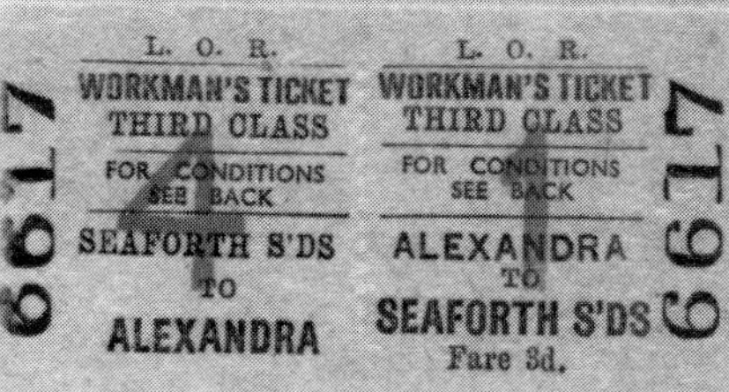
6617
L. O. R.
WORKMAN'S TICKET
THIRD CLASS
FOR CONDITIONS SEE BACK
SEAFORTH S'DS
TO
ALEXANDRA
L. O. R.
WORKMAN'S TICKET
THIRD CLASS
FOR CONDITIONS SEE BACK
ALEXANDRA
TO
SEAFORTH S'DS
Fare 3d.
6617

RETURN WEEKLY
M T W T F S
THIRD CLASS
L.O.R.
Expiring on Saturday following date of issue.
DINGLE to
CANADA and BACK
Available for One Journey each way—the Outward by trains leaving the starting point up to 8.30 a.m and the Return Journey by any train each day.
Fare 3s.6d.
OUTWARD M T W T F S
2898

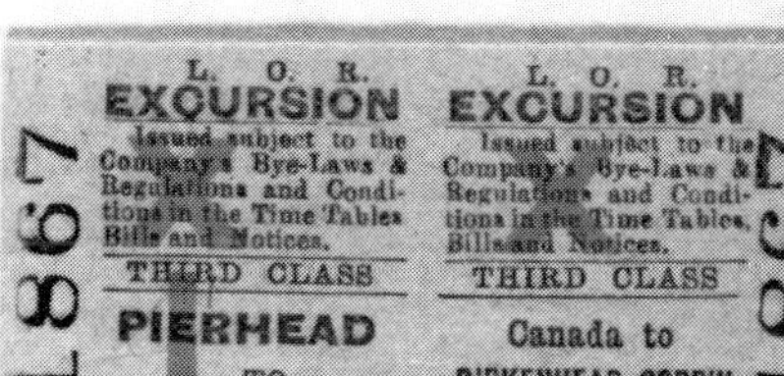
1867
L. O. R.
EXCURSION
Issued subject to the Company's Bye-Laws & Regulations and Conditions in the Time Tables Bills and Notices.
THIRD CLASS
PIERHEAD
TO
CANADA
L. O. R.
EXCURSION
Issued subject to the Company's Bye-Laws & Regulations and Conditions in the Time Tables, Bills and Notices.
THIRD CLASS
Canada to
BIRKENHEAD CORP'N BUS ROUTES
Via Woodside Ferry
Fare 11d. (See Over)
1867

0404
L. O. R.
PARTY
Issued subject to the Company's Bye-Laws and Regulations and Conditions in the Time Tables, Bills and Notices
THIRD CLASS
NEW BRIGHTON to
LIVERPOOL L. STAGE
(Via Wallasey Ferry)
FARE 11d.
L. O. R.
PARTY
Issued subject to the Company's Bye-Laws and Regulations and Conditions in its Time Tables, Bills and Notices
THIRD CLASS
LIVERPOOL L. STAGE to
(Via Wallasey Ferry)
NEW BRIGHTON
FARE 11d.
0404

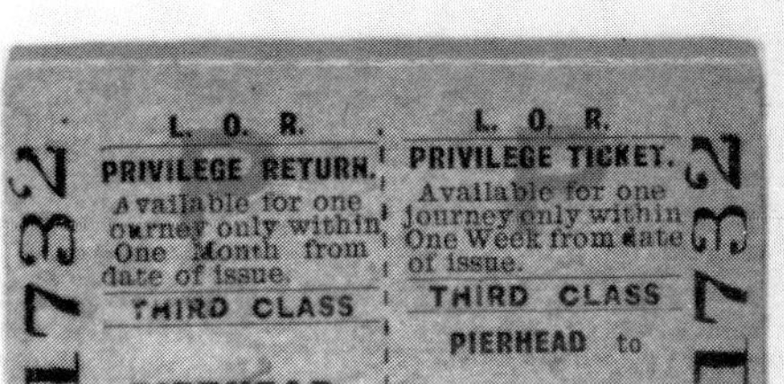
1732
L. O. R.
PRIVILEGE RETURN.
Available for one Journey only within One Month from date of issue.
THIRD CLASS
PIERHEAD
L. O. R.
PRIVILEGE TICKET.
Available for one Journey only within One Week from date of issue.
THIRD CLASS
PIERHEAD to
Fare s. d.
1732

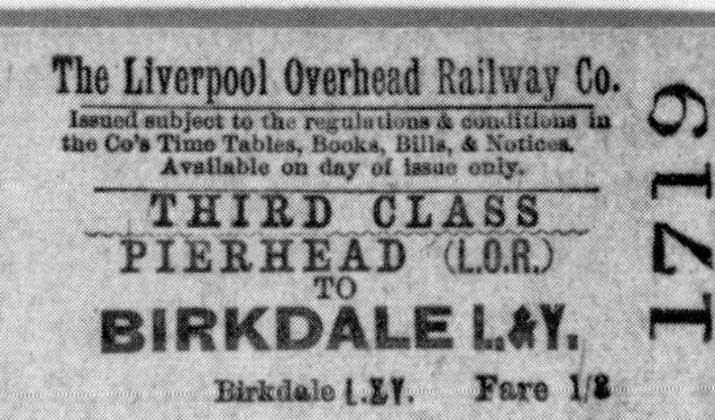
The Liverpool Overhead Railway Co.
Issued subject to the regulations & conditions in the Co's Time Tables, Books, Bills, & Notices.
Available on day of issue only.
THIRD CLASS
PIERHEAD (L.O.R.)
TO
BIRKDALE L.&Y.
Birkdale L.&Y. Fare 1/8
1719

Scotland, the nearest railway station being in Newcastle-on-Tyne. The journey from Leicester was easy, but from Newcastle northwards the route could be continued only by road or sea. Several visits by Thomas Cook were necessary to effect the preliminary arrangements; as on many previous occasions, he was accompanied by his twelve-year-old son, John, already a seasoned traveller.

In that year, 1846, some 350 persons availed themselves of the opportunity to visit the country made famous by the poems of Burns and the novels of Sir Walter Scott. They journeyed to Fleetwood by rail, thence to Ardrossan by steamer, and from Ardrossan by rail to Glasgow and Edinburgh. The contents of the handbook prepared for the trip were as comprehensive as its title: *Handbook of a Trip to Scotland: including Railway Glances from Leicester, via Manchester, to Fleetwood; Views on the Lancashire Coast and the Lakes of Cumberland; Voyage from Fleetwood to Ardrossan; Trip on the Ayrshire, and Edinburgh and Glasgow Railways; Scottish Scenery, and Descriptions of Edinburgh, Glasgow, &c., &c.'*

Having made all the necessary arrangements for the trip, and having compiled the handbook, Thomas Cook was still concerned that the trip should be to the absolute satisfaction of the travellers. He wrote towards the end of the preface:

> Having undertaken the arrangements of an excursion to Scotland, he [Thomas Cook] cheerfully steps forward to communicate such information as he conceives will be found most useful for those who avail themselves of a privilege which no previous generation had ever offered to them — an opportunity of riding from Leicester to Glasgow and back, a distance of about 800 miles, for a guinea.

The only complaint which those intrepid explorers could reasonably have voiced would have been about the inadequacy of the steamboat accommodation between Fleetwood and Ardrossan. Any discomfort they had, however, was more than compensated for when the party reached Glasgow. A salute of guns was fired as they entered the railway station, and a brass band waited to escort them to the Town Hall. It must have been with great reluctance that they left the city after such an enthusiastic welcome. They journeyed to Edinburgh by special train, where the citizens greeted them with equal fervour and extreme cordiality.

By the year 1861, Cook's tours to Scotland had become so popular that during the holiday season alone, more than 5,000 excursionists were making the journey. The monopoly for the whole system of tourist tickets throughout Scotland was in Thomas Cook's hands. Long railway journeys had ceased to be a subject of apprehension, and were instead regarded as pleasure trips. Arrangements had been made with most of the railway companies of the Midlands, the North of England, the Eastern Counties, and some of the Southern lines; interchanges of traffic had become quite commonplace. The various railway companies had begun to make excursion traffic a regular feature of their travelling arrangements.

In September 1868, Thomas Cook published a handbill advertising a 'HALF-DAY HOLIDAY TRIP From LEICESTER TO MELBOURNE'. The occasion was the opening of a line, connecting Derby with Melbourne, which afforded facilities for visiting one of the most delightful spots in the lowlands of

An historic building, which still stands in Gallowtree Gate, Leicester, but is no longer occupied by its original owners. Thomas Cook & Son built the premises in 1894, using three of the four floors. Because of the bas-reliefs on the façade, depicting typical locomotives of the 1841-94 era, it is now a listed building.

Derbyshire. As the distance was within a railway ride of an hour and a half from Leicester, Cook declared, 'It is convenient for a pleasant afternoon Trip, in harmony with the arrangements of the HALF-DAY HOLIDAY MOVEMENT.' The handbill went on to state that since Melbourne was the native place of the Agent for Midland Railway excursions, he [Cook] was anxious to have the privilege of arranging the First Excursion to that town.

The Company authorised him to advertise 'A SPECIAL EXPRESS TRAIN to leave LEICESTER at 2-30 p.m. ON THURSDAY NEXT, SEPT. 10th, FOR MELBOURNE Returning from Melbourne Station at 8-30 p.m.' The fares there and back were First Class, 4s, Covered Carriages 2s. Children above 3, and under 12-year-of-age, were allowed to travel at half-fares, and tickets were to be had at the station. The train ran direct from Leicester to Melbourne, not stopping at Derby, the route beyond Derby being by way of Chellaston, Swarkestone, and across the Trent to King's Newton, the station being situated between Newton and Melbourne. Mr Thomas Cook accompanied the part of excursionists on a promenade of the famed Melbourne gardens, and the parks and grounds surrounding Melbourne Lake.

The reverse side of the handbill gave particulars of what was to be seen and done in Melbourne. Details of population, market-days, and the extensive manufactories of silks, gloves, stockings, and shoes were quoted, and the town was alleged to have the most fertile and extensive market gardens in the Midland Counties. The comprehensive list of places likely to interest the excursionist included: 'A NEW CEMETERY, situated midway between Melbourne and Newton.' Although hardly a tourist attraction it undoubtedly created the precedent for the reduced fare concessions made to battleground pilgrims after World War I.

The final item, No 8 on the list, states,

> THE NEW LINE OF RAILWAY which crosses the Trent, near Weston Cliff, and skirts the hamlet of King's Newton, passing the residence of Mr. Briggs, the talented Historian of Melbourne and author of other popular works. The Station is on the road leading to Donington Park, about a mile from the Melbourne Market Place. Omnibuses will run between the station and the town; and Mr. Warren, of the New Inn and Melbourne Arms, will place at the disposal of Mr. Cook his cabs and other vehicles.
>
> In consideration of the peculiar interest of this Excursion, as the first Trip by Railway to Melbourne, from Leicester MR COOK will take the opportunity of giving a Short Address to the Visitors and Inhabitants, in the Athenaeum, at half-past 7 o'clock, retrospective of his 40 years' absence from his native town, his 28 years of Excursion and Tourist life, [it was, in fact, 27 years], and anticipatory of his approaching Trips to Italy, Egypt, and the Holy Land.
>
> With a determination to make the best of the few hours allotted to this Half-day Holiday Excursion, Ladies and Gentlemen, Traders and their Assistants, are respectfully invited to accompany to Melbourne their long-patronised and appreciative servant,
>
> THOMAS COOK
>
> Leicester, Sep. 7, 1868.

A *Cook's Tours through the Trossachs* leaflet, issued in July 1933, highlights the tremendous progress in railway excursion traffic engendered by the firm. In 1850, John Cook was entrusted by his father with the responsibility of conducting the first large party ever to attempt the journey from Stirling to Glasgow in one day via the Trossachs and Loch Lomond. The 1933 leaflet lists a longer itinerary which takes in those two towns, and almost casually comments that the whole journey could be easily made in one day. The Tour through the Trossachs via Aberfoyle and 'Rob Roy Country' was by London and North Eastern Railway Routes, and was divided into several smaller tours. A typical escorted day tour left Edinburgh or Glasgow on Tuesdays, Thursdays and Saturdays during the season. Passengers were met by Cook's Guide at Edinburgh's Waverley Station where they caught the 9.15am train to Aberfoyle, via the Forth Bridge. On arrival, they joined a coach which motored them through the Trossachs to Loch Katrine. A steamer awaited to ferry them up to Stronachlachar for another coach ride to Inversnaid. From here, the day trippers caught the Loch Lomond steamer to Balloch Pier, and thence by rail to Glasgow, and returning to Edinburgh by 9.18pm. For their day's outing, for which they were provided with rail, steamer, and coach tickets, luncheon, sightseeing fees, and the services of a guide, third-class passengers were charged an inclusive fare of £1 13s 9d.

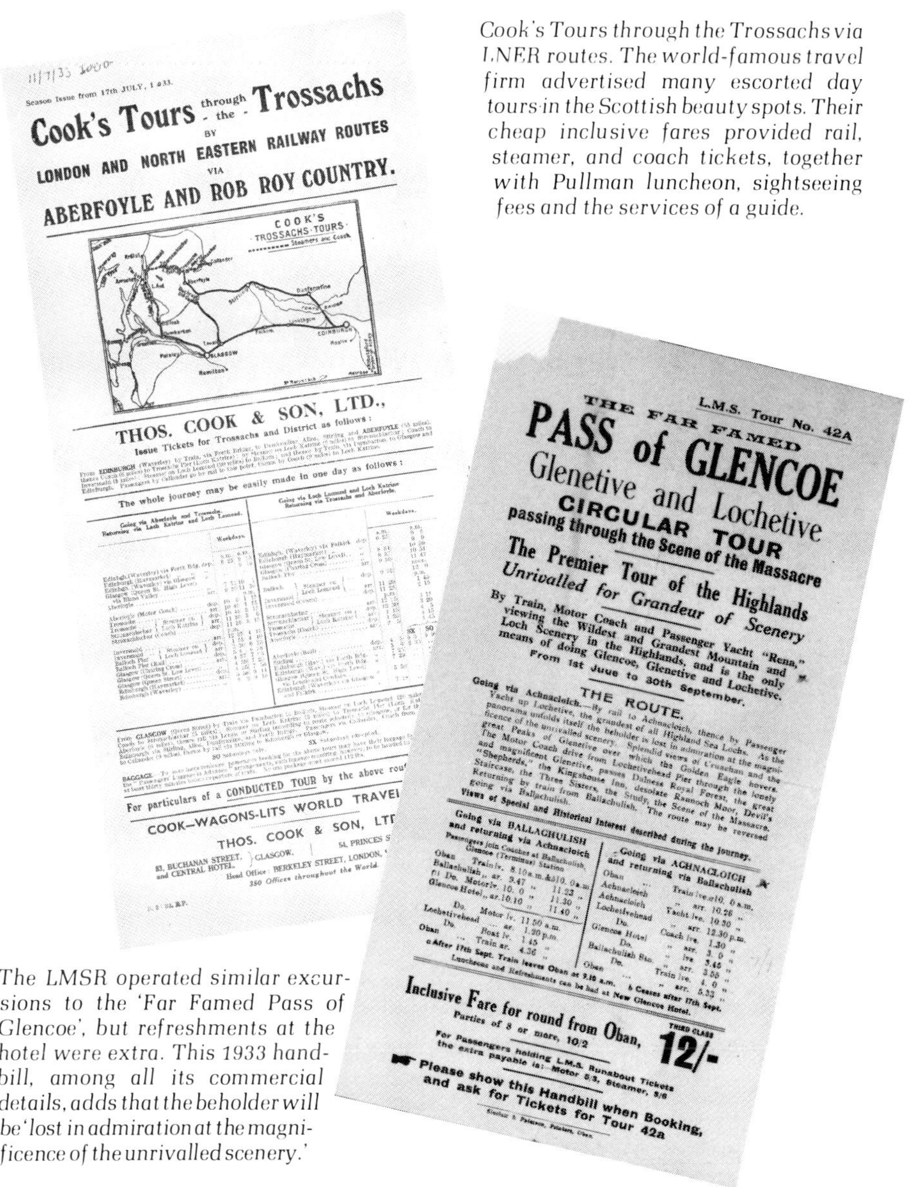

Cook's Tours through the Trossachs via LNER routes. The world-famous travel firm advertised many escorted day tours in the Scottish beauty spots. Their cheap inclusive fares provided rail, steamer, and coach tickets, together with Pullman luncheon, sightseeing fees and the services of a guide.

The LMSR operated similar excursions to the 'Far Famed Pass of Glencoe', but refreshments at the hotel were extra. This 1933 handbill, among all its commercial details, adds that the beholder will be 'lost in admiration at the magnificence of the unrivalled scenery.'

In the same year, by arrangement with Southern Railway (noted for its cheap fares), Cook's were running day excursions at half-day fares. For as little as 5s 6d return, a third-class passenger could travel to Brighton from London (Victoria); the sum of 8s would take a third-class day tripper from Waterloo to Yarmouth, Isle of Wight. In all probability, specially printed tickets for these trips would not have been necessary, the standard excursion ticket for the journey being all that was required.

If Wales had been virtually inaccessible when Thomas Cook's excursionists

COOK'S SATURDAY TRIPS

(For Monday Excursions, see previous pages)

July 22nd, 29th, August 12th, 19th, 26th, September 2nd, 9th, 16th, 23rd and 30th

To—

BRIGHTON

RETURN FARES—THIRD CLASS.

From	Fare
VICTORIA, LONDON BRIDGE	6 6
Clapham Junction and New Cross Gate	6 3
Wandsworth Common, Forest Hill and Balham	6 0
Streatham Common and Norbury	5 9
Thornton Heath and Selhurst	5 6
East Croydon	5 3
Sydenham, Penge West and Anerley	5 9
Norwood Junction	5 6
Tulse Hill	6 3
Crystal Palace	5 9

To—

HOVE

SHOREHAM-BY-SEA

WORTHING

WEST WORTHING

RETURN FARES—THIRD CLASS.

From			
VICTORIA, LONDON BRIDGE	6/6	7/3	7/9

For Conditions of Issue of Tickets, see page 3

WORKS AND DAY OUTING PARTIES.—Special Trains and Times arranged to suit the convenience of Parties visiting resorts on the Southern Railway. Cheap Fares inclusive of Sightseeing Drives, Meals, etc., if desired. Ask for COOK'S DAY OUTINGS PROGRAMME.

THOS. COOK & SON, LTD.

Head Office: BERKELEY STREET, Piccadilly, LONDON, W.1.

LONDON BRANCH OFFICES:

Travel Cheaply by SOUTHERN RAILWAY

COOK'S MONDAY TRIPS

At Half-Day Fares

(For SATURDAY Day Excursions, see back page.)

July 17th, 24th, 31st, August 14th, 21st, 28th, September 4th, 11th, 18th and 25th

CORRIDOR & RESTAURANT CAR EXCURSION

To—

Destination	Third Class Half-Day Return Fares from all Stations (s. d.)
WINCHESTER	5 6
SOUTHAMPTON* (WEST), BROCKENHURST, LYMINGTON TOWN (C)	6 6
BOURNEMOUTH (CENTRAL), POOLE	7 0
WAREHAM, CORFE CASTLE	7 6
SWANAGE	8 0
YARMOUTH (I.W.) (C)	8 0

RESTAURANT FACILITIES.

Luncheon will be served on the outward journey and Supper on the return. 2s. 6d. each meal. Meal Tickets should be taken in advance at Cook's Offices shown on back page.

July 17th, 24th, 31st, Aug. 14th, 21st & 28th

ALLHALLOWS-ON-SEA

Change at Gravesend Central.

Return Fare Third Class All Stations 4 0

As listed on this 1933 4-page handbill, issued by the Southern Railway, Thomas Cook & Son organised a wide variety of excursions. The cheap fares, to places as far apart as Margate and Swanage, were inclusive of sightseeing drives and meals; for the longer journeys luncheon and supper tickets could be obtained from Cook's offices.

first visited the mountainous Principality, then it did not remain so for very long. Many years before 1896, the date of one of the earliest surviving advertisements, the North Wales Narrow Gauge Railway (later incorporated into the Welsh Highland Railway) in conjunction with the London and North Western Railway, was organising cheap excursions to Snowdon. The scene of Cook's inspiration for his Welsh Tours could be visited from any of the principal stations in the United Kingdom. Tourist tickets, valid for a period of two calendar months, were issued between May and October, and allowed the holders of such tickets to break their journey at any of the North Wales pleasure resorts; they could complete the outward journey 'any fine day'.

The Great Western Railway later operated a similar scheme, advertising a 'Tour of the Welsh Highland Railway Through Glorious Welsh Mountain Scenery including Snowdon and the Famous Pass of Aberglaslyn.' The Midland Counties line, later a constituent company of the Midland Railway, eventually ran its metals out to the port of Caernarfon. When, after re-grouping, it became part of the London, Midland and Scottish Railway, with a branch line to Dinas Junction, it too offered cheap circular tours and excursions. A special timetable issued in 1935 showed rail links between the LMS, the Welsh Highland Railway, and the Festiniog Railway — '22 miles through a Riot of Splendour'.

Not nearly so glamorous and luxurious as the 'Northern Belle' of the 1930s, the North Wales Land Cruise (W668) is seen entering Caernavon Station on 26 August 1954. A rather dirty GWR 0-6-0 locomotive, No 3207, from the Portmadoc Shed hauls a rake of standard coaches. (The Late J.W. Dunn)

To quote the final sentence of W. Fraser Rae's biography of Thomas Cook — 'It is no exaggeration to say that the Jubilee of the firm of Messrs. Thomas Cook and Son is an event of note as well as interest in the social history of the nineteenth century.' The firm had many imitators, not the least of whom were the railways themselves. They saw the immense popularity of the excursions and, calling on Cook's vast experience and knowledge, they set out to organise their own trips on similar lines.

At the same time that Thomas Cook was organising one of the earliest trips to the Continent over the lines of the Eastern Counties Railway, by way of Harwich, the company was taking a leaf out of his book. On Monday, 16 July 1855, a dance was held in the ballroom of Rye House, the gardens of which were open to the public. The Eastern Counties Railway produced a delightful pictorial ticket for their excursion to the house and gardens. The tickets were headed by a drawing of one of the company's locomotives hauling two first-class coaches and two second-class coaches. The fare, 'There and Back, 2s. 6d. Each', included admission to the ballroom. In Gothic type-face it was noted that 'A Quadrille Band and Masters of the Ceremonies are engaged'.

In 1853, only two days after its opening, the Deeside Railway was keeping its promise to afford the inhabitants of Aberdeen the opportunity of breathing fresh air. The local paper, the *Aberdeen Herald*, carried advertisements announcing special excursions to Banchory, at that time a favourite beauty spot of the Aberdonians. Less than one week after its opening, in collaboration with the Temperance Society of Aberdeen, the railway company was running excursion trains, some composed entirely of first-class coaches. In making this early bid for the tourist traffic, the directors of the Deeside Railway did not forget the less fortunate citizens of

Aberdeen. In a magnanimous gesture during the summer of 1854, they offered the use of a third-class carriage gratis, for an excursion to Banchory for the benefit of 'Blind Persons attending the Asylum for the Blind.' To cater for the Aberdeen annual holiday traffic, the Deeside Railway announced in July of the same year that excursion tickets to all stations on the line would be issued from Aberdeen.

Bank holidays were first established by Sir John Lubbock's (later Lord Avebury) Parliamentary Act of 1871. The railway companies saw in the newly legalised holidays a chance of taking extra revenue by running excursions. For several years, however, the North Western Railway fought shy of the idea; its directors considered the notion of organising such trips as a nuisance, with the running of special trains upsetting the tidiness of their standard timetable. Presumably, they had such a weight of ordinary traffic that they considered the running of 'extras' as an unbusinesslike proposition.

Fortunately for their shareholders, few railway companies still thought in such negative terms; most took advantage of the business opportunities offered by the natural amenities around them. One such opportunist company was the Severn and Wye and Severn Bridge Railway, who, in 1890, advertised excursions to the Forest of Dean. Pleasure parties wishing

---

Offering the traveller a return journey as part of the same trip at a price slightly less than two singles seems also to have inspired ticket designers. Everything from straightforwardly simple to extravagantly colourful designs have been used.

0403 London & North Eastern Railway Ferry (toll paid), brick-red with horizontal dark red overprint, issued 24 June 1981, more than 33 years after nationalisation.

1529 Great Western Railway monthly return, light blue goemetric pattern safety background, unissued.

4850 Sligo, Leitrim, and Northern Counties Railway six-day return, light blue overprint on white card. The SL & NCR was authorised in 1875, and opened in sections between 1879 and 1882.

4356 London & North Eastern Railway monthly return, light green with overprint red 'R', unissued. A simple easy-to-read design.

767 Waterford & Limerick Railway first class return, yellow, unissued. The company was authorised in 1826, but not brought into being until twenty years later as the Waterford, Limerick, and Western Railway. It opened in sections between 1848 and 1895, and became part of the Great Southern of Ireland Railway in 1924.

464 Londonderry & Lough Swilly Railway third class, horizontal red overprint on white, unissued. The company was taken over in December 1887, by the mortgagees, the Dublin Board of Works.

0102 Manx Electric Railway, one return journey, period unspecified, date of issue unknown. With red diagonal overprint on white, the ticket is printed, 'Punch' style. The MER was formed in 1902, bringing together the Manx Electric and the Snaefell Mountain Tramway.

8203 Festiniog Railway third class, light green, unissued. Built to service the slate quarries of the Blaenau Ffestiniog district, and opened in 1836, it was the first narroe-gauge railway in the world.

2370 Sheffield Corporation, LMS & LNER Railways Joint Omnibus Committee, slate blue with red overprint. The ticket, of Punch type, was available for one journey in each direction on the stage indicated by the punch hole.

1640 Corris Railway third class one week (privilege ticket), light blue horizontal overprint, issued 29 January 1909. The line was opened in 1859 to serve the Corris Slate Quarries, and in 1864 changed its name from Corris, Machynlleth, and River Dovey Tramroad Company. The first passenger train ran on 18 June 1883.

L. N. E. R. FERRY
TOLL PAID
TRAILER
Under 5 Cwts.
NEW HOLLAND PIER
TO
HULL (C. PIER)
PAID INC. TOLL 6s.2d.P
For conditions of issue see back.
L. N. E. R. FERRY
(TOLL PAID)
TRAILER
Under 5 Cwts.
HULL (C. PIER)
TO
NEW HOLLAND PIER
PAID INC. TOLL 6s.2d.P
For conditions of issue see back.
0403

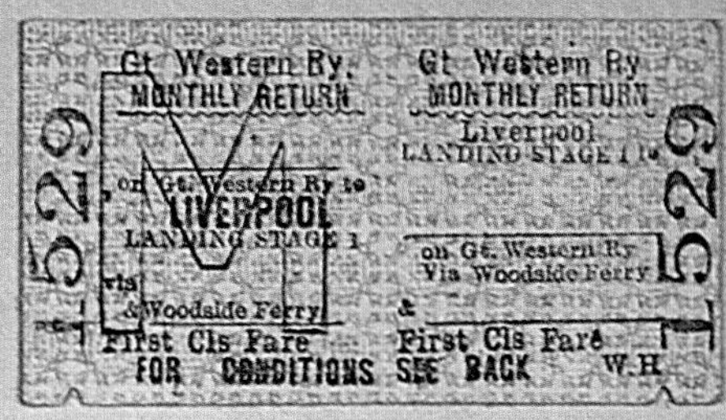
Gt. Western Ry.
MONTHLY RETURN
LIVERPOOL
LANDING STAGE 1
via Woodside Ferry
First Cls Fare
FOR CONDITIONS
Gt. Western Ry.
MONTHLY RETURN
Liverpool
LANDING STAGE 1
on Gt. Western Ry
Via Woodside Ferry
First Cls Fare
SEE BACK
1529

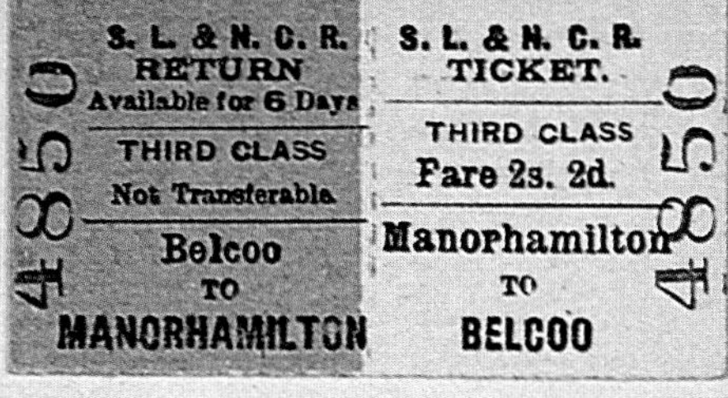
S. L. & N. C. R.
RETURN
Available for 6 Days
THIRD CLASS
Not Transferable
Belcoo
TO
MANORHAMILTON
S. L. & N. C. R.
TICKET.
THIRD CLASS
Fare 2s. 2d.
Manorhamilton
TO
BELCOO
4850

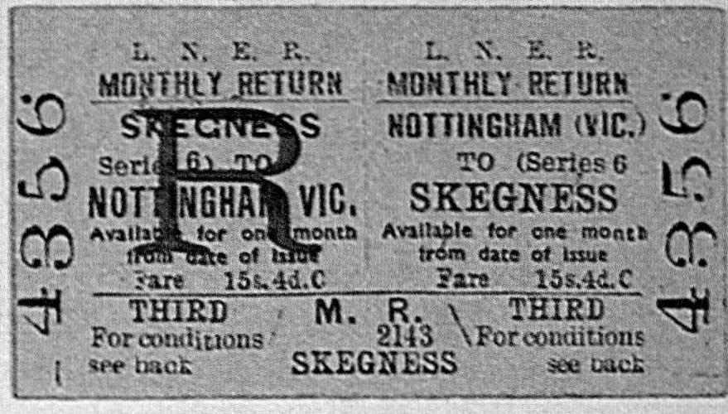
L. N. E. R.
MONTHLY RETURN
SKEGNESS
NOTTINGHAM VIC.
THIRD
For conditions see back
L. N. E. R.
MONTHLY RETURN
NOTTINGHAM (VIC.)
TO (Series 6
SKEGNESS
Available for one month from date of issue
Fare 15s.4d.C
THIRD
For conditions see back
M. R.
2143
SKEGNESS
R
4356

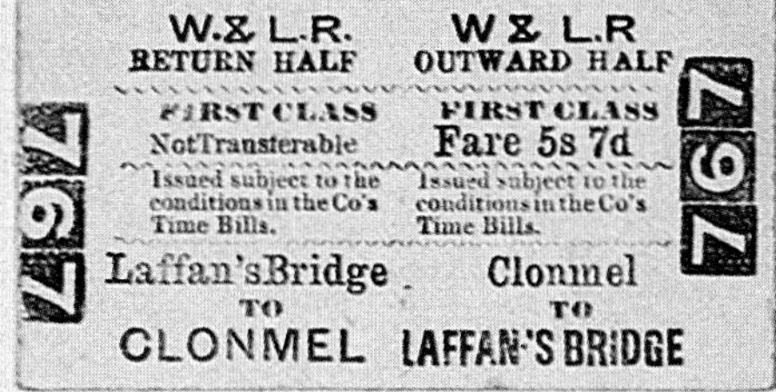
W.& L.R.
RETURN HALF
FIRST CLASS
Not Transferable
Issued subject to the conditions in the Co's Time Bills.
Laffan's Bridge
TO
CLONMEL
W & L.R
OUTWARD HALF
FIRST CLASS
Fare 5s 7d
Issued subject to the conditions in the Co's Time Bills.
Clonmel
TO
LAFFAN'S BRIDGE
767

L. & L. S. Rlv.
SAT to MON RETURN
THIRD CLASS
Available from Saturday or Sunday to Monday
Not Transferable
Kincasslagh Rd
to LETTERKENNY
L. & L. S. Rlv.
SAT to MON TICKET
THIRD CLASS
Fare
Letterkenny to
KINCASSLAGH RD
Kincasslagh Rd
464

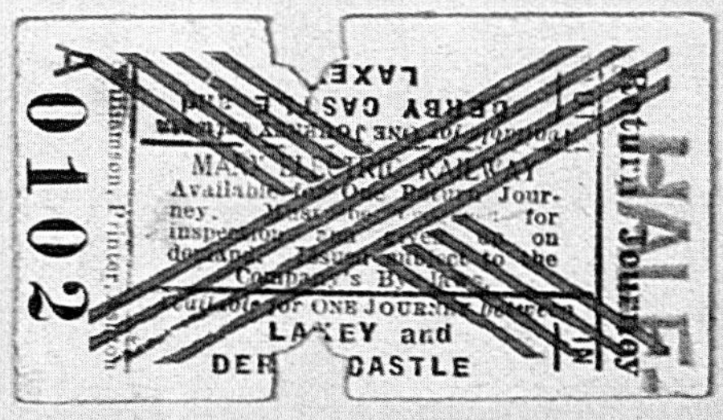
0102
HALF
LAXEY and
DERBY CASTLE

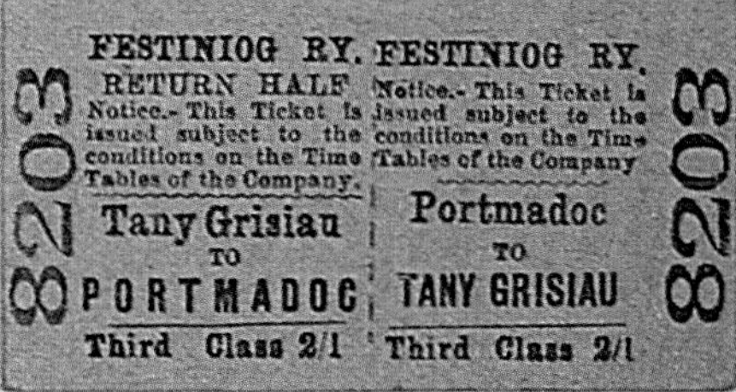
FESTINIOG RY.
RETURN HALF
Notice.- This Ticket is issued subject to the conditions on the Time Tables of the Company.
Tany Grisiau
TO
PORTMADOC
Third Class 2/1
FESTINIOG RY.
Notice.- This Ticket is issued subject to the conditions on the Time Tables of the Company
Portmadoc
TO
TANY GRISIAU
Third Class 2/1
8203

E 2370
2/5
RETURN
RETURN TICKET
1 2 3 4 5 6 7 8 9 10 11 12
13 14 15 16 17 18 19 20 21 22 23 24

Corris Railway.
P.T.
Available One Month
Aberllefeni
2 TO
MACHYNLLETH
Third Class
3d.
Corris Railway
Available One Week
P.T.
Machynlleth
TO 1
ABERLLEFENI
Third Class
3d.
1640

D.&B.J'nt Line
Cabin & Third Class.
Garelochhead (N. B.) TO DUMBARTON
Via Craigendoran
1
(Over.) Garelochhead N.B.
D.&B.J'nt Line
Third Class & Cabin.
Dumbarton TO GARELOCHHEAD (N. B.)
Via Craigendoran
Actual Fare 3/3
1271

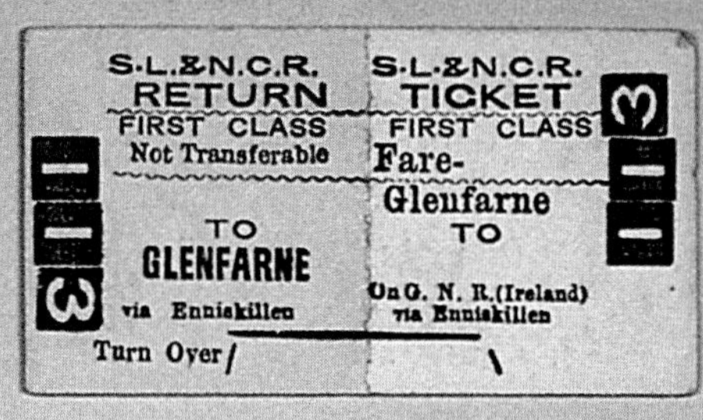
S.L.&N.C.R.
RETURN
FIRST CLASS
Not Transferable
TO
GLENFARNE
via Enniskillen
Turn Over
S.L.&N.C.R.
TICKET
FIRST CLASS
Fare-
Glenfarne
TO
On G. N. R. (Ireland)
via Enniskillen

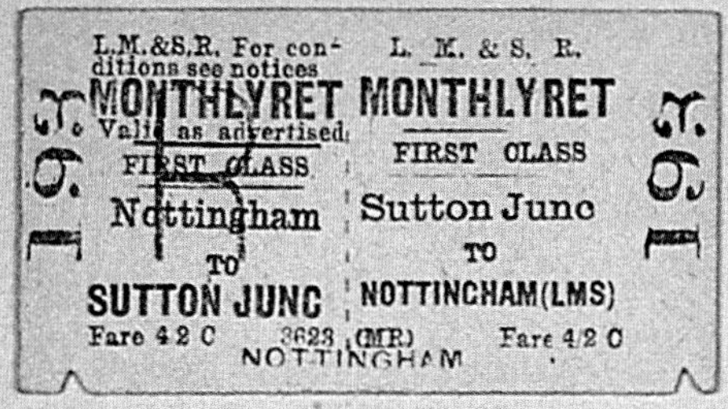
L.M.&S.R. For conditions see notices
MONTHLYRET
Valid as advertised
FIRST CLASS
Nottingham
TO
SUTTON JUNC
Fare 4/2 C
L. M. & S. R.
MONTHLYRET
FIRST CLASS
Sutton Junc
TO
NOTTINGHAM(LMS)
Fare 4/2 C
3623 (MR)
NOTTINGHAM
193

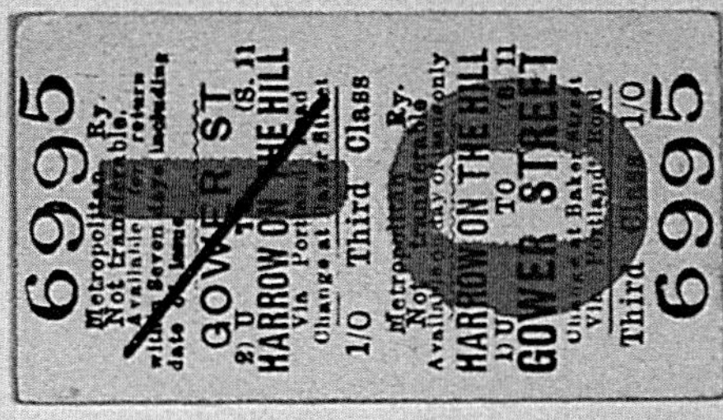
6995
GOWER ST
HARROW ON THE HILL
1/0 Third Class
HARROW ON THE HILL
TO
GOWER STREET
Third Class 1/0
6995

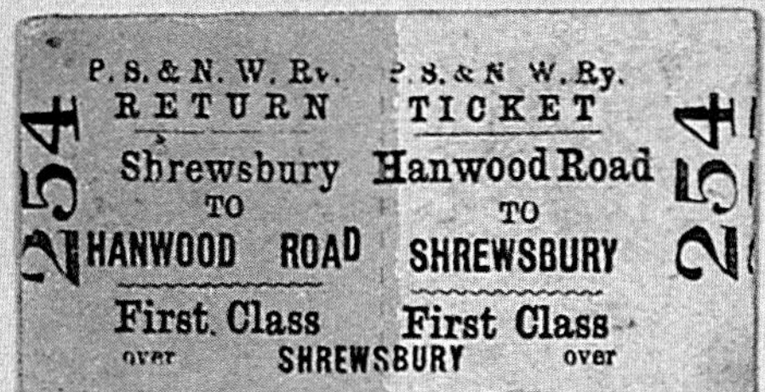
P. S. & N. W. Ry.
RETURN
Shrewsbury
TO
HANWOOD ROAD
First Class
over
P. S. & N. W. Ry.
TICKET
Hanwood Road
TO
SHREWSBURY
First Class
over
SHREWSBURY
254

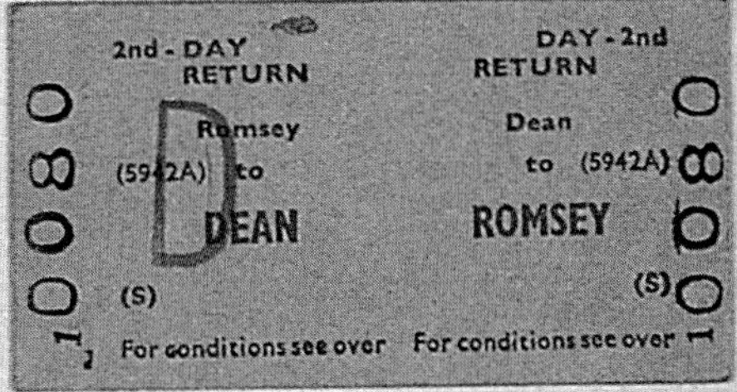
2nd - DAY
RETURN
Romsey
(5942A) to
DEAN
(S)
For conditions see over
DAY - 2nd
RETURN
Dean
to (5942A)
ROMSEY
(S)
For conditions see over
10080

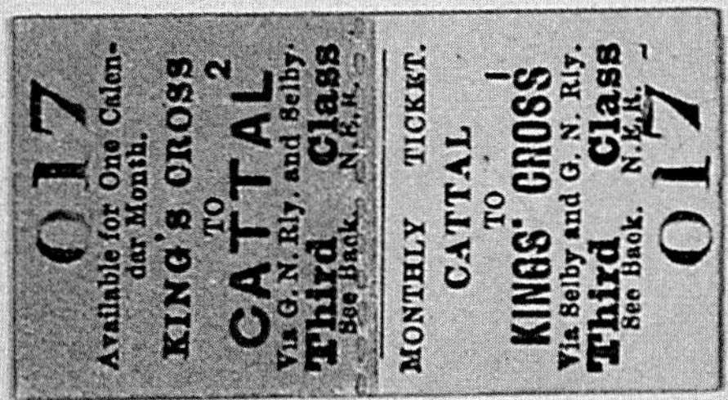
017
Available for One Calendar Month.
KING'S CROSS
TO
CATTAL
Via G. N. Rly. and Selby.
Third Class
See Back.
N.E.R.
MONTHLY TICKET.
CATTAL
TO
KINGS' CROSS
Via Selby and G. N. Rly.
Third Class
See Back.
N.E.R.
017

M. S. J. & A. R.
MONTHLY RETURN
SALE
(Series 16) TO
ALTRINCHAM and BOWDON
Available for one month from date of issue
Fare 8½d.P
THIRD
For Conditions see back
M. S. J. & A. R.
MONTHLY RETURN
ALTRINCHAM and BOWDON
TO (Series 16)
SALE
Available for one month from date of issue
Fare 8½d.P
THIRD
For Conditions see back
M. R.
1982
SALE
1221

L. N. E. R.
MERCANTILE
KING'S CROSS
TO
HULL
Via Doncaster
Available for three months from date of issue
FIRST
For conditions see back
L N E R
MERCANTILE
HULL
TO
KING'S CROSS
Via Doncaster
Available for three months from date of issue
FIRST
For conditions see back
SPECIMEN
0962

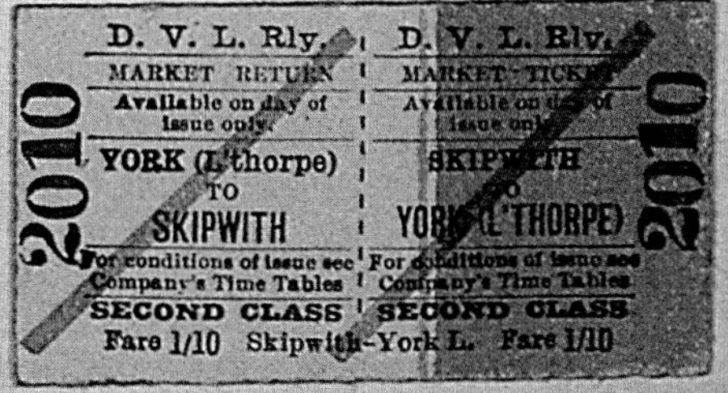
D. V. L. Rly.
MARKET RETURN
Available on day of issue only.
YORK (L'thorpe)
TO
SKIPWITH
For conditions of issue see Company's Time Tables
SECOND CLASS
Fare 1/10
D. V. L. Rly.
MARKET TICKET
Available on day of issue only.
SKIPWITH
TO
YORK (L'THORPE)
For conditions of issue see Company's Time Tables
SECOND CLASS
Fare 1/10
Skipwith-York L.
2010

The 'Northern Belle', seen here near Glenfinnan, was a first class 1930s cruising train. Throughout the summer it left London for a week's tour of the most famous Scottish beauty spots. The special tickets were kept as prestigious souvenirs. (Photo: Gallaher Limited).

Return tickets.

1271 Dumbarton & Balloch Joint Line (third class & cabin). Originally part of the North British, West Highland, and LNE Railways, the company operated to connect with the Loch Lomond steamers.

113 Sligo, Leitrim & Northern Counties Railway first class, yellow overprint on white, unissued.

193 London, Midland & Scottish Railway first class monthly, white, unissued.

6995 Metropolitan Railway third class, light brown with red overprints and black station cancellation, issued 25 September 1904. Vertical printing was done on a random basis, receiving a mixed reception from the ticket staff.

254 Potteries, Shrewsbury, & North Wales Railway first class, yellow overprint on white, unissued. The company was formed in 1865 as an amalgamation of two companies, later taking over the Oswestry and Llangynog line.

0080 British Railways Board day return, pink with green overprint, issued 27 September 1983.

017 North Eastern Railway third class monthly, light brown with drab overprint, unissued. The ticket was intended for use on the lines of the Great Northern Railway (incorporated 1846). The North Eastern came into being through amalgamations made between 1854 and 1865.

1221 Manchester, South Junction & Altrincham Railway third class monthly, green with red 'R' overprint,unissued. Incorporated in 1845, the line was electrified in 1931, being the first in Great Britain to operate on the DC system.

0962 London & North Eastern Railway mercantile (three months' return), stone coloured with red 'R' overprint. This ticket was not issued, but instead, stamped as 'specimen' and sent to the line superintendent for issue to the booking office for a further supply of similar tickets. 'Mercantile' type tickets were for the use of merchant seamen.

2010 Derwent Valley Light Railway second class market return, light green overprint on light brown with red diagonal lines, unissued. The DVLR was opened during the year 1912-13, by which time it had passed into the hands of the North Eastern Railway. It closed to pasenger to traffic in 1926.

The camping coaches provided a novel kind of holiday situated in beautiful localities. Under the charge and supervision of the local station-master, they were fully equipped.

to make the journey could hire a picnic carriage, to seat about twelve persons, on application to the general manager at Lydney. For the modest sum of about 1s 9d per head in addition to the first-class fare, parties could have the use of dinner and tea services, plate, glass, linen, and even an attendant. They allowed the special carriage to be left at pre-selected sidings which gave easy access to various picturesque areas of the forest. Whether distinctive non-standard tickets were printed for the excursions does not seem to have been recorded.

This idea, somewhat similar to the camping coaches of later years, was extended by the London and North Eastern Railway in 1933 with their 'Northern Belle' Land Cruises. These were something in the nature of the railway company's answer to the then current fashion of liner cruising. They became an immense success, with four cruises being run during the month of June each year. Each cruise was just over 2,000 miles, and the passengers (no more than sixty in number) paid £20 for a week's holiday by train. The 'Northern Belle' steamed out of King's Cross Station at 9 o'clock on Friday night, a single 'Pacific' type locomotive hauling fifteen first-class coaches full of excited passengers to the delights of a holiday in the Scottish Highlands. For the part of the cruise actually in the Highlands, two locomotives were used to haul the train, which carried its staff of twenty-seven and a 'host' in their own quarters. Special tickets were issued for the 'Northern Belle' which were afterwards retained as souvenirs by the passengers. The 'Northern Belle' was almost as self-contained as a liner, and was indeed a luxury hotel on wheels. That it was the most luxurious train in Europe is a matter for conjecture, but certainly it was the most unusual. There was a lounge and observation saloon, a writing room with a postbox (letters could be sent from and received on the train), and a special retiring-room for ladies. The train also included among its many facilities a

A picture which illustrates how careful conversion could transform an ordinary railway carriage into a camping coach for a family party. It is taken from a 1936 Holiday Haunts *handbook published by the GWR, whose several hundred pages list boarding houses, hotels, and other tourist facilities available throughout the area served by the railway company. The other three of the 'Big Four' railways published similar volumes.*

One of many kinds of bookmarker issued by the GWR. These were given away with the more expensive company publications, but could be purchased separately. They advertised special tourist areas covered by the railway company, gave timetable and fares details, or had calendar information.

shop, which was a combination of a provincial newsagent, tobacconist and sub-post office.

Before commencing their Scottish cruise proper, the passengers were taken on a motorcoach trip of the English Lake District, rejoining the

'Northern Belle' at Penrith Station and leaving for Montrose at 7.15pm. During the following week, passengers went on extensive coach and steamer tours through the Scottish Highlands. While the passengers spent many happy hours cruising on the lochs, the train continued round the coast to await them at Ardlui or Craigendoran Piers. On the beautifully scenic journey between Mallaig and Fort William, the 'Northern Belle' stopped half-way across the Glenfinnan Viaduct so that passengers could admire the splendid views along Loch Shiel and the glen.

With the number of passengers on these land cruises being limited to 240 per year, it became almost a fashionable social event, with few people being able to boast of having been a member of a 'Northern Belle' cruise party.

In the same year that it introduced the land cruise, the London and North Eastern Railway Company also pioneered the camping coach. As the land cruises catered for the holiday-maker who demanded luxury on wheels, with cost of no great concern, so the camping coach met the requirements of those who wanted an inexpensive vacation. The project was surprisingly popular. The other three members of the 'Big Four' copied the idea in 1934, and in less than two years the number of coaches available throughout Britain jumped from ten to more than two hundred, with the number of campers running into several thousands.

The camping coach, located at some fixed spot, was an obsolete passenger coach converted into a holiday home for six persons, for which an average of £3 per week was paid. Remaining as it did on some quiet branch line siding, the camping coach gave the campers a new look at the British scenery. Sites were available throughout most of the traditional beauty spots in the British Isles, allowing campers the chance to enjoy every variety of scenery from the moors of Cornwall and Devon, the Welsh mountains, the English Lakes and Fens, to the Highlands of Scotland. Each of the 'Big Four' railway companies made it a rule that parties hiring a camping coach had to travel to the site by rail, for which special tickets were issued.

With Thomas Cook having firmly established the idea of railway excursions, and the Bank Holiday being a firmly established concept, it is hardly surprising that the railways, for the most part, took up the challenge offered to them, and organised excursions for every conceivable occasion to every possible venue. Special tickets were produced in prodigious numbers, adding to already swollen stocks, with timetable handbills joining the massive printing output of the companies. To judge by the popularity of the majority of these excursions, the extra printing could hardly have been an economic detriment. Even newly founded railways made an immediate bid for the tourist traffic. Early in 1881, the Swindon, Marlborough, and Andover Railway was opened, and in August of the same year its directors took the alarming step of suspending the ordinary train services. The reason for this extraordinary action was so that special trains, running at ninety minute intervals, could convey Bank Holiday picnickers to Savernake Forest, returning to Swindon in the evening. The line was later incorporated into the Midland and South Western Junction Railway.

The railway companies did not only promote holiday excursions, but

THE WONDER OF 1851!

FROM YORK

TO LONDON AND BACK FOR A CROWN.

THE MIDLAND RAILWAY COMPANY

Will continue to run

TWO TRAINS DAILY

(Excepted Sunday, when only one Train is available)

FOR THE GREAT EXHIBITION,

UNTIL SATURDAY, OCTOBER 11,

Without any Advance of

RETURN SPECIAL TRAINS leave the Euston Station on MONDAYS, TUESDAYS, THURSDAYS, & SATURDAYS at 11 a.m., on WEDNESDAYS and FRIDAYS at 1 p.m., and EVERY NIGHT (Sundays excepted) at 9 p.m.

First and Second Class Tickets are available for returning any day (except Sunday) up to and including Monday, Oct. 20. Third Class Tickets issued before the 6th instant are available for 14 days, and all issued after the 6th are returnable any day up to Monday the 20th.

The Trains leave York at 9-40 a.m. every day except Sunday, and also every day, including Sunday, at 7-20 p.m.

Fares to London and Back:—

1st Class 15s. 2nd, 10s. 3rd, 5s.

The Midland is the only Company that runs Trains Daily at these Fares.

Ask for Midland Tickets!

Children above 3 and under 12 years of age, Half-price. Luggage allowed—112 lbs. to First Class, 100 lbs. to Second, and 56 lbs. to Third Class Passengers.

APPROVED LODGINGS, of all classes, are provided in London for Passengers by Midland Trains. The Agents will give Tickets of reference on application, without charge, and an Office is opened in London, at DONALD'S WATERLOO DINING ROOMS, 14, Seymour-street, near Euston Station, where an agent is in regular attendance to conduct parties who go up unprepared with Lodgings.

The Managers have much pleasure in stating that the immense numbers who have travelled under their arrangements have been conducted in perfect safety—indeed in the history of the Midland Lines, *no accident, attended with personal injury, has ever happened to an Excursion Train.* In conducting the extraordinary traffic of this Great Occasion the first object is to ensure *safety*, and that object has hitherto been most happily achieved.

With the fullest confidence, inspired by past success, the Conductors have pleasure in urging those who have not yet visited the Exhibition, to avail themselves of the present facilities, and to improve the opportunity which will close on the 11th of October.

All communications respecting the Trains to be addressed to the Managers, for the Company,

John Cattle & John Calverley, Wakefield;
Thomas Cook, Leicester.

October 2nd, 1851.

T. COOK, PRINTER, 28, GRANBY-STREET, LEICESTER.

Handbill printed and published by Thomas Cook advertising twice-daily trips on 'Return Special Trains' for the Great Exhibition in London in 1851. More than 160,000 of Cook's excursionists were taken by rail to see the famous Crystal Palace.

coaxed their passengers into Saturday afternoon and Sunday trips. During the early 1900s, the Somerset and Dorset Railway organised afternoon excursions to the Mendip Hills. Passengers on these excursions were especially informed of the picturesque scenery, and were encouraged to alight at Wells to visit the magnificent cathedral.

A fine colourful advertising give away by the Caledonian Railway; the exuberant descriptions are a delight, especially the cartouche on the right of the illustration. The reverse of the card carries details of tickets and 'New Trains De Luxe', tourist literature, a picture of Glasgow Central Station, and a calendar for 1906.

As mentioned previously, the Great Western Railway Company was famous for its publicity artwork. The traditional beauty spots of the West Country, from the Cornish Riviera to the rolling Downs of Wiltshire, were all covered by the company, known affectionately as 'God's Wonderful Railway'. Publicity artists of high calibre were employed by the company to exploit this scenic advantage, while cunningly worded advertisements draw passengers' attention to special excursions. During the summer months, in various parts of the Great Western territory, 'Pic-Nic and Pleasure Parties' were especially catered for with the issue of one day only tickets. For parties of not less than six first-class, or ten second or third-class passengers, reduced rates were available; in order to obtain the concession fare, a member of the party was required to apply for the necessary tickets three days before the advertised date of the excursion.

But excursions were not organised solely to beauty spots. If an annual event was promoted within easy access of the company's territory, that was reason enough to organise an excursion, issue special tickets in vivid colours, and print handbills and timetables to advertise it. One such event was the August Onion Fair held in Birmingham. Another, more widely known event, the Henley Regatta, was the venue for a Great Western excursion in the 1890s from Hereford. Special handbill timetables announced the details under the boldly printed sub-heading: 'At about a Single Fare and a Quarter for the Double Journey'.

After Thomas Cook's initial venture with railway excursions, the idea had become so much of a social habit that independent organisations regarded the whole activity as something commonplace, something to be taken for granted. In the year of the Great Exhibition, when Cook had taken more than 160,000 excursionists to see the famous Palace of Glass, the *London Directory* was published. The publication ran to more than 900 pages of very fine print, and included a 25-page section entitled 'Excursions to the Vicinity of London'. Clearly, the concept of excursions, pioneered by

Thomas Cook a decade previously, was a socially acceptable pursuit. The reader was informed that 'The neighbourhood of London abounds in the many-varying objects of interest for the instruction and pleasure of the stranger and the native.' The introduction goes on to say: '. . . we are yet desirous of adding to our task by inducing the stranger, by means of our railways, to visit the following places — particularly gratifying to persons of taste and refinement.' Then follows detailed descriptions of the surrounding countryside, which was accessible by the Great Western or South Western Railways. The reader was also apprised of Oxford and Cambridge, which could be visited by the Great Western and Eastern Counties Railways.

The directory has some very interesting and revealing things to say about the railways of the day. Eight main stations are enumerated and 'a small but highly valuable link in the general system of railway traffic, viz, the Birmingham and East and West India Docks Railway, is hardly complete enough to justify our doing more than thus to call attention to the many very remarkable and beautiful works comprised within its length.' The Paddington terminus of the Great Western Railway is described as 'ill-considered' in its arrangements even though acknowledged as being temporary. At this stage in their history the Great Western Railway was not, apparently, publicity conscious.

Travellers approached the Great Western Railway booking office from Bishop's Road, by an incline betweeen the canal on the east, and the goods station on the west. There were two departure lines, one reserved for long, and the other for short trains. Spare lines were laid under cover, to hold the trains already made up for departure, and the carriages being held in readiness for use. The distribution of luggage was regarded as the best in London, being 'ingeniously and effectually supplied by a series of traversing platforms.'

This is in direct contrast to the Dover, Brighton, and South Coast Railway whose casual indifference in their treatment of passengers' luggage and effects was the subject of much contemporary satire. The luggage was 'seized upon' at the time of departure, and carried by the porters to the vans or carriages. Once inside the luggage vans it was left to chance, 'for no precaution is taken to protect the contents of the luggage vans against the attacks of the London thieves.' The London terminus at this time housed the booking offices of the North Kent Railway, and the Greenwich Railway; the Dover booking office, although in the same building complex, was separate from the booking-office of the Brighton and South Coast Line. It would seem that there was a strong case for the railway companies to have amalgamated their ticket issuing systems, with the advantage of all tickets being available at a central office.

The London and North Western Terminus had been the subject of much alteration, its original design and function having been surpassed by the phenomenal development of the railways. By the year 1851, thanks to the company's directors having taken the precaution of buying more land than they needed at the time, much-needed building extensions were completed. The compiler of the *London Directory* reckoned the accommodations to have kept pace with the demands for them, and cited the terminus as being the most perfect and the most commodious of any. The passenger station occupied a site of about twelve acres near Euston Square, and each day, not less than eighteen trains each way were despatched and received. If all the trains had been filled to capacity the booking office clerks would have been rushed off their feet issuing tickets. But apparently 'The operations necessary . . . are carried on with so little noise, confusion, or semblance of bustle, that it would almost seem that these complicated arrangements acted of their own accord.'

Fourteen years later, anxious to preserve its reputation for efficiency and service, and in response to repeated requests, the North Western Railway inaugurated its Scottish 'Tourist' express. A stop was made at Greenock which allowed passengers to board the steamer *Iona*. This was the first direct link to Scotland, and was run jointly with the Caledonian Railway, for which tickets allowing passage throughout were issued. The 'Tourist' express proved to be extremely popular, and for several years ran throughout August until late October.

Earlier, when discussing platform tickets, and later, when describing the scene of Cook's first excursion, reference was made to non-travellers crowding on to station platforms. Thoughts on this subject had occurred to the compiler of the *London Directory*,

> The entrance to the station is through the gigantic and very absurd Doric Temple placed in the centre line of Euston Square; facing it is a large, massive, plain range of buildings containing the offices, waitingroom, and board and meeting-rooms of this Company [London and North Western Railway]. Passengers pass firstly into an immense and beautiful hall, with a ludicrous cage for the sale of refreshments in the centre; those who intend to travel by the main northerly lines, proceed to the booking-offices on the east side; those who intend to travel by the midland lines, proceed to the booking-offices, &c., on the west side, from which also it is usual to start the express trains. The booking offices are very fine specimens of architecture, but the waiting rooms are far from corresponding with them in magnificence. At foreign railway stations passengers are not allowed to go upon the platform until just before the time for departure; in England, the practice is to allow the public access to all parts of the station devoted to the dispatch of the trains.

Quite extensive information concerning the London and North Western Railway was listed in the 1851 *Directory*, most of it concerned with the architectural merits of the buildings and the wisdom of the company's directors in foreseeing the development of the traffic. But among the eulogies about the locomotive sheds and the carriage repair shops there is nothing about tickets and administration.

The site of the Great Northern Railway station was on that of the old Fever Hospital in King's Cross, although at the time of the compiling of the *Directory* it was not yet in its permanent form. The temporary station was set on a wide road leading from King's Cross on the north side of the Regent's Canal, and the booking-offices and waiting-rooms were placed parallel to the outgoing line.

The terminus of the Eastern Counties Railway Company, although small and confined, was approached from the street by a spacious court. This gave access to the company's offices and the booking-offices. The ticket

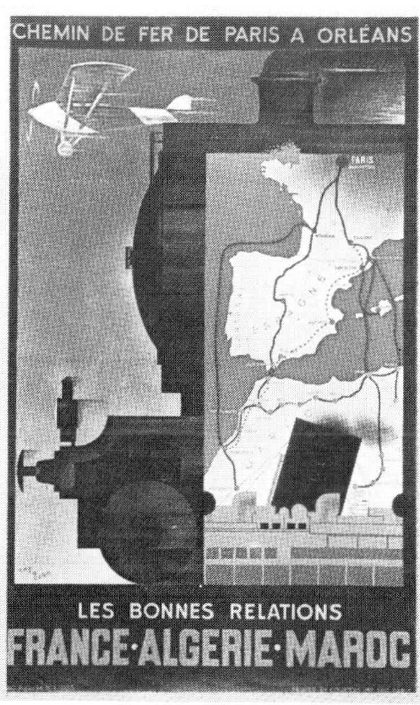

Four examples of French railway advertising from the early 1930s. Like their British counterparts, famous and outstanding artists of the day were specially commissioned to produce the pictures which were then printed and bill-posted on some convenient hoarding. They were works of art in their own right, many of them chromo-lithographed, and yet their ultimate fate was to be torn down, or pasted over with some other public notice.

platform was situated on the arrival line, but the company had just begun to adopt the plan of collecting tickets at the last station on the line before arriving in town. This was generally regarded as a wise move, since it saved the passengers at least ten minutes unnecessary delay. Such delays were commonplace on the other railway lines where tickets were collected at a station established solely for that purpose.

If the Eastern Counties Railway had been wise and efficient in its business in 1851, such commendation could not be given to a line which they later bought out. The directors of the Norfolk Railway, which was opened in 1845, saw the tremendous impact of excursion traffic, and they were determined to have their share of it. An excursion from Norwich to Yarmouth was organised for 30 June 1846, and was widely advertised in the local papers. Perhaps a little inexperienced in railway management, and not a little greedy for extra custom, the directors sought to attract excursionists by charging an absurdly low fare — the return fare for children was only 3d! The response to the advertisements was staggering, for almost six thousand people took advantage of the offer, which must have overwhelmed the booking clerks. There does not appear to be any record of if this vast crowd was supplied with tickets or how it was conveyed on the advertised trip, but the mistake was never repeated.

The passenger station of the Blackwall Railway Company was described as a building 'very plain and unpretending in character', set in a crowded part of the town, and with an 'access of great difficulty'. The booking office was on the ground floor, with staircases leading to and from the arrival and departure platforms. With the use of a complicated system of slip-coaching, and two through crossings without any turn-table whatever, arrivals and departures were effected every fifteen minutes, in each direction. Considering that the 'terribly cramped position of the station' in Fenchurch Street served two railway companies, whose trains had to arrive and depart on the same line, this was excellent service. Quite obviously the booking office had to match such efficiency with its ticket distribution. The compiler of the *Directory* commented, 'the branch line suburban traffic becomes so far exceptional in their arrangements, even more than those of the lines with more regular traffic.'

Despite the proven success of Thomas Cook's excursions, there was much opposition to this form of travel from both the public and the railways. The Church was very much against commercial activities on Sundays, which tended to lure congregations from their worshipful duties. At one of the preliminary hearings held in connection with the proposed Railway Act of 1842, a clergyman declared that all excursions by railway, held on a Sunday, were 'trips to hell, at seven shillings and sixpence per head'. A Mr Plumptre put forward a proposition aimed at prohibiting all forms of railway activity on 'any part of the Lord's Day'.

During the 1850s, the major railway companies were engaged in a price war. It became their aim to increase regular services rather than to provide price concessions for excursions. Under certain conditions, they reasoned, a loss in takings on regular services could be caused by the provision of price reductions on special trains. Thomas Cook had proved that the excursion train, even with its drastic fare reductions, could be operated at an acceptable profit because of the increased demand. The Parliamentary

The date of this advertising pamphlet is unknown, but is more than likely from the turn of the century when palmistry was very much in fashion. As can be seen, the GCR publicity department was on hand to inform its prospective passengers.

Act which allowed regular holidays for all was as yet twenty years away; only the wealthier members of the public could afford regular travel by train, nor did they need concessionary fares. The working class were very limited as to when, or if, they could indulge in holidays, and they were, in their demands for special trains, very much in the minority. The railways' main objection to excursion trains and the issue of special tickets was that the demand was seasonal, and within certain definable limits during that period.

Eventually the railway companies' objections were either overruled or outdated. The Railway Clearing House (of which more later) was responsible for the member railway companies reaching an agreement, after many meetings, for the development of excursion services. That their proposals were a success can be judged from the fact that in the summer of 1851 a railway journal was able to comment that the countryside was 'alive with excursion trains'.

These railway companies which had previously spurned the operation of excursion specials, acting upon recommendations from the Clearing House, or spurred by competitors' successes in the price war, changed their tactics and began to cater for excursion traffic. The North Eastern Railway, after success with excursions to small resorts along the East Coast, commenced in September 1870 to operate regular runs to Scarborough. This East Coast town, which had been a health resort as long ago as 1620, received a steady influx of visitors brought by train after train. Indeed, so heavy was this excursion traffic, that in 1908 a special station was built to deal with it. On the original excursions, the number of carriages per train was limited and special tickets equal in number to the carriage accommodation were issued. In a strictly enforced regulation only those passengers who held the special excursion tickets were allowed to travel on the train. In the 1930s, evening excursions were run from Leeds, Wakefield, and Hull to Scarborough, the fare being only a few shillings.

In later years the North Midland and Great Northern Joint Railway held an extremely good reputation for their operation of long distance excursions. Running from Norfolk, they were ready to go anywhere, any time; it was not unusual for such trips to finish up in Wales on the metals of the Cambrian Railway. On trips of such magnitude, it was necessary for corridor coaches to be used, most often those of Midland Railway stock. The company did of course operate excursions to more local destinations, which were equally popular. In 1909, they organised 'Combined Tours of the Norfolk Broads by Rail and Motor Launch'. The tours were operated on a weekly basis throughout the season, and a special ticket was issued.

The popularity of the excursion specials in the early years is quite remarkable when one considers the conditions under which passengers had to travel. On regular service trains, third-class passengers travelled for a concession fare, and so they rode in open wagons. Despite the conditions of the 1844 Railway Act, the railway companies treated them as of little account, except when they wanted their support for excursions. The South Eastern Railway ran an excursion to Herne Bay on Whit Monday, 1865, from Charing Cross station; to tempt would-be travellers, they offered a return fare of 2s 6d, and the journey by covered carriage.

The Great Northern Railway had similar promotions when running cheap day excursions to London, King's Cross. Advertisements appeared simultaneously in the London, Manchester, and Liverpool papers, and details were given in timetable form, the fares being quoted at 5s for a closed carriage. In conjunction with through trains to London, the company provided express omnibuses which operated between Liverpool and Garston to convey passengers to the trains, and to meet them on their return.

In 1879 the North British Railway introduced excursions to Dublin from Glasgow, via Silloth, and issued special tourist tickets. These were available for a period of two calendar months from the date of issue. They

The Bournemouth Express, about 1905. London & South Western expresses between London and Bournemouth covered the 108 miles in 2 hours 6 minutes. These trains were exceedingly popular for day and weekend excursions. The picture shows two versions of early Drummond 4-4-0 engines.

were issued to and from Dublin, by way of the stations listed in the timetables, for journeys via the first-class passenger steamer *North British*, or other fast-sailing steamers. Passengers had the option of returning by any steamer during the period for which the ticket was valid. The tickets had to be stamped on board the steamer during the outward journey; passengers were warned that unless such endorsement was received, the company would refuse to recognise the ticket on the return journey. No payment was required of the passenger for the transfer of luggage to and from the steamer. Notice was given on the timetables for the Dublin excursions, of excellent hotels at Silloth, 'where Passengers will meet with every comfort and attention'.

During the period between the turn of the century and the outbreak of World War II, the railway excursion reached its peak. A special ticket was issued by the Great Western Railway for the journey between Aberystwyth and the famous Devil's Bridge. It was a combined 'Rail and Scenery Ticket' which allowed passengers to visit the spectacular waterfalls and picturesque scenery of this Welsh beauty spot. This was but one of many such places on the Great Western system which, in the 1920s and the early 1930s, was covered by tourist ticket facilities. Special tourist programmes were published on a regional basis which gave full details of the tourist tickets available for specified areas throughout the GWR territory.

Eighty years previously, the London and South Western Railway had taken a leaf out of Thomas Cook's book and was running combined rail and sea excursions which proved to be very popular. More than 400 passengers per train set out for Southampton from Nine Elms station. On arrival they embarked on a chartered steamer for an eight-hour cruise round the Isle of Wight. The fare for this remarkable journey was 20s.

Another company which was deservedly famous for its excursion specials was the Southern Railway. Race meetings, regattas, and football matches were sufficient excuse for the operation of a 'Special'. For its Continental service, the all-Pullman 'Golden Arrow' was introduced in

D 613

TRAVEL L M S

WHITSUNTIDE HOLIDAYS, 1931

Whit Monday, May 25th, 1931

Cook's DAY EXCURSIONS to

LONDON (St. Pancras)

FROM	Times of Starting.			RETURN FARES (Third Class). Day Excursion (Rail to St Pancras and back only).	Day Excursion (including Rail & Bus travel in London) (see note)	RETURN ARRANGEMENTS.
	a.m.	a.m.	a.m.	s. d.	s. d.	
Kegworth	—	—	8.25	12 0	14 0	Passengers return same day from LONDON (St. Pancras) at 11.20 p.m. for Kettering (only), at 12.10 midnight for Loughboro' and Kegworth (only) and at 12.15 midnight for all other stations.
Loughboro' ("Mid.")	—	—	8.35	12 0	14 0	
LEICESTER	—	8. 5	—	11 0	13 0	
Nuneaton (Trent V.)*	—	6.42	—	11 0	13 0	
Hinckley	—	6.53	—	11 0	13 0	
Elmesthorpe	—	7. 0	—	11 0	13 0	
Narborough	—	7.12	—	11 0	13 0	
Market Harboro' ...	—	8.30	—	10 0	12 0	
KETTERING ...	3.40	8.50	—	9 1	11 1	
Higham Ferrers ...	—	8.23	—	8 7	10 7	
Rushden	—	8.27	—	8 6	10 6	
Wellingboro' (Mid. R.)	—	9. 2	—	8 3	10 3	
Irchester	—	9. 7	—	7 11	9 11	
London (St. Pan.) arr.	5.29	10.40	11.19			

CHILDREN under three years of age, free; three years and under fourteen, half-fares.

SIGHTSEEING IN LONDON—TRAVEL IN OMNIBUSES AND ON UNDERGROUND RAILWAYS.

Available for any journey on:—DISTRICT RAILWAY—(3rd Class)—Bow Road to Putney Bridge, Ealing, Hounslow or South Harrow. METROPOLITAN RAILWAY—(3rd Class)—Aldgate to South Kensington, and Bishops Road to Hammersmith and Addison Road. LONDON ELECTRIC RAILWAY—Elephant and Castle to Queen's Park, Hammersmith to Finsbury Park, and Kennington to Highgate and Edgware. CITY AND SOUTH LONDON RAILWAY. CENTRAL LONDON RAILWAY—Liverpool Street to Wood Lane. OMNIBUSES:—GENERAL (L.G.O.C.); METROPOLITAN (M.E.T. Co.); BRITISH (T. & B.A.T., Ltd.); THOS. TILLING, LTD.; PUBLIC.

The LEICESTER CORPORATION is arranging for 'Buses and Trams to meet the return excursion train at Leicester Station to convey passengers along the various routes. Fare: Adults 6d. (Children 3d.). Passengers must obtain the 'bus and tram tickets at the station, or at the office of Thos. Cook & Son, Ltd., Gallowtree Gate, Leicester, or at Humberstone Road Station, before commencing the outward rail journey.

CONDITIONS OF ISSUE OF EXCURSION TICKETS AND OTHER REDUCED FARE TICKETS.

Excursion tickets and tickets issued at fares less than the ordinary fares are issued subject to the Notices and Conditions shewn in the Company's Current Time Tables.

Passengers holding day or half-day excursion tickets by special trains are not allowed to take any luggage, except small handbags, luncheon baskets, or other small articles intended for the passenger's use during the day. On the return journey only, passengers may take with them, free of charge, at Owner's Risk, goods for their own use not exceeding 60 lbs.

The L.M.S. Company, by arrangement with the Omnibus Companies with which it is associated, is in a position to fix up road tours for passengers travelling by Day and Half-day Excursions to Morecambe, Lake District, Matlock, Bakewell, Birmingham, Worcester, Derby, Nottingham, Sheffield, etc.

Organisers of parties desirous of information in respect of Motor Coach Tours between any points should communicate with the Station Master or Agent at the Station from which they propose to travel, or with Mr. Ashton Davies, C.X.D. Department, L.M.S. Railway, Derby.

Passengers are requested to OBTAIN their TICKETS IN ADVANCE as this will assist the Company in the provision of accommodation.

TICKETS CAN BE PURCHASED at the STATIONS; at the Office of THOS. COOK & SON, LTD., Gallowtree Gate; PICKFORDS, LTD., 3, Welford Place; the LEICESTER CO-OPERATIVE SOCIETY, LTD., High Street; at the Enquiry and Advance Booking Office, London Road, or at Humberstone Road Station, Leicester.

At LOUGHBORO' from A. ALTHAM, LTD., 46, Market Street.

DAY, HALF-DAY and PERIOD EXCURSION TICKETS can be obtained in advance from COUNTESTHORPE, SYSTON, WIGSTON (Glen Parva, Magna and South), Kirby Muxloe and Blaby Stations, AVAILABLE FROM AND TO LEICESTER ONLY.

*—Passengers travelling from Nuneaton (Trent Valley) station may obtain their tickets at Nuneaton (Abbey Street) Station, if more convenient.

All information regarding Excursion Trains on the London Midland and Scottish Railway can be obtained on application to the Divisional Passenger Commercial Superintendent, New Street Station, Birmingham, and General Superintendent (Passenger Commercial), Derby.

PLEASE RETAIN THIS BILL FOR REFERENCE.

May, 1931. J. H. FOLLOWS, Vice-President.

12,000 H., 150 P. Bemrose & Sons Ltd., Derby and London.

This London, Midland & Scottish Railway excursion handbill is typical of those also issued by other railway companies. It is interesting to read the details of the return arrangements; how many corporation bus crews of today would meet excursion trains at 12.15am?

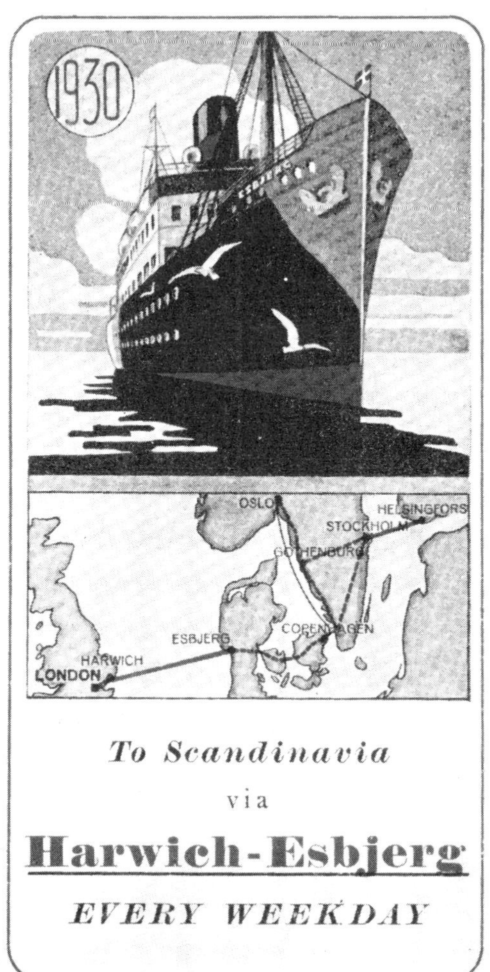

An advertising give away, issued jointly by the United Shipping Co Ltd, the Danish Tourist Bureau Ltd, and the London & North Eastern Railway; the reverse bears a calendar for 1930. (Stuart Underwood collection)

1929; it was extremely popular with the public, but not with the railway men who called it the 'White Elephant' because of its unevenly distributed weight. The Southern Railway had an extensive seaboard trade built up over many years from the pre-grouping era, and owned a fleet (in 1939) of forty-six steamers. One of its predecessors, the South Eastern Railway, operated ten Continental services daily, with trains running from London to Folkestone and Dover. Special through tickets were issued jointly between the South Eastern Railway and the Northern Railway of France.

Most railway companies operated a Continental service, particularly during the 1930s, when tours of all descriptions were available. They varied from one day and weekend tours, to those which lasted for one month; special tickets were issued in all cases. A big factor in the popularity of these tours was the fact that passports were not required for the one day or weekend tours.

In the early 1900s, the London and North Eastern Railway introduced '1,000 Mile Coupon Tickets'; it was the only company to do so. Each coupon was for each mile of travel, and the cost averaged out at approximately 1¼d per mile. The same company, in 1933, introduced a 'Holiday Runabout Ticket' (on which British Rail based its 'Rail-Rover Ticket') which became so popular that it caused severe disruption of the operation of the standard service schedules. This upsurge in excursion traffic could only be accommodated in one way, and so the company built new rolling stock to deal with it. The new stock was made into special trains with a rake of twelve coaches, which included two buffet cars. Each train was capable of carrying 600 passengers in bucket-type seats. For less than two years these trains remained as completely integrated 'Tourist Specials', and then regrettably they were broken up, and the coaches widely dispersed.

EXCURSION HANDBILLS

The handbills which have been preserved show an astonishing variety of reasons why special trains were run. These bills were printed by the million to advertise the many special trains operated by a company during the year. As well as being a record of a company's operating schedules for special trains, they provide an interesting social chronicle.

The sales and advertising techniques so flamboyantly exploited today were being used as standard business procedures by the railways more than fifty years ago. Long before dispensing racks were used for the distribution of promotional literature, a simple nail was all that was needed by a stationmaster to display the handbill that advertised an excursion. At the end of a season, the walls of the booking hall near the ticket window contained countless nail holes. Solitary nails sticking from the panelling bore silent testimony to the long-departed sheaves, crisp and colourful, which once hung from them.

These excursion notices were displayed with great seriousness; each of the 'Big Four' companies printed a small circle (about three millimetres diameter) in the top centre of the notice to indicate where the hanging nail should be driven! On many of the LMS handbills this tiny circle was printed directly above a note: 'Please retain this Bill for Reference', although it is not clear for whom the note was intended - the Stationmaster, the booking clerk, or the passenger.

As well as announcing the usual holiday excursions, these handbills also advertised more unusual events. For instance on Easter Monday, 18 April 1938, the London and North Eastern Railway ran a special train from Leicester, via Ingersby, John o'Gaunt, and Tilton, to Hallaton for the Annual Bottle Kicking and Hare Pie Scramble. Visitors to this centuries-old festival set out from Leicester at 9.55am, having paid a fare of 2s 1d, and returned (possibly filled with ale and hare pie) at 8.15pm.

For the Whitsuntide holidays in 1936 half-day excursions were operated from Leicester to Skegness, Mablethorpe, and other east coast resorts. Excursionists were invited to 'Meet the Sun on the East Coast', and were advised to book early. They were assured that this 'will assist the Railway Company in making arrangements FOR YOUR COMFORT if you TAKE TICKETS IN ADVANCE'. In co-operation with the LNER, the Leicester Corporation arranged for buses and trams to meet the return half-day excursion train;

LNER publicity. The beautiful German city of Heidelberg gives its name to a range of printing machines. An enterprising publicity agent inserted this delightful and colourful advertisement in an early 1930s printing trade magazine. All the railway companies commissioned leading artists to paint publicity pictures.

---

the bus and tram tickets had to be obtained at the Leicester (Belgrave Road) Station, or at advance booking agents, before commencing the outward journey. The handbills advertising these trips carried a footnote explaining the conditions of issue of the excursion tickets. It is interesting to note that then, and right up to the outbreak of war, Melton Mowbray was still listed as a Great Northern and LNWR joint station.

In March and April of the same year, day excursions were run to the Belvoir Hunt point-to-point meetings at Long Clawson, from Melton Mowbray via Scalford. The journey was only ten minutes long, and the course was but five minutes walk from Long Clawson station. Racegoers were sure of arriving at the course at least 40 minutes before the first race.

For the Easter Holidays of April 1930, Dean and Dawson organised a three to fifteen day excursion to Douglas (Isle of Man), and the London and North Eastern Railway published a handbill. It carried a cartoon heading showing a bespatted, cigar-smoking gent striding along a platform towards a ticket collector, who stood with outstretched hand for the proffered tickets. Behind the gent was (presumably) his wife, walking clear of the cigar smoke. She wore a knee-length coat with heavily furred collar and lapels, and a 'pudding-basin' hat. Held firmly in tow was a gym-slipped, velour-hatted schoolgirl and her two brothers, both wearing berets. Staggering and sweating at the rear was a porter pushing a trolley laden with the family's luggage.

After giving the dates and destination of the excursion, the handbill requested the holder to 'See Other Side for Times, Fares, etc.' Then followed

These colourful trade cards, cheaply printed by chromo-lithography, published by the railroad company and issued by the ticket agent, are an interesting variation on the handbill. The reverse, advertising the Great Central Route (part of the Grand Trunk Railway), lists four express trains daily leaving Niagara Falls 'for Detroit Grand Rapids, Chicago, San Francisco and the Great West.' Passengers were allowed to stop off and view the greatest natural wonder of the continent, 'The Falls and Scenery of Niagara'. Tickets for various journeys on the route between New York and the West Coast could be purchased from several agents, some of whom actually travelled on the trains to obtain sales. The cards, from 1880, are historic in that the suspension bridge built in 1855 was replaced in 1895 with a single-span steel arch, the new bridge being built around the old. It was, at the time, the largest single-span bridge ever built.

in very close type the conditions of issue of the 'Excursion Tickets and other Tickets issued at Fares less than Ordinary Fares'. These tickets were issued subject to the conditions of issue applicable to ordinary passenger tickets, and also to further limiting conditions. The most important of these extra conditions was listed first. It read:

> Neither the holder nor any other person shall have any right of action against the Company or any other Railway Company or person owning, working or using any railway, vehicles, vessels or premises (whether jointly with the Company or otherwise) upon which such tickets may be

available in respect of (a) injury (fatal or otherwise), loss, damage or delay however caused, or (b) loss of or damage or delay to property however caused.

As stated previously, the issue of an Insurance Ticket entirely negated this and other restrictive conditions which induced the passenger to waive his rights.

Further conditions imposed for the Douglas excursion concerned the availability of the excursion ticket, and its usage for the outward and return journeys. If a ticket was used in contravention of these conditions, the holder was required to pay the difference between the sum actually paid for the ticket, and the full ordinary return fare between the stations named on the ticket. Accompanied children under the age of three were allowed to travel free, while children of three years of age and under fourteen years of age could travel at half-fare, the minimum fare being one penny.

As with all other rail journeys at concession rates, restrictions on the conveyance of passengers' luggage were imposed. The limits of such restrictions varied according to the class of travel and the extent of the excursion, whether half-day or period. For the outward journey on a half-day excursion, passengers were allowed to take (free of charge) only small handbags or luncheon baskets, but for the return journey could take goods from 60lb to 120lb according to class. On period excursions the weight limits ranged from 100lb to 150lb according to class, on both the outward and return journeys. Exceptions to these arrangements included linoleum and mailcarts, 'and other similar articles for which special accompanied rates are in operation', although it is difficult to understand why anyone would wish to take linoleum or mailcarts on a holiday excursion.

The Easter holidays for 1939 produced the usual spate of handbills advertising excursions, plus a half-day excursion for the football match between Notts County and Port Vale. The bill advertising this football excursion also carried an outlined notice below the timetable section — 'Get your Holiday Handbook From L.N.E.R. Stations, Offices and Agencies. The Herald of the Holiday Season'. On 30 April 1938, Huddersfield Town played Preston North End for the Football Association Cup at Wembley Stadium. The London and North Eastern Railway ran Cup Final Specials to London (Marylebone) and Wembley. The fares were inclusive of conveyance between Marylebone and Wembley.

Conveyance of passengers from their destination station was always high on the list of a company's priorities when promoting an excursion. A London and North Eastern Railway handbill published in November 1936, gave details of 'Private Motor Saloons for the convenience of Parties arriving at or departing from King's Cross'. The saloons could accommodate ten passengers with the usual quantity of luggage, and could be engaged on the following terms: 'Any distance up to 3 miles . . . 8s. 6d. Each additional mile . . . 3. 0d.' All charges were increased by one quarter between specified off-peak hours. The saloons could be booked in advance, and applicants were requested to supply the King's Cross stationmaster with details of where the saloon was required, dates and time, train travelling and destination, and the number of passengers requiring transport. The handbill also carried a photograph of one of these saloons —

heavy balloon tyres, a bulbous looking body with a built-in ladder for access to the roof-rack, very upright and sedate, and yet charmingly quaint, if perhaps a little inelegant to modern eyes.

Despite the restrictions of wartime, the Whitsun holidays of 1940 were catered for by the LNER who tempted northern area passengers to spend a day at Belle Vue, Manchester. The excursion handbill, printed on orange-coloured paper, gave no hint of the war or its restrictions. The many attractions of the extensive zoo and gardens were advertised in detail, as were also the scenic and miniature railways, and the Speed Aces of the World who exhibited their skill in 'Speedway Racing on Britain's Finest Track'.

For the 1936 Motor Show, and the Cycle and Motor Cycle Show, both held at Olympia, the London and North Eastern Railway issued special season tickets. They were available for a minimum period of seven days, commencing from any day of the week. Extra days were charged pro rata.

It is not known what was so special about Melton Mowbray shops on early closing days between 7 July and 22 September 1938, inclusive, but the London, Midland and Scottish Railway evidently thought them worthy of a visit since they advertised 'Half-Day Excursion Tickets (at Exceptional Fares)', from Birmingham, Derby, and Peterborough.

Cheap day return tickets were issued by the same company from 28 March until 6 July 1929, for journeys to Matlock Bath, Matlock, and Rowsley (for Chatsworth). Excursionists departed for these Derbyshire beauty spots from 7.19am from Alsager, Etruria, and Meir in the Potteries, returning at 6.22pm the same day. The return fare, third class, ranged from 3s 6d to 7s 9d.

In conjunction with the LMS, Cook's organised half-day excursions to Worcester and Great Malvern, and day excursions to London, on Whit Sunday, and Whit Monday 1931. Seats could be reserved to Worcester and Great Malvern from Leicester for a fee of 1s per seat, extra to the fare of 4s 6d. Excursionists to London (St Pancras), setting out from Kegworth, Loughborough, Leicester, Hinckley, and Kettering, paid fares ranging from 12s to 9s 1d. For an extra 2s they could go sightseeing by rail and bus in the metropolis. The special tickets issued were available for any journey on the District Railway, Metropolitan Railway, London Electric Railway, City and South London Railway, and the Central London Railway, third class and over specified routes.

The Great Western Railway introduced 'Something Unique in Travel for 1930!!!' with their land cruises by rail and road. Throughout the season, which ended on 22 September, three six-day tours were in operation. For an all-in fare of 12 guineas, passengers were given first-class rail travel, motors, hotels, sightseeing fees, and gratuities. The Tour No 1 roamed through Oxford, Gloucester, Cambrian Coast, and the Shakespeare Country; Tour No 2 visited Torquay, South Devon, Dartmoor, the Cornish Riviera, Lands End, and Plymouth, &c; Tour No 3 explored the 'Lorna Doone' Country, Westward Ho!, Cheddar Gorge, and Bath. A representative of the GWR was advertised to conduct each tour personally, the details of which could be obtained upon application to the superintendent of the line, at Paddington Station.

5
BEHIND THE BOOKING OFFICE WINDOW

Having purchased his ticket to the next village, big city, or some faraway holiday haven, the passenger is only concerned that the train will be on time for both departure and arrival, and will convey him to his destination safely, and in comfort. The booking clerk, behind the barrier of glass, was and is a creature impersonal, as remote as the engine driver. To the passenger, the business, economics and administration of the railway are given little thought — except when the train is late.

Railway administration is a vast subject about which many learned volumes have been written. It presents quite a different picture of travel when viewed from the company's side of the booking office window. Railways were created by Parliament, later re-grouped, and then nationalised. The various Railway Acts laid down administrative procedures for the companies to raise and encourage investments, to fix rates, and to make rules and regulations.

Passenger traffic, as distinct from the carriage of goods and freight, includes, in addition to the conveyance of passengers, such items as personal luggage, mail, and animals. Statistics show that a very large percentage of railway receipts has always been derived from such traffic. In 1870 the total number of passengers carried on the railways of Great Britain was more than 336½ million, their contribution to the gross receipts being 42.8 per cent of the total. By 1923, when the railways were re-grouped, this percentage had risen to 46.1, having been as high as 58.5 in 1919 while the railways were still under state control.

A Fellow of the Royal Statistical Society, J. Holt Schooling, writing in 1896, presented some interesting railway facts in fancy frames. He illustrated his text by using diagrams in ticket form to show the proportional division of related facts. For the year 1894, he observed that receipts from passenger traffic had reached the staggering total of £36,495,488, which represented 45.7 per cent of the total traffic receipts. Third-class passengers, so long scorned by the railways, proved to be the mainstay of the companies, providing 78 per cent of all classes carried. Third-class passengers brought to the railway companies six times as much revenue as was contributed by first-class passengers, and nearly nine times as much as second-class passengers. Of every one thousand travellers who got into a railway carriage, 901 rode third-class; clearly, these passengers were by far the most important customers of the railways.

More than 911 million passengers were conveyed during the year 1894,

A view of the booking office on platforms 12 and 13, Manchester Victoria station, Lancashire & Yorkshire Railway, about 1914. In the background to the left can be seen a waiting train, and just around the corner, a chocolate-vending machine. Beyond the platform sign the newsagent's stand displays books and magazines; placards announce 'Hopes of Peace' and ' Womens' Threats' over the franchise. (National Railway Museum)

Interior of a Manchester Victoria (L & YR) booking office, about 1914, showing the ticket racks. To the right of the window can be seen an Edmondson ticket dating machine. Most of the stacks of tickets have one on display at the front, the first in the series, numbered '0000'. This ticket would later be used by the booking clerk for the ordering of further supplies. (National Railway Museum)

A scene inside the booking hall of St Pancras station, Midland Railway, about 1912. Many features can be seen which have disappeared from the modern railway operation. The train departure indicator reveals one train every seven minutes to parts of the MR network as far apart as Edinburgh and Folkestone, while the station-master checks his rosta. The pictures and posters on the walls are now collectors' items; the wooden panelling and cast-iron chandelier are also marks of a bygone age. (National Railway Museum)

this figure excluding the 1.2 million season ticket holders. In other words, the number of first-class passengers was about equal to the then population of Italy, in excess of 29 millions; the entire population (more than 60 millions) of the United States represented the total of second-class passengers, while nearly all the nations in Asia would be required to equal in number (nearly 821½ millions) the third-class passengers conveyed by the railways of the United Kingdom. During the two years 1893 and 1894, the number of third-class passengers conveyed by the railways of Britain exceeded by one million the population of the whole world.

As the railways increased their passenger traffic, they became more aware of safety and reliability. In 1875 the total number of passengers was equal to the combined population of England and Wales, out of whom but one was accidentally killed; twenty years later only one passenger was killed out of every 57 millions carried.

But when accidents happen they ruin good records and reputations. Such was the case in 1879, the year of the Tay Bridge disaster, when seventy-three persons were killed. This drastically reduced the proportion of passengers conveyed in safety to 7½ millions for every one killed. The founding principle of the early railways was that they would form an improved system of highways along which any person would have a right of vehicular passage, upon payment of a toll to the railway company. For example, the Great Western Railway was sanctioned by the Act of 1835, with the proviso that 'All persons shall have free liberty to pass along and upon and to use and employ the said railway with carrriages properly constructed as by this Act directed, upon payment only of such rates and tolls as shall be demanded by the said company. . . .' The Act also empowered the company to use locomotive engines, and 'in carriages or wagons drawn or propelled thereby to convey all such passengers as shall be offered, and to make such reasonable charge for such conveyance as they may from time to time determine upon.'

The early railways gave a simple and unsophisticated service which is reflected in their timetables. On the opening day (4 July 1837) timetable of the Grand Junction Railway there appears an item which gives a very revealing insight into the times. In describing the trains available it states that 'The First Class Trains will consist of Coaches carrying six inside, and of Mails carrying four inside, one compartment of which is convertible into a Bed-carriage, if required. The Mixed Train will consist of both First and Second Class Coaches, the latter affording complete protection from the weather, and differing only from the First Class in having no lining, cushions or divisions of the compartment. Both kinds have seats on the roof for those who prefer riding outside.' Subsequent development of the railways showed the necessity of intensifying that service to meet the local requirements at each station along the line. Fast trains were an absolute must, and as the trains became more varied and the territory of the company extended, the character of the company's service underwent radical changes. The principle of the fast or express train continued up to and beyond the time of the regrouping. The inauguration of express train services had a tremendous publicity value which played a conspicuous part in the competition between the railway companies.

In later years the introduction of cross-country traffic, by co-operation

FOR CHEAP EXCURSIONS TO LONDON, *see other Side.*

MIDLAND RAILWAY.

IN CONNECTION WITH COOK'S SPECIAL TRAINS TO LONDON,

ON MONDAY, SEPTEMBER 19TH, 1881,

Passengers will be Booked to

PARIS, SWITZERLAND, HOLLAND, BELGIUM, & THE RHINE,

From the undermentioned Stations of the **Midland Railway,** at the following

Through Fares for the Double Journey. Tickets available for Sixteen Days:—

STATIONS.	TO PARIS, *Via* London Brighton and South Coast Railway.		TO PARIS, *Via* London Chatham & Dover, or South-Eastern Railways.		TO ROTTERDAM or ANTWERP, and Back, via Harwich. *		TO BRUSSELS and Back, via Harwich and Antwerp.		Circular Tour to Rotterdam, Cologne, the Rhine, and Mayence, returning via Aix-la-Chapelle, Brussels, Antwerp, and Rotterdam.	
FROM	3rd cl. to London, 2nd cl. beyond.	1st cl. and Saloon.	3rd cl. throughout.	1st cl. to London, 2nd cl. beyond.	3rd cl. to London, 2nd cl. beyond.	1st cl. and Saloon.	3rd cl. to London, 2nd cl. beyond.	1st cl. and Saloon.	3rd cl. to London, 2nd cl. beyond.	1st cl. and Saloon.
	s. d.	s. d.	s. d.	s. d.	s. d.	s. d.	s. d.	s. d.	s. d.	s. d.
CARLISLE	45 0	66 0	49 6	77 0	42 0	70 0	46 4	75 9	85 0	122 0
CARNFORTH ... / LANCASTER (G. A.)	44 6	66 0	49 0	77 0	41 6	70 0	45 10	75 9	84 6	122 0
GIGGLESWICK ...	43 0	64 0	47 6	75 0	40 0	68 0	44 4	73 9	83 0	120 0
SKIPTON ... ... / COLNE ... ... / KEIGHLEY ...	42 0	62 0	46 6	73 0	39 0	66 0	43 4	71 9	82 0	118 0
BRADFORD ... / LEEDS ... ... / NORMANTON ... / WAKEFIELD ... / YORK ... ... / HULL	42 0	61 0	46 6	72 0	39 0	65 0	43 4	70 9	82 0	117 0
BARNSLEY ... ... / SHEFFIELD ... / MASBORO'	40 0	60 0	44 6	71 0	37 0	64 0	41 4	69 9	80 0	116 0
CHESTERFIELD ...	39 0	59 0	43 6	70 0	36 0	63 0	40 4	68 9	79 0	115 0
LIVERPOOL (Mid.) / WARRINGTON ... / STOCKPORT (Tiviot) / MANCHESTER ... / GUIDE BRIDGE ...	42 0	61 0	46 6	72 0	39 0	65 0	43 4	70 9	82 0	117 0
LINCOLN	38 0	58 0	42 6	69 0	35 0	62 0	39 4	67 9	78 0	114 0
NOTTINGHAM ... / DERBY ... ... / BURTON ... ... / BIRMINGHAM ...	37 0	56 0	41 6	67 0	34 0	60 0	38 4	65 9	77 0	112 0
WOLVERHAMPTON	39 0	58 0	43 6	69 0	36 0	62 0	40 4	67 9	79 0	114 0
WALSALL	38 0	57 0	42 6	68 0	35 0	61 0	39 4	66 9	78 0	113 0
LEICESTER... ...	35 6	53 0	40 0	64 0	32 6	57 0	36 10	62 9	75 6	109 0

* Passengers can be booked to Rotterdam *via* Queenboro' and Flushing at an additional charge of 6s. 2nd Class, and 5s. 1st Class.

Passengers by Excursion to London and Paris as above may avail themselves of Cook's Cheap Tourist Tickets to Switzerland, at the following Fares for the Swiss Tour, in addition to the above Fares to Paris and back;—From PARIS to Fontainebleau, Dijon, Neuchatel, BERNE, Thun, Interlacken, Fribourg, Lausanne, GENEVA; returning *via* Culoz, Amberieu, Macon, and Dijon, to PARIS. First Class, £5 10s. 6d.; Second Class, £4 4s. 0d. (This Circular Tour may be reversed beyond Dijon.)

Tickets good fo returning to London by any Train or Steamer of the Route within 14 days from the date of issue.

Passengers can break their journey in London going or returning, so that they complete the journey by returning from St. Pancras Station, London, by any Ordinary Train within 16 days from date of Tickets.

The Tickets to **PARIS**, *via* **London, Brighton, and South Coast Company's Route**, are available by the Night Service, leaving London Bridge at 8·0 p.m., and Victoria at 7·50 p.m., any evening (except Sundays), Train arriving in Paris following day as per Tidal Table; returning from Paris by Night Service at any time within Fourteen Days. The Boats used for the Night Service, *via* this Route, are the regular Passenger Boats. Passengers by this Route can break the Journey at Brighton, Newhaven, Dieppe, and Rouen.

Tickets to **PARIS**, *via* **London, Chatham, and Dover and South-Eastern Companies' Routes**, are available by the Night Service, leaving Holborn Viaduct any evening at 6·25, Ludgate Hill 6·22, Victoria 6·25, Charing Cross 6·15, and Cannon Street 6·28 p.m., and allow Passengers to return from Paris by the Night Service at any time within 14 days.

Tickets to **HOLLAND, BELGIUM,** and **GERMANY**, by the **Great Eastern Company's Route**, are available for starting from Liverpool Street Station, for Rotterdam, daily (except Sundays) at 7·10 p.m.; returning from Rotterdam daily (except Sundays) at 6·0 p.m. For Antwerp, from Liverpool Street Station, at 7·10 p.m., on Mondays, Tuesdays, Thursdays, and Saturdays; returning from Antwerp every Monday, Wednesday, Thursday, and Saturday at 4·15 p.m.

Tickets to **ROTTERDAM** or **ANTWERP**, *via* **QUEENBORO'** and **FLUSHING**, are available for starting from Victoria at 8·30 p.m., Holborn Viaduct at 8·25, and Ludgate Hill at 8·26 p.m. daily; returning from Rotterdam and Antwerp daily.

Tickets can be obtained at any time previous to the running of the Excursions at the following Offices and Agencies of THOS. COOK & SON:—

MANCHESTER—61, Market Street.
LIVERPOOL—11, Ranelagh Street.
BIRMINGHAM—Stephenson Place.
WALSALL—Post Office Buildings, The Bridge.
WOLVERHAMPTON—27, Queen Street.
LEEDS—1, Royal Exchange.
BRADFORD—8, Exchange, Market Street.

SHEFFIELD—Change Alley Corner.
NOTTINGHAM—16, Clumber Street.
LEICESTER—51, Gallowtree Gate.
BARNSLEY—Messrs. T. & C. Lingard, "Chronicle" Office.
HULL—Mr. W. Adams, Bookseller, 23, Market Street.
SOUTHPORT—Mr. J. W. Howarth, 36, London Street.
BOLTON—Messrs. Beckett & Rothwell, Town Hall Square.

N.B.—Passengers booked at Midland Stations for the Continent must exchange their vouchers at the offices of THOMAS COOK and SON, Ludgate Circus, before leaving London.

The Fares do not in any case include transit across London.

HOTEL COUPONS FOR PARIS and all parts of the Continent, at 8s. per day, will be issued in connection with the above. Tickets for Carriage Drives in Paris, &c., can be obtained at Reduced Fares.

COOK'S GUIDE TO PARIS. With Map. One Shilling.

For full particulars of Continental arrangements apply to the Agents of the Companies:—

D. 413/81. **THOS. COOK & SON,** Tourist Offices, Ludgate Circus, London.

FOR PERSONALLY CONDUCTED EXCURSIONS TO PARIS, *see other Bills.*

A handbill giving details of a continental excursion promoted by Thomas Cook & Son in 1881, using the facilities of the Midland Railway. The prices for the various tours would seem to be astonishingly cheap, but bearing in mind the changes in the social structure and the valuation of currency, it is difficult to make easy comparisons. The other side of the bill advertises cheap excursions to London on the same date to link up with the holiday trains.

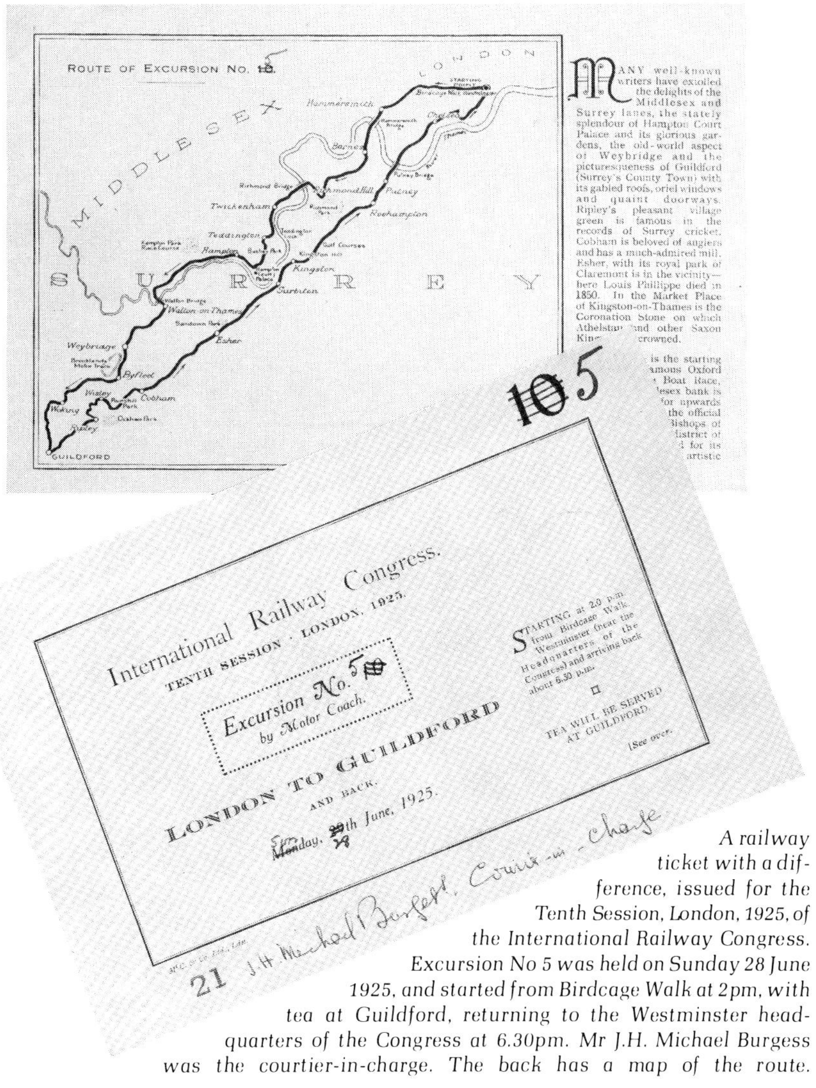

A railway ticket with a difference, issued for the Tenth Session, London, 1925, of the International Railway Congress. Excursion No 5 was held on Sunday 28 June 1925, and started from Birdcage Walk at 2pm, with tea at Guildford, returning to the Westminster headquarters of the Congress at 6.30pm. Mr J.H. Michael Burgess was the courtier-in-charge. The back has a map of the route.

---

between the various companies, gave a more convenient service to passengers. The running of through coaches, and frequent trips by short trains were further improvements in the services offered to the travelling public. The Act which engendered the regrouping was a further development in the search for increased efficiency, and the wider variety of services was to be seen in the complex timetables subsequently produced.

As the train services increased, the timetables had to keep pace. The production of the by now bulky volumes necessitated the continuous employment of time-bill clerks. The responsibility for the preparation and revision of the timetables was held by the superintendent of the line.

The general arrangement of a timetable was basically simple, although in appearance to the passenger it was somewhat complex. In most cases, the main lines were shown sectionalised; the first section related to London and its suburbs, and thence to the principal towns and stations throughout the system. Each section included all the branch stations together with the connecting services; with the aid of references given at the beginning of each section, it was easy to determine the services available.

As always, the revision of connections made the altering of a timetable a difficult task. Even with regrouping the task was little diminished, but before then, all changes in a timetable which affected other companies' services needed much negotiation before the final agreement could be reached. Any significant alteration in the running times of just one train could involve a score or more of consequent alterations. Railways have always had their critics, but few of the complainants realise the difficulties in timing a train, and fewer still could work out an ideal service for their particular section of line. Prior to the running of the first summer train services of the regrouped companies in 1923, the *Daily Express* commented,

> For months timetables experts have been busy working out intricate plans to cope with the rush of traffic which the railways expect, and to make these arrangements fit the accelerated speeds which holiday travelling demands. They have had to budget for hundreds of new trains in so ingenious a way that there shall be as little duplication as possible, and, above all, no delay. In order to achieve this miracle of organisation, they have had to bear in mind the number of locomotives and carriages available at the starting-places; the engine power and probable loads; the train staff and the connections at junctions.

Timetable revision is made somewhat easier by using a specially prepared graph. The various stations and junctions are represented by horizontal lines set apart in proportion to the distance between one place and another. Intersecting vertical lines indicate time intervals, the hours being divided into five-minute units, the course of the trains and their different classes being represented by coloured lines of distinctive form, ie solid, dashed, or dotted. At first sight, graphic timetables seem complicated, but in fact, they are quite easy to read. The entire traffic passing through any section during a twenty-four hour period can easily be seen. Any imperfections in previous revisions can be seen more clearly. These timetable diagrams can be used to show the effect of dividing trains during busy holiday seasons; gradients and sidings may also be readily shown.

The superintendent of the line authorised the reissue of the timetables whenever it was necessary to adjust train services. During the winter, services were not so intense as during the summer, and the need for train mileage economy meant the discontinuing of certain trains, and the consequent revision of the timetables. Experience was the guide, and for reference time-bill clerks used the issue of a timetable for the corresponding period of the previous year. Before such revisions could be effected, general meetings of the traffic officers were held to discuss the contemplated changes. With the approval of the superintendent of the line, the proposed changes were formally submitted to the general manager for his sanction. For drastic changes in the train workings, final consent had to be obtained from the board of directors who reviewed the possible effect on the company's revenue. With the final consent the superintendent would issue

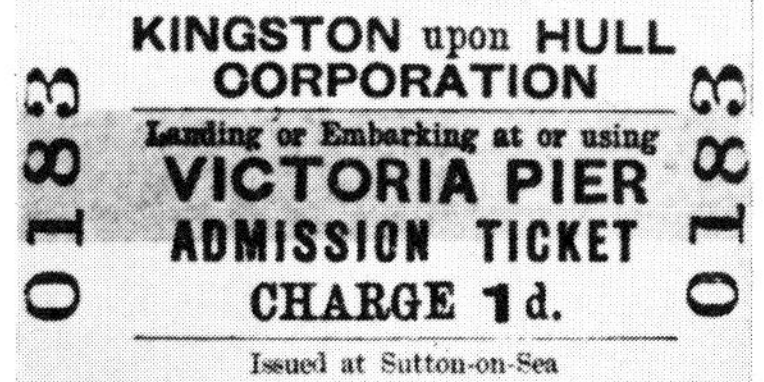

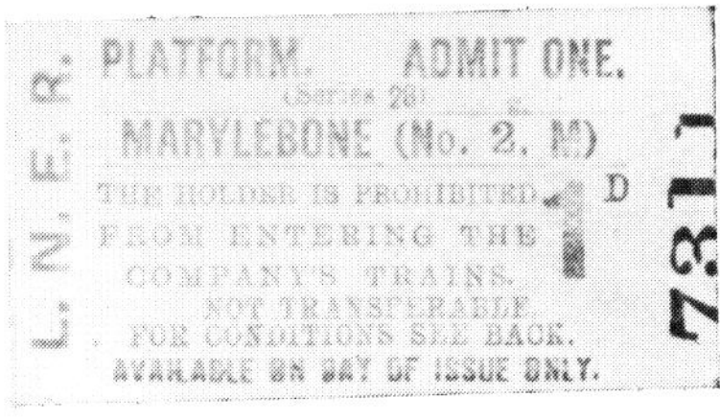

Platform tickets
0183 Admission ticket was for the ferry service, issued by the LNER in 1934.
7311 LNER ticket, the restriction details are printed in red with the serial number in black.
1530 LNER free ticket, about 1930. The linear clock was punched in the appropriate time space upon issue.
0736 A typical GWR design of the mid-1930s, with blue horizontal bands on white board.
3366 An unusual LM & SR ticket which allowed non-travellers to enter the station premises and to make use of the station dining room. In contrast to the other tickets of Edmondson standard, the Great Eastern Ticket No 28 is most unusual. It is made of pressed brass with the words and serial number space in relief against a black enamelled background. (Ipswich Ticket: P.B. Whitehouse collection)

instructions for the preparation of the revised timetables.

The time-bill clerks set to work on the necessary alterations, and in the course of time would receive printers proofs of the new tables. These were sent for checking to other companies who were concerned with the times of connecting trains. On return they would be resubmitted to the printer for final production. At one time, most of the railway companies did their own printing, both of tickets and timetables, but as the work grew more complex it became necessary to contract out to specialist printers. The formes containing the set-up type used to be kept year after year, but modern printing techniques have since obviated the necessity for such practice.

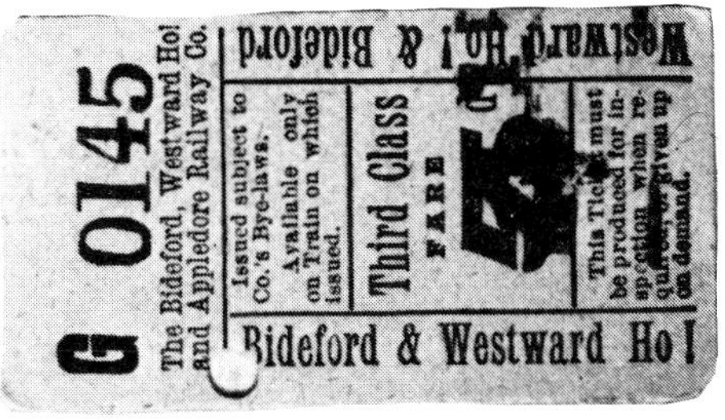

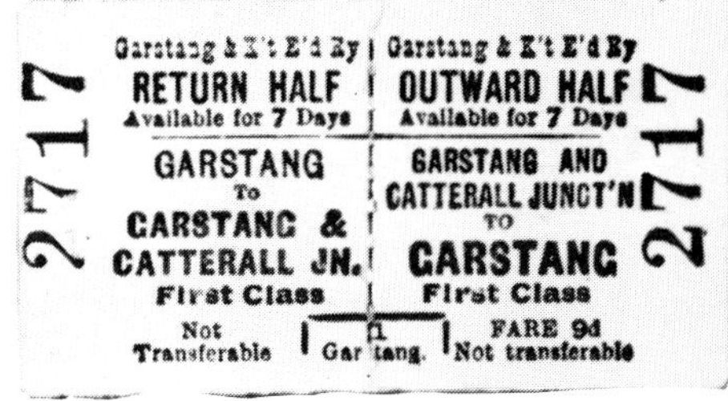

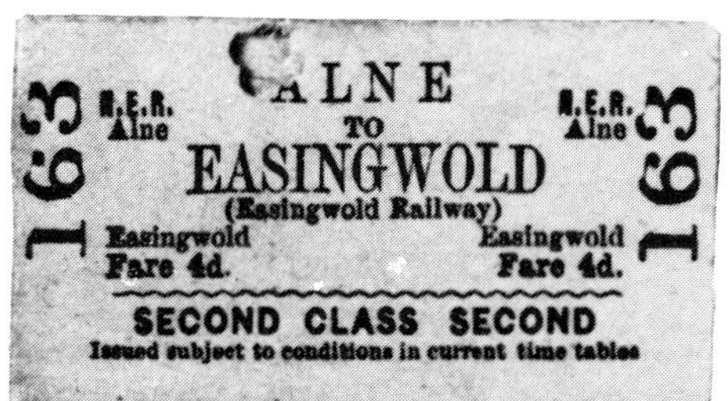

In railway histories the part played by light railways is sometimes overlooked; they have been condescendingly referred to as 'toy railways', the Festiniog Railway being a case in point. Their intricate networks in remote country areas, sometimes originating as quarry lines, were important interconnectors with the main lines.

3301 Kent & East Sussex Railway third class single. The company was authorised in 1904, becoming part of British Railways in 1948.

3398 Lynton & Barnstaple Railway first class single issued in 1905. Given the Royal Assent in 1895, and opened in 1898, the company was purchased by the London & South Western Railway in 1922, and the following year became part of the Southern Railway.

G0145 The Bideford, Westward Ho! and Appledore Railway Company third class single. This romantically-named line had three locomotives; its tickets were of the punch type, similar to those issued on omnibuses.

2717 Garstang & Knot End Railway first class return. Sanctioned in 1864, the first seven miles of line were opened in 1870. Closed down in 1872, it re-opened in 1875, and at the regrouping was absorbed into the London, Midland & Scottish Railway.

163 North Eastern Railway second class single to connect with the Easingwold Railway. The latter company was incorporated in 1887, and opened for traffic four years later. It was closed, just after nationalisation, in 1948.

(Patrick B. Whitehouse collection)

The legal implications in a published timetable have varied throughout the history of railways. In general, the issue of a timetable by a particular company was held to be a legal contract to run trains as shown; this also applied to any connecting services, with the same company or in conjunction with another. This became the subject of lawsuits, and as mentioned earlier, provision was made to guard against future actions at law. The railway companies gave notice on their timetables disclaiming any liaibility for failing to provide any or all of the services as advertised; reference to this was also made on the tickets.

Each of the four major companies, using slightly different phraseology, notified passengers that the timetables only fixed the time at which tickets could be obtained for any journey. The company guaranteed that the train would not start before the appointed time, but they did not guarantee that the train would either start or arrive at the time indicated in the timetables. No liability was accepted for loss, inconvenience, or injury arising from delays caused by the negligence of the company's servants or by any other cause. As previously stated, when the passenger paid his fare and accepted a ticket in return, this made a special contract between the railway company and the passenger, subject to the conditions or reference to conditions printed on the ticket. The railway companies were not obliged to convey passengers without conditions, and any person without a travelling ticket could lawfully be prevented from boarding a train.

It was the company's duty to convey passengers to their destination in a reasonable time. Circumstances determined what was 'reasonable', and passengers could only claim to be conveyed by the ordinary route in the company's system. If delays occurred because the company deemed it unsafe for a journey to continue, then no claims could be upheld.

Before 1914, each railway company had its own methods for the layout and production of timetables; publication dates varied, leading to considerable confusion among the travelling public. With Government control during World War I, frequent alterations to the services were necessary. Wartime paper and printing restrictions eventually led to a cessation in the issue of timetables. When eventually the Government relinquished control of the railways, and subsequently with the regrouping, the publication of timetables was standardised at July and October.

With the regrouping in 1923 significant changes were effected in both the compiling of timetables and the operation of many service schedules. The principle of sectional timetables became impractical, and in the summer of 1924 each of the new companies issued single-volume tables to cover all routes in the respective systems.

As may be understood, company timetables catered for the running of regular service trains; but they also needed to be sufficiently flexible to allow for the insertion of special trains operating at irregular times. Such trains fall into three main categories: relief trains, special traffic, and excursion trains.

Relief trains were used at holiday periods, in certain cases to augment ordinary services. The stationmasters at the more important stations were responsible for gauging the intensity of traffic, and the consequent operation of extra trains. Special procedural manuals were published which itemised the necessary steps to be observed. The special traffic trains were usually granted priority. For example, trains which met the Atlantic liners were infiltrated into existing service schedules, and telegraphed instructions preceded them, notifying the principal stations en route of their departure times, and requesting an absolutely clear road for the trains.

Excursion trains were, as a rule, pre-arranged, and station staff were

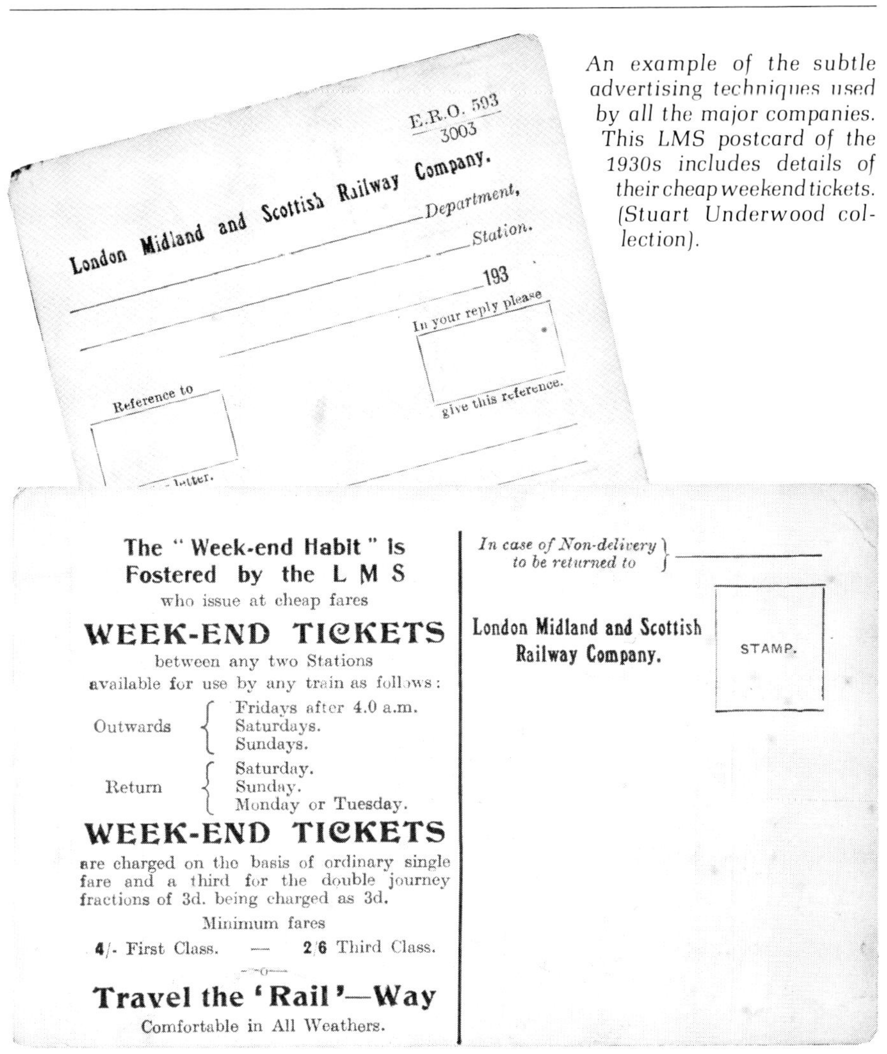

London Midland and Scottish Railway Company.

E.R.O. 593
3003

Department,

Station.

193

In your reply please give this reference.

Reference to Letter.

The "Week-end Habit" is Fostered by the L M S

who issue at cheap fares

WEEK-END TICKETS

between any two Stations

available for use by any train as follows:

Outwards { Fridays after 4.0 a.m. / Saturdays. / Sundays.

Return { Saturday. / Sunday. / Monday or Tuesday.

WEEK-END TICKETS

are charged on the basis of ordinary single fare and a third for the double journey fractions of 3d. being charged as 3d.

Minimum fares

4/- First Class. — 2/6 Third Class.

—o—

Travel the 'Rail'—Way

Comfortable in All Weathers.

In case of Non-delivery to be returned to

London Midland and Scottish Railway Company.

STAMP.

An example of the subtle advertising techniques used by all the major companies. This LMS postcard of the 1930s includes details of their cheap weekend tickets. (Stuart Underwood collection).

given notice of them. This was given in the weekly and fortnightly notices. Full details were given, including the purpose of the train, its allotted time, and general arrangements necessary. Charter trains, which could, for a special charge, be requisitioned at a few hours notice, obviously were not featured in the notices. At the time of their despatch all stations en route were notified by telegraph.

For the Royal Train, it was usual for regular services to be temporarily suspended; this was usually for a period of about thirty minutes. A 'pilot' train ran in advance of the Royal Train by about fifteen minutes to 'clear' the signals. Queen Victoria's train averaged about forty to forty-five miles per hour, the Queen having an intense dislike of speed. Every possible precaution was taken to ensure an undisturbed journey, and every stationmaster was required to be on duty in full regalia to see both the 'pilot' and the Royal Train pass through his station.

With all train-working arrangements, rolling stock and engines had to be 'balanced', since the traffic through a given section was rarely uniform. For example, workmen's trains did not run at week-ends, and excursion trains were mainly seasonal in their operation. Then, as now, coaches hauled on a particular journey had to be returned to their depot regardless of whether or not they ran occupied. Coach and engine working programmes were regularly prepared, needing close liaison between the traffic and locomotive departments.

With the introduction of the eight-hour day for railwaymen, it became very difficult to balance trains and their crews. The reduction in the working day meant a necessary reduction in the distance a crew could travel. It was the usual practice to work long-distance train crews through to the train's destination, but the new working hours necessitated the changing of crews at intermediate points. An eight-hour day did not mean that a locomotive could be run for that period of time. At least an hour was required by the driver and fireman to prepare the engine at the sheds, with extra time to run from the sheds to the departure station. Similar time was required at the end of the day, so that it was rare for an express engine crew to work on train hauling for more than five hours per day.

Train logs had to be compiled by the crews, a special journal form, which when completed gave a full working record of any particular train. A typical passenger train journal was headed with a description of the train, its original departure time, destination, date, and a serial number for the sheet. A list of stations and dividing points was given, with the actual times of arrival and departure entered; any time late away from a station was also shown. Minutes lost were shown under various headings: 'By Station Work Wtg. Connections, By Engine, By Signals, By Exceptional Causes'. The number of vehicles attached or detached, together with a description of the types of vehicles was also required to be shown; the number of wheels at any standing point and where the load was altered was likewise entered in the journal. A detachable summary slip was filled in on the front section of the form. The rear of the sheet carried details of the

---

Long before the turn of the century, the word 'Excursion' on a ticket means that apart from obvious special occasions, a journey could be undertaken at a discount fare, provided the traveller used specified trains.

880 Isle of Man Railway first class, with centre section red vertical overprint, unissued. The IOMR was authorised in 1872 and opened the following year.

4222 Cork, Blackrock, & Passage Railway first class. Red vertical lines overprint on cream coloured card, unissued. The CB & PR was originally authorised in 1837, abandoned, and after several applications, finally sanctioned in 1846. It opened in 1850, became part of the Great Southern Railway in 1924, and closed in 1933.

439 Typical of Great Western design with two green horizontal overprints on white.

4618 Isle of Man Railway Company first class, maroon overprint on lilac card.

0045 Great Northern & London & North Western Railway Companies third class local long date. The outward half is coloured with a narrow red vertical band between two blue sections, while the return half is a reverse of this pattern. The reverse of the ticket is printed in lilac.

7107 Yet another variation on an IOMR ticket. Overprinted light green on light brown card, both halves bear the Manx symbol together with two narrow horizontal light blue lines.

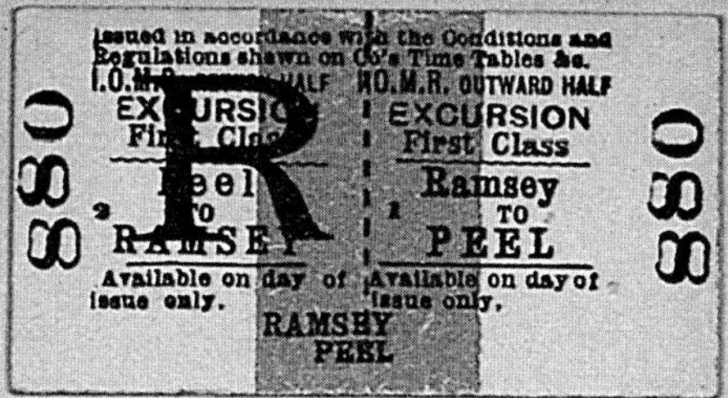
880
Issued in accordance with the Conditions and Regulations shewn on Co's Time Tables &c.
EXCURSION
First Class
Peel
TO
RAMSEY
Available on day of issue only.
I.O.M.R. OUTWARD HALF
EXCURSION
First Class
Ramsey
TO
PEEL
Available on day of issue only.
RAMSEY
PEEL
880

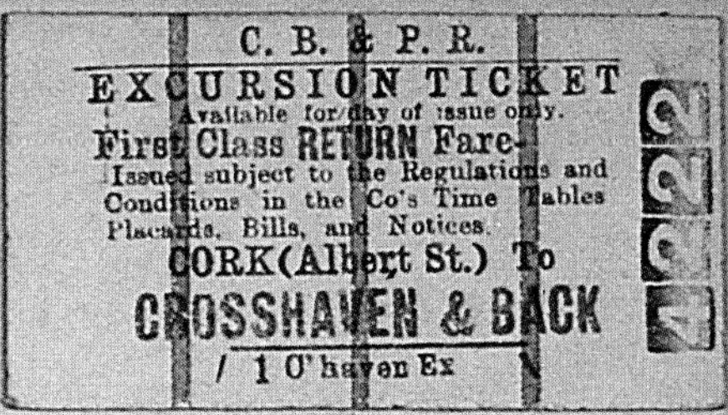
C. B. & P. R.
EXCURSION TICKET
Available for day of issue only.
First Class RETURN Fare
Issued subject to the Regulations and Conditions in the Co's Time Tables Placards, Bills, and Notices.
CORK (Albert St.) To
CROSSHAVEN & BACK
/ 1 C'haven Ex
4222

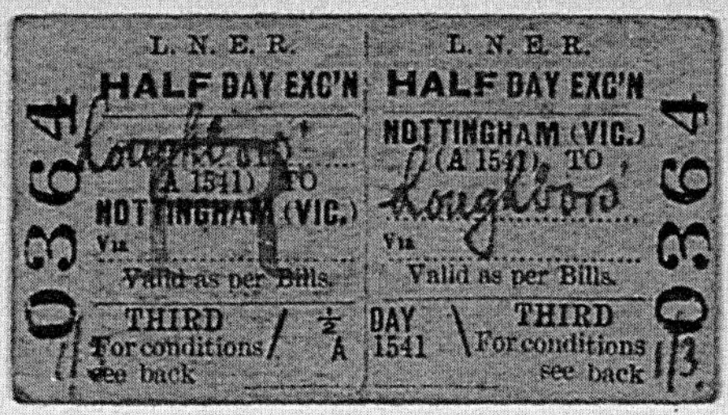
0364
L. N. E. R.
HALF DAY EXC'N
Loughboro'
(A 1541) TO
NOTTINGHAM (VIC.)
Via
Valid as per Bills.
THIRD
For conditions see back
½ A
L. N. E. R.
HALF DAY EXC'N
NOTTINGHAM (VIC.)
(A 1541) TO
Loughboro'
Via
Valid as per Bills.
DAY 1541
THIRD
For conditions see back
1/3
0364

439
Gt. Western Ry
Gt. Western Ry
HALF DAY EXCURSION
RETURN TICKET
BirminghamSH2 BirminghamSH2
TO
GT. MALVERN
AND BACK
via Cradley & Worcester
Third Class Fare
(See back)
Great Malvern
Great Malvern
439

219
L. N. E. R.
EVENING EXCURSION
to
SHIREOAKS
Via
Valid as per Bills.
THIRD
For conditions see back
EVENING EXC.
Shireoaks
L. N. E. R.
EVENING EXCURSION
SHIREOAKS
to
Via
Valid as per Bills.
THIRD
For conditions see back
219

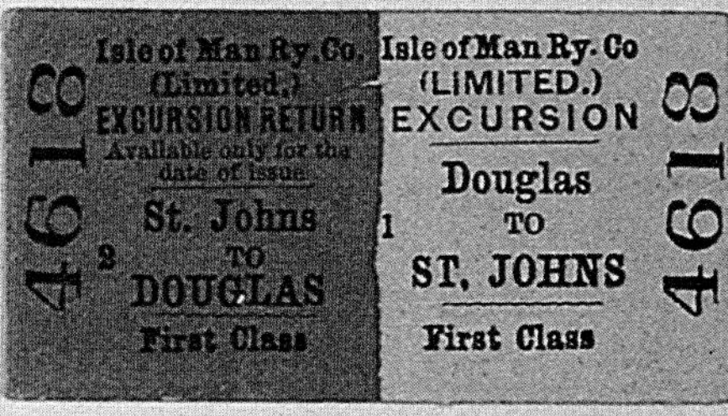
4618
Isle of Man Ry. Co.
(Limited.)
EXCURSION RETURN
Available only for the date of issue.
St. Johns
TO
DOUGLAS
First Class
Isle of Man Ry. Co
(LIMITED.)
EXCURSION
Douglas
TO
ST. JOHNS
First Class
4618

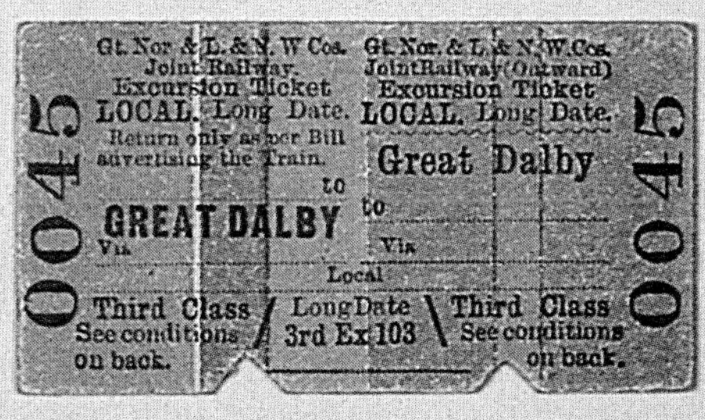
0045
Gt. Nor. & L. & N. W. Cos.
Joint Railway.
Excursion Ticket
LOCAL. Long Date.
Return only as per Bill advertising the Train.
to
GREAT DALBY
Via
Third Class
See conditions on back.
Local
Long Date
3rd Ex 103
Gt. Nor. & L. & N. W. Cos.
Joint Railway (Outward)
Excursion Ticket
LOCAL. Long Date.
Great Dalby
to
Via
Third Class
See conditions on back.
0045

160
L.M.&S.R.
HALF DAY EXC'N
Valid as advertised
Third Class
Birmingh'mNS
3754
TO
LEICESTER (LMS)
FOR CONDITIONS SEE BACK
LM&SR For conditions see back
HALF DAY EXC'N
Norths 3754 Agency
Leicester
TO
BIRMINGHAM (NEW ST)
Third Class
160

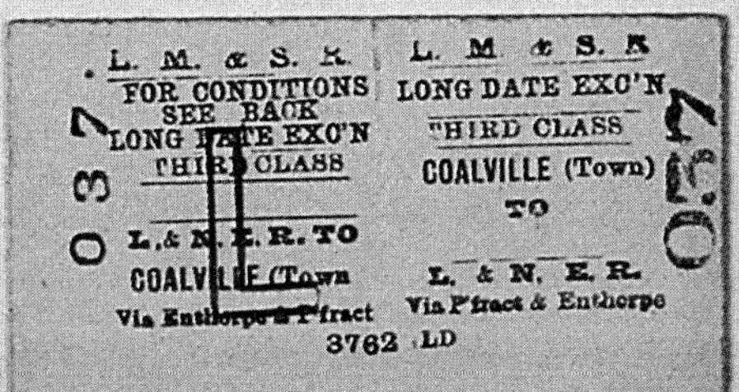
037
L. M. & S. R.
FOR CONDITIONS SEE BACK
LONG DATE EXC'N
THIRD CLASS
L. & N. E. R. TO
COALVILLE (Town
Via Enthorpe & P'fract
L. M. & S. R.
LONG DATE EXC'N
THIRD CLASS
COALVILLE (Town)
TO
L. & N. E. R.
Via P'fract & Enthorpe
3762 LD
037

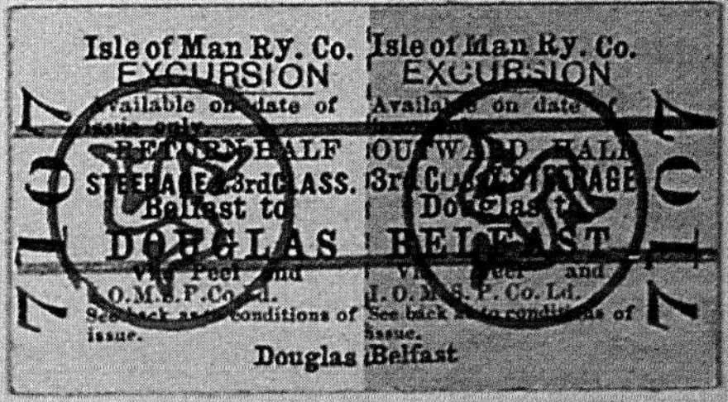
7107
Isle of Man Ry. Co.
EXCURSION
Available on date of issue only.
RETURN HALF
STEERAGE 3rd CLASS.
Belfast to
DOUGLAS
Via Peel and I.O.M.S.P. Co. Ld.
See back as to conditions of issue.
Douglas
Isle of Man Ry. Co.
EXCURSION
Available on date of issue only.
OUTWARD HALF
3rd CLASS STEERAGE
Douglas to
BELFAST
Via Peel and I.O.M.S.P. Co. Ld.
See back as to conditions of issue.
Belfast
7107

G. N. R. (I) EXCURSION
Issued subject to this Companys regulations and to the conditions in its Time Tables.
NotTransferable Available for day of issue only
24th. NOV. 1906.
Messrs T. COOK & SONS
Dublin(Amiens St) to
BELFAST
AND BACK. via Tanderagee
THIRD CLASS
AVAILABLE BY SPECIAL TRAIN ONLY
108

G C. & M. JOINT C.
Not Transferable
MARKET
ON DATE OF ISSUE ONLY
Stockport(T-D)
TO
ROMILEY
via Woodley or Bredbury J.
THIRD CLASS
CHILD
Fare 3d.
Romiley
TO
STOCKPORT(T.D)
THIRD CLASS
CHILD
FOR CONDITIONS SEE BACK.
3553

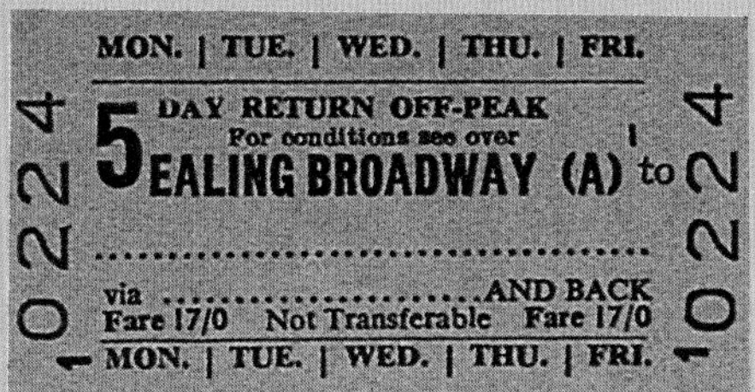

MON. | TUE. | WED. | THU. | FRI.
5 DAY RETURN OFF-PEAK
For conditions see over
EALING BROADWAY (A) to
via .... AND BACK
Fare 17/0 Not Transferable Fare 17/0
10224

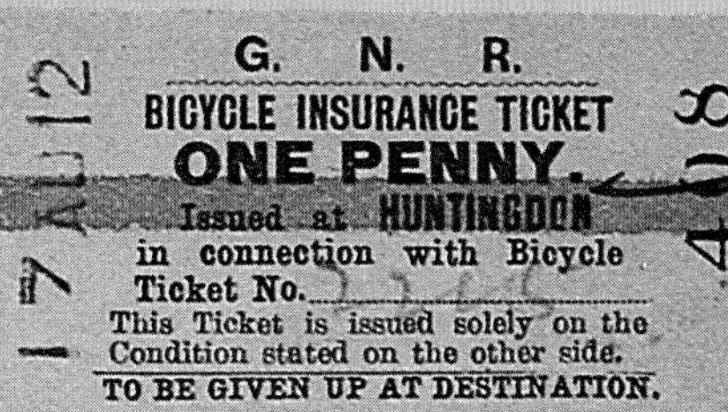

G. N. R.
BICYCLE INSURANCE TICKET
ONE PENNY.
Issued at HUNTINGDON
in connection with Bicycle
Ticket No.
This Ticket is issued solely on the Condition stated on the other side.
TO BE GIVEN UP AT DESTINATION.
408

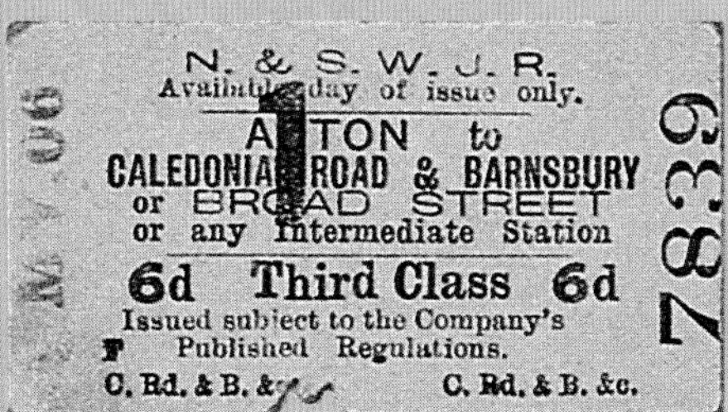

N. & S. W. J. R.
Available day of issue only.
ACTON to
CALEDONIAN ROAD & BARNSBURY
or BROAD STREET
or any Intermediate Station
6d Third Class 6d
Issued subject to the Company's Published Regulations.
C. Rd. & B. &c. C. Rd. & B. &c.
7839

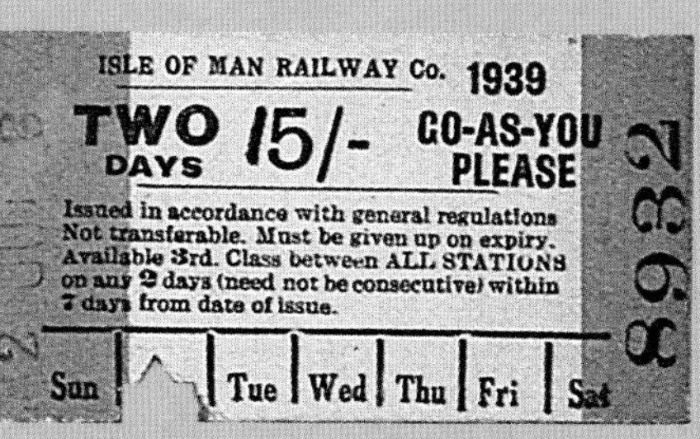

ISLE OF MAN RAILWAY Co. 1939
TWO DAYS 15/- GO-AS-YOU PLEASE
Issued in accordance with general regulations
Not transferable. Must be given up on expiry.
Available 3rd. Class between ALL STATIONS on any 2 days (need not be consecutive) within 7 days from date of issue.
Sun Tue Wed Thu Fri Sat
8932

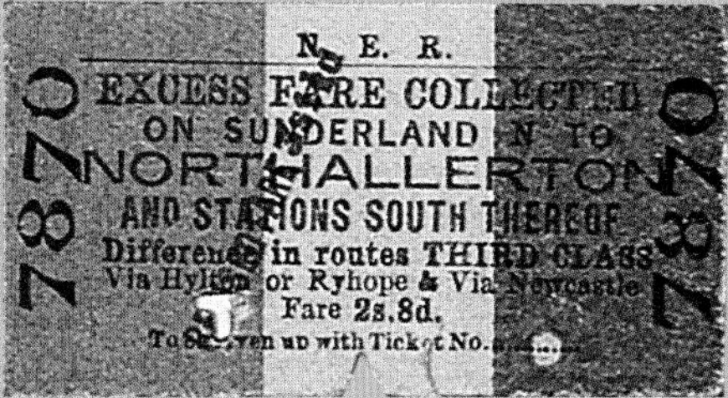

N. E. R.
EXCESS FARE COLLECTED
ON SUNDERLAND TO
NORTHALLERTON
AND STATIONS SOUTH THEREOF
Difference in routes THIRD CLASS
Via Hylton or Ryhope & Via Newcastle
Fare 2s.8d.
7870

LYNTON & BARNSTAPLE Ry.
(S.4.) CHELFHAM
TO
BARNSTAPLE TOWN
Chelfham Barnstaple T'n
Third Class
Fare 4½d. See Over Fare 4½d.

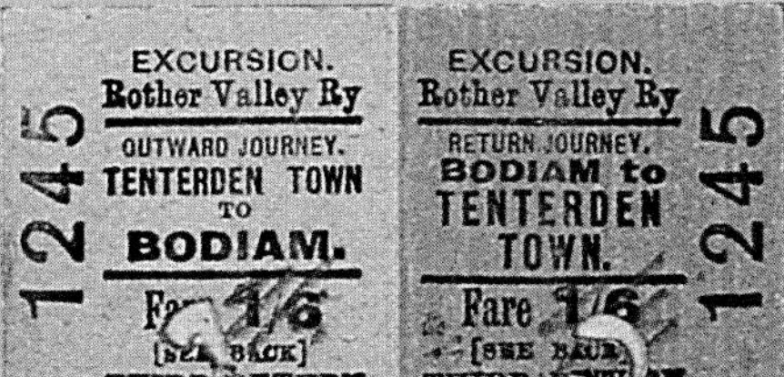

EXCURSION.
Rother Valley Ry
OUTWARD JOURNEY.
TENTERDEN TOWN
TO
BODIAM.
Fare 1/6
[SEE BACK]
THIRD RETURN
EXCURSION.
Rother Valley Ry
RETURN JOURNEY.
BODIAM to
TENTERDEN
TOWN.
Fare 1/6
1245

British Railways Board (M)
The A4 Locomotive Society Ltd.
17th June, 1972
SUPPLEMENTARY TICKET
ONE PACKED MEAL
ON SPECIAL TRAIN
FROM
NEWCASTLE
0395

working of guards, ticket collectors, etc, with their respective names, grade, destination and journey, and their home station. Further details were listed concerning the formation of the train at the commencement of the journey, with the vehicles shown 'In Order From Engine'. Branch passenger train crews filled in a similar but slightly less comprehensive journal.

These daily journals were sent variously (according to their importance) to the divisional officer and/or the superintendent of the line. By this record of each train's running, the working was kept under continual review; a steady flow of information was thus secured, necessary for any revision in the timetables.

The Railway Companies (Accounts and Returns) Act of 1911 set out in detail the statistical requirements of the various companies, since prior to its operation, the information compiled by each company differed considerably. The North Eastern Railway Company was one of the few who compiled comprehensive information. With the Railway (Re-grouping) Act of 1921, further revision was made in these requirements as a result of discussions between the Ministry of Transport and the Railway Companies' Association.

Assorted categories.
108 Great Northern Railway (Ireland) dated excursion, green with three vertical red stripe overprints.
3553 Great Central & Midland Railway Joint Committee market return (child), light red and green block overprints on white, with dark red vertical bar overprints on each, issued 6 May 1935.
0224 London Transport day return off-peak, pink.
408 Great Northern Railway bicycle insurance, buff coloured with horizontal red band overprint, issued 17 August 1912.
7839 North & South Western Junction Railway third class single, buff coloured with black station code overprint, issued May 1906. Incorporated 1851, opened in 1853, the line was closed to passenger traffic in 1902, but became part of the LMS in 1921.
8932 Isle of Man Railway two days 'Go-As-You-Please', two vertical light blue bands at either end. Although intended for issue in 1939 this particular ticket was not issued, with impressed date, until 2 June 1968.
7870 North Eastern Railway excess fare, pink and light blue block overprints on white with revised fare overprint in red, issued 22 March 1923.
9881 Lynton & Barnstaple third class single, lilac, issued 11 August 1922. The line was opened in 1898 with more than 19 miles of narrow gauge (1ft 11½in) track. It became part of the Southern Railway in 1923, was closed in 1935 and dismantled in 1936.
1245 Rother Valley Railway excursion return, brick red overprint on buff coloured card, issued 20 July 1944. Under a Light Railway Order the line was opened in 1900 and changed its name to Kent & East Sussex Railway in 1904.
0395 British Railways Board (Midland Region) dated supplementary ticket. Red outline overprint on light yellow card.

6
TICKET TYPES & FARES

After the Parliamentary sanction for the formation of a railway company, it was left to the company to formulate its own by-laws necessary for the efficient operation of train services. These laws provided that no one could board a train for the purpose of travelling, without having obtained the necessary ticket. The ticket has stood the test of time as being the best and simplest means of proving that the required fare has been paid. As has been previously shown, there were many varieties of passenger ticket in use by the different companies, but they may be classified into five main groups, viz, Ordinary tickets, Tourist tickets, Cheap Ordinary tickets, Excursion tickets, Season or Contract tickets. It was required by statute that all railway companies carried servicemen and police at less than ordinary fares.

ORDINARY TICKETS

Although each company was empowered at its foundation to charge reasonable fares, the variations allowed differed considerably between the companies. In 1855, such differences ranged from 3d to 9d per mile for first-class fares. Further differences, exclusive of the Government duty, were determined by the type of travel, ie express or ordinary train. Generally, fares were charged upon a distance travelled basis, but with the outbreak of war in 1914, railway fares underwent a complete revision.

Except for the third-class Parliamentary fare, none of the railway companies had a uniform fare. In 1913, the Great Western Railway charged

Obverse and reverse of an ivory free pass issued by the Midland Counties Railway to one of its directors. Note the heraldic wyvern which was later used by the Midland Railway. The Midland Counties was effectively amalgamated into the MR at the first general meeting held at Derby on 16 July 1844.

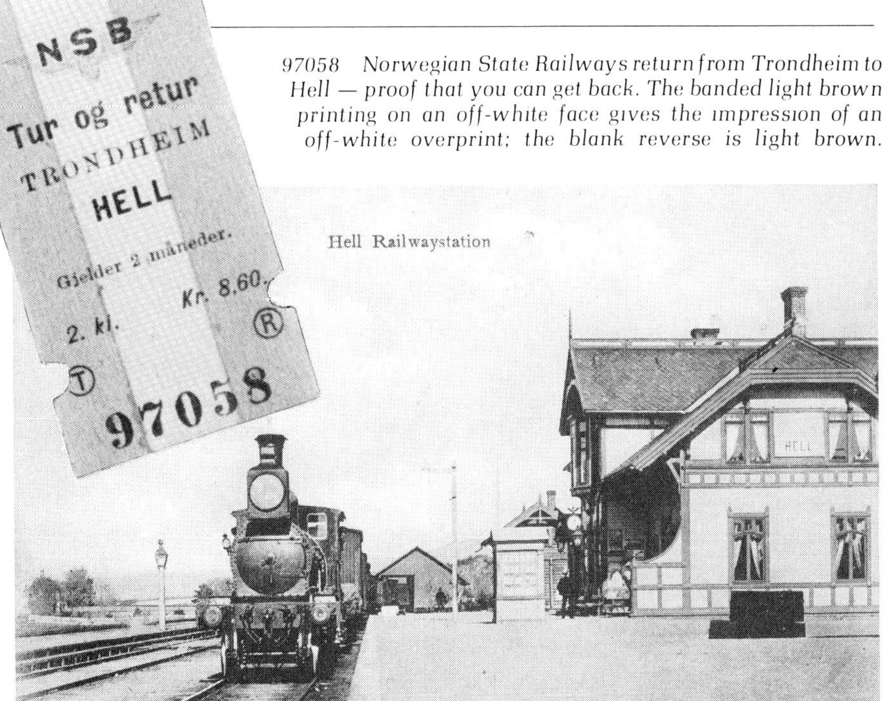

NSB
Tur og retur
TRONDHEIM
HELL
Gjelder 2 måneder.
2. kl.
Kr. 8,60
97058
Hell Railwaystation

97058 Norwegian State Railways return from Trondheim to Hell — proof that you can get back. The banded light brown printing on an off-white face gives the impression of an off-white overprint; the blank reverse is light brown.

Hell Railway Station. A picture postcard showing the station and train in 1909.

return fares at twice the single rate for third-class, and one and three-quarters of the single fare for first-class. Some of the companies charged a similar rate for third-class fares, but not for first-class; others charged one and three-fifths single fare for first-class, or even double for return fares.

After Government assumption of control of the railways on 4 August 1914, the fare structures of all the companies underwent radical alterations. The proposed changes, however, were not put into effect until January 1917. The 50 per cent increase in fares empowered by the December 1916 Order in Council, did not seek to swell the railways' coffers, but rather to discourage passenger traffic, in order that more troops and material could be conveyed over the rail network. Exceptions to the general increases were workmen's tickets, season tickets, traders' tickets, and zone tickets; existing arrangements were allowed to stand.

With the establishment in 1919 of the Ministry of Transport, a Rates Advisory Committee was set up to investigate 'any interest affected by alterations to rates, fares, tolls, dues, and other charges'. Subsequent to a public inquiry held to determine the best means for the railways to obtain increased revenue, a report on passenger fares was forwarded to the Ministry of Transport. A 75 per cent increase above the pre-war charge was recommended, and operated from 6 August 1920.

The travelling public did not take at all kindly to such gross increases, and when the Government relinquished control of the railways in 1921, there was an immediate outcry for fare reductions. The various companies announced that fares would be reduced to a figure 50 per cent above the pre-war charge. At the same time, fare standards, where necessary, were introduced. The 1921 Railway Act laid down procedures for the fixing of

LONDON AN…

PROPRIETOR'S

(FREE.)

On presenting this Ticket to the Guard at the London Terminus, the BEARER and FRIEND will be allowed on any one day *before* the to go by any Croydon Train to Croydon, and from thence to be conveyed by the Atmospheric Train, when at work, to the Forest Hill (Dartmouth Arms) Station, and back to Croydon, after which they may return to London by any Locomotive Train *on the same day*, when this Ticket *must be delivered* to the TICKET COLLECTOR at the London Terminus.

London and Croydon Railway free ticket. The company operated the atmospheric railway along a single line, with the leading carriage in every train carrying a piston along a 15in pipe laid between the rails. Speeds of 75mph were said to have been attained. Brunel laid an atmospheric track between Newton Abbot and Teignmouth, the trains regularly travelling at 70mph. The L & CR was amalgamated into the London, Brighton, and South Coast Railway during 1846.

fare schedules, these having to be approved by the Railway Rates Tribunal before being put into practice.

The London & North Eastern Railway, Great Northern Section, Special Train Arrangements, January to June 1936 volume, and issued from the District Manager's Office, Nottingham, contains the following items.

> Circular No. P.M. 935.
> London & North Eastern Railway (Southern Area).
> Instructions to Stationmasters, Booking Clerks and all others concerned respecting Reduced Fare Bookings by Ordinary Trains for Special Events, etc.
> Sunday, 9th February, to Saturday, 15th February, 1936, inclusive.
>
> Return Tickets at Ordinary Single Fare and One-Third.
> Return tickets may be issued upon presentation of vouchers, as shown below: third class at ordinary single fare and one-third for the double journey (fractions of 3d. reckoned as 3d.) — first class at 50 per cent above the third class fare (fractions of 3d. reckoned as 3d.).

The event which occasioned the above instruction was a 'Hotels Holiday Makers Re-Union', held between the 8 and 15 February 1936. Tickets were issued to London, and were available for one calendar month.

Following upon this instruction was another which concerned the issue of day return tickets for several events taking place between 8 February and 22 February. The events ranged from a Masonic meeting in Liverpool and a music festival in Barnsley, to the reunion of the 16th Battn (CLB) The King's Royal Rifle Corps Old Comrades Association. Tickets were to be issued from any station upon surrender at the time of booking of vouchers

Admission ticket 0183 was issued by the LNER acting on behalf of the Hull Corporation under the Kingston upon Hull (Victoria Pier) Scheme, 1934. It was required to be produced on demand by the railway company's ticket examination staff. Ordinary return 7026, issued by British Railways Board, bears a similar broad, horizontal red band overprint.

signed by a person named. The return fare was the same as the third class at the ordinary single fare (plus fractions of 1d), while the first class fare was 50 per cent above the third class fare with the same qualification. Both ticket issues were subject to the train service allowing the outward and homeward journeys to be performed the same day.

British Industries Fair, 1936. London & Birmingham.
17th to 28th February.

In connection with the above, it has been agreed to the issue of 'Monthly Return' tickets to Exhibitors and Buyers making direct out and home journeys either to London or to Birmingham via London or vice versa: at the single fare and one-third; First Class fares being 50 per cent over the Third Class. In the case of triangular journeys, tickets may be issued under circular tour arrangement at approximately three-fourths of the ordinary fare, Third class. First class fares 50 per cent over Third class, from point to point upon application to the local station before commencing the journey; the tickets being available for three months.

Vouchers were not required in the case of:
(a) Visitors from Ireland and Channel Islands.
(b) Journeys between places in Great Britain where the fares were below the 'monthly return' tickets minima.

The format of the railway ticket voucher for the British Industries Fair was shown. It was addressed to the booking clerk, station and railway company to be specified. He was required to issue tickets as per the instructions, and on the voucher he entered the number of the ticket issued, the fare paid, and added his signature.

From the beginning, no Railway Act had ever required a company to issue return tickets, which was regarded as being a sales gimmick. As has been described previously, the companies found that fare reductions tended to bring about an increase in passenger traffic. A Parliamentary Committee in 1846 sought verification that the London and Birmingham Railway had made several reductions in their fares. The committee was told that in September 1844, the through fares between London and Birmingham were 32s 6d for the mail train, and 30s for the ordinary first-class. In October they were reduced to 30s and 27s respectively, and by

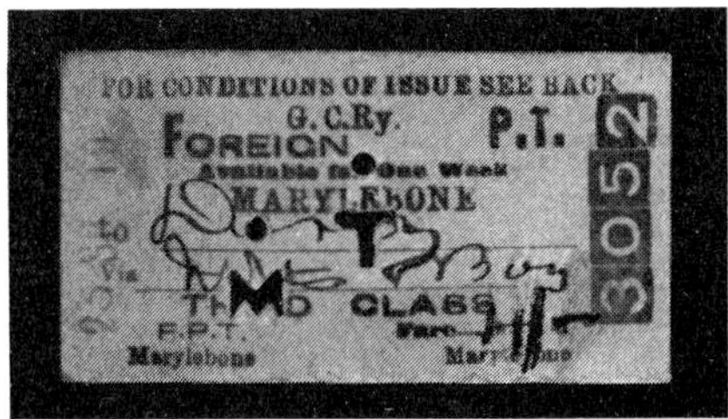

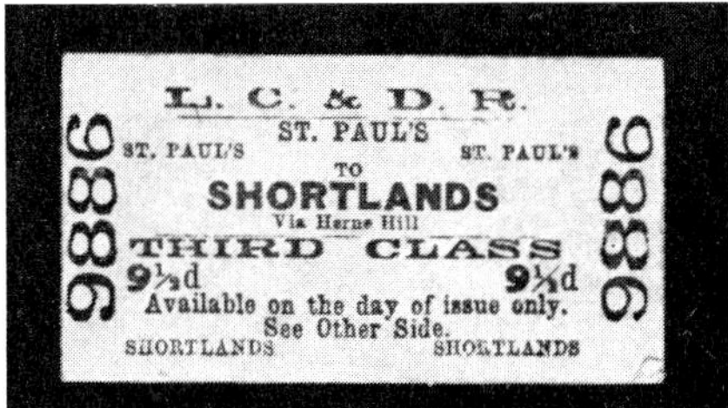

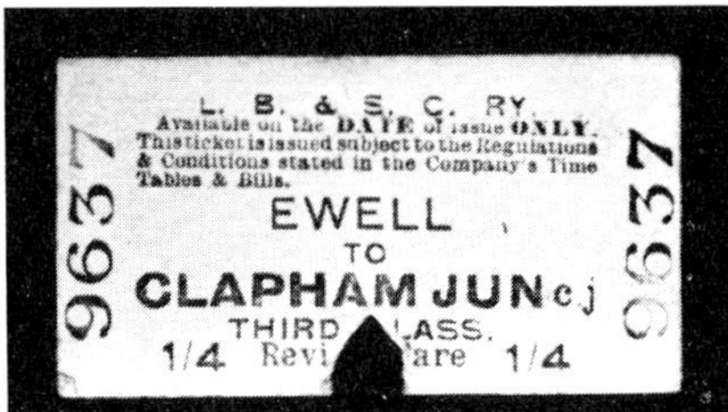

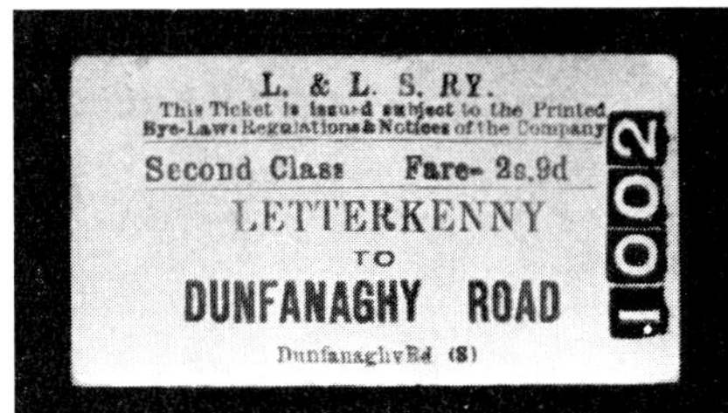

3052 Great Central Railway foreign privilege ticket, third class. Issued in September 1910, it was intended for use only by company servants, their wives or children in accordance with the special regulations. Light blue.
9886 London, Chatham & Dover Railway third class single. Light green, issued 1898. Some of the fiercest competition in British railway history was between the LC & DR and the South Eastern Railway. Both operated services to Dover to connect with the Calais boats, for passengers bound for Paris.
9637 London, Brighton & South Coast Railway third class single, revised fare. Journeys for which excess ticket stocks had been printed would not have required specially printed issues, the old fares being crossed out by the booking clerk.
1002 Londonderry & Lough Swilly Railway second class. Light blue, this ticket was not issued. Opened in 1863, the L & LS included the Letterkenney and Burtonport Extension in 1903.

January 1845, the first-class fare dropped to 20s. The committee asked if such reductions had 'been attended in any instance with a loss of revenue'. They were assured that there had been in fact an increase in first-class passengers of 19.5 per cent, with an increase in the number of second-class passengers of 61.2 per cent. The figure quoted for the increase in third-class passenger traffic was a staggering 259 per cent!

Special conditions were operated with the issue of ordinary tickets. As with other types of ticket, these conditions were printed, or referred to, on the ticket. As a general rule ordinary single tickets, and the outward halves of ordinary return tickets were available on the day of issue only. Return halves could be valid for a period of two days, or over a week-end. Much support was given to the notion that tickets should be issued without time limitations, and to this end several unsuccessful Bills were placed before Parliament.

Ticket scalpers were a type of railway criminal peculiar to American railroads alone. They started in the early days, when it used to be said that a company's revenue was decided by the conductors of the various trains. It was alleged that at the end of the day they threw the day's receipts against the roof of the carriage, and 'whatever stuck was turned in to the Company'.

NOT TRANSFERABLE SEE NOTE (1) BELOW. Army Book 422.

WAR OFFICE RAILWAY WARRANT

for use of Military personnel travelling on duty and for Guns, Vehicles and Horses when accompanying troops, and for Horses travelling unaccompanied.

CHARGES PAYABLE BY
*The Command Paymaster, Aldershot.
or

This Warrant is ~~not chargeable~~ chargeable* against the public. (See Note 5.)
Initials of Issuing Officer

97

Nº 310368

Military Station Wordsley Date 22nd May 1942
To the concerned Railway Company.

Please convey without charge to Bearer the passengers and other traffic shown below via the ~~recognised direct and cheapest route.~~ most expeditious route

From Stourbridge
To Birmingham (Snow Hill) Single. ~~Return.~~

†Returning same day.
†Returning on

and debit the charges at ~~Ordinary~~* Military fares and rates as indicated above.

Signature of Issuing Officer H. Wynn Kennine
Rank and Corps *Major, R. A.*
Military Registrar.

MILITARY SECTION
22 MAY 1942
WORDSLEY EMERGENCY HOSPITAL
STOURBRIDGE

Stamp of Issuing Office.

The particulars on the back of this Warrant must be fully completed	Number (in words) to be conveyed. (To be filled in by Issuer)	To be filled in by Railway Company: Ordinary Fares	Military Fares	Amount payable £ s. d.
FIRST CLASS— Officers, Wives, Children 14 years and over, Children of 3 and under 14				
THIRD CLASS— Officers, W.O.'s and other ranks, Wives, Children 14 years and over, Children of 3 and under 14	ONE			

	No.	Weight including contents. (See Note 7) Tons. cwts. qrs.	Mileage	Rates
GUNS, LIMBERS, VEHICLES, &c. (other than mechanical). MECHANICAL VEHICLES (For details, see other side).				
HORSES OR MULES (See Note 8). In Horse Boxes— *By Passenger Train; *By Special Troop Train. In Cattle Trucks— *By Special Troop Train; *By Merchandise Train	Numbers (in words) to be conveyed.			
BICYCLES (See Note 8).				
MOTOR BICYCLES (See Note 8).				
			TOTAL £	

To be filled in by Railway Company.

Number(s) of ticket(s) issued .... Date 19
Route via .... Issued by ....

*Strike out words not applicable.
†Complete as necessary.

IMPORTANT.

(1) This Warrant is not transferable. It must be presented at the Booking Office of the Station from which the journey is authorised to be commenced, when a Railway ticket or tickets will be issued in exchange. Such tickets are not transferable.

(2) Children under 14 to be entered as "Half passengers," no entry to be made for children under 3 years of age, as carried free.

(3) Any alteration on this Warrant must be initialled by the Issuing Officer.

(4) This Warrant will become null and void if not used within one calendar month from the date of issue.

(5) Where Warrants are issued on repayment, the instructions in paragraph 1074, King's Regulations, 1935, must be strictly complied with.

(6) Animals (other than Horses and Mules), Sewing Machines, Perambulators, Go-carts and Pictures, &c., should not be entered on Warrants.

(7) The weight of baggage and stores not packed in Army vehicles must be excluded. Separate forms (Carriers' Notes) to be used for traffic not so packed.

(8) Only Horses or Mules, or Bicycles and Motor Bicycles entitled to be conveyed at the public expense to be entered.

(9) Attention is directed to paras. 4 and 8, Instructions relating to Conveyance of Army Personnel and Baggage, 1934, regarding the issue of warrants for single, return and through journeys.

This type of railway warrant could be used as, or in exchange for, an appropriate ticket. The old-fashioned phrase 'most expeditious route', written by the issuing officer, indicates that wartime restrictions on passenger trains frequently meant re-routing and altered timetables. (Patrick B. Whitehouse collection)

The practice of the scalpers was to buy the return sections of the coupon tickets, and then to re-sell them at inflated prices. The traveller at any large, important railway station had to run the gauntlet of rows of scalpers' 'offices'. Each, trying to be brighter than its neighbours, carried flamboyant banners and placards loudly advertising ticket bargains.

The nuisance eventually reached such proportions that the Pinkerton Detective Agency was called in by the railroad companies to combat such conditions. For years they worked as undercover agents among the operating personnel of the railroads, before they evolved the ticket barrier inspection and collection systems used from the early days on English railways.

TOURIST TICKETS

These are not to be confused with cheap ordinary tickets; they were a special issue for the convenience of passengers on tour. Such passengers had the right to break their journey, usually at specified stations, and the tickets were valid for periods of one week and more. As long ago as 1852, it was possible to travel to Ireland on a ticket valid for one month; tourist travellers in Great Britain used a ticket which was available for a period of three weeks. By 1916, when the issue of tourist tickets was suspended, the period of validity had been extended to six months. Tourist tickets were eventually reissued in 1921 with a two month limit.

At the time of the original introduction of tourist tickets, the charge was established as one and a half times the single fare, being later increased to one and three-quarter times the single fare. Such tickets were of course only available for first-class passengers, but in 1872 they were generally introduced; the third-class fares for journeys covered by such tickets were charged on the same basis as the other classes. Two subsequent major fare revisions affected the issue of tourist tickets. The first revision was in 1900, part of an overall restructuring of fare schedules. By rounding-up odd pence to the nearest shilling the tourist fares were established at one and three-quarter times the single fare, plus fractional parts of a shilling. The second revision was caused by the after-effects of the settlement of the 1911 rail strike. Subject to the provision that ordinary fares would not be exceeded, a 5 per cent increase on third-class tourist fares was agreed.

Initially, the issue of tourist tickets had been restricted to the summer season, but this was gradually extended into the winter months. Agreement was reached by the various companies that tourist tickets should only be issued to certain places, these being known as 'Recognised Tourist Resorts'. The addition of a resort to the lists published in each company's tourist programme had to be approved by the Railway Clearing House at an annual meeting.

CHEAP ORDINARY TICKETS

Quite early on in the Government control of the railways during World War I, many cheap travelling concessions were withdrawn. The Railway Executive Committee issued the following notice on 29 March 1915:

Special Railway Notice
Withdrawal of Excursion and Cheap Fare Facilities

> On and from Monday, 29th March, 1915, and until further notice excursion and cheap fare facilities (with certain exceptions) will be withdrawn.

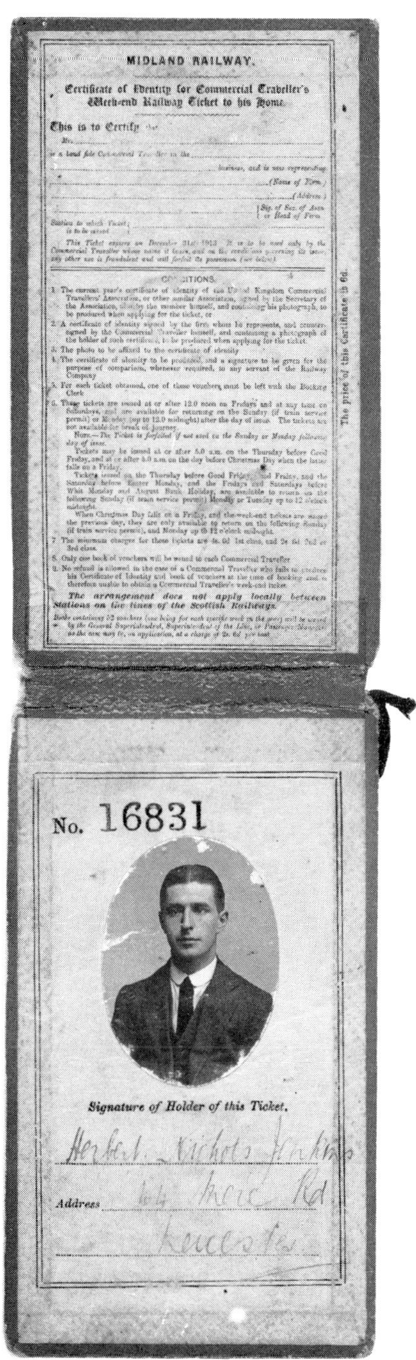

MIDLAND RAILWAY.

Certificate of Identity for Commercial Traveller's Week-end Railway Ticket to his Home.

This is to Certify that

Mr. ....

is a bona fide Commercial Traveller in the .... business, and is now representing

.... (Name of Firm.)

.... (Address.)

.... { Sig. of Sec. of Assn. or Head of Firm.

Station to which Ticket is to be issued ....

This Ticket expires on December 31st 1913. It is to be used only by the Commercial Traveller whose name it bears, and on the conditions governing its issue; any other use is fraudulent and will forfeit its possession (see below).

CONDITIONS.

1. The current year's certificate of identity of the United Kingdom Commercial Travellers' Association, or other similar Association, signed by the Secretary of the Association, also by the member himself, and containing his photograph, to be produced when applying for the ticket, or
2. A certificate of identity signed by the firm whom he represents, and countersigned by the Commercial Traveller himself, and containing a photograph of the holder of such certificate, to be produced when applying for the ticket.
3. The photo to be affixed to the certificate of identity.
4. The certificate of identity to be produced, and a signature to be given for the purpose of comparison, whenever required, to any servant of the Railway Company.
5. For each ticket obtained, one of these vouchers must be left with the Booking Clerk.
6. These tickets are issued at or after 12.0 noon on Fridays and at any time on Saturdays, and are available for returning on the Sunday (if train service permit) or Monday (up to 12.0 midnight) after the day of issue. The tickets are not available for break of journey.

   Note.—*The Ticket is forfeited if not used on the Sunday or Monday following day of issue.*

   Tickets may be issued at or after 5.0 a.m. on the Thursday before Good Friday, and at or after 5.0 a.m. on the day before Christmas Day when the latter falls on a Friday.

   Tickets issued on the Thursday before Good Friday, and Friday, and the Saturday before Easter Monday, and the Fridays and Saturdays before Whit Monday and August Bank Holiday, are available to return on the following Sunday (if train service permit) Monday or Tuesday up to 12 o'clock midnight.

   When Christmas Day falls on a Friday, and the week-end tickets are issued the previous day, they are only available to return on the following Sunday (if train service permit), and Monday up to 12 o'clock midnight.
7. The minimum charges for these tickets are 4s. 0d. 1st class, and 2s. 6d. 2nd or 3rd class.
8. Only one book of vouchers will be issued to each Commercial Traveller.
9. No refund is allowed in the case of a Commercial Traveller who fails to produce his Certificate of Identity and book of vouchers at the time of booking and is therefore unable to obtain a Commercial Traveller's week-end ticket.

The arrangement does not apply locally between Stations on the lines of the Scottish Railways.

Books containing 52 vouchers (one being for each specific week in the year) will be issued by the General Superintendent, Superintendent of the Line, or Passenger Manager as the case may be, on application, at a charge of 2s. 6d. per book.

The price of this Certificate is 6d.

No. 16831

Signature of Holder of this Ticket.

Herbert Nichols Jenkins

Address

For some reason, this splendid Midland Railway commercial traveller's weekend railway ticket was never issued. Mr Herbert Nichols Jenkins, of Leicester, for whom it was intended, was required to provide a photograph of himself, together with a certificate of identity signed by the firm he represented, when applying for the special ticket. It is bound in imitation Morocco leather, coloured light green, with the titling and year date embossed in gold. (Stuart Underwood collection)

Great Central Railway.

Weekly ZONE Tickets

SHEFFIELD DISTRICT.

On and from September 13th, 1920.

ZONE TICKETS

will enable you to travel between ANY Stations indicated on the diagram

AS OFTEN AS YOU LIKE FROM SUNDAY MORNING UNTIL SATURDAY NIGHT

FOLLOWING THE DATE OF ISSUE.

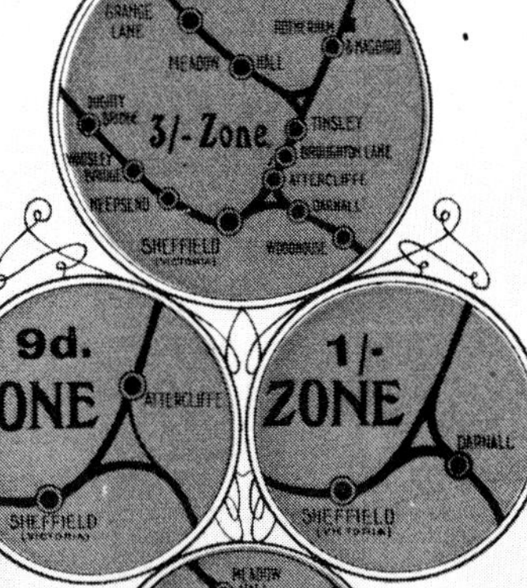

ZONE TICKETS

are only available . at the Stations . . shown in the . respective Zone Areas, and their use is restricted to Trains calling at those Stations.

ZONE TICKETS ARE NOT TRANSFERABLE, and must be produced to any servant of the Company upon request, and failing such production upon any journey, the Full Ordinary Fare for such journey must be paid.

These Tickets are issued at a reduced rate, and in consideration thereof are accepted by the passenger on the express condition that the liability of the Company to make compensation for injury or otherwise in respect of the passenger shall be limited to a sum not exceeding ONE HUNDRED POUNDS, and that the amount of compensation payable in respect of any such passenger shall, subject to such limitation, be determined by an arbitrator to be appointed by the Board of Trade, and not otherwise.

These Tickets are issued at the Stations on any day of the week, but will not be available beyond the Saturday following the date of issue.

Marylebone Station, London, N.W., September, 1920. L.1875.—3,100. **SAM FAY,** *General Manager.*

CHAS. SEVER, Printer, Lithographer, &c., 40, King St. West, Manchester.

Great Central Railway weekly zone ticket handbill. These tickets were intended to supplement the ordinary weekly tickets by providing facilities similar to those available with standard season tickets, but with the standardisation of such tickets in 1918 the system proved to be costly and cumbersome.

Great Central Railway.

ZONE TICKETS

The GREAT CENTRAL RAILWAY COMPANY hereby give notice that on and after Sunday, 30th October, 1921, the issue of Zone Tickets will be discontinued.

The Season Ticket Rates which have hitherto been based on the sum of the Zone Fares will be cancelled also, and the Ordinary Season Ticket Rates, as published in the Company's Pamphlets, will apply.

On and from Monday, 31st October, Workmen's Weekly Tickets, available for six days, i.e. from Monday to Saturday inclusive, and for one journey in each direction in third class carriages on each day while in force by certain specified trains, particulars of which may be obtained at the Stations, will be issued between points where Zone Tickets were available.

SAM FAY, General Manager.

Marylebone Station, London, N.W. 1.
October 20th, 1921. 100

Knapp, Drewett & Sons Ltd., 30, Victoria St., S.W., and Kingston-on-Thames.—1421 G.C.

One year after introducing the zone ticket system, the Great Central Railway announced that the issue would be discontinued.

Particulars of the Reduced Fare Bookings which will remain in operation can be obtained at the Railway Stations.

By Order of the
Railway Executive Committee
London, March, 1915.

Although there were several exceptions to this order, effectively only HM Forces, war-workers, and those whose living depended on their travelling by rail were given reduced fare concessions. Strangely enough, these and other restrictions had less than the desired effect in reducing passenger traffic. Subsequent to the cessation of hostilities, an attempt was made to restore prewar services. An almost endless variety of reduced fare concessions were made available, catering for everybody from Anglers to Strolling Players, Bell Ringers to Shipwrecked Mariners, Concert Parties to Battlefield Pilgrims.

The conditional issue of the cheap ordinary tickets was aimed at increasing passenger traffic. Each of the 'Big Four' launched widespread advertising campaigns, with company representatives canvassing prospective travellers. Groups and associations were charged ordinary single fare for a round trip, with a minimum charge for twelve adult fares.

With weekend passenger traffic on the increase, the companies introduced special weekend tickets available for all classes of passengers. Commercial travellers, on presentation of a voucher to which their photograph was affixed, had long been granted cheap weekend return tickets. The weekend tickets were issued at a single fare and a third for a return journey, available between specified times, and with conditions relating to the amount of free luggage carried by passengers. Certain types of weekend ticket were issued as combined rail and hotel tickets. For an inclusive charge, passengers could stay at a high-class hotel, with full board from Saturday luncheon to breakfast on Monday.

It is almost impossible to draw a distinction between the tourist ticket and the ultimate development of the cheap ordinary ticket. The railways offered diverse facilities for tourists, enabling passengers to travel to one station, and return from another. The journey was made by ordinary trains, within territorial limits of 60 miles radius from the station of departure, tickets being issued at half the ordinary single fare for the round trip. Combined rail and road, or rail and steamer daily walking tours, and steamboat circular tours, were some of the tourist facilities offered; the tickets were available over different periods, and fares were at cheap rates. The 'Save to Travel' scheme introduced by the LNER was used for the purchase of tickets for journeys to the Continent via the company's steamship routes, and LNER stations and town offices would accept 'Save to travel' stamps or vouchers in payment or part payment for such fares.

The instructions noted in the fortnightly circulars had to be followed in accounting for all tickets issued in exchange for stamps or vouchers.

EXCURSION TICKETS

The excursion ticket is, by general definition, a form of cheap ordinary ticket issued usually in connection with special trains. The period of validity for such tickets ranged over a wide field; basically the divisions

London Midland and Scottish Railway Company.
WEEKLY SEASON TICKET. THIRD CLASS
No. 9172 AVAILABLE BETWEEN
ST. PANCRAS & LUTON
L.N.E.
Also available King's Cross for through
to and from and Luton journeys only.
UNTIL
Signature of Holder
FOR CONDITIONS SEE BACK.

9172 *London, Midland & Scottish Railway Company third class weekly season ticket. The multi-dot safety background and the LMS motif are printed in green on glossy white card. Main ticket and destination details are printed in black; the extra availability information is in red.* (Stuart Underwood collection)

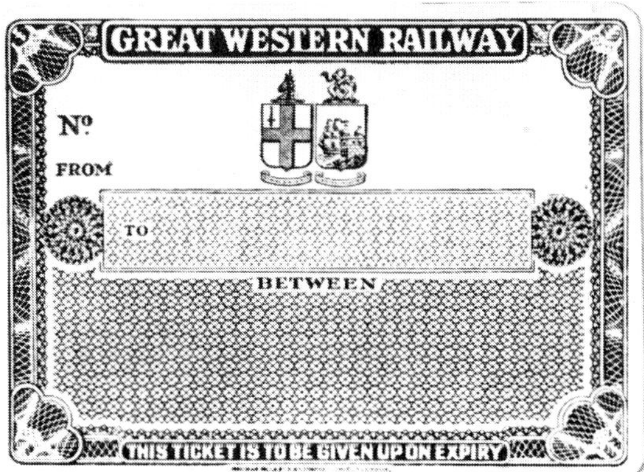
GREAT WESTERN RAILWAY
No.
FROM
TO
BETWEEN
THIS TICKET IS TO BE GIVEN UP ON EXPIRY

Great Western Railway season ticket blank; the delicately engraved design was introduced in 1928. The use of banknote-style printing for this category of ticket was an innovation intended to provide a safeguard against forgery. Steel-plate printing was used for this design of high artistic merit, a process rarely used in this country other than for the then newly-issued Bank of England notes. In station stock the blank was over printed with the necessary details in appropriate colours.

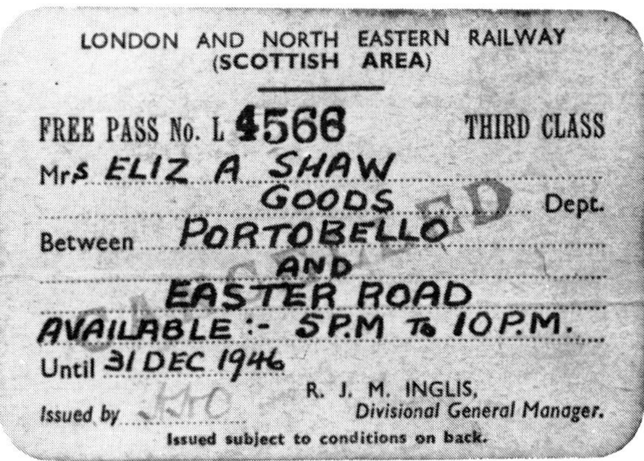
LONDON AND NORTH EASTERN RAILWAY
(SCOTTISH AREA)
FREE PASS No. L 4566 THIRD CLASS
Mrs ELIZ A SHAW
GOODS Dept.
Between PORTOBELLO
AND
EASTER ROAD
AVAILABLE :- 5PM To 10P.M.
Until 31 DEC 1946
R. J. M. INGLIS,
Issued by ...... Divisional General Manager.
Issued subject to conditions on back.

L4566 *London and North Eastern Railway (Scottish Area) third class free pass. Printed overall in green, this type of free pass, with a time limit for its usage, was issued to carriage cleaning staff.*

were half-day, day, short period, and long period. Conditions for the use of excursion tickets were displayed in the advertisements, and infringement of these conditions required the passenger to pay the full ordinary fare.

The Railway Traveller's Handy Book commented that 'Excursion tickets are of varied kind and character; the leading idea is, however, to afford an opportunity of enjoying the greatest amount of pleasure at the smallest possible cost.' It went on to comment that excursionists were expected to

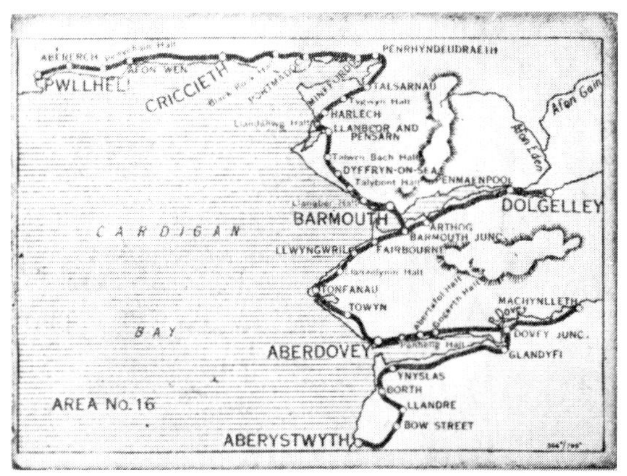

The reverse of this Great Western Railway holiday season ticket is a perfect example of the graphical representation of a company's system on its tickets. As well as providing information for the traveller concerning the zonal availability of the ticket, its clarity is such that it could stand as a guide map in its own right. Printed in black on a light brown background. (P.B. Whitehouse collection)

Stockton & Darlington Railway.

SEASON TICKET.

First Class.

To Mr. ______________________

DARLINGTON AND REDCAR.

From the ________ **day of** ______________ **inclusive,**

to ________ **day of** ______________ **inclusive.**

______________________ ***Secretary.***

The holder of this Ticket is subject to the same Rules and Regulations as other Passengers.

Stockton & Darlington Railway season ticket blank. Printed in black on pink card, its date is unknown, but certainly prior to 1865. (John E. Shelbourn collection)

abide by the restrictions which limited the quantity of their luggage.

Subsequent to the regrouping, the four major companies operated two classes of excursion trains. The first included trains which ran on schedules promoted entirely by the company, while the second comprised 'guaranteed trains' which were operated on a charter basis. An independent promoter chartered such a train, guaranteeing not less than 300 passengers for fares less than 10s, and where the amount was greater than this, the promoter was required to guarantee 200 passengers. With such charter trains the company paid a commission of not more than 7 per cent on all bookings. Guaranteed trains were advertised solely by the promoter, but excursions organised by the railway company utilised the full resources of that company.

It was usual for most types of excursion to be operated at third-class only, but special exceptions ran with first-class bookings, the fares being something in the region of twice the third-class excursion rate. Prior to the regrouping, the method of calculating excursion fares had differed from one company to another, but subsequently, a generally uniform system was introduced. Broadly speaking, ordinary single fares were charged for a double journey on half-day and day excursions. For period bookings the rate was ordinary single fare and one third. In 1920, the Rates Advisory

E.R.O. 43570/2

London Midland and Scottish
RAILWAY COMPANY.

No. 42

MANCHESTER & NORTH WALES
CLUB SALOONS.

is a Subscribing Member to the Manchester and North Wales Travelling Club, and is entitled with his First Class Season Ticket to travel between the points indicated thereon in the Special Club Saloons.

This Ticket is operative till April 30th, 1941, is **Not Transferable,** and is to be given up on expiry.

.... *for L. M. & S. Rly. Co.*

.... *Secretary to the Club.*

London, Midland & Scottish Railway Company first class season ticket. As with the commercial traveller's ticket and other similar issues, the company was not stinting in its production. Although produced during the war there is no hint of austerity in their presentation .
42 Manchester & North Wales Club Saloons blank which was required to be signed by official representatives of the railway company and the Travelling Club. The cover is of light tan imitation Morocco leather, the company crest and ticket title embossed in gold.

Committee reported to the Ministry of Transport that they considered excursion, weekend, and tourist rates should be a higher proportion of ordinary rates than had been the case before the war.

SEASON OR CONTRACT TICKETS

Where passengers regularly travelled on standard services, the railway companies accorded them the privilege of purchasing a season or contract ticket, the rates being low. Most holders of season tickets, then as now, made one round journey per day, although it was not unknown for more frequent journeys to have been made.

At one time, few of the railway companies published fare details for season tickets, but, quite naturally, prices were competitive. Eventually, business sense prevailed, and pamphlets were published which specified the fares, and the attendant conditions. Many companies issued special half-price season tickets, available to people between the ages of 12 and 18. The North Staffordshire Railway required applicants for such tickets to produce a birth certificate; this was not unusual, since most companies required certificated proof of the applicant's age. This was supplied by the applicant's parent, guardian, teacher, or employer; in the case of the employer, he was also required to certify that the applicant's wage did not

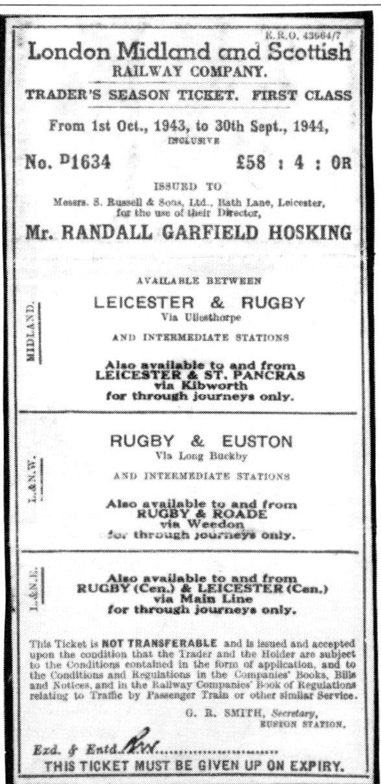

E.R.O. 43664/7

London Midland and Scottish
RAILWAY COMPANY.

TRADER'S SEASON TICKET. FIRST CLASS

From 1st Oct., 1943, to 30th Sept., 1944,
INCLUSIVE

No. D1634 £58 : 4 : 0R

ISSUED TO
Messrs. S. Russell & Sons, Ltd., Bath Lane, Leicester,
for the use of their Director,

Mr. RANDALL GARFIELD HOSKING

AVAILABLE BETWEEN

MIDLAND.

LEICESTER & RUGBY
Via Ullesthorpe
AND INTERMEDIATE STATIONS

Also available to and from
LEICESTER & ST. PANCRAS
via Kibworth
for through journeys only.

L.&N.W.

RUGBY & EUSTON
Via Long Buckby
AND INTERMEDIATE STATIONS

Also available to and from
RUGBY & ROADE
via Weedon
for through journeys only.

L.&N.E.

Also available to and from
RUGBY (Cen.) & LEICESTER (Cen.)
via Main Line
for through journeys only.

This Ticket is NOT TRANSFERABLE and is issued and accepted upon the condition that the Trader and the Holder are subject to the Conditions contained in the form of application, and to the Conditions and Regulations in the Companies' Books, Bills and Notices, and in the Railway Companies' Book of Regulations relating to Traffic by Passenger Train or other similar Service.

G. R. SMITH, *Secretary*,
EUSTON STATION.

Exd. & Entd..........................

THIS TICKET MUST BE GIVEN UP ON EXPIRY.

D1634 Trader's season ticket. This ticket is unusual in several respects. It was issued for a twelve-month period, specially printed with the bearers name and his company, together with the fare paid. In the details of the routes of availability, the ticket is most interesting. Each of the three sections has supplementary information printed in red. The first two refer back more than twenty years to pre-grouping days, while the third refers to travel over the lines of one of the other members of the 'Big Four'. The cover is of red leather, and embossed in gold. A cut-out in the central panel positively displays the expiry date. (Stuart Underwood collection)

exceed 18s per week. Some companies granted further reductions in the issue of season tickets where two or more such tickets were purchased by members of the same family. Such rather extravagant concessions were withdrawn in 1918 when the issue of season tickets was standardised.

The season ticket was no stranger to conditions of issue; indeed, the conditions were much more varied and complex than for most other types of ticket. For example, they could be issued for periods of up to one year, or for broken periods corresponding to school terms in the case of teachers. In this latter case, the teacher, supplying bona fides, applied for a ticket to cover the actual period of the terms (which had to exceed a total of three calendar months), and odd days were charged at a proportionate rate. The basic condition of a season ticket was that it was not transferable, and could be used on any ordinary service train. The destination and departure stations were listed, together with any further conditions relating to the section of line for which it was valid.

In keeping with the issue of other types of tickets, the season ticket had to

Midland Railway first class season ticket, personally signed by James Allport, General Manager. The year of issue, 1866, is printed in light red, as part of the background, on each half of the ticket; this confirmed the date of validity, and was a further safeguard against the risk of forgery. Its case is of red Moroccan-style leather, embossed in gold with the company's emblem. (George Dow collection)

be produced on demand of an authorised servant of the company. A passenger who could not produce his season ticket was liable for payment of the full ordinary fare. Season tickets could be renewed, but if not surrendered to the company on the date of expiry, renewal from any other date was not possible. It is only human nature to want something for nothing, but one must marvel at the gall of passengers who, being dilatory in the renewal of their season tickets, claimed upon the company for a refund of full ordinary fares paid by them in the interim.

Loss of a season ticket had to be notified immediately to the company, who inserted details concerning the ticket in the weekly and fortnightly notices. Duplicates were only issued at the discretion of the company, but such procedure was rare; on such occasions, a charge of not less than 2s 6d was levied in the case of three-monthly tickets.

Refund was possible if the ticket was used for a few days only, but was subject to certain conditions. The death of the holder of a season ticket required only the production of the medical certificate for full value of the unused period to be refunded, without further conditions.

Season tickets were, and still are, very popular, and received much publicity. Although the usual notice required before the issue of season tickets was one week, some companies went so far as to make them available on demand at certain stations. In the vicinity of coastal resorts, some companies issued special holiday season tickets, for use in that area.

A less familiar version of the season ticket was that issued to traders. Firms whose goods traffic over a company's lines equalled £450 per annum were granted the concession of one ticket; more tickets would be issued for an annually sustained traffic, the value of which was in multiples of that amount. The traders' season tickets were issued after completion of a special application form countersigned by a director or the secretary of the

An interesting free pass issued by the Lyon, Mediterranean Railway to M. Toni Fontenoy, Chief Engineer of the St Rambert & Grenoble Railway. The ticket, looking like an invitation to a state banquet, allowed the Chief Engineer free travel over the entire LM network. Both the LM and the St R & G became amalgamated into the Paris, Lyon and Mediterranean (PLM) Railway. (Photo: La Vie Du Rail)

firm. They were valid for a minimum period of six months for use for genuine business purposes only. Where there had been discrepancies in the standards used by the different companies for the issue of season tickets, and tickets in general, peculiarly, the issue of traders' season tickets was governed by an agreed scale of charges in use by the major railway companies since 1888.

The London *Evening News*, Monday 31 January 1972, carried a news item which shows that despite the high initial cost, season tickets were still regarded as value for money. Above a photograph of two smiling men was the headline: 'Bargain season ticket costs them £840 each'. The *Evening News* reporter explained that the season ticket purchasers considered that the main attraction of such tickets was 'saving money'. Doubtless, they appreciated the other benefits, like being able to avoid booking office queues, and receiving VIP treatment at ticket barriers. The special gold-lettered tickets, which cost £842.40 each per year, were issued at the Euston headquarters of the London Midland Region.

Until 1971 it was possible to purchase an all-regions runabout ticket; the fare was £600 for first class or £400 second class. The scheme proved to be uneconomical so it was scrapped, but existing ticket holders were reassured that further renewals could be made for as long as they were required.

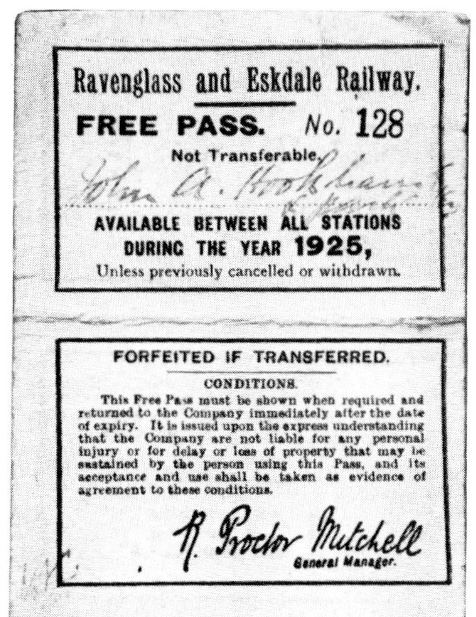

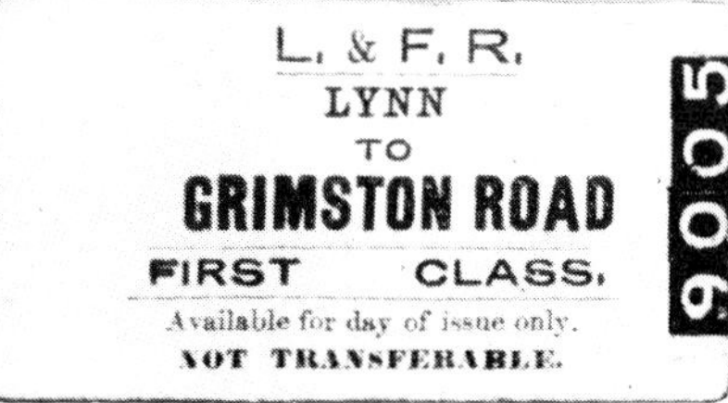

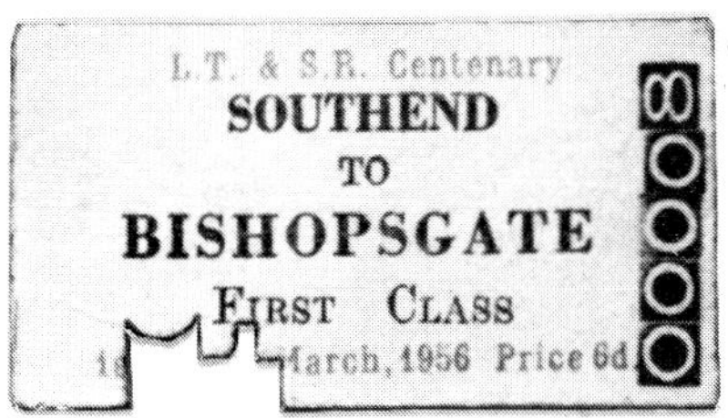

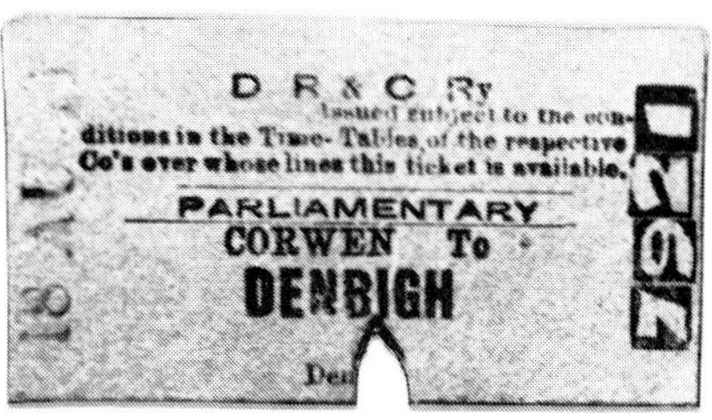

128 Ravenglass & Eskdale free pass. This all stations pass is of special interest, being made out in favour of Mr John A. Hookham, one-time locomotive superintendent of the North Staffordshire Railway.

1658 Manchester, Sheffield & Lincolnshire Railway Locomotive Department, workman's free ticket. Such a ticket was similar to a privilege or pass; the classification 'steerage' was surely an almost contemptuous demeaning of status for a journey merely between either terminus of a river ferry. (George Dow collection)

9005 Lynn & Fakenham Railway first class single. After amalgamation in 1883 with the Yarmouth & North Norfolk Railway, the L & FR became known as the Eastern & Midlands. Eventually, these and other lines became absorbed into the Midland & Great Northern Railway under its Joint Managing Committee with headquarters at King's Lynn.

00008 London, Tilbury & Southend Railway Centenary first class single. The ticket is a souvenir replica of the original issue with the centenary details in red overprint on buff coloured card.

7921 Denbigh, Ruthin & Corwen Railway Parliamentary. Date of issue is uncertain. The numbering is very crudely printed.

To replace the runabout ticket a new type of ticket was introduced, known as 'Tickets by Arranged Contract'. It was this type of 'season' ticket which had been bought in the *Evening News* report. Arranged contract tickets would appear to be little different from the traders' season tickets introduced more than 85 years ago.

Supplementary & special category tickets.

020 Great Northern & London & North Western Joint Railway supplemental ticket blank. Such tickets would be purchased at the same time as the ordinary ticket, and presented to the guard or ticket examiner on boarding the train.

0089 Southern Railway special pass, issued in September 1938, and clipped, according to instructions, on the outward journey.

431 LNER overprint on Great Central Railway requst stop ticket blank, on white card. This type of ticket was uncommon; originally it would be presented to the guard immediately prior to the passenger boarding the train.

Privilege Tickets and Passes were not issued to railway staff alone, but also to company guests who were accompanying company's servant.

056 London, Midland & Scottish Railway exchange voucher blank printed on lilac-coloured card. The passenger was allowed to travel by motor without charge; the motor concerned was a local omnibus, its company and the railway having a commercial arrangement. The conditions on the reverse of the ticket stated that the railway company disclaimed any liability for ' any occurence however arising off their own Coaches'.

0234 LNER blank issued at Snelland date of issue smudged, probably around 1935. It is very difficult to see the red 'R' overprint against the dark brick-red coloured card.

2419 LNER blank from Whitby; the ticket dates from the late 1920s but is printed in the style of the pre-grouping era.

PASSENGER DUTY

In 1832 the railway companies of Great Britain were required by an Act of Parliament to pay ½d per mile for every four passengers carried. Because of the tremendous administration difficulties involved, and after much Parliamentary lobbying, the Act was revised in 1842; the new conditions required a payment of 5 per cent of the gross receipts from passenger traffic.

The author of a book published in 1852 declared that the open third-class carriages met the rain from whatever quarter it came. He likened them to a 'species of Horizontal shower-bath, from whose searching power there is no escape'. Third-class trains were inconvenient, slow and the public were actively discouraged from using them. As a result of considerable public and Parliamentary agitation, the 1844 Railway Act set conditions for the operation of third-class services, and introduced the Parliamentary fare. This was tantamount to Governmental blackmail of the railway companies, since, if they complied with the order, they were automatically relieved of the passenger duty for these cheap trains. Various revisions of the conditions of this Act occurred until the Cheap Trains Act of 1883, sometimes erroneously known as the 'Bargain Act'.

The effect of the 1883 Act was that railway companies were no longer required to run Parliamentary trains. Instead, they had to provide a proportional increase in the third-class accommodation, and fares were not to exceed 1d per mile. Passenger duty was not required to be paid on single journey fares which did not exceed 1d per mile. Because of the reduction in fares which this condition engendered, the travelling public received tremendous benefit. The railway companies became obliged to provide workmen's trains, and to increase concessions to military and police forces.

The real origin of the workmen's trains lies in the Railway Act of 1864. The Great Eastern Railway wished to extend Liverpool Street Station, the scheme involving the demolition of several terraced houses. The law at that time required the rehousing of ejected people within one mile of their original residence, but to do so in the centre of the City of London was impractical. The company therefore made a compromise with the Government. In return for the powers to construct the station, they agreed to convey workmen daily to and from Edmonton and Walthamstow. A concession fare of 2d was charged for the journey, a distance of approximately 10 miles.

Despite the revisions recommended by the Rates Advisory Committee in 1920, workmen's trains were, generally speaking, uneconomic. In general terms, 'workmen' has never been clearly defined, although an Act in 1889 made provision for the penalties against the improper use of a workman's ticket. A Select Committee of 1905 stated that the railways had been generous in their application of the term, often carrying passengers who were not really eligible for the concession. A further report by the Rates Advisory Committee in 1920 amplified the view that it was neither desirable nor practical to define the term; their recommendation that the workmen's trains be known as 'Cheap Early Trains' was adopted by all the principal railway companies.

As has been previously mentioned, fraud was a major problem for the railway companies. Multi-journey tickets (or as the Americans called them, 'so many ride passes') and workmen's tickets, both of weekly availability, were particularly prone to fraudulent usage. These tickets, of Edmondson standard, were issued at reduced fares. In the case of the workmen's tickets, it was essential to issue them quickly, and also to make them easily identifiable at the ticket barrier. To this end, in an attempt to minimise fraud, the number of the week was clearly shown. Most British railway companies frequently used a large overprinted numeral for this purpose. The calendar week number and the ticket week number never tallied.

The following items are extracts from The London & North Eastern Railway (Southern Area), GN Section, Special Train Arrangements volume, January to June, 1934:

Circular No. P.M. 806

OVERSTAMPING OF WEEKLY TICKETS AND WEEKLY WORKMEN'S TICKETS. In connection with the arrangements whereby Weekly Season Ticket Roster numbers are used for overstamping Weekly Tickets (vide page 180 of G.E. Section London Suburban Time-table), and Weekly Workmen's Tickets. The following are the numbers which will operate during the year 1934:-

For Week ending 1934		Number to be used
6th January	.. .. ..	27
13th January	.. .. ..	50
20th "	.. .. ..	4
27th "	.. .. ..	18

The table for the rest of the year was set out in a similar manner. Ticket week One did not occur until week ending 25 August.

The District Manager's Office at Nottingham evidently considered that the use of a single numeral for nine of the ticket weeks could possibly lead to confusion. Circular No PM 807 contained the following remedial instruction:

OVERSTAMPING OF WEEKLY TICKETS AND WEEKLY WORKMEN'S TICKETS.

With reference to notice appearing in Passenger Manager's Weekly Circular No. 806, week ending 13th January, 1934. All concerned to note the following amendments to the numbers to be used for overstamping Weekly Tickets and Weekly Workmen's Tickets referred to.

Week ending to be used		No. to be used	Week ending		No.
20th January	.. ..	04	25th August	..	01
10th February	.. ..	09	15th September	..	03
2nd June	.. ..	07	20th October	..	05
21st July	.. ..	02	10th November	..	06
			15th December	..	08

F.R.3/48678. G.C.

7
SYSTEMS & THE RAILWAY CLEARING HOUSE

The ticket barrier is a very important link in a very long chain of service provided by the railway company. Through its richly ornate, cast-iron canopied arches of the Victorian era, its elegant Edwardian panels, or the tubular steel turnstiles of the twenties, pass all the channels of that service. The ticket of the outward bound passenger is inspected and clipped, and he is directed to the correct platform and train. At the barrier of his destination station, surrender of the ticket is the proof that the company has safely conveyed him to his journey's end. The ticket is accounted for, and the necessary details entered in company statistics; this has been the basic pattern throughout the history of the railways.

There have been several different systems of accounting for the tickets, from the checking by hand of the number of tallies in a leather bag, to reading the indicators on a digital computer. But in the 1920s, the booking clerk's life was fuller than a leather bag, but not so sophisticated as a computer. The booking clerk compiled several returns of all ticket stocks in his care. In a register known as a Train Book he made a daily record of the ticket details as soon as possible after the issue of a ticket. A typical page in such a register was headed with the day, date, month, and year. Columns below, when completed, read as follows:

Train	Station	Commencing Number	Closing Number	No of Passengers	Class	H/Day Rate	Amount and Total by Each Train
5	London	13	16	3	3rd	6/6	19/6

The book was balanced at the end of the day, and the pages countersigned by the chief clerk; at certain stations it was possible to balance the book immediately after the departure of the train. A similar book, known as a Proof Book, was used as a weekly record of ticket and cash transactions. A further record, the passenger classification, was prepared on a monthly basis. It included details of particular ticket stocks, and an account of any non-issues of ticket series, both card and paper blanks.

An LNER instruction of 1934 stated that the various types of tickets, such as cheap day, monthly returns, workmen, etc, had to be entered in successive order; fares, routes and 'Grouped' stations to be given in full, and in the same order, as in PM Circular No 808. The instruction went on to say: 'It is important that three months' stock of tickets be always on hand;

(continued on page 200)

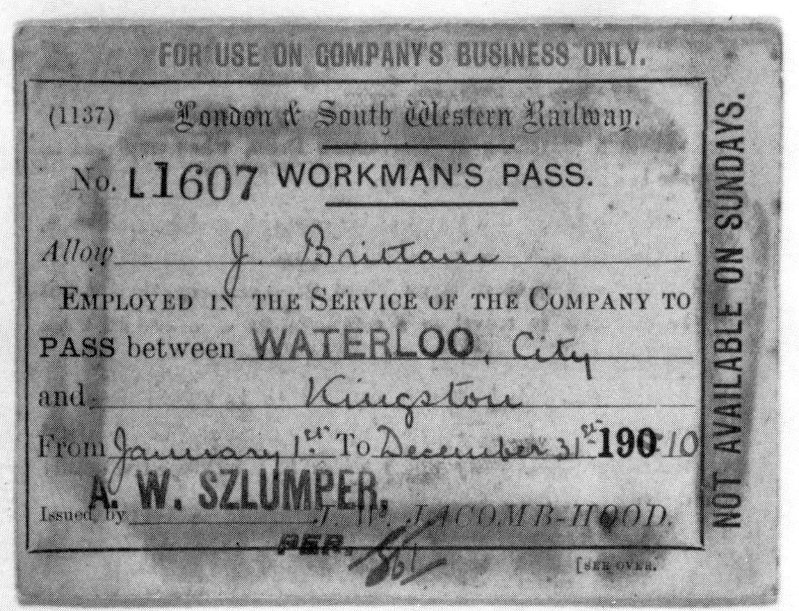
FOR USE ON COMPANY'S BUSINESS ONLY.
(1137) London & South Western Railway.
No. L1607 WORKMAN'S PASS.
Allow J. Brittain
EMPLOYED IN THE SERVICE OF THE COMPANY TO
PASS between WATERLOO, City
and Kingston
From January 1st To December 31st 1910
A. W. SZLUMPER.
Issued by J. W. JACOMB-HOOD.
PER.
[SEE OVER.
NOT AVAILABLE ON SUNDAYS.

0693
Bradford Corporation
Nidd Valley Light Rly.
Workman 3rd Class
LOFTHOUSE
TO
WATH
Return Fare 4½d.
Issued subject to time tables and to Corporation's rules and regulations in force relating to the said Railway.
SINGLE Fare for Return Journey. Available on day of issue only.
Bradford Corporation
Nidd Valley Light Rly.
Workman 3rd Class
WATH
TO
LOFTHOUSE
Return Fare 4½d.
Issued subject to time tables and to Corporation's rules and regulations in force relating to the said Railway.
SINGLE Fare for Return Journey. Available on day of issue only.
0693

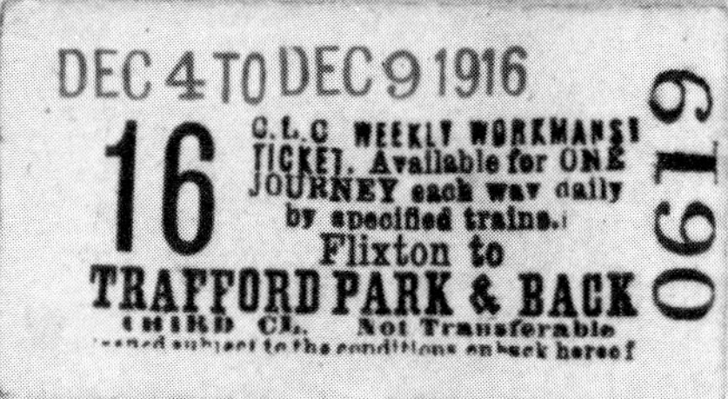
DEC 4 TO DEC 9 1916
16
C.L.C. WEEKLY WORKMANS' TICKET. Available for ONE JOURNEY each way daily by specified trains.
Flixton to
TRAFFORD PARK & BACK
THIRD CL. Not Transferable
0619

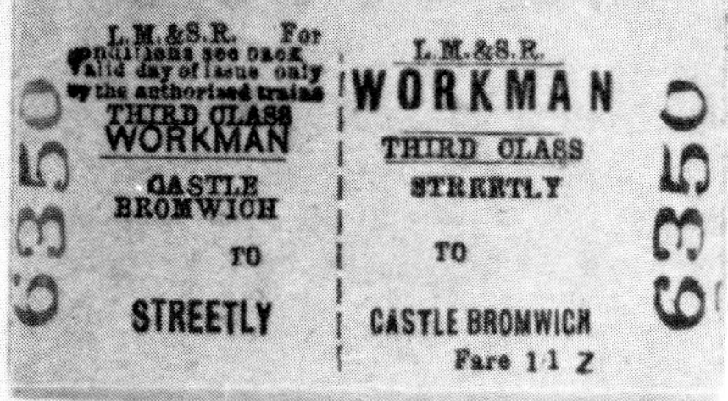
6350
L.M.&S.R. For conditions see back
Valid day of issue only by the authorised trains
THIRD CLASS
WORKMAN
CASTLE BROMWICH
TO
STREETLY
L.M.&S.R.
WORKMAN
THIRD CLASS
STREETLY
TO
CASTLE BROMWICH
Fare 1/1 Z
6350

1 2 3 4 5
L. N. E. R.
WORKMAN'S 5-DAY WEEKLY TICKET
Third Class Price 4s.9½d.Z
For conditions see back.
LUTTERWORTH to
RUGBY (Central) and BACK
Issued at Rugby (Central)
Available for one return journey on each of 5 week days of week ending as dated.
1 2 3 4 5
0693

Workman's tickets and passes. By the Cheap Trains Act of 1883 the Board of Trade was empowered to demand that railway companies provide adequate numbers of workmen's trains at cheap rates between 6am and 8am. The number of these trains depended upon the number of workmen in the district served by the particular company. The railways decided that if they were to provide cheap transport then the extent of their liability in the case of accident was also limited. Some companies were granted private Acts of Parliament in order that they could pare down liability to the absolute minimum, and could quote a precise sum regardless of amounts offered by other companies. By an Act of 1893, the Metropolitan District Railway limited its liability to passengers travelling on 'Workmen's Tickets' to £100, whether the ticket was issued by them or by another company having booking arrangements over the same tracks.
L1607 The reverse of this pass for 1910 reveals some interesting conditions. The pass was to be used only by workmen travelling in workmen's dress, and when employed on the business of the company. The holder was required to travel third class when third class carriages were on the train; if there was no third class carriage, the holder could travel in a compartment of a second class carriage selected by the guard.
0693 LNER, light orange with light blue overprint.
0619 CLC, lilac, with station code number.
6350 LM & SR, slate grey.
0693 Bradford Corporation Nidd Valley Light Railway, green and red overprints on white with red skeleton 'R'. Opened in 1907, the line was built during construction for the Bradford waterworks supply, and was the only such railway to operate a passenger service; it closed in 1929.

Furlough or leave tickets. Such tickets were issued to members of HM forces and other uniformed services as required by Statute. A concession of approximately three-quarters ordinary fare was granted. Similar to the furlough tickets were those issued to HM Forces on duty, a post-grouping development of the Government agreed rate ticket originally issued to volunteer militia on manoeuvres. Most tickets in this category were usually issued with a three months' period of validity.
0371 Palestine Railway first class military, buff-coloured with the word 'Military' as a red overprint. An example of bilingual printing (the conditions of issue on the reverse are also printed in Arabic), the ticket was issued 19 June 1945, the date being impressed.
43 Midland Railway travel warrant, lilac paper. Note that even shipwrecked mariners qualified for the issue of the warrant, but these warrants were not available on the Irish and Scotch Mails. The Irish Mails, of which there were two each day and night, were the railway descendents of the 'New Holyhead Mail Coach' of the 1830s. This travelled from London in 27 hours, the mail taking at least another day to reach Dublin.

Special circumstances demanded special measures, and these two tickets are not to Edmondson's standard.
79510 London, Midland & Scottish Railway special ticket, pink thin card. Date of issue unknown, possibly 1939. Similar tickets were issued to wartime evacuees.
British Railways pantomime express blank, light blue thin card. Designed on the American coupon system, this excursion ticket with a difference tells its own tale.

PALESTINE RAILWAYS
HAIFA EAST
CAIRO
CLASS
MILITARY
0371A
L.N.E.R. FURLOUGH
L.N.E.R. FURLOUGH
KING'S CROSS TO NOTTINGHAM (VIC.
NOTTINGHAM (VIC. TO KING'S CROSS
Available for three months from date of issue
THIRD
Fur. Rtn.
2143
KING'S CROSS
For conditions see back
8045
BRITISH RLYS (W)
H.M. FORCES ON LEAVE.
Liskeard TO LOOE
THIRD CLASS
FOR CONDITIONS SEE BACK
2903
L.M.&S.R. FOR CONDITIONS SEE BACK
NAVY ARMY & AIR FORCE on LEAVE
THIRD CLASS SINGLE
NARBORO TO
BLABY
CHILD
Rly
Via
FARE.... S. D
035

MIDLAND RAILWAY. A. B. 7.

This ticket is issued subject to the published conditions and arrangements of the Company, and on the condition that they incur no liability in respect of any loss whatever that may be sustained by any passenger beyond the amount limited by the Merchant Shipping Acts, nor for any loss whatever caused by perils of the sea or weather.

COUNTERFOIL.

FOR SOLDIERS, SAILORS, POLICE, &c.

No. 43 July 1 1895

From Defford Co

Via

.........Officers.............	1st Class.	Rate.........		
.... ,, Wives	1st	,, ,, ...		
.... ,, Children ...	1st	,, ,, ...		
.........{Soldiers or Naval Seamen}	3rd	,, ,, ...		
.... ,, Wives	3rd	,, ,, ...		
.... ,, Children ...	3rd	,, ,, ...		
.........Volunteers	1st	,, ,, ...		
.... ,, ...	3rd	,, 3/4 ,, ...	1	1½
One.....Police	3rd	,, ,, ...		
.........Prison Official......	3rd	,, ,, ...		
.........Prisoners	3rd	,, ,, ...		
.........Merchant Seamen	3rd	,, ,, ...		
.........Shipwrk'd Mariners	3rd	,, ,, ...		

Total No. Miles......... Total £ 1 1½

No. of Warrant 5 [signature], Booking Clerk.

Not available by Irish or Limited Scotch Mail Trains unless stated in the Company's Time Tables and notices to be so. Through tickets in cases where the journey is not continuous do not include the cost of transfer between Railway Termini in towns, or between Railway Stations and Steam Boats.

N.B.—This ticket must be shown and given up when required.

79510

L. M. & S. RAILWAY SPECIAL TICKET

NOT TRANSFERABLE.

AVAILABLE FOR ONE PERSON ON DAY OF ISSUE ONLY.
TO BE RETAINED UNTIL COMPLETION OF JOURNEY.

FROM STATION OF ISSUE BY

L. M. & S. RLY. TRAIN

AND THENCE TO FINAL DESTINATION

THE STRICT CONDITION OF THE ISSUE OF THIS TICKET IS THAT THE HOLDER SHALL COMPLY WITH ALL INSTRUCTIONS GIVEN BY OFFICIALS.

ISSUED SUBJECT TO BYE-LAWS, REGULATIONS AND CONDITIONS OF THE RAILWAYS.

BRITISH RAILWAYS—N.E. Region

DINING-CAR PANTOMIME EXPRESS

to NEWCASTLE, FEBRUARY 13th, 1952

Please provide

ONE RESERVED SEAT (DRESS CIRCLE)

AT THEATRE *To be exchanged on Train*

BRITISH RAILWAYS—N.E. Region

DINING-CAR PANTOMIME EXPRESS

to NEWCASTLE, FEBRUARY 13th, 1952

Please provide ONE TEA as arranged

BRITISH RAILWAYS—N.E. Region

DINING-CAR PANTOMIME EXPRESS

to NEWCASTLE, FEBRUARY 13th, 1952

Please provide ONE SUPPER as arranged

BRITISH RAILWAYS—N.E. Region

DINING-CAR PANTOMIME EXPRESS

to NEWCASTLE, FEBRUARY 13th, 1952

Available for ONE RETURN JOURNEY

THIRD-CLASS

....to NEWCASTLE and back

For conditions on which this set of Coupons is issued see reverse

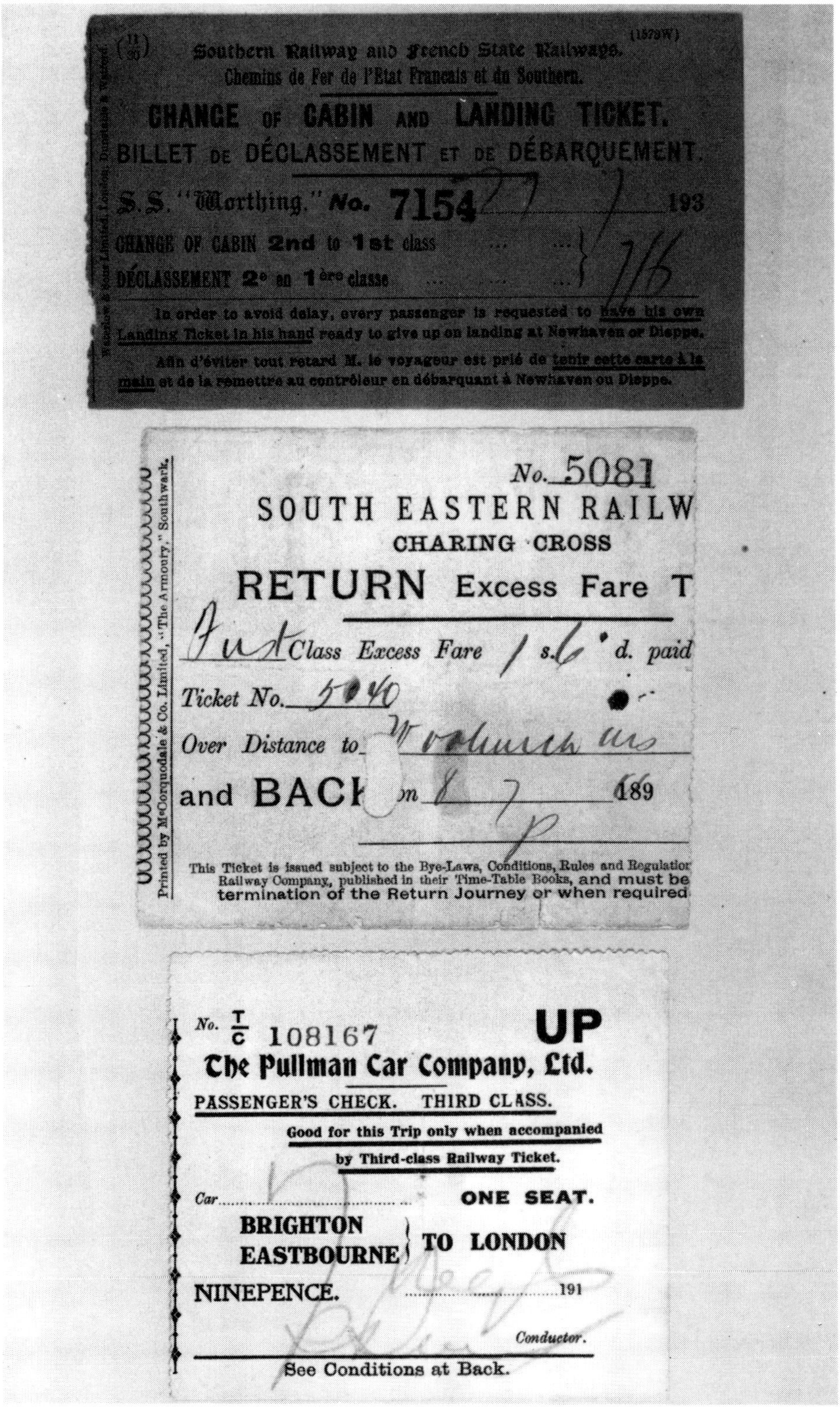

(11/30) Southern Railway and French State Railways. (1579W)
Chemins de Fer de l'Etat Francais et du Southern.

CHANGE OF CABIN AND LANDING TICKET.
BILLET DE DÉCLASSEMENT ET DE DÉBARQUEMENT.

S.S. "Worthing." No. 7154 27/7 193
CHANGE OF CABIN 2nd to 1st class ... ... } 7/6
DÉCLASSEMENT 2e au 1ère classe ... ... }

In order to avoid delay, every passenger is requested to have his own Landing Ticket in his hand ready to give up on landing at Newhaven or Dieppe.

Afin d'éviter tout retard M. le voyageur est prié de tenir cette carte à la main et de la remettre au contrôleur en débarquant à Newhaven ou Dieppe.

Waterlow & Sons Limited, London, Dunstable & Watford.

No. 5081
SOUTH EASTERN RAILW
CHARING CROSS
RETURN Excess Fare T

First Class Excess Fare 1 s. 6 d. paid
Ticket No. 5040
Over Distance to Woolwich Ars
and BACK on 8 7 189

This Ticket is issued subject to the Bye-Laws, Conditions, Rules and Regulation Railway Company, published in their Time-Table Books, and must be termination of the Return Journey or when required

Printed by McCorquodale & Co. Limited, "The Armoury," Southwark.

No. T/C 108167 UP
The Pullman Car Company, Ltd.
PASSENGER'S CHECK. THIRD CLASS.
Good for this Trip only when accompanied by Third-class Railway Ticket.

Car .... ONE SEAT.
BRIGHTON } TO LONDON
EASTBOURNE }
NINEPENCE. 191
Conductor.
See Conditions at Back.

Despite Edmondon's attempts to standardise tickets, the stage-coach methods had not died in the 1930s as these non-standard examples show.

7154 Southern Railway and French State landing ticket, blue paper, issued in the 1930s The SS Worthing *was one of the Southern's most powerful steamers at 14,500hp, crossing between Newhaven and Dieppe along with more than 140 other steamships. They were described as ocean liners in miniature.*

5081 South Eastern Railway, white paper. The passenger's half of this excess fare ticket is shown as possibly being issued in 1901.

108161 The Pullman Car Company Ltd, light yellow paper. In 1874 the Midland Railway introduced Pullman cars from America, a startling new concept in which the carriage was not divided into compartments, but contained easy chairs and a long passage down the centre of the coach. British designers put the passage, or 'corridor' down the side of the coach. The independent PCC owned many first and third class cars for which it paid rental to the railway companies for inclusion in their trains. The 'Brighton Belle' was reckoned to be the only electric multiple unit Pullman car train in the world.

Assorted categories.

020 Great Northern & London, and North Western Joint Railway supplemental ticket blank, lilac.

3369 Metropolitan Railway first class single, lilac with red bar overprint, issued 6 April 1906.

4988 London Electric Railway revised fare, cream coloured.

2766 Metropolitan Railway merchandise ticket, slate blue and light red overprints, issued 9 August 1932.

9626 London & North Eastern Railway permit. Although the ticket was originally printed for issue when the Humber Ferry Service was suspended, this particular ticket was issued on the last day of public sailing, 24 June 1981.

B 2440 London, Midland & Scottish Railway excess fare, grey paper.

920 LM & SR reserved seat, light yellow.

4297 Isle of Man Railway market ticket third class return, brick red block overprint on buff coloured card.

72185 Victorian State Railways weekly periodical (second class), light red with station code overstamped purple.

8989 Baker Street & Waterloo Railway third class (Metropolitan), buff coloured with vertical light blue overprint, issued 3 June 1908.

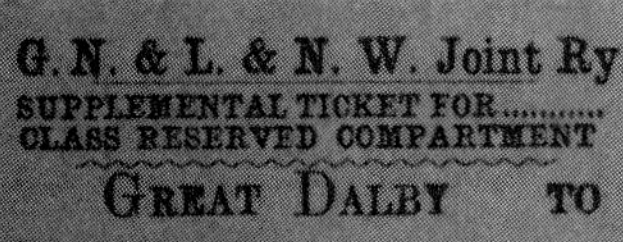
G. N. & L. & N. W. Joint Ry.
SUPPLEMENTAL TICKET FOR..........
CLASS RESERVED COMPARTMENT
GREAT DALBY TO
020
NOT VALID EXCEPT ON PRODUCTION
OF.........ORDINARY........CLASS TICKETS
COVERING THE JOURNEY MADE.
TURN OVER)
Fee 5/-

Metropolitan Railway.
NOT TRANSFERABLE
Available on day of issue only
3369
BAKER STREET
BAKER STREET BAKER STREET
H TO Series 1
HIGH ST.(KENSINGTON
High St. (Kensington) High St. (Kensington)
VIA BAYSWATER
FIRST CLASS 3d
3369

UNDERGROUND
London Electric Ry.
Issued subject to the Companies' Bye Laws Regulations and advertised Conditions
4988
DOWN STREET
TO
STRAND
or GOODGE STREET
or intermediately
Via Leicester Square
REVISED FARE
Available day of issue only.
2d
4988

METROPOLITAN RAILWAY
TICKET FOR MERCHANDISE &c.
IN CHARGE OF PASSENGER
MONUMENT to
EDGWARE RD. WEST HAMPSTEAD
SOUTH KENS or FINSBURY P'K (MET.
Via Mark Lane
Description
Weight not exceeding 56lbs.
Carriage Paid 4d.
See conditions on back
12766

L. N. E. R.
Issued at Hull Corporation Pier (2)
PERMIT.
The bearer holding a ticket available by the Humber Ferry Service is allowed to travel by rail throughout Via Doncaster or Retford without additional charge on account of the Ferry Service being suspended.
SEE BACK
9626

B 2440
London Midland and Scottish Railway.
RECEIPT FOR
FARE
1d
2
EXCESS
PAID AT
Kentish Town.

920
L. M. & S. R.
RESERVED SEAT
TRAIN
FROM GLASGOW (CENTRAL)
DATE
COACH
SEAT No
CLASS
BACK to ENGINE
For conditions see back FEE 1/-
920

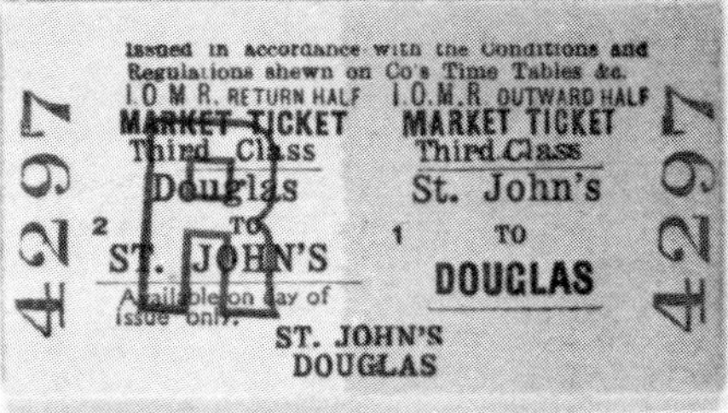
Issued in accordance with the Conditions and Regulations shewn on Co's Time Tables &c.
4297
I.O.M.R. RETURN HALF
MARKET TICKET
Third Class
Douglas
TO
ST. JOHN'S
Available on day of issue only.
I.O.M.R. OUTWARD HALF
MARKET TICKET
Third Class
St. John's
TO
DOUGLAS
ST. JOHN'S
DOUGLAS
4297

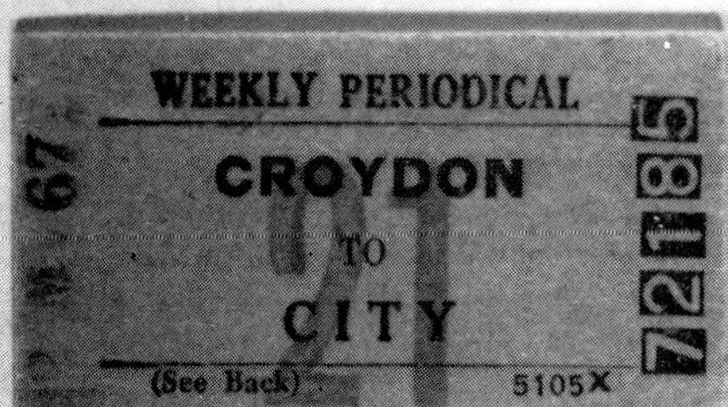
WEEKLY PERIODICAL
67
CROYDON
TO
CITY
(See Back)
5105X

Baker Street & Waterloo Ry.
3 JUN 08
Trafalgar Square
19
TO (No. 1)
WEST HAMPSTEAD
(MET. RY.)
Change at Baker Street
3rd. CLASS on METROPOLITAN RY
Fare 4d.
3989

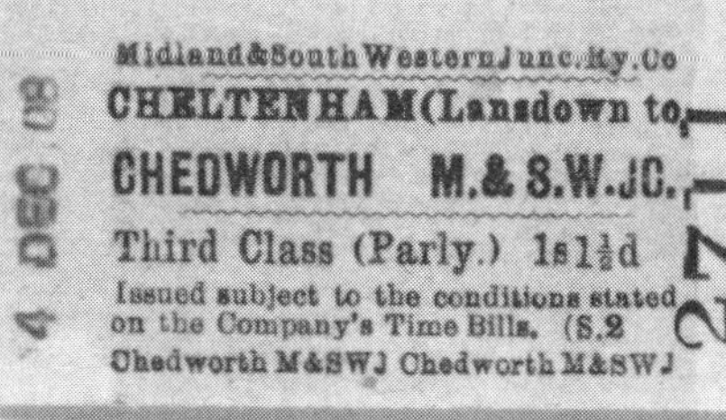
Midland&South Western Junc. Ry. Co
CHELTENHAM (Lansdown to
CHEDWORTH M.& S.W.JC.
Third Class (Parly.) 1s1½d
Issued subject to the conditions stated on the Company's Time Bills. (S.2
Chedworth M&SWJ Chedworth M&SWJ
4 DEC 09
2711

Golden Valley Railway.
PONTRILAS
TO
HAY
THIRD CLASS PARLY 1/7
6568
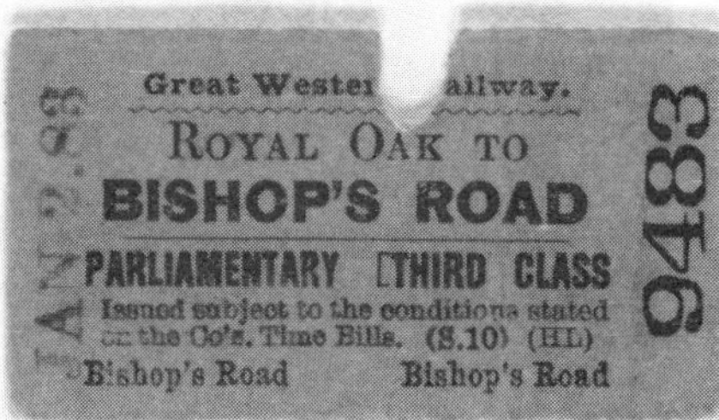
Great Western Railway.
ROYAL OAK TO
BISHOP'S ROAD
PARLIAMENTARY THIRD CLASS
Issued subject to the conditions stated on the Co's. Time Bills. (S.10) (HL)
Bishop's Road Bishop's Road
9483

RHYMNEY RAILWAY.
PENGAM & FLEURDELIS
THIRD CLASS PARLY.
CHILD
832
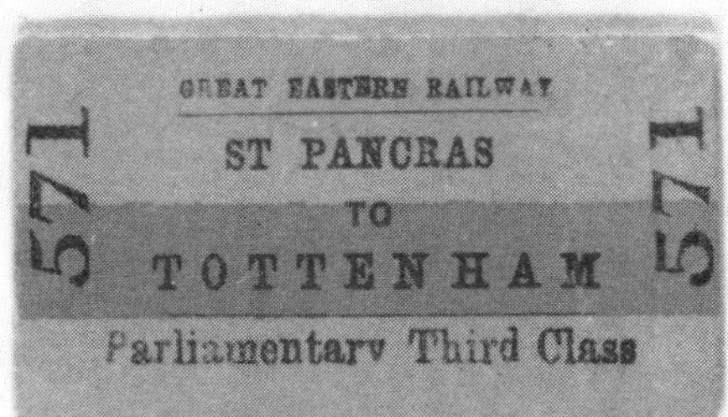
GREAT EASTERN RAILWAY
ST PANCRAS
TO
TOTTENHAM
Parliamentary Third Class
571
571
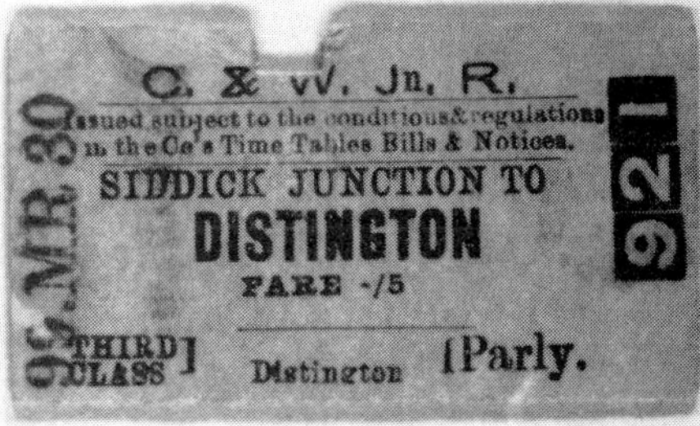
C. & W. Jn. R.
Issued subject to the conditions & regulations in the Co's Time Tables Bills & Notices.
SIDDICK JUNCTION TO
DISTINGTON
FARE -/5
THIRD CLASS
Distington
Parly.
96 MR 30
921

C. K. & P. R.
KESWICK
TO
PENRITH
PARLIAMENTARY
Penrith
FARE 1/6.
JU 13 95.
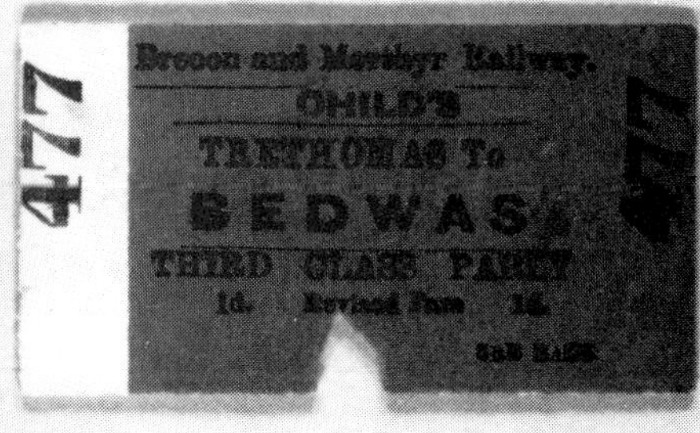
Brecon and Merthyr Railway.
CHILD'S
TRETHOMAS To
BEDWAS
THIRD CLASS PARLY
1d.
477
477
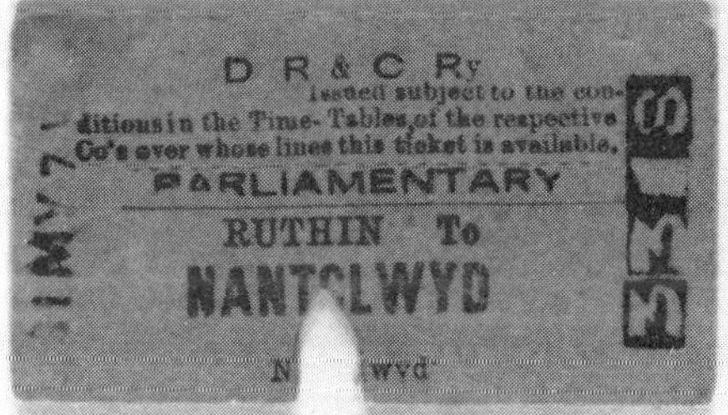
D R & C Ry
Issued subject to the conditions in the Time-Tables of the respective Co's over whose lines this ticket is available.
PARLIAMENTARY
RUTHIN To
NANTCLWYD
5315

GLASGOW
to
HELENSBURGH
PARL'Y—Closed Carriage.
25 AU

Parliamentary ('Parly'). With the introduction of the 'Parliamentary Fare' Act (Railway Regulation Act, 1844), trains, with seats protected against the weather, travelling at not less than 12mph (including stoppages at every station), were required to be run each weekday, except Christmas Day and Good Friday. Even light railways like the Festiniog had to provide 'Parliamentary' trains. In return, the companies were relieved of the passenger tax for these trains. After many years of legal wrangling the House of Lords recommended the repeal of the Act. A Select Committee considered that the class for whom the enactment had been designed were being victimised by its conditions. Subsequently, the Cheap Trains Act of 1883 removed the anomalies created by the repeal.

2711 Midland & South Western Junction Railway, pink, issued thirty-two years after the repeal of the 'Parly'.

6568 Golden Valley Railway, green, unissued. The GVR was opened between 1881 and 1889, but fell into financial difficulties from which it was rescued by the GWR in 1901. It was closed in 1941 and dismantled in 1952.

9483 GWR, green, issued 2 January 1883.

832 Rhymney Railway, overprinted dark green bands on white. Opened in stages between 1858 and 1909, the 77 miles of track give access to several collieries and other large industries.

571 Great Eastern Railway, green with horizontal slate-grey overprint, issued 1 May 1873.

921 Cleator & Workington Junction Railway, green, issued 30 March 1899. Between 1876 and 1878, authorisation was given for 21 miles of track; a further 20 miles was authorised during 1881-3. By an Act of 1877, operational powers were given to the Furness and the London & North Western Railways.

7802 Cockermouth, Keswick & Penrith Railway, green, issued 13 June 1895. Opened in 1865, the CK & PR linked Cockermouth and Penrith through the Cockermouth and Workington Railway and the Lancaster & Carlisle Railway.

477 Brecon & Merthyr Railway, dark green with white vertical band. Having been incorporated in 1859, the B&MR was really part of several lines. Some amalgamation was authorised in 1865 but was later declared void, and control of the company was taken by the Midland Railway in 1874.

3318 Denbigh, Ruthin & Corwen Railway, dark green, issued 31 May 1871. The DR & CR was a 17-mile line, opened in 1862, and which became part of the London & North Western Railway in 1879.

3279 Glasgow, Dumbarton & Helensburgh Railway, pink. Date of issue uncertain, but at least forty-nine years after the repeal of the 'Parliamentary Fare' Act.

Dog tickets. The complex issues of the Carriers Act (1830) and The Railway and Canal Traffic Act (1854) meant that many railway companies introduced liability disclaimers in the form of bye-laws, particularly with reference to dogs and other animals. Such bye-laws declared that the companies were not 'Common Carriers of Dogs', and also stipulated that 'Except by permission of a guard of the train, no person shall take . . . any dog . . . into any passenger carriage'. Several test cases at law during the late nineteenth century upheld the view that although companies were not bound to be common carriers of dogs, they were bound by the Carriers Act to carry them on reasonable terms.

421 LM & SR, purple.

265 Great North of Scotland Railway, with yellow cross overprint.

385 London & South Western, vertical green overprints at either end, with two vertical purple bands in the centre.

0260 LNER, brick red.

4842 Kent & East Sussex Railway, horizontal pink overprint on white,

79255 County Borough of Bournemouth, pink, with red overprint.

0457 Bermuda Railway Company, drab.

101 L & NWR, top half red overprint on yellow card, issued 21 September 1886, with date impressed.

567 LM & SR, slate blue.

152 Kingston-upon-Hull Corporation (LNER), horizontal pink overprint on white.

L. M. & S. R.
ONE DOG (ACCOMPANIED BY PASSENGER)
LIABILITY NOT EXCEEDING £2
Bagworth&Ellistown to
R
Carriage Paid s. d.
This ticket must be given up on arrival
TURN OVER)
42

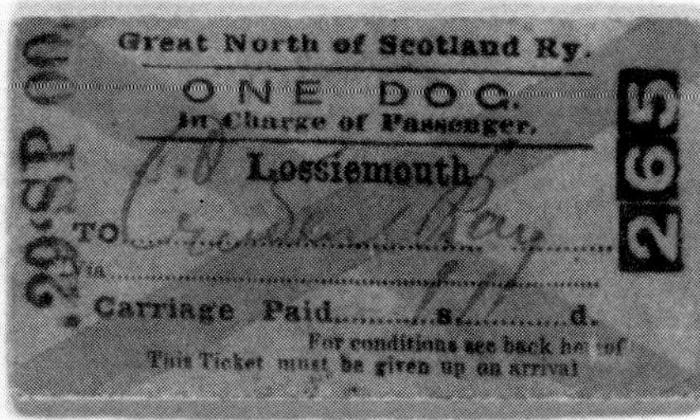
Great North of Scotland Ry.
ONE DOG.
In Charge of Passenger.
Lossiemouth
TO
Via
Carriage Paid s. d.
For conditions see back hereof
This Ticket must be given up on arrival
29 SP 09
265

London & South Western Ry.
ONE DOG
RICHMOND NEW to
KINGS CROSS
Metropolitan Railway
Via Hammersmith The Grove
S.1 FARE 6d See over
AU 14 189
385

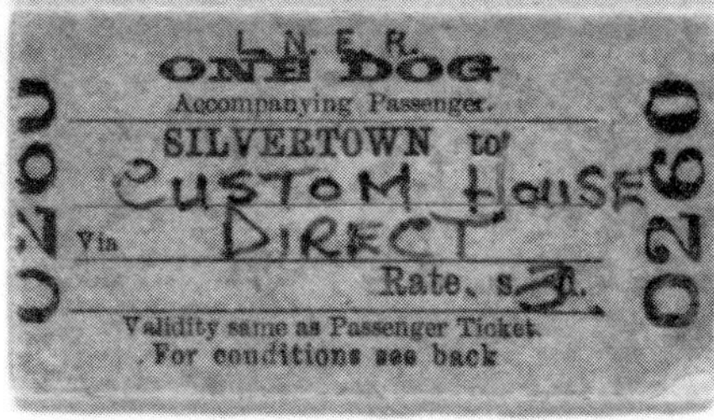
L.N.E.R.
ONE DOG
Accompanying Passenger.
SILVERTOWN to
CUSTOM HOUSE
Via DIRECT
Rate, s. d.
Validity same as Passenger Ticket.
For conditions see back
0260

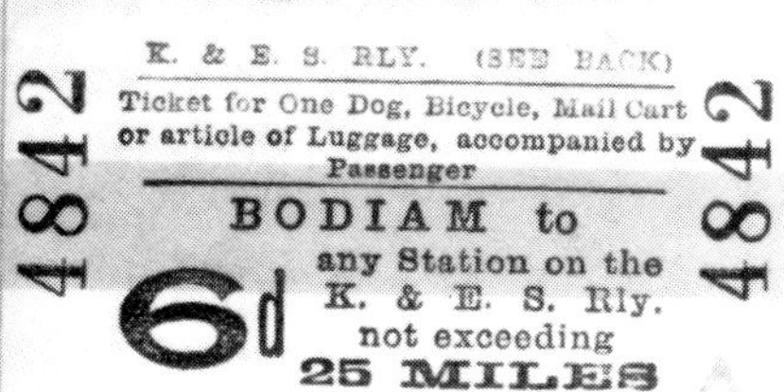
K. & E. S. RLY. (SEE BACK)
Ticket for One Dog, Bicycle, Mail Cart or article of Luggage, accompanied by Passenger
BODIAM to
any Station on the
K. & E. S. Rly.
not exceeding
25 MILES
6d
4842
4842

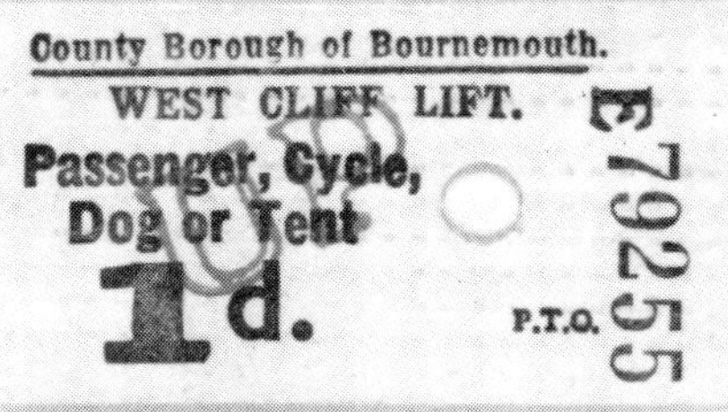
County Borough of Bournemouth.
WEST CLIFF LIFT.
Passenger, Cycle,
Dog or Tent
1d.
P.T.O.
E79255

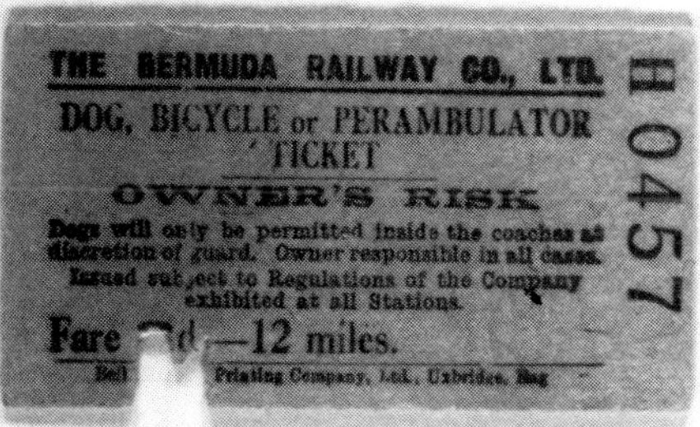
THE BERMUDA RAILWAY CO., LTD.
DOG, BICYCLE or PERAMBULATOR
TICKET
OWNER'S RISK
Dogs will only be permitted inside the coaches at discretion of guard. Owner responsible in all cases.
Issued subject to Regulations of the Company exhibited at all Stations.
—12 miles.
H 0457

L&NWR LIABILITY NOT EXCEEDING £2.
This ticket must be given up on arrival
Bicester To
Ry
ONE DOG
The above is delivered to the Company solely on
Turn over

DOG
s. d.
L. M. & S. R. ONE DOG. CARRIAGE PAID
TO BE GIVEN UP AT THE DESTINATION STATION
Manningham to
LIABILITY NOT EXCEEDING £2.
567

KINGSTON upon HULL
CORPORATION
Landing or Embarking at or using
VICTORIA PIER
DOG or BICYCLE
ADMISSION TICKET
CHARGE 1d.
Issued at Barrow Haven
152
152

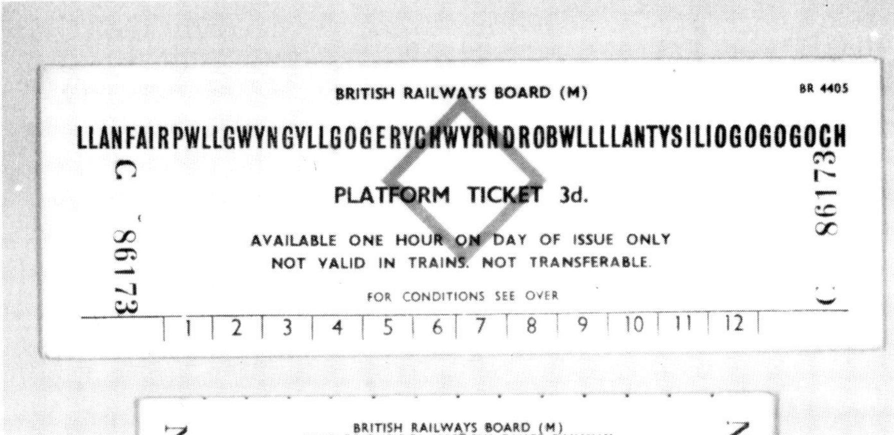

The introduction of platform tickets allowed people other than passengers access to stations; by keeping loiterers from the platforms there was a consequent increase in efficient train working. It was an established rule of law that stations were private premises and, therefore, people not holding a ticket of some description could not be permitted to enter. Numerous devices were introduced in an attempt to discourage the fraudulent use of the platform ticket. Apart from the obvious notion of distinctive design and bold overprints, one idea used extensively in France, and later developed by the GWR, was to limit the period of availability of the ticket. A linear clock-face was printed on to the edges of the ticket and the appropriate space was punched when the holder entered the station. Some European railways issued season platform tickets printed in book form.
C86173 and 0515 Each of these tickets is printed black on white card with a red diamond overprint. Both the Llanfair and the Devil's Bridge tickets are really little more than souvenir tickets in offical guise.

HM Forces ticket.
5871 Southern Railway, green with 'GR' (Government Rate) red overprint. This ticket was not issued until 1968.
0005 Belfast Steamship Company, blue with red overprint.
000 Whitechapel & Bow Railway, pink with black diagonal bar on return half. The first in a series, this would have been issued sometime between 1938 and 1941. Opened in 1902, and electrified in 1905, the company came under the control of the Midland Railway in 1912.
054 North Eastern Railway, outward half light orange overprint on white, return half light green overprint on white, with skeleton 'R' overstamped purple.
0244 Great Central & North Staffordshire Railways Committee, light green with red overprint.
8113 Glasgow Corporation Transport (Underground), light brown with horizontal light green overprint in central panel, paper. After much opposition the line was opened in 1896, and owing to an accident, closed down for one month, reopening in January, 1897. In 1923 the line passed into the ownership of the Glasgow Corporation.
6143 Liverpool Overhead Railway, blue with red overprint.
0137 London Transport, buff coloured.

SOUTHERN RAILWAY.
GOVERNMENT RATE
Westgate-on-Sea to
ANDOVER
Via WATERLOO
Third Class
5871
For Conditions see back of Ticket
H. M. FORCES ON DUTY
Third Class
Single Fare
5 MAY 1941
0005
3rd Cl W&BR
CIVIL DEFENCE & HOME GUARD
CHEAP DUTY TICKET
East Ham
to BOW ROAD
Bow Road
To
EAST HAM
NOT TRANSFERABLE
Fare 7d
000
Gt. Western Ry.
H.M. FORCES ON LEAVE
BRISTOL T.M.
TO
NEWPORT H.ST.
via Severn Tunnel
THIRD CLASS
NEWPORT H.St.
TO
BRISTOL T.M.
FOR CONDITIONS SEE BACK
9453
054
Soldier on Furlough
Foreign To
KIRBYMOORSIDE
Via
THIRD CLASS
See back. N.E.R.
SOLDIER on Furlough
KIRBYMOORSIDE
Foreign To
SOUTHERN RAILWAY.
OFFICER ON LEAVE.
Available for Three Days including Day of issue
Cranleigh to
BARNARDS
Via
First Class.
FOR CONDITIONS SEE BACK
0354
G.C.&N.S.Rlys Com.
SERVICE
MILITARY ETC.
to
BOLLINGTON
Via
Available for three months from date of issue
THIRD
For conditions see back
S.M. Etc. R. 2231
BOLLINGTON
to
Via
0244
Glasgow Corpn. Transport (Underground)
FARE
1d
H.M. FORCES
SPECIAL TICKET
Available for a FULL JOURNEY on One Circle
Jk 8113
L.O.R.
FORCES RETURN
Issued subject to the Company's Bye-Laws and Regulations and Conditions in the Time Tables, Bills and Notices
FIRST CLASS
ANY L.O.R. STATION
TO
ANY L.O.R. STATION
Fare 9d
6143
FORCES LEAVE TICKET
Fare Paid 1/10
Fare Paid 1/10
BAKER STREET (E)
Baker Street (E)
Baker Street (E)
To any one of L.T. stations shown on fares list at an ordinary SINGLE FARE of
2/6
2/6
2/6
For conditions see over
10137

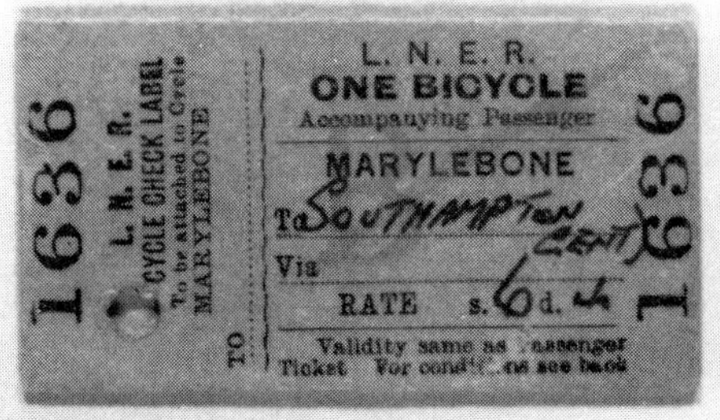
L. N. E. R.
ONE BICYCLE
Accompanying Passenger
MARYLEBONE
RATE
Validity same as Passenger Ticket
1636

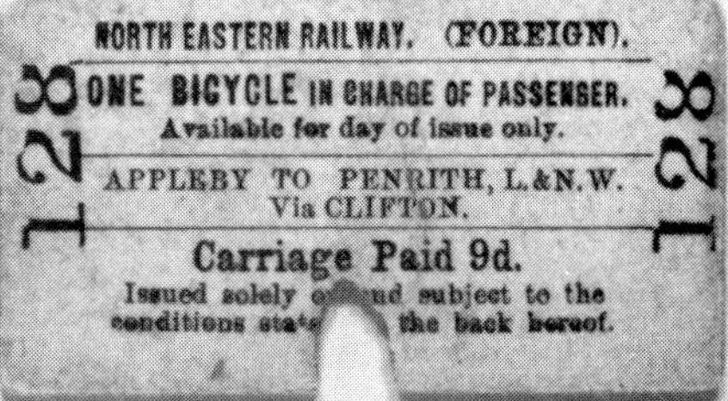
NORTH EASTERN RAILWAY. (FOREIGN).
ONE BICYCLE IN CHARGE OF PASSENGER.
Available for day of issue only.
APPLEBY TO PENRITH, L.&N.W.
Via CLIFTON.
Carriage Paid 9d.
128

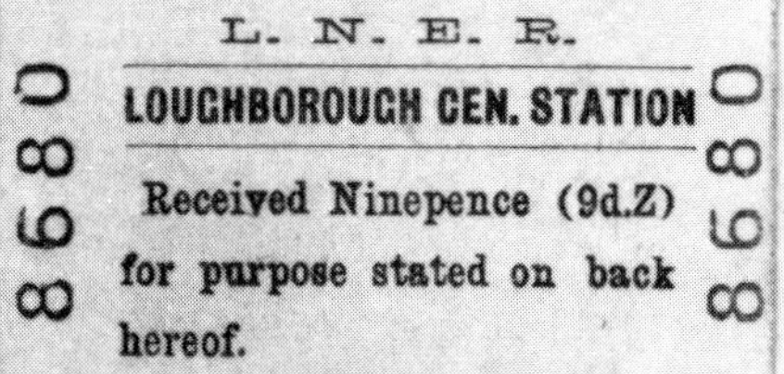
L. N. E. R.
LOUGHBOROUGH CEN. STATION
Received Ninepence (9d.Z)
for purpose stated on back
hereof.
8680

Mid. & G. N. J'nt Committee.
CYCLE CHECK TICKET.
Cycle Ticket No.
CROMER BEACH to
(TO BE ATTACHED TO CYCLE.)
For instructions see other side.

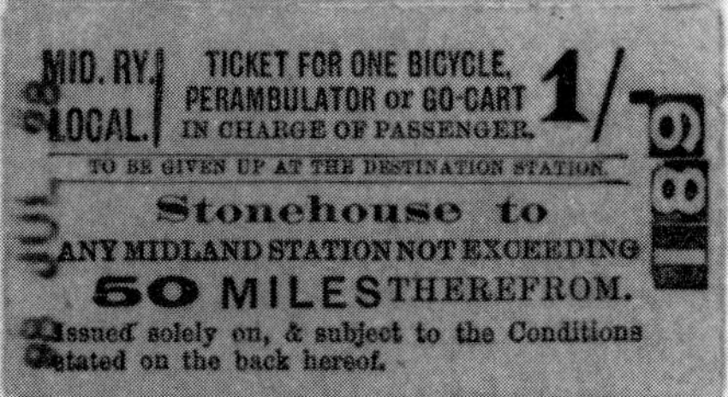
MID. RY.
LOCAL.
TICKET FOR ONE BICYCLE,
PERAMBULATOR or GO-CART
IN CHARGE OF PASSENGER.
1/-
TO BE GIVEN UP AT THE DESTINATION STATION.
Stonehouse to
ANY MIDLAND STATION NOT EXCEEDING
50 MILES THEREFROM.
Issued solely on, & subject to the Conditions
stated on the back hereof.
189

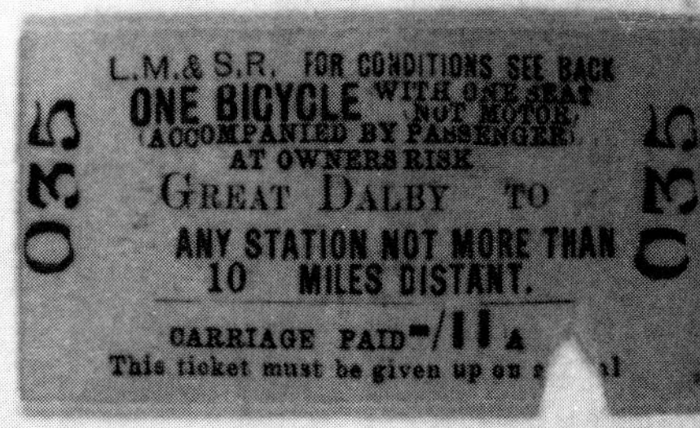
L.M.& S.R. FOR CONDITIONS SEE BACK
ONE BICYCLE WITH ONE SEAT
NOT MOTOR
(ACCOMPANIED BY PASSENGER)
AT OWNERS RISK
GREAT DALBY TO
ANY STATION NOT MORE THAN
10 MILES DISTANT.
CARRIAGE PAID
035

002

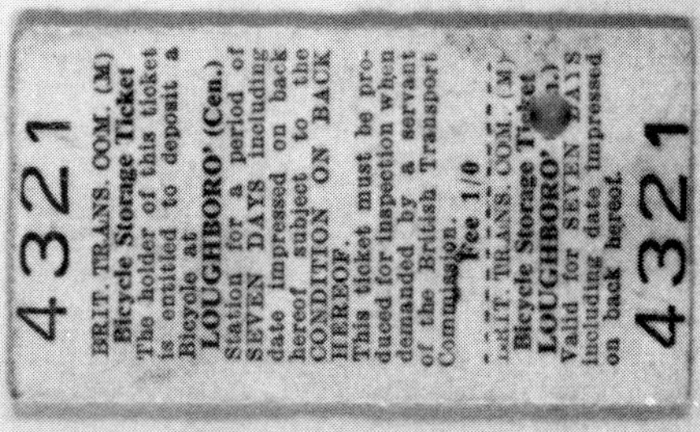
BRIT. TRANS. COM. (M)
Bicycle Storage Ticket
LOUGHBORO' (Cen.)
Fee 1/0
4321

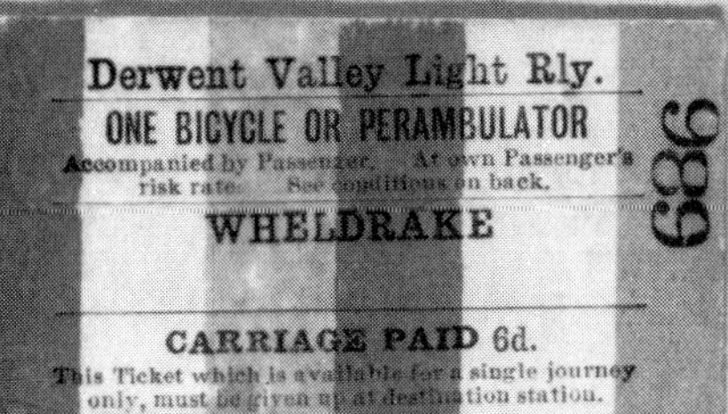
Derwent Valley Light Rly.
ONE BICYCLE OR PERAMBULATOR
WHELDRAKE
CARRIAGE PAID 6d.
686

CARDIFF RAILWAY.
WHITCHURCH
TO
Penarth
CARRIAGE PAID
See conditions on back
123

Bicycle tickets. Until 1899 it was generally considered that an article could be classed as personal luggage if it was being taken for the immediate personal use of the passenger at the end of the journey. However, in a lawsuit of 1899 against the Great Northern Railway it was decided that a bicycle was not 'ordinary luggage', and that a passenger could not require a railway company to carry it without extra charge.

1636 LNER, light orange with red overprint; the stub of the ticket was intended to be fastened to the bicycle.

128 North Eastern Railway, printed black on cream card.

8680 LNER, black on white card. The ticket, issued 7 August 1949, entitled the holder to leave a bicycle on the company's premises for seven days at his own risk. Midland & Great Northern Joint Committee, green.

189 Midland Railway Local, lilac, issued 28 July 1898.

035 LM & SR brick red.

002 GWR Extra Insurance, dark blue, issued 7 August 1926. 4321 British Transport Commission, printed black on white. Compare with 8680 issued from the same station.

686 Derwent Valley Light Railway. Both halves of the ticket are overprinted pink and light blue on white card, producing a most patriotic effect.

123 Cardiff Railway, light brown, issued 12 March 1935. In 1897 the Bute Docks Company changed its name to the Cardiff Railway Company, with authority to construct a further 12 miles of track in the Cardiff district. After further powers the line opened in 1910, and transferred to the GWR in 1922.

Vehicles and toll tickets. Rail and road travel often come together in one journey, in many ways and for a variety of reasons.

011 Motor Ticket, issued by the LMS, for use on the old Midland 'Red'. The issue of such a ticket is a puzzle, as the bus and train stations at Leicester were more than a mile apart, the road journey is absolutely direct and there never was a railway station at Mountsorrel Green, only a fare stage bus stop.

0507 No doubt about what sort of vehicle was accompanying the passenger with this pictorial ticket. Several railway companies used the same idea, particularly with 'Dog' tickets.

Apart from 'souvenir' type issues, platform tickets have appeared in many designs and colours, as this selection shows.

9657 Top and bottom green/blue oveprints on white card.

0513 Printed red on white card.

6313 Printed black on lilac card.

1872 Horizontal yellow band on white card.

000 Printed black on buff coloured card.

4937 Printed black on green card, with station name in red.

1854 Printed black on blue card.

0244 Printed black on coloured background (two bands light red with central band pink). The reverse of the card is white.

8995 Printed black on pink card.

2454 Printed black on white card.

MOTOR
FOR CONDITIONS SEE BACK
HALF DAY EXCURSION
L. M. & S. ISSUE
Leicester to
MOUNTSORREL GREEN
By MID. RED MOTORS
017

0373
ONE MOTOR CYCLE & SIDECAR
(ACCOMPANYING PASSENGER)
Hull (Corporation Pier) to
NEW HOLLAND PIER
(N) TOLL PAID Charge 10/0
For conditions see over
0373

018
L.M.&S.R. FOR CONDITIONS SEE BACK
Valid on day of issue only
PARKING TICKET FOR
MOTOR CYCLE
AT
LEICESTER (WEST BRIDGE)
Registration No.
Fee 1/6 Z
018

De statl. järnvägs. ..l.
Biljett
för
VELOCIPED,
tvåhjulig utan motor
från
KALMAR C
Kr. 1.00
Oemballerad eller
bristfälligt emballerad
0507

3356
KINGSTON upon HULL
CORPORATION
Landing or Embarking at or using
VICTORIA PIER
ONE MECHANICALLY PROPELLED
VEHICLE or TRAILER
ADMISSION TICKET
CHARGE 1s.0d.C
Issued at Hull (Corporation Pier)
3356

MERSEY TUNNEL
JOINT COMMITTEE
NT 1911/20
This Ticket is issued subject to the Joint Committee's Bye-laws, Rules and Regulations, is available for One Single Journey on day of issue only and must be shown on demand
To BIRKENHEAD K.4
TOLL AS PER SCHEDULE
TOLL 2/- PTE
VEHICLE
14.SEP.36
AFT'NOON

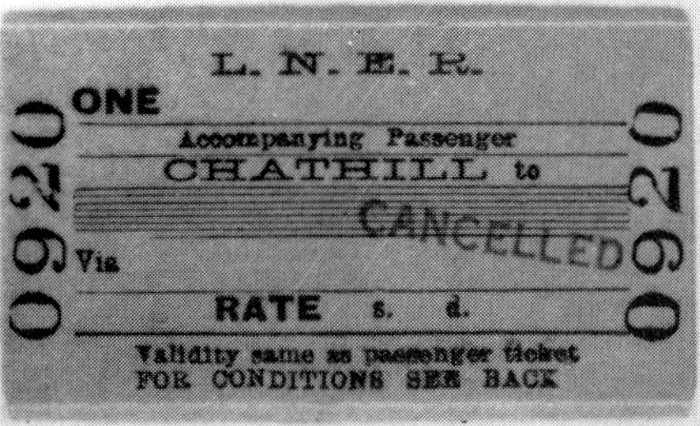

0920
L. N. E. R.
ONE
Accompanying Passenger
CHATHILL to
CANCELLED
Via
RATE s. d.
Validity same as passenger ticket
FOR CONDITIONS SEE BACK
0920

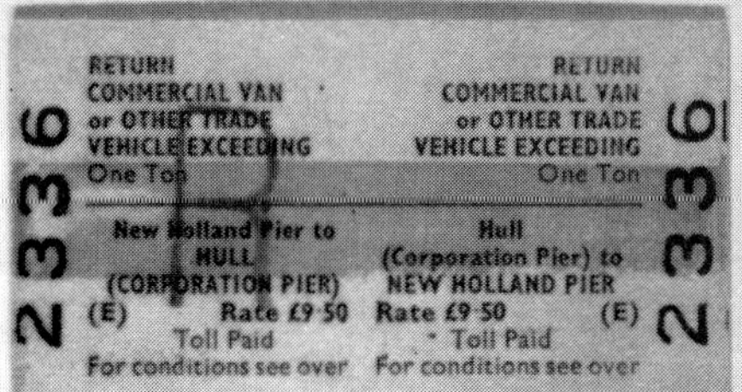

2336
RETURN
COMMERCIAL VAN
or OTHER TRADE
VEHICLE EXCEEDING
One Ton
New Holland Pier to
HULL
(CORPORATION PIER)
(E) Rate £9·50
Toll Paid
For conditions see over
RETURN
COMMERCIAL VAN
or OTHER TRADE
VEHICLE EXCEEDING
One Ton
Hull
(Corporation Pier) to
NEW HOLLAND PIER
Rate £9·50 (E)
Toll Paid
For conditions see over
2336

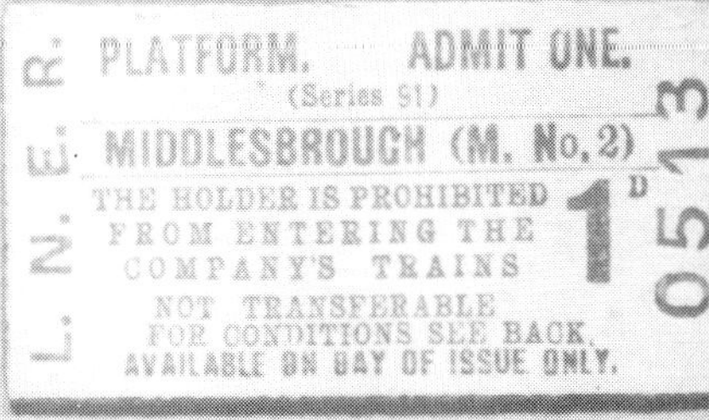

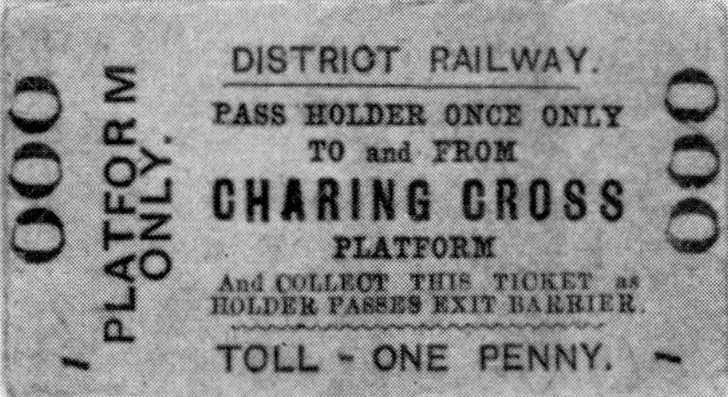

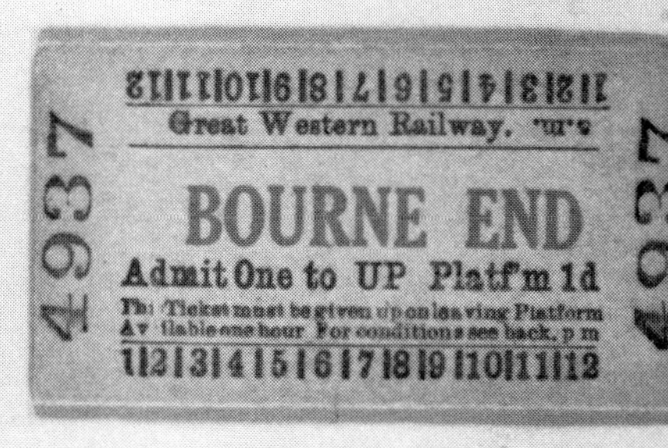

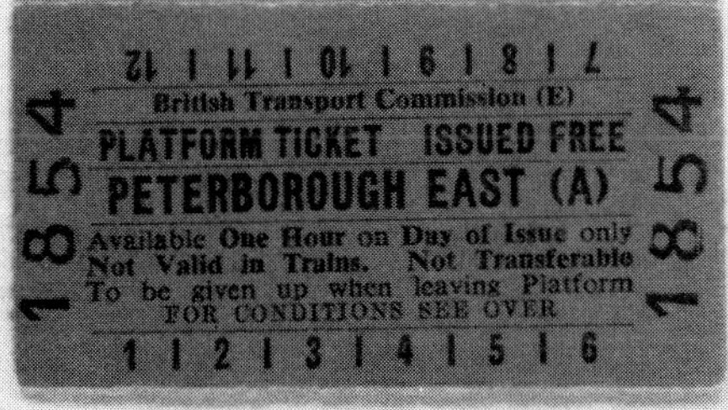

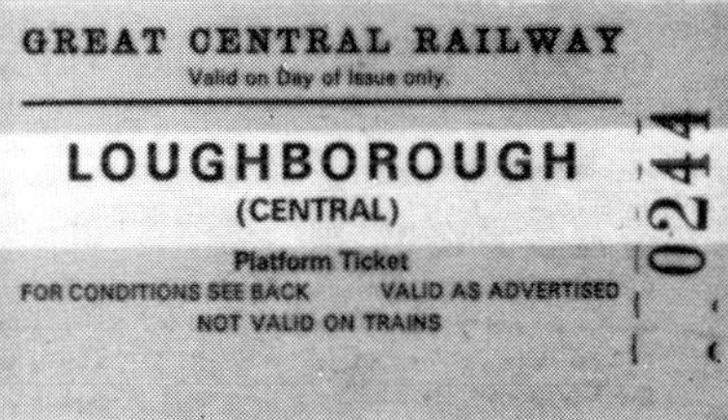

3995
Great Western Railway
CARDIFF GENERAL U
STATION
Pass Bearer to Station
3995

2454
1 | 2 | 3 | 4 | 5 | 6 | 7 | 8
L. M. & S. R.
Admit ONE to PLATFORM. Valid ONE HOUR
Day of issue only. Ticket must be given up
when leaving PLATFORM. CHARGE 1d
LEICESTER (B)
Issued subject to the Bye-Laws,
Regulations Notices and Conditions
published in the Company's Bills & Notices
9 | 10 | 11 | 12
2454

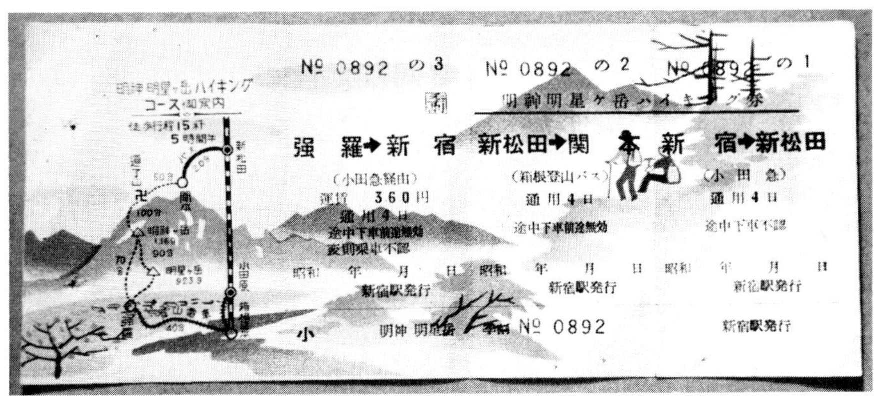

This Japanese paper coupon ticket is colourfully printed in orange and light blue in the best traditions of Eastern art. Issued by the Odakyu Electric Railway as a hiking ticket, discount return, the route over which it was valid is indicated by the diagram on the left-hand coupon. It is generally thought that the first representation of a railway system on tickets was on those issued for the 1885 Exhibition in Antwerp. The essential art of designing such a map of the system lies in preserving the clarity of the route within the small space available. (George Dow collection)

special orders owing to shortage of stock tickets dislocates the organisation of the printer.' When exceptional circumstances necessitated an immediate supply of stock tickets, a separate requisition was sent.

Railway Clearing House classifications were prepared for the issue of various types of ticket (excursion, tourist, etc), where the journey was made over the rails of another company. This was necessary for the proportional division of receipts. Further statistics were made on a local and regional basis for use in the Company's audit office.

Entries in the various registers had to be correct; the daily remittances had to tally with the book. It was not unusual in the early days of the railways, and at least up to the turn of the century, for clerks to be debited for any errors they made. From the regrouping era the company withstood any losses, but not without severe criticism of the individual responsible. It was usual for the booking clerk, in turn responsible to the stationmaster, to be responsible for other cash receipts, eg platform tickets, cloakroom, lavatory, and parking tickets, together with any excess fares.

With the introduction of automatic and semi-automatic ticket-issuing machines the manual operations necessary by the booking clerk became much reduced. Although the machines provided an automatic register for all tickets issued, the hand of the booking clerk was still required to check in cases where tickets had been incorrectly issued. All tickets issued were recorded on a continuous control slip, and those tickets issued in error were retained, and credited in when the day's takings were remitted. The machine system was generally superior since it provided a check against the day to day work of the booking clerk, allowed a reduction in office fittings, and above all, simplified much of the administration.

Mighty oaks from little acorns grow, and the vast web of railway administration grew from the issue of the tiny slip of pasteboard. As the

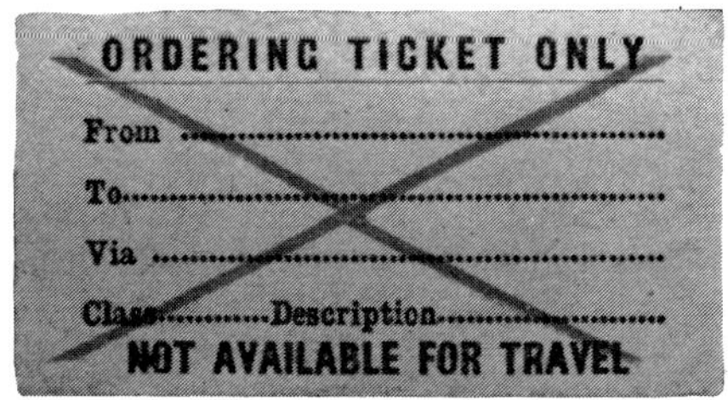

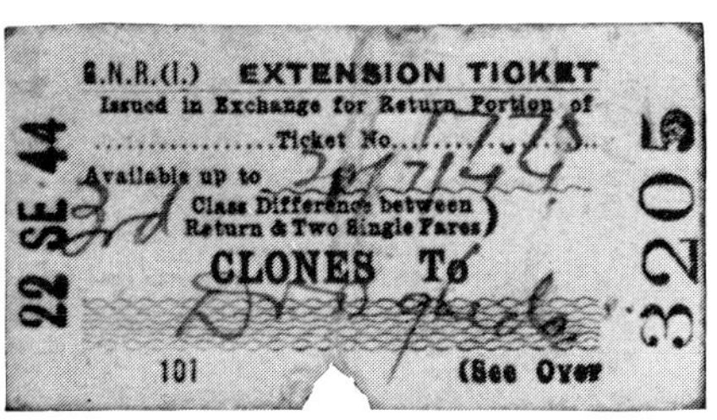

The ordering ticket (company unknown – several companies used a similar style) was used for small local orders to replenish stocks which were infrequently used.
1610 Midland & Great Northern Joint Committee platform ticket, printed in light red on white card.
3205 Great Northern Railway (Ireland) extension ticket or exchange voucher issued on the same conditions as the original ticket. It was forfeit if used for any other station or if transferred, and the full fare was charged.
464 Londonderry & Lough Swilly Railway three day return, quartered horizontally by pink stripes.

ticket was the almost perfect record that a passenger had paid his fare, it was imperative that the collection of tickets be equally efficient. The ticket collector's lot was not a happy one, since at one time it was considered 'clever' by some passengers to avoid production or surrender of their ticket. Certain stations were classified as 'open', that is, passengers were free to come and go as they pleased, and the tickets were collected on the train or at a nearby station. Naturally, this sort of situation gave rise to careless examination or collection of the tickets, with a consequent rise in the fraudulent use of tickets.

Travelling examiners and collectors made frequent checks on long-distance trains to prevent third-class ticket holders travelling in first-class compartments. The Great Western Railway introduced a system whereby the collectors had ticket punches, distinctively marked, for each station in a section. The ticket, when clipped, embossed a number which indicated to the collector the various stages through which the traveller had passed during his journey. The system allowed for the punching of tickets at all stopping-places, and although somewhat complicated, it proved to be remarkably practical.

Many systems were tried in an attempt to evade payment of the proper fare, and just as many were operated as counters to the frauds. Surprise checks on trains, and supervision of the examination and collection of tickets did much to eliminate the abuse of tickets; none were wholly successful.

The platform ticket system, although remunerative to the company, had opponents who claimed that the issue and usage of such tickets actually encouraged fraud. Passengers who had travelled without a ticket or payment of the proper fare could leave the station premises merely on the surrender of a platform ticket previously purchased for this purpose. As a counter to such practices, many companies limited the availability of platform tickets. The sides of the ticket were printed to indicate the hour of the day or night; upon issue, the appropriate time space was punched, and at the time of the ticket's surrender it was easy to determine whether or not the ticket still remained valid. It was the practice on some Continental lines to issue season platform tickets.

An ingenious ticket system was instituted at Crewe Station, and was operated successfully. The station was a 'closed' one, and passengers were issued with a platform ticket as they entered the premises. These tickets, on surrender at the booking office (there was a booking office on each of the several platforms), allowed the would-be passenger to obtain an ordinary service ticket. Crewe was a large exchange centre with a continual flux of passengers changing trains and re-booking. If a traveller arrived at Crewe without a ticket, having the intention of obtaining a ticket to cover the remainder of his journey, he was stalled by the system. His failure to produce a service or platform ticket meant that he could not be issued with a service ticket, and awkward questions were asked. The booking offices refused to issue service tickets except in exchange for a similar one to Crewe or a platform ticket which had been issued there. It was thus impossible for anyone to leave Crewe Station without surrendering one or the other type of ticket.

Sir Felix J. C. Pole, General Manager of the Great Western Railway, writing in 1927, declared that 'Integrity is an essential characteristic' in the appointment of men as collectors and examiners of tickets. He was also of the opinion that 'Ticket collectors should be carefully instructed in their duties — i.e., the conditions of availability of tickets, how to act in the varying and difficult circumstances that often arise in the examination of their duties, &c.' Adequate staff was necessary at collecting stations in order that the various duties were correctly performed, and encouragement to staff was offered in order to increase the collection of excess fares. Collectors and examiners who distinguished themselves in the detection of fraud were rewarded.

The collected tickets were cancelled and sent daily to the Audit Office, and for this purpose were arranged in numerical and/or alphabetical order. The 'end numbers' of the tickets provided a check on the returns listed in the passenger classifications.

THE RAILWAY CLEARING HOUSE

Behind and beyond the booking office window lay perhaps the most important link in the chain of railway administration, namely, the Railway Clearing House, which was responsible for checking railway transport revenue.

Prior to the nationalisation of the railways in Britain, it was possible for a passenger to enter a station and book a journey anywhere in Great Britain, in the sure knowledge that the ticket he purchased was valid over the lines of companies other than the issuing company. In the early days of railways there was no provision for through booking, and passengers had to suffer the inconvenience of changing trains even on short distance journeys. At the preliminary meetings prior to the establishment of the Railway Clearing House it was firmly stated that passengers must be enabled to travel within the limits to which continuous railway access extended. It was held that passengers should not be required to change carriage (from one Company's train to that of another), nor should they be inconvenienced or burdened with their luggage, etc. Numerous letters to the press were written by irate passengers who had undergone this 'Trial by Journey'. They all declared that, rather than suffer such discomforts, they would travel by the old stagecoach.

Traders and merchants, too, had their problems. Through traffic for goods was not possible, the same wagon could not be used for the entire journey. Goods had to be unloaded and reloaded from one company's wagons to those of another; this inevitably meant losses and delays, to the

A rare family portrait type of photographic postcard, from about 1905. The gentleman is believed to be a Mr Dutton of Walsall, who worked for the London & North Western Railway as a ticket collector. Status was always very important among the uniformed staff of railway companies.

Ticket shredding machine, as used on the Lancashire & Yorkshire Railway. After accounting at the Railway Clearing House and internal audit, companies shredded the tickets to prevent their re-issue and misuse, but also because there was nowhere to store the accumulating bulk of the card. (National Railway Museum)

dissatisfaction of the merchants. Questions were asked in Parliament, and the railways were forced to evolve a system which met the demand for through-invoicing of goods. But in solving one problem, they created another. Who was to pay for the carriage of goods in wagons running over the metals of other companies? When a traveller bought a ticket from one company and journeyed to a station served by another company, how was the ticket money to be distributed between the two companies.?

Opinions differ as to who had the original idea to set up a central office which would deal with both passenger and goods through-accounts. Mr George Carr Glyn (who afterwards became Lord Wolverton), being a banker, was familiar with the methods of the Bankers' Clearing House; he gave his full support to the idea. Mr Robert Stephenson, the engineer, and Mr Kenneth Morison, head of the audit department of the London and Birmingham Railway, had both expressed firm and enthusiastic support for such administrative action. The general manager of the Midland Railway, Sir James Allport, was also a keen supporter of the idea.

With a staff of four men to conduct its business, the Railway Clearing House was established on 2 January 1842, being later incorporated by Acts of Parliament in 1850 and 1897. The initial premises were situated in Drummond Street, London; they were vacated in 1848 for a larger building in Seymour Street, Euston Square. The Drummond Street premises were near to the Doric Arch of the London and North Western Railway, so scornfully referred to by the compiler of the 1851 *London Directory*.

The first meeting of the board of the Railway Clearing House was held on 26 April 1842. At that first meeting the representatives of nine railway companies were admitted to discuss the business. The original membership was the London and Birmingham, the Midland Counties, Manchester and Leeds, Leeds and Selby, Hull and Selby, the Birmingham and Derby Junction, North Midland, York and North Midland and the Great North of England Railway Companies. These companies, along with others, later amalgamated into the constituent companies which formed either the LMS or the LNER.

The original chairman of the Railway Clearing House was George Carr Glyn who continued in that office until his death in 1873. He was the longest serving chairman of the Railway Clearing House, and it says much for his enthusiasm and capabilities that he should have been elected annually to this office for such a long period. The undoubted success of the Railway Clearing House owed a lot to his efforts and his personality. The first secretary of the Railway Clearing House was Mr Morison.

The early difficulties which beset the RCH lay in the various shapes, sizes, colours, and materials of the tickets; some were still of the paper type, while others were to the new Edmondson standard. Different methods of issue, usage, and collection, by the member companies increased the difficulties of the Clearing House staff; some companies collected their tickets before the passenger commenced his journey, while others used special collecting stations. As previously mentioned, such diverse practices led to increases in both fare evasion and the forging of tickets.

Naturally enough, it was not long before the Edmondson standard was adopted by all the member companies, since it simplified the Clearing House work routines. A proposal was laid before the board of the Railway Clearing House that only companies which used the Edmondson standard tickets should be admitted to membership. It was even recommended that Edmondson himself should have the monopoly of printing all the tickets used by each member company, but this was not done.

The idea of the Railway Clearing House was not too well received at first, and in the first three years of its existence, the number of railway companies admitted as members to the RCH system had increased to only sixteen; the route length of track served by them extended to 656 miles. Ten years later there were seventy-three members, and in 1868 the jurisdiction of the RCH extended over 13,000 miles of rail. By 1876 the number of companies using the Clearing House was ninety-four, and the mileage had increased to 15,000. The railway companies were very tardy in their payment of dues to the Railway Clearing House, and a Parliamentary Act of 1850 empowered the RCH to sue defaulting companies in the courts. The powers contained in the Act had the desired effect and all consequent payments were settled promptly. By the year 1851, Clearing House staff were sorting through more than 12,000 tickets per week, each ticket being received, examined, and returned to the issuing company.

Four main departments controlled the work of the Clearing House — goods, mileage, coaching, and accounts. If a first class carriage travelled from Euston to Edinburgh the Scottish railway company was bound to

Printed fare tickets. It was common practice for joint issues to be made where the journey lay over common lines. Apportioning of the percentage of returns from the fare was determined by arrangement with the Railway Clearing House.

690 Oldham, Ashton & Guide Bridge Junction Railway first class single. White, date of issue unknown. The OA & GBJR was opened in 1861, connecting the London & York Railway with the London & North Western Railway.

017 London & North Western Railway first class blank. Attention is drawn to revised fare, yet nowhere is the original charge displayed, a situation which gave rise to misuse.

014 Otley & Ilkley Joint Line Committee third class single. The line was opened in 1865 a joint venture between the Midland and North Eastern Railways. Date of issue of the ticket is unknown, but is obviously post-1923.

7169 Great Northern & London & North Western Joint Railway third class single. Light green, date of issue unkown.

7824 North Eastern Railway third class single. Unissued. Light green.

5290 Midland & Great Northern Joint Committee third class single, light green. Not issued until 1958! The use of vast stocks of pre-nationalisation tickets was commonplace on economic grounds, but must have been the ticket collectors' nightmare.

9097 South Eastern & Chatham Railway third class single, green. Ticket issued sometime in 1908.

6149 Metropolitan & Midland Railways third class single, light green. Issued in June 1905, this ticket was available by Midland trains only on the joint line.

return it immediately, either full or empty, or a demurrage charge of 10 shillings per day was made for its detention. Proportionately lower rates were charged for second and third class carriages and goods wagons, these latter being charged at three shillings per day. In order to check this detention, employees of the Clearing House were located at each major junction to note the numbers of 'foreign' rolling stock, and the dates of arrival and departure. Any unnecessary delay in the return of other company's stock was charged against the offending company. Each daily list was the subject of careful scrutiny and cross-checking, and its information analysed.

The monthly settlement of accounts between the Railway Clearing House and the various companies was a prodigious task, even more remarkable when one considers the modern business methods and equipment which were lacking in those days. To meet this monthly schedule meant that the regular preparation of accounts and statistics sheets of immense size, numbering in excess of 16,000, and each hand-prepared in triplicate! Such a huge administrative undertaking demanded that extraordinary measures be taken in order to comply with the inexorable monthly deadline. Senior staff were instructed to take home the statistics sheets for copying purposes, and for their extra work were paid an additional salary. The system of differences, then a standard banking clearing house system, was used by the Railway Clearing House in the monthly settlement of its accounts.

Each day, every member company received from all stations in its network, booking returns listing the daily transactions. These records, of passengers booked through (either in company or private carriages), horses and cattle transported, parcels, goods, and laden or empty wagons which had arrived or been despatched, were forwarded to the Clearing House. Each return was the subject of careful scrutiny and cross-checking, and its information analysed.

By an Act of Parliament in 1897 the Railway Clearing House was fully incorporated. The RCH Committee, under the chairmanship of Mr Glyn, was formed of the chairmen of all the member companies, the constitution of the committee only allowing one delegate from each company. Under the Railway Clearing House Amalgamation Scheme of 1922, changes were made. Four delegates from each of the four amalgamated companies, and one from each of the other companies, the London Passenger Transport Board, Mersey Railway, the lines of the Joint Committes, and the Irish Companies, formed the new corporation. From the delegates of the corporation an executive or superintending committee of eight members was elected.

In contrast to the 1845 membership figures, those of 1935 show that the number of companies working under the Clearing House system was fifteen; this apparent drop in membership conceals the fact that several mergers had taken place during the ninety-year period. The total route length of track served by the 1935 member Companies was in excess of 23,000. By the 1930s, the work had been streamlined, and the Clearing House divided into three departments — merchandise, coaching, and secretarial.

The coaching department, which dealt with passenger traffic, was

Tickets surrendered to the railway staff collectors were despatched to the Railway Clearing House every month. Some idea of the enormity of the task of determining traffic returns of the different railway companies can be gauged from this picture.

Highly skilled staff sorting tickets in the Railway Clearing House. Their nimble fingers and sharp eyes helped to apportion receipts of the traffic on Great Britain's 23,000 miles of rail routes.

divided into two sections, a 'two companies' group and a 'three companies' group. The first dealt with the tickets issued for journeys where only two companies were involved. Each type of ticket (ordinary, tourist, excursion, etc) was processed separately. The booking company showed details of a particular transaction on its daily returns, together with information concerning the other company's proportion of the receipts from that booking. The Clearing House then credited the amount to the company to which it was due, and debited the booking company. A copy of the returns was forwarded to the non-booking company for agreement.

The 'three companies' group operated in a similar way, with the passenger traffic details being supplied by the booking company as before, but proportioning of the receipts was not shown. By an agreed method, the booking company, having possession of the cash, retained its proportion of the total receipts, and forwarded the remainder to the Railway Clearing House.

For monthly receipts which were less than £3 for a particular route, arrangements were made by means of what was known as a 'Light Fund'. This fund was apportioned pro rata to a division of similar passenger traffic receipts taken from four selected months before the month of settlement.

Checking of the passenger traffic returns was made by examination of the tickets collected at the end of the journey. In a vast hall, overlooked by a supervisor in an ornate wooden-grilled cubicle, were numerous tables under pendant lamps with 'Chinese coolie' celluloid shades. Young women, sitting on uncomfortable chairs, twelve to a table, sorted through piles of tickets which would be the envy of a present-day collector. The prospect of riffling through a never-ending stack of tickets must have been somewhat monotonously grim, even though the job demanded nimble fingers, and wits to match; perhaps the monotony was relieved by the occasional vase of flowers which sprouted among the tickets.

Parcel traffic was another important section of work dealt with by Clearing House staff; quarterly Post Office accounts, and payments for the loans of coaching and wagon stocks were also made.

In the first year of its establishment, the Railway Clearing House receipts were £193,246; by 1847 this total had risen to £793,701; in 1868 receipts were in excess of £11 million, and in 1873 the figure reached an astonishing £15,402,814; for 1933 the amount exceeded £34 millions, a rather striking comparison.

The general section of the secretarial department, from the days of the foundation of the Railway Clearing House, dealt with the administration of the establishment; this department provided the virtual control of the RCH. From the very early days of the railways it had been necessary for company officers to meet on a regular basis on common ground; the advent of the Clearing House fulfilled admirably that very need. Matters affecting the railway companies and their workings were of obvious consideration. But the companies realised the value of the Railway Clearing House for the purpose of considering the thousand and one questions, the solution to which lay between the railways and their travelling patrons.

A comment in the 1876 Edition of the '*London & North Western Railway Co's Official Tourists' Picturesque Guide To The Principal Tourists Districts in Great Britain & Ireland*' is of interest. This handsomely bound, blue buckram, gold embossed volume with gilt-edged pages, 'Specially Prepared for the Use of American Tourists', stated: 'Though the Clearing House is a wonderful monument of commercial intelligence, skill, and exactness, and upon whose existence so much of the public service depends, we advise the tourist to be content with admiring its splended system of adjusting contra accounts, its calculations almost infallible, and its balances, in which no discrepancy is detected; to be grateful for the power which its existence gives him of passing on from line to line without delay or hindrance in the shape of re-booking, changes of carriage, and shifting of luggage; and not to consider the Clearing House an institution to be visited out of curiosity as a show place.' It further commented upon the twelve hundred clerks being deeply interested in an many calculations, and 'the presence of a stranger only seems to disturb the monotonous routine, perfect exactitude, and supreme silence.'

The Railway Clearing House was the final link, the common bond between the companies and their service to the public; a network of iron roads with a colourful history firmly anchored in the tiny slip of pasteboard, the unpretentious card.

8
FURTHER DEVELOPMENTS

This is the end of the line on what I hope has proved to be an enjoyable journey, to discuss a neglected aspect of railway history.

Since the beginning of railways as a commercial venture, in particular that section concerned with the transport of passengers, many systems have been evolved to account for their movements and the revenue they brought to the various companies. The ticket has proved supreme in this field, and yet, curiously, its final form has still to be decided. It has ranged from the laboriously hand-written flimsy paper receipt and way-bill, to the multi-coloured pre-printed card issued from an electrically driven machine. New developments in the systems of ticket issue have brought the unpretentious card full circle. The paper coupon-tickets with safety background, and continuous roll tickets printed and issued instantaneously, now in use, are but modern descendents of the machines and tickets of the 'twenties and early 'thirties.

More advanced systems are being debated in railway committee rooms throughout the world. One such system was considered by British Rail and London Transport. In the autumn of 1971, the Opinion Research Centre conducted a survey for the London *Evening Standard* on the whole aspect of commuter traffic within the London area. As a result of the investigations a bold idea emerged, which, if it had been put into operation, would have drastically changed the present fares system.

Generations of railway travellers have dreamed of free journeys, wherever and whenever they desire. The only ones, in general, who achieve that dream are chairmen and general managers of railway companies. It is a Utopia where booking office queues and ticket barrier crushes are non-existent. Someone has to pay for the service, and the obvious source of revenue to pay for the operation of the scheme is the taxpayer or ratepayer. Not surprisingly, only a small percentage of the ratepaying commuters who were interviewed for the poll were in favour of the idea. Those who supported the scheme claimed that its advantages lay in the savings in terms of ticket issuing machines, and the different types of ticket staff at present employed.

In cities like New York, Paris, and Moscow, flat rate fares systems for some journeys are in operation. The advantages of such a system is that the passenger is saved time at the booking office, while the administration is much simplified; reductions in staff and equipment are also possible. The London Transport authorities agreed that such a system could work on selected routes. The survey found that among the advantages of the flat rate system, advance selling of tickets at a discount was possible, but this is by no means a new idea.

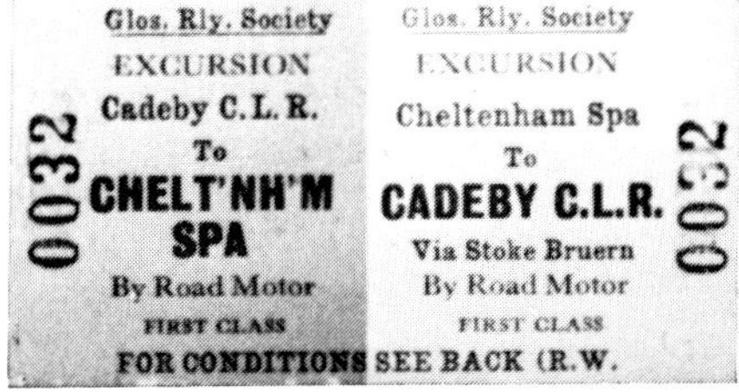

Imitation Edmondson tickets. It has long been an unwritten tradition in the world of the railway enthusiasts and preservationists to issue tickets based on upon those printed in the 'good old days' of steam, and for them to be retained as souvenirs.
Of especial interest is the Whitbread Flowers ticket. It was issued on 22 August 1969 to mark the re-naming of the Railway Hotel, Ambrose Street, Cheltenham, as the St James Hotel. It thus perpetuates the name of the Great Western Railway station which stood nearby from 1847 to 1966.
The Gloucestershire Railway Society excursion ticket is the one referred to in the Foreword; the return half is overprinted orange on white card.
Great Western Railway colour and style have been copied for the Hutton House Museum ticket.
The Cadeby Light Railway in the grounds of the Cadeby Rectory is one of the few steam railways in operation for which no Parliamentary Enactment was made – hence the category of ticket!

The Great Eastern Railway, in 1905, was the first to sell packets of tickets, with one ticket being valid for each day of the week. The Midland Railway extended the idea to the issue of workmen's tickets. By the 1930s, most railways in Britain issued bulk tickets at reduced rates; the LNER issued bulk travel tickets and bargain travel tickets which were virtually the same thing. The same company also sold exchange tickets which were issued against distance coupons.

Another idea (which perhaps could have been used on commuter lines) underwent extensive trials by road transport operators throughout the world, and was an electronic echo of the mechanical systems introduced on the London Underground fifty years ago. The system used the 'Videmat' Self Service Ticket Machine, which was passenger operated. Using the machine was simple. The passenger inserted his money in a coloured aperture at the top of the machine, an adjacent button was pressed, and the ticket issued from the front of the machine. The ticket face carried the details of destination, date, and serial number, while on the reverse side was a photocopy of the coins inserted.

The railway insurance ticket is an example of an old idea that has been reintroduced. In the 1930s, the Paris Nord-Sud Railway issued tickets of double the Edmondson standard size in a special envelope; the envelope was in fact an insurance policy, valid for *Un Seul Trajet.* The 'Railway Passengers Assurance Company All Accidents Insurance Ticket (Journey)', formerly issued by British Rail, is not so much a ticket as a postal card. Of conventional postcard size, when issued it had a code and serial number, benefits and conditions, together with the name of the issuing station and the date of issue. The purchaser was required to sign the ticket-cum-card, and then to post it to a relative or a friend. For a premium of 1s, the sum assured was £2,000; hundreds of thousands of these insurance tickets were printed in Great Britain prior to decimalisation.

Photographs of American trains in the mid-1930s often show the conductor/guard with one foot on the platform and the other on the steps of the coach, about to give the signal for departure. There was a reason for this, other than to make a nicely posed picture. Many American super-trains, including the famous 'Comet' of the New New York, New Haven and Hartford Railroad, were fitted with automatic doors and steps. When the doors opened the steps automatically projected, and as the doors closed the steps folded up. Controlled by electro-magnetic valves and a compressed air system, it was impossible to close the doors while the guard was standing on the steps. The doors and steps control gear was also connected to the Westinghouse Air Brake system, and the train could not be started if any door was open. Present-day research into electro-magnetic locks and keys could well evolve a magnetic key-ticket which would operate a similar system. With his electronically programmed key-ticket, the traveller of the future could board the streamlined express train, the coach doors opening only to the signal from the electronic ticket. Compartment doors of the different classes would operate in the same way, thus preventing fraud; the conductor would, of course, carry a master key ticket.

There is one story which even relates to sex descrimination among tickets. A letter in the London *Evening News,* for 18 October 1971, urged travellers, when purchasing a ticket, to be sure that it was of the correct sex! The wife of the writer had bought his weekly season ticket for him on a Sunday. The following Tuesday, he was prevented from boarding his train by a keen-eyed inspector. The inspector explained that the traveller had no authority to make a journey on a ticket which was not his. The season ticket had a small 'w' stamped on it; it had been issued to a woman, and clearly, the writer was not of that sex. Despite explanations, the inspector demanded the return of the ticket as the property of the British Rail. The traveller refused and went to see the station manager, and asked for his authority to cancel the troublesome 'w'. Apparently, matters were not quite that simple, and the manager suggested that the whole affair was the fault of the passenger who would have to prove that the season ticket was his. Since the wife had purchased the ticket, and the husband had signed it, the 'Non-Transferable' law was being broken, but the writer, was eventually allowed to board the train. He made enquiries of the booking clerk who had issued the ticket, and was told that the booking clerk issued a 'w' ticket to a woman purchaser and he had not thought it necessary to ask which sex ticket was required.

Even in the 1930s, the Philadelphia Rapid Transit Company was issuing tickets marked 'male'. Such tickets were in the form of sheets of coupons; they had a continuous safety background, and were issued as booklets. They were widely used for short journeys.

In his work, *Passenger Tickets*, Professor Wiener includes an illustration of a ticket in use before the railway era, circa 1790. Issued by Monsieur E. Monier, who operated a staging coach between Beauraing and Dinant, the ticket is approximately twice the size of the Edmondson standard. Superimposed on perforations across the centre of the ticket is the day of issue, and each half carries a printed serial number, the type-face of which is fairly common even today. In a centre panel on each half-ticket is listed the staging points of the journey, under the heading *Aller;* under the heading, *Retour,* the list is reversed. Thus either half of the ticket could be presented on the outward journey.

In my opinion, the time is long overdue for another International Railway Congress to reconsider some of their pre-war proposals. To judge by some of the tickets issued on modern railways the world over, it is no wonder that there is a dearth of timber on this planet of ours; the paper used in some Continental and American issues is nothing less than extravagant waste. If Thomas Edmondson were to revisit the railway scene, he would shake his head in disbelief and despair, wondering why he bothered solving the problem of cumbersome tickets in the first place. He would certainly consider that, even allowing for the modern miracles of science, the stagecoach booking clerk with his triplicate waybills did not seem to have such a hard task after all!

To conclude this final chapter, I can do no better than to quote part of the last paragraph of Professor Wiener's fascinating book.

'Lest we gloat over progress achieved . . . let us look at a . . . still older ticket which is a kind of ancestor of all others. This stage-coach ticket of the 18th century will come as a surprise to many, for it already embodied many of the features which still appear in the tickets produced'. . . more than 190 years later.

BIBLIOGRAPHY

Passenger Tickets, Prof Lionel Wiener, (The Railway Gazette, 1939)
Great Central, George Dow, (Ian Allan, three volumes 1959-65)
The Business of Travel, W. Fraser Rae, (Thomas Cook & Sons, 1891)
Carriage by Railway, Henry W. Disney (Stevens & Sons, 1912)
The Midland Railway, Frederick S. Williams (Bemrose & Co, 1876)
Modern Railway Administration, (Gresham Publishing Co Ltd, 1927)
Railway Clearing House in the British Economy, Philip S. Bagwell, (Allen & Unwin, 1968)
The Royal Deeside Line, A.D. Farr, (David & Charles, 1968)
The Campbeltown and Machrihanish Light Railway, Nigel S.C. Macmillan, (David & Charles, 1970)
The Welsh Highland Railway, Charles E. Lee, (David & Charles, 1970)
The North Midland & Great Northern Joint Railway, A.J. Wrottesley, (David & Charles, 1970)
The North Staffordshire Railway, R. Christiansen & R.W. Miller, (David & Charles, 1971)
The Railway Magazine, Various issues, 1930
Railway Wonders of the World, Various issues, 1935

INDEX

Page numbers in **bold** refer to illustrations